The
TWIN ELEMENTAL EFFECT

KUSHAQXI

 Kushite Publishing Co.

Publisher's Cataloging-in-Publication Data

Names: Kushaqxi, Derrick, author.
Title: The twin elemental effect / Derrick Kushaqxi.
Description: Houston, TX: Kushite Publishing, 2024.
Identifiers: LCCN: 2024923616 |

ISBN: 979-8-9871089-8-7 (hardcover) 979-8-9871089-9-4 (paperback) | 979-8-9919483-0-2 (epub)
Subjects: LCSH Soul mates. | Parapsychology. | Spirituality. | Spiritual life. | Love. | Self-help. |
BISAC BODY, MIND & SPIRIT / Afterlife & Reincarnation | BODY, MIND & SPIRIT / Healing /
General | BODY, MIND & SPIRIT / Inspiration & Personal Growth | BODY, MIND & SPIRIT
/ Mindfulness & Meditation | BODY, MIND & SPIRIT / New Thought | SELF-HELP / Personal Growth /
General | FAMILY & RELATIONSHIPS / Love & Romance
Classification: LCC HQ801 .K87 2024 | DDC 646.7/7--dc23

INTERIOR & EXTERIOR DESIGNS BY KUSHAQXI
https://kushitepublishing.com/
www.TwinElementalsoulmates.com

Kushite Publishing Co.
17350 STATE HWY 249, STE 220
#12879 HOUSTON, TEXAS 77064

Overview

Those who haven't cultivated their astral or psychic senses for discerning the spirits of the people around them are like the blind fumbling in darkness. In this evolving world, it's essential to train yourself to recognize the ensouled elemental's you are connected to while cultivating detachment from temporal, ego-driven attachments.
Much like having a crystal ball, this ability will aid in identifying who and what serves as assets, liabilities, energy vampires, or lightworkers in your life. Above all, understanding the Twin Elemental effect is like acquiring the philosopher's stone for the emotionally relating alchemist.
~ Kushaqxi

Contents

Dedication	VII
Introduction	VIII
Preface (Extended Version)	XIII
Epigraph	XXX
PART I	1
1. Wash | Rinse | Repeat	2
2. Love, Lust & Attraction	37
3. The Timeline	70
4. Generations	131
5. Soulmate Psychology	176
6. Religion & Reincarnation	200
7. A Case for Past Life Recall	210
8. Leaders in the Field	226
PART II	251
9. Twin Elementals	252
10. TWIN FLAMES	292
11. TWIN FLOODS	307
12. TWIN WINDS	321
13. TWIN PLANETS	338

PART III		362
14. Conscious Relating	MASTER CLASS Pt.1	363
15. Conscious Relating	MASTER CLASS Pt.2	417
About the author		469
Also by the Author		470

Dedication

To my Tribe
The Creatives, Intuitives, Healers and Empaths
who wear their hearts and desires on their sleeves.

Most of all, to the twin elemental soulmates
who married and or procreated with me.

and finally,
veneration to those who came before me
and laid a path so that I could be.
May you find my offerings worthy.

Introduction

Quote: This place is a dream. Only a sleeper considers it real. Then death comes like the dawn, and you wake up laughing at what you thought was your grief. —RUMI

At some point, you may have asked yourself, Why am I constantly encountering extremely disagreeable people? Should I just be alone for peace of mind? Perhaps you've wondered why your pain and grief feel so overwhelming at times, almost as if they're suffocating you? Maybe you've wondered why you're so invested in someone who doesn't seem to reciprocate, even as a friend. You may have felt regret over some of the decisions you've made along the way. Perhaps you've wondered how to replicate the energy you've generated when you've encountered super magical people. If you have wondered about any of those scenarios, this book was written especially for you.

The question I've often asked myself, however, is how can I build a compelling case for identifying the patterns that manifest those karmic soul ties who infiltrate your life under the color of friendship, romance, and any interpersonal relationship for that matter? A case so compelling indeed that it heightens an individual's psychic sensitivities upon revelations.

The Answer Is: Present a detailed forensic analysis of all the elements involved, elucidating an entire model that would uncover the intricate connections and hidden dynamics at play. This involves meticulously unraveling the threads that bind the souls for understanding the profound implications of such connections. By exploring the subtleties and complexities of these soul ties, one can illuminate the complex spiritual properties in motion , bringing to light a comprehensive model that resonates, intrigues, and empowers.

Now, here's a question for you. Have you ever felt that your words fall short of conveying what you truly mean? When relating to others, it can be challenging to articulate our thoughts and feelings, often resulting in miscommunication, misunderstandings, and conflict. This book aims to provide the candid language needed to express the ideas and emotions many people struggle to convey, enabling more intelligent communication for more advanced social exchanges. As we mature and understand ourselves, we can learn to express what was previously inexpressible. Simply put, the tools found in these pages will help you understand and communicate your thoughts more clearly.

To fully appreciate this book, readers are advised to approach it with patience and an open mind, without of preconceptions. If we were in a lecture hall, I'd probably ask for a show of hands, firstly, from those that are teachable, but then I'd ask if you were familiar with a photomosaic. If you didn't raise your hand, I'd then proceed to inform you that a photomosaic is when several individual photos or images are arranged to form a larger, often more complex image when viewed from a distance.

The purpose of that inquiry and use of it as an example would be to illustrate how the information in this book is designed to mentally converge into a coalescence. Like a photomosaic, this body of work unfolds as a holographic compendium, facilitating a pan-dimensional awareness by intertwining knowledge across various realms of time and consciousness. It embarks on a journey through the psychological, spiritual, emotional, and beyond, using intuitive and analogical reasoning. What remains is a cohesive idea much like that of an intricate photomosaic.

Moreover, this book fosters integrative thinking and conceptual synthesis, leading the reader through a harmonious examination of divergent ideas and concepts, merging them into comprehensive insights for a deeper understanding. It showcases how amalgamating esoteric concepts enhances problem-solving and creativity, which aims to cultivate advanced cognitive abilities for seamless navigation and connection of complex spiritual information.

So what does all of that even mean?

For context – Let's simplify!

Holographic Compendium: A book that combines several different pieces of abstract information into one mental picture, much like a photomosaic.

Pan-Dimensional Awareness: Understanding things from many different perspectives.

Integrative Thinking: Putting different ideas together to find better solutions.

Conceptual Synthesis: Mixing various ideas to understand them in a new way.

Cohesive Examination: Looking at different ideas carefully and seeing how they connect.

Comprehensive Insights: Gaining a deep and full understanding of something.

Esoteric Concepts: Special ideas understood by a few people, often related to spiritual awareness.

Intuitive Reasoning: Understanding things by feeling or instinct.

Analogical Reasoning: Understanding by comparing things to other similar things.

In short, this publication connects many ideas from different times, dimensions, and ways of thinking, helping us understand our minds, behaviours, feelings and our souls much better, through using reason, intuition, comparisons, and instinct. Some might wonder, Why not just say that from the start? Here's why: because **Language Matters.** In the ideas found in The Twin Elemental Effect, each passage is carefully crafted to convey specific ideas with precision so that the insights gained are authentic and unmistaken. As the reading progresses, new insights start to coalesce, revealing patterns that had previously been hidden, offering readers a rich and multifaceted perspective. The experience promises an immersive, alchemic mental process that amplifies problem solving with innovative solutions.

On a different note, I was recently advised that to reach a much wider audience, a great writer must present their work as if presenting to third graders. While this is common, seeing as though the essence of communicating ideas lies in simplicity

INTRODUCTION

and creativity, this book does not dilute its content, respecting the intelligence of its audience. It aims to serve as a tool for advancing the reader's mental framework, yet requiring the reader's active engagement for effective integration.

The concepts presented are accessible yet profound. They are intended for a discerning audience capable of deep insights. Unlike traditional texts read sequentially from cover to cover, this book invites non-linear exploration, encouraging you to revisit chapters as you might with sacred texts. Mystical and rich with enigmas, subjects like twin elementals are meant to illuminate the mind and uplift the spirit. This iterative approach fosters a deeper connection, allowing layers of understanding to gradually unfold.

Starting with practical concepts and gradually increasing in complexity, this book challenges and expands the reader's perspectives. It combines extensive topics into a cohesive narrative, balancing directness and playfulness for clear, intelligent information without unnecessary details. Structured as candid conversations, it blends an academic and conversational tone, speaking authentically—as if talking with friends over a glass of wine. This reflective approach often leads to 'eureka' moments, epiphanies, and breakthroughs bringing about profound clarity and enlightenment.

This book unites content from three distinct areas into a cohesive guide, creating an in-depth educational experience in a single volume. Offering a vast storehouse of information for conscious and subconscious processing, it balances direct honesty with a touch of playful banter and an occasional dad joke. My aim isn't to peddle unicorns or feel-good fluff, but to provide a straightforward, no-frills blueprint for massive transformation.

Above all and most importantly, this book will reveal a path to profound detachment from the subconscious patterns that shape how we relate to others. With each step of release, you'll find greater clarity and deep acceptance of your true self, discovering who you are beyond ego-driven definitions. As you detach from egoic identity and embrace pure awareness, the impermanence of everything around you becomes unmistakable—and less unsettling. You'll realize that all that comes and goes is not you—or your reality, a truth that will anchor you in a world defined by constant change.

Impermanence in relating, often a source of anxiety, will come to feel natural, accepted as the state of all things. Observing this flow reminds you that you exist beyond fleeting events or emotions. With 'Equanimity,' you can meet both joy and challenge, unaffected by external forces. Releasing attachment to specific outcomes allows you to focus on intentional, aligned action, bringing serenity to life. Losses and gains, joys and sorrows are met with quiet dignity, knowing your true essence remains undisturbed by passing changes. Practicing non-reaction grounds you, transforming triggers into moments of calm, as even the most intense events can flow by without stirring compulsive reactions.

Over time, you'll cultivate space to breathe, reflect, and respond with intention rather than reaction. This awareness deepens personal peace and fosters harmony in relationships. By breaking habitual patterns and choosing non-reaction, you free yourself from cycles of suffering, embracing your journey as pure consciousness. Each act of non-reaction strengthens your awareness, blending consciousness and existence until they are unified. In this state, life unfolds from within as an expression of your true self—cosmic consciousness. Every moment then becomes an opportunity for boundless freedom and unshakable peace.

Consider this your forewarning. This won't be a rushed or condensed publication; instead, it's crafted to avoid ruthless compression. It won't just skim the surface; it will in fact dive deep, ensuring no vital nuances, context, or real-world applications are left unexplored, thus vibrantly bringing the subject to life. In addition, please bear with me as I address imperfections in this independent, self-published, self-edited manuscript. For those engaging with the audiobook version of this publication, we kindly ask for your understanding regarding any mispronunciations that may occur due to the digitally generated narration.

Finally, I encourage you to approach this book as if preparing to teach it. Engage deeply, question, and explore each concept to fully understand and articulate it. By studying with the mindset of both student and teacher, you'll not only grasp the content more thoroughly but also internalize it, empowering you to share it confidently. This approach will enrich your learning and enable clear communication of these ideas in discussions, writing, or personal reflection.

The insights you gain here are not just lessons but stepping stones to a life lived in alignment with your highest vibrational self. Embrace the journey ahead, and feel free to continue with the extended preface before delving into the chapters that follow.

Preface (Extended Version)

> We are caught in an inescapable network of mutuality, tied in a single garment of destiny. Whatever affects one directly affects all indirectly.
> —*Martin Luther King Jr.*

WHAT AND WHY THIS BOOK?

Throughout our lifetimes, we inevitably encounter certain individuals whose magnetic presence draws us in, compelling us in ways we can't always explain. These enigmatic connections—whether with family members, mentors, friends, or lovers—possess a unique power. The shared experiences we have with them seem to defy ordinary understanding, yet they can profoundly influence the trajectory of our personal narratives. These relationships, charged with a mysterious energy, often act as catalysts for transformation, pushing us toward self-discovery, growth, and even moments of revelation. In their wake, we are left to reflect on the nature of destiny, questioning whether these encounters are random or part of a larger cosmic design, forever shaping who we are and who we become.

While at times these relationships—whether personal or professional—may appear casual, coincidental, or born out of mere happenstance, we often come to realize they are far more than chance encounters. What may seem like a fleeting or surface-level connection gradually reveals itself as something serendipitous yet intricately woven into the fabric of our lives. These bonds are not just random; they are guided by the unseen hands of fate, perhaps even destiny itself. They arrive in our lives at precisely the right moment, offering lessons, opportunities, or challenges that shape our path in ways we couldn't have anticipated. Over time, we begin to see that such encounters, however unexpected, are purposeful—each one playing a vital role in the unfolding of our personal story, as if we were always meant to meet, learn, and evolve through them.

What if I told you that everything in the seen world has an unseen counterpart, like the images and sounds on your electronic devices, which are in fact nothing more than invisible ones and zeros projected as waves through Bluetooth technology? Imagine that your entire body, world, and life are simply projections from an unseen source, much like data streaming over Bluetooth. Moreover, what if your life was entirely pre-scripted, just as the songs, movies, games, and other invisible streams of data that appear in real-time on your devices?

This would include the enigmatic relationships you experience, wouldn't it? These connections, magnetic and transformative, are not random. They, too, are part of a larger, prewritten design woven into the fabric of your existence. For the sake of clarity, this unseen program, the invisible force behind these profound connections, is what we've come to understand as soul ties.

Soul ties are often described as deep emotional, spiritual, or psychological bonds that form between two people, typically through intense or intimate experiences. The concept is most commonly associated with romantic or sexual relationships, but it can also occur in friendships, family connections, or other significant relationships.

In the context of past life reincarnation and related spiritual beliefs, soul ties are often thought to be deep, enduring connections between souls that transcend time and space, continuing across multiple lifetimes. These ties are believed to persist as part of a broader spiritual journey, where individuals are linked together through various reincarnations.

Whether experiencing intense grief, regret, anger, liberation, or acceptance, it is often only after deep reflection and introspection that you begin to understand the true purpose behind these soul-tying experiences and their influence on your life. It is through the insights and realizations that you integrate these experiences for transcendent growth and ultimately evolve into a more enlightened version of yourself.

When discussing soul ties, the subject of soulmates will inevitably come up, and when soulmates are explored, the conversation often leads to twin flames and similar concepts. Though widely unpopular and seen as distinct, this work will demonstrate that within the realm of soul ties, all soul connections— including twin flames—are essentially forms of soulmates. This controversial perspective may challenge enthusiasts and spark debate, but it will lay out a clear blueprint to support this perspective, inviting deeper exploration of the interconnectedness of these relationships.

In discussions about twin flames and soulmates, some perceive soulmates merely as subjects of idealistic, romantic notions, overlooking the fact that a soulmate can be anyone with whom one shares a predestined soul tie or karmic connection. Many individuals explore the ideas of soulmates and twin flames within both romantic and transactional relationships through an emotional lens. The insights they arrive at frequently originate from their own experiences, showcasing a variety of personal perspectives for projecting as the ultimate truth.

In the field of cognitive-behavioral therapy, or **CBT**, the process of arriving at conclusions based solely on one's emotional reactions, despite contrary objective evidence, is known as emotional reasoning. This cognitive distortion leads individuals to believe that their feelings accurately reflect reality, treating their emotions as facts. For example, I'm upset, so I'm correct, or because I'm so angry, I must be right. Emotional reasoning is a common pattern that can significantly impact decision-making and self-perception, often requiring intervention to develop more realistic and objective viewpoints.

I have observed numerous debates about whether soulmates and twin flames are are the same, often entangled with mythical explanations and interpretations backed by emotional reasoning as the evidence. This work draws inspiration from those many debates and aims to establish itself as the definitive authority on the subject. Stemming from the identification of recurring patterns, not only in interpersonal relationships but also in the fundamental structures of diverse relationships across cultures and throughout history, this study seeks to offer an exhaustive analysis.

Recognizing these recurring patterns has inspired a drive to leverage their potential for transformative effects. It is through the acknowledgment and subsequent adaptation of these patterns that the Twin Elemental Model, formally acknowledged as the twin flame, was developed. You will soon learn that a twin flame is much more than a simple romantic connection; in fact, it supersedes romance all together and is designated as an agent for unsuspecting transformation.

Furthermore, the concept of 'Twin Elementals' cannot be understood without the awareness of the realm of souls and the study of reincarnation. When souls become embodied, grasping how they connect with one another requires an understanding of attraction programming and the levels of consciousness each ensouled avatar operates within. All these factors converge to form a point of singularity from which relating can begin. This book challenges the current paradigm surrounding magnetic soul pairings, soul families, and soul ties. It presents a compelling argument for reincarnation and its influence on the many interpersonal relationships you will encounter in your lifetime.

This exploration delves into the notion that ensouled humans often reincarnate with each other over many lifetimes, highlighting the lasting connection between individuals across successive incarnations. Much of the available information on these topics remains vague, offering little beyond feel-good fluff, often for the sake of emotional gratification. For these reasons, the idea of soulmates are generally considered the bright-eyed fantasy found in fairytales.

While the concept of soulmates is often associated with romantic relationships, it actually encompasses a broader range of karmic soul ties, including connections with colleagues, grandparents, pets, best friends, or neighbors. These relationships are believed to be grounded in intimate pre-birth contracts, designed to bring individuals together in various capacities beyond just romantic partnerships. In life, we can sometimes forget that an interpersonal relationship does not have to be solely romantic to be beneficial or fulfilling.

Within the context of soulmate philosophy, many individuals do offer genuine insights, based on psychic intuition, transcendental meditation, hands-on experience. This along with a profound understanding of the human condition can distinguish them from those with a subjective view. Essentially, it's all just a matter of intuitive perspective and interpretation. Yet, as you seek high vibrational information, it is not uncommon to sometimes find yourself surrounded by an abundance of enthusiastic optimism, overzealous positivity and inflated confidence regarding studied subjects.

This kind of chatter can be remarkably motivating and inspiring, much like the fiery sermons of a southern hell and brimstone preacher at a summer tent revival, where dopamine flows as freely as a flood. Yet, once the show concludes and the dopamine levels recede, it can become apparent that the experience often lacks real-world applicability or useful education that equips individuals with the necessary tools to consistently enhance their lives and evolve their spiritual intelligence.

PREFACE (EXTENDED VERSION) xvii

Exercising discernment is vital when on a quest for right knowledge. It's perfectly fine to draw inspiration and motivation from uplifting speeches with positive affirmations. However, it's crucial to evaluate whether the information presented is grounded in evidence and offers practical insights for real-life use, fostering lasting transformation. Enlightenment and personal growth have effects that reach far beyond a fleeting surge of dopamine. They result in enduring positive changes in behavior, attitudes, and mindset. High vibrational consciousness projected through the filter of one human being can cause a quantum ripple effect throughout the space of an entire galaxy. Case and point, Isa, also known as Yashuah, also known as Jesus, also known as Buddha, Tammuz and a few others, depending on your geographical location.

Hence, it is essential to prioritize authentic, high-vibrational knowledge that can be consistently applied to enhance both our individual lives and our contributions to our communities and society at large. As we relentlessly expand our understandings, we must do so with an open mind and a willingness to question our own beliefs and assumptions. This approach allows us to develop a more thorough and nuanced perspective, firmly grounded in evidence and thoughtfully balanced by wisdom and intuition. I bring up these points to introduce a new model of reasoning that may challenge what you've been taught so far.

In this book, Chapter One opens by sharing my personal journey, setting the stage for a deeper examination. This narrative then unfolds into the science of attraction followed by a comprehensive historical exploration, offering readers a thorough understanding of the evolving nature of interpersonal relationship culture through the ages. This approach not only enriches our discussion with a solid empirical foundation but also bridges the gap between past and present, shedding light on the unchanging aspects of human connections shaped by pre-life agreements and soul contracts. As we navigate through this exploration, we anchor our insights in the concrete, moving beyond mere theoretical speculations to a more profound comprehension of the intricate web of relationships defining our existence.

In addition, a religious context is provided to offer a comprehensive view encompassing various belief systems, recognizing that a significant portion of humanity derives their knowledge of culture, history, and society from their religious background. This inclusive approach recognizes various sources of evidence and understanding, highlighting the importance of religious perspectives in shaping cultural knowledge and societal norms regarding relating souls.

Our goal is to uncover the roots of human relationship patterns and behaviors, often overlooked by many. By exploring our history, readers gain insight into the evolution of real time human connections, crucial for navigating future relationships. This manuscript then delves into parapsychology and the transformative world of hypnosis, unveiling past life accounts that impact present relationships. This exploration, fueled by a lifelong passion, adds depth to the work.

Armed with this foundational understanding, we will shine a light on the Twin Elemental traits inherent in all soulmate connections. We will dive deeper into the unique phenomenon of twin flames, enhancing our comprehension of both soulmates and twin flames through the lens of preordained karmic ties. Following this, we will venture into a thorough examination of the diverse spectrum of all twin elemental archetypes, offering a nuanced perspective on these profound connections.

Take note that, on each page turned, you'll discover a multitude of methods and models for recognizing the traits within yourself and others that trigger life-altering experiences. Furthermore, you'll gain access to the tools needed to consciously transcend these traits like a true alchemist while embracing various empowerment systems. As we embark on this shared journey as writer and reader, my aim is not only to engage your intuition but also to challenge your logical mind, reasoning abilities, and highest intuitive intelligence.

You'll often hear me use the term "interpersonal" in the context of twin elementals. An interpersonal relationship refers to the connection, interaction, and association between two or more individuals. These relationships vary in nature and intensity, from casual acquaintances and friendships to intimate bonds like family relationships, romantic partnerships, and professional connections. Interpersonal relationships involve communication, emotional exchange, and mutual influence, playing a significant role in shaping our social lives and personal development. When you hear "interpersonal," think of terms like mutual, reciprocal, communal, consensual, socioemotional, or interactive. Refer to this section whenever the word appears in the text.

Why is this book necessary?

PREFACE (EXTENDED VERSION)

Throughout the various seasons of our lives, we incarnate, projecting the consciousness of our souls to embody flesh-made avatars for a brief few decades. Immersed in countless narratives, we accumulate karmic experiences that compound like ripples in a crystal-clear ocean, waves gently washing ashore on pristine, white-sanded beaches. Rarely, however, do we **pause to reflect on the quantified pain cost** of our emotional and spiritual ignorance. It's said that the wise man knows he knows nothing, yet, while knowing what we think we know, and not knowing what we don't know, we consistently fall prey to imperceptible yet massive collateral damages. Unfortunately, we often navigate through life, oblivious and accepting of our damaged, unbalanced and unhealthy reality as a normalized setting. It's ironic—never do we see a T-shirt or meme declaring, *"Normalize Dysfunctional Living,"* yet it remains our proudly accepted reality.

Regarding normalized dysfunction for example, particularly In the realm of romantic relationships, consider the widely known fact that far over 50% of marriages end in failure. Despite this, many individuals enter marriage without any proactive plans to mitigate these high failure rates or adapt to changes in social behavior. It prompts a pertinent question: Would you willingly board a flight with an airline and pilot boasting a success rate far below 50%?

To the alpha-proud man who might dismiss a book like this, consider a study conducted at Stanford University, revealing that over 70% of divorces are initiated by women. This particular disruption in life catches most men off guard, often leading to a downward spiral into depression. Research indicates that life post-divorce is emotionally and physically more demanding for men, suggesting a more traumatic and or challenging experience than for women, feel free to look it up, as Numbers don't lie. If 70% of your paycheck was missing, would it not matter? Would it not initiate a micro-trauma?

Whether facing a 50% or a 70% chance of divorce catching you off guard, would an alpha man consciously opt for clinical depression and witness his life unravel, forfeiting all that he's invested in and accumulated to maintain a fairly decent lifestyle? Bear in mind that with each passing day, his mind and body grow older and weaker, while his testosterone declines with each passing year. You don't need to be a forensic accountant to predict how this scenario will likely play out for most people. But would a man willingly accept the tangible pain-cost and loss that result from failing to maintain sound insights, or take advantage of a blueprint for nurturing healthy connections with loved ones, and potentially gain an edge over those plotting against them? The wisdom of Sun Tzu's "The Art of War" has already taught us that the best way to win a war is to essentially never truly enter it in the first place.

The famous psychologist Carl Jung once stated, "One does not become enlightened by imagining figures of light, but by making the darkness conscious." I believe that once you have seen the light, it is impossible to unsee it. Enlightenment is crucial if we aim to alleviate the significant pain costs and unseen collateral damage previously discussed. Just as each link in a chain contributes to its strength, every individual must do their part to evolve humanity as a whole. To further exemplify, envision a nation characterized by fractured social connections, lacking the integration of soulmate bonds essential for personal soul evolution.

A depressed and deprived, ignorant populace teetering on the brink of rage and extreme spiritual poverty. Now, contrast this with an enriched civilization where a harmonious culture thrives, and individuals are spiritually and systematically developed as well as emotionally interconnected like lightning-fast synapses in the brains of superconscious beings. In the ladder scenario, they'de be emotionally integrated and in alignment with divine purpose, causing manifestation potential to become inherently compounded and radically exponential. If this were the case, it would imply that the world around you would appear noticeably different, perhaps resembling an alternate dimension on a significantly higher vibrational timeline.

The manuscript before you serves as the catalyst for this transformation, as it all starts with your understanding of the interconnected nature of souls. It provides the essential insights needed to begin your journey of deeper self-awareness and connectivity. You'll discover a pragmatic framework that not only helps you recognize and alleviate the thresholds of negative stress by demystifying soul ties but a framework that also provides a contextual foundation for the evolution of your soul consequently initiating a trickle down effect throughout your lifetime positively affecting everyone you cross paths with and the world at large. For these compelling reasons alone, my beloved friends and family, this book is undeniably necessary.

Here's what's truly interesting. Amidst the myriad relationship narratives, the anecdotes provided transcend the romantic realm. They unfold within the broader canvas of social engagements with interpersonal encounters that stretch far beyond the confines of romance. In the grand tapestry of your life, you're not just navigating romantic encounters; you're mingling with a diverse array of souls in countless contexts. These interactions become pivotal, acting as disruptors in your life's timeline, often triggering exposure to the shadow self and injecting the vital energy needed for the evolution of your soul. It's a dynamic journey where every choice you make and every connection you forge, serves as a vibrant brushstroke on the canvas of your existence. Now, multiply that with countless lifetimes in several dimensions presenting as various personalities.

Even if you're a hardened criminal serving a life sentence in prison, understanding the significance of the souls you encounter beyond a romantic context is crucial for navigating socio-political interactions. All interactions carry a predestined spiritual depth, even if they're with your arch-nemesis. After all, who is Superman without Lex Luthor or Batman without the Joker, more aptly Luke without Darth Vader—an undeniable and apparent soul connection. No pun intended with the word "a-parent." Some would passionately assert that the soul's journey towards evolution remains unfinished unless accompanied by the emergence of a soul-polarizing shadowed twin elemental charged with nemesis-like energy for orchestrating a symphony of spiritual equilibrium.

This book adopts a polymathic approach, drawing on a broad spectrum of sources to forge a comprehensive understanding of the soul's nature. It incorporates peer-reviewed studies by top researchers, historical records, behavioral studies, and data analytics, including surveys from the Marist Institute for Public Opinion. The goal is to deepen your understanding of why soul-tied-mates exist and how intimate relationships form across a spectrum of mirrored reflections impacting the trajectory of your life's timeline.

As you journey through these pages, you'll explore the complex dynamics of emotion, attraction, intimacy, and social interaction, gaining insights into the elemental forces that shape these relationships. You'll also uncover the mystical reasons behind your destined encounters with certain individuals. This exploration will enhance your understanding of twin elemental characteristics in pre-destined soulmate connections. It offers new perspectives on your interpersonal relationships across lifetimes and dimensions, while clarifying the patterns that influence your soul's evolution.

Many people are unfamiliar with the twin flame concept, and fewer still understand the additional elemental types such as Twin-Floods, Twin-Winds, and Twin-Planets, each offering a unique perspective alongside the well-known Twin-Flames. These elemental relationships, although lesser-known, significantly enhance our understanding of soul connections and have profound, life-altering impacts similar to the butterfly effect.

Exploring these relationships enables us to appreciate their influence on our life's journey and to recognize aspects like Carl Jung's concept of the shadow self. This understanding fosters enhanced self-awareness, greater spiritual intelligence, deeper personal growth, and ultimately, richer interpersonal connections. This book provides tools and insights to navigate the complexities of these relationships, helping you to build and maintain fulfilling social and personal bonds.

Furthermore, intelligent entities, including corporations, employ meticulous protocols when evaluating potential partners. They check character references, conduct background checks, review financial histories, and even use methods like psychological tests, natal chart readings, and DNA analysis for some. In a world where a simple résumé is no longer sufficient, ensuring successful ventures requires conscious, intentional engagement when forming new connections.

In our bonus chapters titled 'Conscious Relating: A Master Class - Parts One and Two,' we will establish and validate the practice of consciously-relating with our many soulmates and loved ones, facilitating spiritual transmutation toward higher states of awareness, regardless of the nature of the bond. In the context of conscious relating, the words "conscious" and "intentional" are often used interchangeably.

As we explore the doctrine of Intentional or **Conscious Relating** and its contrasting counterpart, **Compulsive Relating**, you may find it concerning to see that in today's social interactions, many people often engage in several relationships, from socializing to falling in love, without real intention or awareness. This pattern is not limited to romantic connections but also includes platonic friendships and business partnerships. The words you'll read extend beyond mere sentimental relationship advice; they offer profound social guidance for humanity's evolution.

The mirrored elemental natures in the souls we encounter daily, whether shadowed or illuminated, hold the potential to disrupt the timelines of our lives. In this context, guidance is crucial for co-creating improved models of relating as to not make decisions based in unconscious compulsions. Compulsive behavior often stems from societal influences and pressures or the fear of loneliness. As individuals, we often become emotionally impassioned about various matters, only to later realize that such fervor may have been unnecessary.

Often times, rather than proactively choosing to "grow" in love, within a partnership, many individuals find themselves "falling" in love instead. They rush into romantic relationships solely driven by strong emotions or physical attraction. However, it's essential to recognize the contrasting impacts of "passion" and "com-passion." While passion has the potential to inflict intense pain, compassion remains unblemished. Some people may carry unresolved emotional wounds or past traumas that propel such behaviors. Regardless of the underlying causes, these impulsive and reactive patterns pose substantial challenges to establishing healthy and enduring relationships.

Additionally, the rapid pace of modern life further fuels our collective compulsions. With social media and dating apps at the forefront of our culture, individuals may prioritize instant gratification and fleeting connections based on illusion, neglecting the time and effort required to forge deep, meaningful bonds. In essence, fostering a healthy and fulfilling relationship necessitates a conscious commitment to cultivating self-awareness, emotional maturity, and effective communication skills. If you have experienced suffering due to similar compulsive behaviors, honesty and accountability will bring clarity, healing, and wisdom. By adopting a deliberate and mindful approach to social interactions, relationships, and even love, individuals can forge profound connections and nurture enduring bonds with their partners and associates.

If we're honest with ourselves, we've all encountered toxic and impulsive behaviors at one time or another. Some have experienced toxic engagements early on, perhaps in their teenage years or early adulthood, while others confronted them later in life. Regardless of the timing, such experiences can have a lasting impact on our emotional and mental well-being, and they aren't confined to amorous or familial relationships alone. Toxic dynamics can manifest in any relationship, whether it's with friends, family, colleagues, and in local environments.

In the conscious relating bonus chapters, I'll present a blueprint for conscious relating as opposed to compulsive relating. The objective is to supercharge your self-awareness, enabling you not only to understand yourself better but also to recognize patterns in others. By doing so, you'll naturally strengthen your psychic sensory and awareness as well as learn to steer clear of toxic entanglements by default, no matter the relational context. Through the practice of conscious relating, you'll cultivate the innate ability to instinctively counteract compulsive relating as your default mental setting.

Conscious relating is of utmost importance to understand because experiencing trauma at any stage in life can lead to the **fragmentation** of one's personality as a defense mechanism for safeguarding mental stability. This phenomenon is widely recognized as **dissociative identity disorder** or (DID), formerly known as multiple personality disorder. Within DID, distinct identities or personality states emerge in response to trauma, allowing individuals to compartmentalize and cope with overwhelming experiences. Make no mistake, micro traumas cause micro states of dissociative identities no matter how low on the spectrum.

At some point, we've all had to adopt different versions of ourselves as a means of self-protection, no matter how minor or seemingly insignificant the adjustments may have seemed. Unfortunately, we often internalize the toxicity projected onto us, adapting to it to ensure our survival. However, if left unaddressed, these numerous micro-adaptations can engrain learned traits within us, ultimately leading to their projection onto others.

In toxic intercourse, one or both parties engage in emotionally or psychologically harmful, controlling, or manipulative behavior. This behavior can manifest in various forms, including verbal or physical abuse, gaslighting, jealousy, possessiveness, a lack of respect for individual autonomy, and a disregard for the other person's feelings, among several other common traits.

Like calloused skin on bruised knuckles, even seemingly insignificant micro traumas can trigger the parasympathetic nervous system, prompting a defense mechanism to shield fragile egos. For instance, when yelled at, a shockwave courses through the nervous system, leading one to shield themselves by adapting their behavior. As a result, they may reflect the same behavior and react outwardly, unleashing subsequent outbursts of yelling without consciously choosing to. Over time, unprocessed trauma compounds, attracting the type of circumstances which lead to several subsequent lifetimes incarnated on earth processing karma. Stop and think about that for a moment, or read it again if you didn't quite understand.

PREFACE (EXTENDED VERSION)

Toxic relationships, be they romantic, platonic, familial, commercial, or otherwise, can have imperceptible, yet detrimental impact on a person's mental and physical health, influencing a divergent timeline in an individual's life. In some cases, the individual may feel isolated, anxious, or depressed, subsequently influencing all other relationships. They may also struggle with low self-esteem, a distorted self-image, and difficulty trusting others which can affect professional relationships and other opportunities. These behaviors contribute to a significant portion of today's young adults suffering from philophobia, 'the fear of falling in love,' and pistanthrophobia, 'the fear of trusting others in a romantic context.' Many young adults openly admit that their romantic and social anxiety can be so debilitating that they appear socially awkward during a seemingly organic social interaction.

Aristotle once said, 'Man is by nature a social animal.' This reflects the idea that human flourishing is deeply tied to social interactions. At the heart of this concept is the theory of social capital, which explains how networks of relationships create value by fostering cooperation, trust, and the exchange of resources. Sociologist Robert Putnam further explored this in his work, 'Bowling Alone,' where he highlighted how strong community connections and vibrant social relationships are essential for both individual well-being and the advancement of society as a whole.

Seeing as though, "People Make the World Go Around," *according to the Stylistics*, and relationships are the glue to social advancement, It is essential to recognize the signs and patterns of toxic relationships, heal from their effects, and take action to address any issues that may have caused them. Ultimately, healthy relationships are founded on trust, mutual respect, authenticity, and effective communication, among other essential elements. Unfortunately, making healthy relationships the norm is not a priority for many. It appears that sometimes individuals would rather terminate their relationships than work on manifesting a more healthy dynamic.

Just as the average house pet may not comprehend the complexities of employment to cover home expenses, some could argue that the average human may not grasp the cumulative and quantitative compound effects of subtle ignorance in behavioral patterns over time. This lack of understanding extends to how factors that constitute compulsive relating dynamics can fundamentally transform one's living timeline and soul evolution.

This book serves as a guiding light to illuminate your awareness, assisting you in effectively shifting your paradigm as if skillfully manipulating it from a consciousness reminiscent of 4th-dimensional awareness. Delving into its contents, you'll find insights and tools for a transformative journey, allowing you to navigate your consciousness beyond the ordinary and embrace the profound.

While co-creating healthy relationships amid inherent disorder can be challenging, exploring the concepts in this book unlocks a level of awareness with the potential to significantly transform your mind and reshape your life. The goal is to inspire you by offering tools for full empowerment and an elevated state of consciousness, providing greater clarity and a deeper understanding of the paradigm that connects esoteric relationships with predestined soul pairings.

As human beings, we are much like sophisticated computers, each of us running a multitude of unconscious programs that govern our thoughts, behaviors, and perceptions. These programs—composed of our ingrained beliefs, habitual behaviors, and automatic thought patterns—operate silently in the background, shaping our reality without us even realizing it. However, just as software can become obsolete in a rapidly advancing technological world, many of these internal programs can become outdated or even detrimental over time. They may have once served us well, but as we evolve and our environments change, they can start to hold us back instead of helping us move forward.

Imagine a computer clogged with old software and riddled with malware—it slows down, becomes inefficient, and struggles to perform even basic tasks. Similarly, our minds can become cluttered with limiting beliefs, negative thought patterns, and outdated ways of thinking that no longer serve our highest potential. These mental "viruses" can hinder our growth, distort our perceptions, and prevent us from accessing the full capacity of our consciousness.

Just as a programmer knows the importance of regularly updating and debugging code to ensure optimal performance, we too must take responsibility for updating our mental "software." This means becoming aware of the unconscious programs running our lives, questioning their relevance, and actively working to replace those that are faulty or obsolete. It's about cleansing our minds of the "malware"—the fears, doubts, and negative narratives—that undermine our potential.

By consciously updating our mental programming, we unlock new levels of awareness and freedom. We liberate ourselves from the constraints of past conditioning, allowing us to think more clearly, act with greater intention, and align more closely with our true selves. This process isn't just about fixing what's broken; it's about proactively upgrading ourselves to thrive amidst constant change. It's an ongoing journey of self-improvement, adaptation, and empowerment.

Embracing this mindset transforms the way we interact with the world. We become more resilient, more adaptable, and more capable of navigating the complexities of modern life. We start to see challenges as opportunities for growth rather than insurmountable obstacles. Ultimately, by taking charge of our internal programming, we pave the way for a more fulfilling, authentic, and empowered existence. Are you ready to become the programmer of your own mind? To debug the system, install new updates, and unlock the fullest expression of who you are? The choice is yours, and the possibilities are as limitless as your willingness to evolve.

In closing.

It is firmly believed that with a more profound understanding of how and why souls attract and interact, individuals can alleviate fears concerning human interaction and eventually overcome duality as well as separation consciousness. In our rapidly advancing era of transhuman technocracies, the potential for meaningful human connection diminishes day by day, as evidenced by social media trends and real world accounts. We don't just experience magic or dysfunction in relationships with our peers; sometimes, it's the deep, complex bonds with estranged family members that cause disruption. These are the quintessential dynamics—like the classic mother-daughter nemesis or the perverse uncle stories we often hear—that can leave lasting effects.

Within this introduction and extended preface, I am sure you have gathered by now that this book transcends simple advice on erotic and sentimental relationships; it's a comprehensive guide covering various aspects of life. Yet, in the realm of romance, it stands out as an invaluable resource, particularly during the exciting courting phase. Can you imagine using it as part of a vibrant date night, offering a deeper experience than the usual 'Net flix and chill.' Would it not shift your perspectives and greatly improve the compatibility vetting process if studied together, subsequently helping you understand each other better and revealing qualities often missed in the early stages of dating. I imagine one might initiate this process as a resource for sniffing out red flags like a well trained bloodhound.

By acquiring a deeper understanding of one another, we can collectively advance toward embracing the reflective love of the universal source within each of us, ultimately nurturing a more spiritually connected world. When exploring the evolution of the soul and its complex social interactions, remember that this knowledge doesn't come with degrees or official certifications. It's not always about relying on experts for validation; sometimes, it's about trusting your own intuition to find your inner truth in the pages you read.

In conclusion, there is a reason you've found your way to this book, and it might not be immediately evident. Every encounter holds a divine purpose and significance. Each meeting is predestined; this one is no exception. Whether it's with a mentor, a romantic partner, or even a chance meeting with a stranger in the park or book store, every soul pairing, no matter how small, carries its own unique energy signature alongside a subsequent ripple effect. In the grand scheme of the universe, every connection between individuals is purposeful, including the connection between a student and a teacher or a writer and a reader. A divine plan is at work and every encounter holds the potential for massive transformation.

It is with immense honor and joy that I share these revelations, insights, and eternal truths through this literary endeavor, aiming to enrich the progression of our world and humanity at large. To you, dear reader, I extend my sincere wishes that you find substantial value and wisdom within this labor of love, as you set forth on a transformative path towards deeper enlightenment.

This book stands as the authoritative source on the topic, offering a comprehensive guide for all related matters. Whether you begin reading from the middle, the end, or jump around from section to section, periodically returning to these pages will significantly enhance your journey—a journey marked by vibrant experiences plus unforeseen developments in every new interaction. So, make yourself comfortable and prepare yourself for an exploration that promises to deeply enrich your awareness.

— Yours in service, Kushaqxi

Thank you for reading and or listening to this extended preface. While this book serves as a valuable introductory course, don't stop here. Dive deeper into this fascinating topic by connecting with us on all social media platforms, including Facebook, YouTube, Instagram, and TikTok, under @TwinElementalSoulmates. See QR codes on the copyright page for real time links. Join discussions, share your experiences, and help our community learn and grow from our collective encounters. Feel free to take the **Twin Elemental Soulmate Quiz** on our website to discover which elemental you and a partner are or may have been. Also, explore our corresponding books, courses and manuals for more content and insights. I encourage you to personally embrace this transformative experience and share it with friends by forming book clubs. This fosters collective appreciation for the joyous and enlightening journey found in immersing oneself in knowledge through reading physical books. Your journey into this subject is just beginning!

EPIGRAPH

*The body is forever changing
and will someday turn into dust.
Thus it is the soul that I will love
and commune with eternally.
To love me with your eyes,
or mind, is a temporal love...
Love me with your soul
and our love will be infinite.
I choose ONLY this.*

—*KushaqXi*

PART I

Chapter One

Wash | Rinse | Repeat

You live and you learn

Quote: "If you love yourself, you love others. If you hate yourself, you hate others. In relationships with others, it is only you, mirrored. — Osho.

Allow me to embark on a tale of a young man's quest for love and happiness. But let's dive right into the heart of it, for there, in the middle, is where this story truly takes shape. This is the narrative of two fated relationships that unfolded over the course of a year, profoundly altering my life and reshaping my perspective on love and human connections forever. Through these experiences, I gleaned invaluable insights about myself, my place in the world, the intricate nature of love, and the myriad challenges that come with encountering a karmic soulmate.

As I navigated through the intricacies of these relationships, I rode the waves of various emotional extremes—moments of sheer ecstasy contrasted with deep despair. I found myself confronting my fears, insecurities, and personal shortcomings head-on, a journey that was often arduous. Yet, in the end, I emerged as a wiser and more self-aware individual, armed with a profound comprehension regarding the true essence of love and being loved in return. This includes the love within and its connection to the source of all souls.

For me, that year represented nothing less than a comprehensive master's course in personal evolution. It was as if I had enrolled in a cosmic university where, upon graduation, my spiritual and emotional being would undergo a profound metamorphosis. The ultimate lesson gleaned from this transformation was the priceless awareness of the relationship I shared with myself. Becoming conscious of the remarkable power of self-love through the reflections provided by a twin elemental entanglement was an immersive, hands-on lesson like no other. An explosive metamorphosis and its subsequent ripple effects were already underway, unbeknownst to me, and about to forever cause a paradigm-shifting disruption to the trajectory of my life's timeline.

This, my friends, is my story.

It all started with the fiery trial of a twin flame experience. Though I had been familiar with the concept of twin flames for decades, my complete enlightenment regarding the dual nature of the following twin elemental experiences felt like the opening of a dogmatic reality, as if a telepathic signal from a satellite star had been intentionally broadcast to me, opening the floodgates to the entire twin elemental program. While healing from the crucible of circumstances that arose from the experiences I'm about to recount, long-forgotten memories from past relationships resurfaced during prolonged meditation, bringing clarity to the esoteric purposes of engaging with a twin flame, or any twin elemental, regardless of the dynamic.

I soon came to the realization that these were not solely my narratives, but they constituted a collective experience shared by many of my peers who were unknowingly entangled in similar situations. Whether in the public eye through high-profile media relationships or within my own family as with siblings, cousins, aunts, uncles, and even grandparents, the patterns observed in their behaviors mirrored an interconnected web of twin elemental engagement.

I mentioned that this story begins during the transitional phase between two relationships because that was the pivotal time that I sought guidance. The transformative insight took place between the end of the first relationship and the beginning of the second, precisely at the midpoint.

Amidst emotional turmoil, I turned to an unconventional yet familiar source for counsel—a long-time friend we'll simply refer to as the Ethiopian tarot reader, or Miss "T." The "T" in her name isn't related to tarot; her birth name coincidentally starts with the letter "T."

She was a beautiful-souled, golden bronzed, gypsy-like woman whom I had known through her craft, as a medium since my late teens. My meeting with Miss "T" would later prove critical in understanding why I was affectionately bonded with the two souls with whom I was entangled.

What I would learn from Miss "T" shocked both of us. It turned out to be the missing piece that brought complete clarity and a deeper understanding of the esoteric nature of the assignment that lay ahead. The message from Miss "T's" cards was simple yet as illuminating as a supernova. While its significance was not immediately apparent yet poignant, I wouldn't realize just how poignant at the time, and so we will return to Miss T and our quintessential reckoning of sorts shortly.

I'd like to take you back, all the way back—five or so years before I officially met the person who would become the first part of the catalysts that spawned what would become an emo-spiritual transformation in my life. I first became aware of the personality I'll call "AJ" through a buddy of mine who had connected with her on Craigslist. They began dating, subsequently establishing a trust level where she would leave him the keys to her apartment when she was out of town.

Mind you, she was possibly in her second or third trimester of pregnancy when she connected with my Sagittarius buddy online. I distinctly remember the first time I learned of her—it was a day when my buddy and I visited her apartment to check up on things. While there, I couldn't help but notice the numerous pork rind bags scattered across her kitchen table and atop the refrigerator. This seemed particularly odd, considering my friend was a strict vegetarian.

Needless to say, this raised an eyebrow. But, in line with my young Sagittarius curiosity, I still needed visual confirmation. A social media profile, or some sort of reference, would help to make sense of it all. I had to gauge her attractiveness and evaluate if the union of their disparate personalities was worthwhile.

I imagine that upon first seeing her, I must have reacted with a skeptical smirk and followed it with a subtle yet squinty-eyed nod of approval, indicating—not bad—not bad at all. She was slender, fairly tall, had a flawless reddish-brown complexion like myself, and featured a symmetrical nose with high cheekbones reminiscent of Queen Nefertiti. You could liken her to a darker version of the Somali-born model Iman, especially when viewed through rose-colored glasses.

I assume my friend must have shown me her social media profile, because, at some point, I definitely sent her a friend request, possibly after recognizing it again by chance, and we soon became digital friends. At that time, I didn't dwell too much on the serendipitous encounter. It appeared to be a random and fleeting event within the vast cosmos. I was largely oblivious to the potential for the compounding power that could ripple from such a brief and seemingly insignificant moment.

Regardless, over the next few years, we found ourselves occasionally commenting on each other's social media posts, sometimes expressing approval with likes on some and probably wrinkling our noses at others. By this time, AJ and my buddy had long gone their separate ways, so there were no restrictions on staying in touch, particularly in a platonic manner.

She was undeniably strong-willed and held firm opinions. From my standpoint, many of her views appeared to lack substantial foundations, perhaps fueled by emotions stemming from past traumas. But, on social media, that's nothing unusual. Naturally, she had every right to cope with life in her own way.

Unfortunately, as the years passed, her vexing rants grew to be quite an annoyance, prompting me to remove her from my friend's list multiple times to safeguard my sanity. Surprisingly, I found myself missing her entertaining antics and frequently pondered her activities, which eventually led to me sending yet another friend request. To my surprising delight, she always graciously accepted. Nonetheless, we often went through extended periods of minimal interaction. I suppose the adage "out of sight, out of mind" held true for both of us. After all, she was just a cute little Chica Morena my buddy used to date.

As fate would have it, then came the day that I unexpectedly bumped into her at the local Barnes and Noble bookstore after a lengthy absence. We were both delighted to see each other, and decided it was an opportunity to catch up. I extended an impromptu lunch invitation, to which her response was, "I never turn down food." Seeing as she maintained nearly zero percent body fat, she could afford to live on the edge like that.

We chose Chipotle, conveniently located just a short walk from the bookstore. Here's the thing: aside from the occasional social media interaction, we didn't really know each other personally. However, there had always been a sense of curiosity and a cautious attraction since day one. It's worth noting that she was undeniably attractive to me, and, without bragging too much, I'd like to think I wasn't too shabby in that department either, or so I've been told. But I digress, let's keep the story moving.

One lesson we acquire with age is that physical attraction doesn't necessarily correlate with the true value of a person, especially when it comes to their spirit or personality. Life's experiences teach us that even the most stunning Hollywood celebrities can harbor poor hygiene, severe drug and alcohol issues, or a self-loathing complex that can make every obnoxious word they utter nauseating and repulsive.

Thankfully, AJ didn't fit that description, yet she was an entirely different breed in her own right. In fact, who am I kidding? She wasn't all that different when I ponder it further. I distinctly recall her once mentioning that her aspiration was to never be sober and to perpetually revel in the bliss of being intoxicated and stoned on a beach somewhere in Miami or Paris.

During that particular time in the past when we had our impromptu lunch date, we didn't delve deeply into each other's inner worlds. Instead, we simply enjoyed our meal, engaged in light banter, and she extended an invitation to visit her at her workplace – a jazz club in the city. I eventually managed to find the time to drop by and see her in her element while working the room as a bottle girl.

To be honest, it wasn't an extremely eventful encounter either, except for two things: firstly, I observed that she was a delightful presence while working the room, and secondly, I received a complimentary drink. Nevertheless, there was always a guarded demeanor about her that made me hesitant, so I didn't linger for long that evening.

This brings me to our actual meeting for our inevitable and predestined bonding per our pre-birth soul contract. It would be over another year or so before we would cross paths again. On a serendipitous late summer night, following a prolonged period of silence between us, I caught sight of a slim, perfectly browned silhouette in a long pencil skirt, and a fresh pixie bob cut, gliding to the back of the 15 items or less aisle while shopping at the local "K.Rogers" grocery market.

As our eyes met, we immediately recognized each other, and in that moment, we shared the most enormous smiles and the warmest, heartfelt embrace. Astonishingly, it felt as though we were reuniting with a cherished, long-lost friend. It had been over five years since I first became aware of the being we're affectionately referring to as AJ.

Throughout the years, there had always been something enigmatic about her, something I couldn't quite put into words. But now, it seemed as if everything had been building toward this very moment. Perhaps, our positions in the cosmos had finally synchronized. After all, there's a preordained time and space for everything beneath the stars.

We were genuinely thrilled to see each other. In that moment, we both realized that it was time to shed our guards, which had been up for far too long. It felt as if, while locking eyes, we both understood the assignment, and that the person before us was genuinely cool. Well, that's open to interpretation, but AJ certainly possessed a fantastic personality when she chose to showcase it.

AJ consistently presented herself with respect and simple courtesy. It had been half a decade of passive vetting, and now the ideal moment had arrived to truly commit to maintaining contact and building a genuine and long-overdue friendship. This was fueled by a strong physical attraction, to say the least, as our gaze into each other's eyes had revealed. If nothing else, we were determined to see where the winds of destiny would carry us this time.

It goes without saying, I was feeling significantly confident these days. I had just moved back to Atlanta from my two-year tour of duty in Harlem, New York, A place I most certainly loved. I was now working three restaurant jobs, one being Highland Bakery which I loved and the others being California pizza and some chicken spot which I loathed. I was also slowly rebuilding my flooring company, and hoping to build credit by financing a luxury vehicle through my credit union amongst other things.

My life was definitely forward moving and on a path to recovery, particularly since the somber divorce from one of the great loves of my life – the mother of my children from my first marriage. That, coupled with a subsequent series of failed relationships, meant that I was long overdue for some good luck. I've always been a lover's lover—Possibly even in love with love. Be it bad and boujee, Yogi Yasmiin, the one that broke my heart, or the beautiful and charismatic Haitian Brooklynite, Kimichie, whose heart I regretfully broke—I was always into something.

I must have been in my early to mid-thirties around this time and was single and always ever ready to mingle. Still, there's always a natural mystic in the air when on the Westside of Atlanta, at a big box grocery store on a late summer's night. Firstly, what were all these people doing shopping at almost midnight? This isn't the village in Manhattan, for gods sake. Secondly, why does summer feel so good when you have money in your pocket, feeling great, and recently reconnecting with an old acquaintance?

My guy, Sio, a buddy who worked with me rehabbing homes from time to time, was riding shotgun that night. He listened as I animatedly recounted the nostalgic details of my encounter with AJ. As we drove, I almost hit an elderly woman in a white sedan while attempting to exit the West Ends K. Roger's" parking lot. I held up my hands in a peaceful posture as to say, excuse my reckless haste, but guess who jumped out of the passenger seat of the sedan, apparently wanting smoke with the impatient driver of the silver BMW X5. I'll give you a moment, go on, take a guess — Bingo. It was none other than the fiery, Ms. AJ. In case I haven't made it clear yet, she was a firecracker with a short fuse and a strong-willed demeanor. Taken aback, I lowered my window and unleashed my charm, offering heartfelt apologies. To my delight, it worked like magic, as she was grinning from ear to ear.

Looking back, I often pondered, what were the odds? There are no random occurrences when the universe is following a meticulously crafted script. AJ reassured her mother that everything was fine. At that moment, I couldn't tell if it was solely my charm or the allure of the so-called luxury vehicle that had an entrancing impact on someone I would later discover to be a shrewd opportunist. Nevertheless, within an hour of our chance encounter, she gave me a call, and roughly an hour later, around 2 am, I was en route to her place.

Upon my arrival, there was an undeniable sense of magic in the air, or perhaps it was just the effect of intense animalistic pheromones. We engaged in a night-long conversation, and around 4 am, she persuaded me to drive her across town to Atlanta's eastside to acquire a unique pack of Indian cigarettes called cloves from a 24-hour convenience store off of 20 East and Glenwood Avenue. Upon our return, our conversation continued until well after sunrise. Allow me to share an unrelated tidbit: I had enlisted the help of a hypnotist six months prior to successfully quit smoking, and it had worked like a charm; I had become smoke-free. Little did I know that her hypnotic sway would be far more powerful.

We lounged, savoring black clove cigarettes, sipping red wine, and locking eyes as we descended deeper into the captivating chemical cocktail of oxytocin, dopamine, serotonin, adrenaline, and quite possibly DMT, because by the time she gave the green light to explore her intimate domain, we were already traveling an enchantingly karmic and cosmic soul network akin to an orgasmic out of body experience, no doubt a journey that culminated in a blissful blackout, only to reawaken and re engage several times.

Later that afternoon, as we headed out for brunch, her neighbor, while washing his truck in his driveway, called her over. He mentioned how earlier that morning a group of neighborhood kids had gathered by the curb on their bikes, genuinely concerned about the strange sounds coming from her open windows. They worried that a wild cat was being subjected to punishment or something – no pun intended!

As expected, the initial two to four weeks were nothing short of mesmerizing. The two of us and her adorable daughter, who was now five, would all hang out sometimes, though the little one often found herself under the care of her grandmother. For context, AJ had been squatting in the house she formally rented for the past six months when we reconnected.

A conspicuous hole in the bathroom floor was gradually expanding, putting the rest of the floor at risk of collapsing. To secure free rent, she had employed her charm to finesse the landlord, who had hesitated to address the many issue for over six months, until just about a month before our reunion. Her landlord had finally had enough and was making preparations to have her legally evicted. Naturally, I "Captain Savior," suggested she move in with me, offering her a safe haven in a newly rented downtown condo.

Fast forward, we were living the dream. Now, make no mistake, there were red flags every day, every hour on the hour, but I was enjoying myself because, dare I say, I was in love (whatever that was). Far from it I'm sure, but undoubtedly, entranced by the chemical cocktail coursing through me, and the allure of a world brimming with novelty and excitement in every direction. Little did I know, I would one day learn that red flags are difficult to see when you're wearing rose-colored glasses.

AJ's unique openness and free-spirited nature resonated deeply with my own disposition. I've always seen myself as a freedom centered individual, with a tendency towards ethical polyamory, but looking back, I think I might have had some insecurities. I often asked her about her past and imagined scenarios in the present, attempting to understand who she was and what exactly was it, we were doing.

Interestingly, I also created hypothetical situations to test her. One memorable example was when I asked her what she would do if she found me intimately involved with the singer from the band with singer Sade' Adu. Her response was humorous and unexpected: she said she'd ask if she could watch and then record the encounter. These moments truly highlighted the entertaining and unique nature of companionship with her.

There were times when acquaintants, familiar with both AJ and I, would discretely offer warnings. They'de label her a "maneater" and a heartbreaker, advising me to stay alert. With a knowing look and raised eyebrows, they'd wish me luck, as if they knew something I didn't. I was aware of the potential risks, yet I chose to live in the moment, cherishing each transient experience. The thrill was so intense that, if possible, I would have captured and sold it, potentially becoming Rolls-Royce rich.

Truthfully, being with AJ felt like living the lyrics of Luther Ingram's R&B song, "If loving you is wrong, I don't want to be right —the irony. Roughly a month into our relationship, I started to observe a gradual but distinct change in her behavior, which became progressively rude and unsettling. Reflecting on this with a sense of honesty and self-awareness, I acknowledged that I had been too accommodating, perhaps even naïve or simple minded and excessively sympathetic - one might even say, quite Simpish. I realized I was investing emotional energy without receiving the same in return, and this dynamic needed to shift.

Taking note of her altered demeanor, I suggested that we both could benefit from some space. I proposed that she move in with her brother, a place where her mother and daughter also lived, believing it might be a healthier environment for us both—It marked the start of our decline. While it might seem like I initiated the breakup to send her a message about her behavior, it felt as though she was the one who distanced herself from me.

Initially, she continued to visit, and we shared a few more brief, intoxicating moments, but eventually, things played out as they were destined to. With each passing day, I found myself growing emptier as I detoxed from the limmerent intoxication of infatuation. I would attempt to hang out with her, sometimes bearing gifts, but honestly, she was always on a date. It was as if she could effortlessly switch partners, like a pirate leaping from one ship to another, without a second thought. She had moved on as swiftly as she had entered my life. It truly felt like a case of energy transference, as she adopted the role I initially believed I would embody.

The pivotal moment in this entire saga occurred on a day when I was feeling exceptionally low, not specifically because of the relationship, but due to a general sense of despondency. I was wandering through downtown Atlanta, wrestling with myriad feelings, and the thoughts of my recent breakup with AJ surged, triggering an outburst of tears. In a moment of emotional release, I looked up to the sky and cried out, "Why me?" Believe it or not, it really wasn't about AJ at all; it was more a deep introspective reflection of myself.

I questioned why I seemed to repeatedly make decisions that created the sort of conditions that put me in less than favorable positions. I was acutely aware of my circumstances and had a clear understanding of who AJ was, so I pondered deeply the spiritual significance of why anyone would make these choices.

It reminded me of a saying from George W. Bush: "Fool me once, shame on you; fool me, uh, um .well, funk it, you can't get fooled again." It was a reminder that, once I was aware of the deception, I was the one responsible for continuing the cycle. I accepted full accountability for my role in co-creating this story. To say that she and I were a mismatch or unequally yoked would be a gross understatement.

Considering her behavior and lifestyle, she was far from the type of woman I typically dated. Most of my friends would raise their eyebrows in confusion when they met her, asking, "Are you sure about this?" Some would acknowledge her cool appearance but emphasized that energy never lies. Despite these warnings, I was captivated by the idea that she offered something entirely different from what I had experienced before. I'm not sure what she was selling, but she sold it well.

It was during this period that I gained my first real understanding of what a true narcissist was. She would often portray herself as a divine gift to humanity, but in reality, and as candidly described by my close friend Shara, she was nothing more than a "Basic Bum Bitch" – Shara's words, not mine, and there was no denying the accuracy of that description.

I won't delve to deeply into the specifics here, but the truth was, her life was in disarray. She seemed to survive by ensnaring men with her charms, a skill she had undoubtedly honed during her early twenties while dancing at the renowned Atlanta gentlemen's club Magic City, and later as a bottle girl at the jazz club. Her existence was marked by perpetual self destructive chaos, evident from the hole in her floor to her fear of sobriety.

There was no judgment from me because, essentially, my life couldn't have been much better seeing as I was her current reflection and yet, when we were together, we felt at peace. The sunburst past the dark clouds of our minds when I would elicit within her the beautiful natural high that comes from the illusion of being in love.

Returning to the crucial realization and the climactic moment after our separation, tears streamed down my face as I grappled with acute disappointment, primarily directed inward towards myself. Crying out in response to personal realizations can be understood as undergoing an emotional breakthrough or catharsis. This reaction often entails confronting deep-seated emotions, memories, or truths about oneself, leading to a release of pent-up feelings through tears. Such moments are integral to the process of self-discovery, healing, and personal growth.

I realized that I had significantly compromised my standard of living by letting someone deeply affect my spirit and dominate my emotional and energetic existence. My feelings weren't of heartbreak or disappointment towards AJ, as I hadn't harbored any substantial expectations from her. Rather, it was a profound sense of inadequacy within myself that surfaced. I recognized that I had been ensnared in a repetitive cycle that hindered my growth and obstructed my path to reaching my full potential. This was a striking and eye-opening realization. I couldn't help but wonder, however, how could I, someone who prided himself on being enlightened and intelligent, subject myself to such a privately humiliating experience? I had poured every ounce of my energy into what I would later acknowledge as a true and living succubus, while neglecting myself. I felt spiritually cheap.

This experience prompted a profound epiphany: the substantial amount of time, energy, emotions, and financial resources that I had been pouring into dating over the years could have instead been invested in myself. This investment would take the form of personal growth and self-improvement, endeavors that could potentially yield returns beyond measure. Even the energy expended in moments of cathartic pleasure could have been regenerated and magnified within my overall magnetism had they been self concentrated. I won't even mention the potential financial gains from self focused improvements. The inverted flames AJ ignited, served as the catalyst that opened the floodgates to numerous epiphanies that had been lurking just beneath the surface of my conscious mind.

I recognized that personal attention, self-mastery, and discipline had the power to draw to me all the things I desired and truly deserved, whether they were material or spiritual, known or yet to be discovered. I felt as though I had been cheated, swindled, and robbed of my own energy, by the most unsuspecting perpetrator – myself. Who does that? Who robs themselves?

I imagine if the Arch Bishop Don Magic Juan was my mentor and minister, he would have directed me to the following scripture: Malachi 3:8: where it states, "Will a man rob God? Yet ye have robbed me. But ye say, Wherein have we robbed thee? In energetic tithes and offerings. To the God within that is. #church

My actions were, at their core, foolish and nonsensical. Nevertheless, there had been a significant transference of energy, and my magic had seemingly vanished, leaving me feeling empty, absent, and lost. The question remains, why did I allow myself to fall in love with Ms. If Red Flags were a person, and knowingly trade my integrity and self respect for an obvious devil in a red dress.

I describe our situation in this manner not to cast shame or blame on AJ, but to paint a picture of what hustling backwards looks like and while fully being conscious of my actions, yet powerless to alter the unfolding events. Like a spectator in the sunken place, It all felt surreal. Could there have been an unseen spiritual significance at play within the atomic simulation of my life?

During this challenging phase, life was particularly tough for me. To add to my struggles, I lost my condo, which compounded the difficulties. "Kick a man while he's down, why don't you?" was my initial sentiment towards AJ, possibly because I felt that I had lifted her up when she was down. I understood however that she had no obligations and owed me nothing. Despite swiftly moving past my entanglement with AJ, I found myself wrestling with a deep, inexplicable heartache. It might have been a withdrawal from the euphoric chemical rush of excitement I had felt.

This pain, however, had a beneficial aspect – a silver lining if you will - it ignited a powerful desire for personal change. In the midst of this turmoil, I began fasting daily, as I was unable to eat or sleep due to the self-inflicted emotional turmoil. My routine transformed drastically; I exercised intensely and found solace in reading, consuming a book a day, sometimes two while digesting multiple audio books on constant rotation.

Despite everything, a peculiar transformation was underway. The pain began to morph into a strangely masochistic form of gratification. It seemed as if my brain was concocting a new chemical cocktail, transforming misery into motivation. There's likely a medical term for this powerful phenomena. The inner work I was doing daily became a source of inspiration, driving me towards becoming a superior version of my former self as I navigated through and emerged from this challenging period.

I was undoubtedly undergoing a process of "Post-Traumatic Growth," characterized by positive psychological changes arising from the struggles with and conquest of adverse life experiences. This transformation involved dopamine detoxification, shifts in perception, intentional interactions with others, personal resilience, and a deepened appreciation for life. As the pain began to dry up, I found myself wrestling with the fear of losing the secret weapon that had bestowed upon me this mystical new superpower. My magic had returned in a way I had never experienced before. I was reborn, like the mythical phoenix rising from the ashes.

One of the books I read, by an author whose name eludes me, contained a statement that struck me. In essence, it conveyed, "I've learned and evolved more in 10 days of agony than I have in 10 years of study." While I'm paraphrasing, this statement profoundly resonated with me and essentially became the cornerstone of my entire healing process.

Although I was making progress, I found myself standing at a crossroads, quite literally. The deity of the crossroads, Eshu Elegba, a recurring theme in various indigenous traditions, played a significant role in my life during this period. And with that, this is where Ms. T, along with her revealing tarot card reading enters the scene. Let's refer to it as 'midterms' in terms of the spiritual lessons I encountered during this phase of my life. It was like the halftime show in the current season of the stage play known as life.

Her place was beautiful and mystical, providing an exquisite setting. Though mostly positive, I cannot recall all of the details from the psychic reading yet one moment stood out vividly which were the cards that pertained to my life and relationship. While apparently channeling my destiny, In a subtle manner, I noticed her slight jump and a hint of shock in her expression. Contrary to her previous demeanor, she, in her low-toned and breathy Ethiopian American accent, declared, "you are going to be back with her."

Forgive my directness, but my response was unequivocally, "No Hell," a down south urban way of saying, no the hell I'm not. My expression communicated a clear message – you might want to reshuffle that deck, sis. She examined the cards once more and affirmed, "you will be with that same spirit and energy, if not her directly. The energy remains, unaltered." Strangely, this pivotal moment validates the entire chapter, namely, the "repeat" part.

In the midst of personal growth, immersed in a shamanistic state of celibacy, focus, flow, and heightened vitality, I discovered that a man's magnetism could draw the attention of various high valued individuals, from local celebrities to married women. That's often how life works when you're off the market and unavailable. Unbeknownst to me, destiny had something else in store, as I was soon to encounter a supervillain in the intricate game of life and love, a final boss, so to speak. "Enter the Butterfly.

If you thought AJ was a beast, Butterfly, an alternative name for the sake of this writing, was a savage goddess. I wouldn't be surprised if the Butterfly ghost wrote the song "You needed me" performed by Rihanna. And I quote, "You was just another one on the hit-list, trying to fix your inner issues with a bad chick. Didn't they tell you that I was a savage, 'F' your white horse and a carriage. — Oh my, If ever there were a song that mirrored the precise events of two real-life relationships, this would be it.

I'm not even sure where to start with this one. My relationship with AJ was precisely three months. My healing period was about a month, and the Butterfly would occupy the rest of the year. Coincidently, I first met the Butterfly at the same Barnes & Noble in East Atlanta, where I had bumped into AJ years earlier. If you hadn't gathered by now, Barnes & Noble was a favored spot of mine for a significant time. With its array of baked goods, coffee, quiet ambiance, and free book reading, it was an inviting happy place for me that was hard to resist. The colorful butterfly sat studying and writing in her notebook, exuding an aura of enchantment and looking like a whole magical fairy touting a halo of destiny.

Her magnetism exuded an otherworldly quality, much like the character Bilquis from the television series "American Gods" with her comparable abilities. I sat as free as an invisible unicorn, capable of appearing as a brilliant, bright black apparition if I so chose. My radiance was pure and righteous. I, too, was studying but found it challenging to focus due to her captivating mystique. I reminded myself not to engage, as I adhered to a hood-like Buddhist lifestyle—celibate, fasting, and with a pure heart and mind. If I had theme music, it would be the tranquil Om chant, accompanied by a faint scent of burning frankincense and myrrh oil in the distance. She, however, sat poised, like a perfectly rehearsed actress ready to perform her scripted actions.

I struggled to resist, but unfortunately, curiosity got the best of me, and like a moth drawn to a flame, I approached her. It felt as if I were observing myself from an omni directional astral perspective as our eyes locked, remaining in that intense gaze for what seemed like timeless seconds. We engaged in a brief conversation, as if we both already understood the predestined journey we were about to undertake. Our communication was laden with allegory, concealed in cryptic banter and seductive body language. We reveled in the delicate balance between formality and spontaneity.

From the moment we made contact, it was as if we needed to possess each other's souls through sorcery and sexuality. After our initial formalities, I walked her to her minivan, noticing something peculiar about how she walked, as if in heat, a natural characteristic i would learn many men noticed in fact. I contemplate now if I should go into the entire story of myself and the honey pot, we're calling Butterfly. Her story deserves an entire book of its own if not a lifetime movie. What you will learn of us is only the tip of the iceberg.

Nevertheless, following our serendipitous encounter that day, we met up later that evening at a cozy, quaint restaurant in midtown. Wait—Pause, let me clarify! I recall her asking over the phone if we were going to hang out that night, mentioning she had another suitor lined up if we weren't. Indeed, it was the following evening when we actually linked up seeing that, the way my bank account was set up that day, well you get the picture. A key maxim and or axiom of a hustler is as long as you've got product, or a skill, you got money, only time and energy separate you.

The intimate midtown setting was perfect for falling in love. We spent over an hour with our heads and faces gently caressing like serene lions nuzzling, before we even began to glance over the menu. I remember most, her soft hair washing across my face like the touch of silk against the skin.

It goes without saying that we soon fell deeply in love, experiencing a whirlwind romance that could rival a classic black-and-white Hollywood film from the 1930s. The intensity between us was overwhelming. On that first night together, we stood hugged up and aroused in a dimly-lit parking lot, I playfully cautioned her that if we didn't quickly put some distance between us, I would soon fill my mouth with her as she was the most tasty little thing I had ever experienced. All jokes of course but whats understood doesnt need to be explained.

My risqué and playful banter ignited within her a passionate longing, driving her into a crazed frenzy of lust and desire. Though spoken in jest, I was young and sexually adventurous, fully aware of the triggers for maximum excitement. Fortunately, we did indeed put space between us that night, but let me be clear: from day one we were inseparable and from day one there were unmistakable red flags that I regrettably chose to ignore. I invited her to a Yoga class at a Buddhist temple with a couple of other friends for a second date a couple days later.

There's an old saying: "Those who fail to learn from their mistakes are destined to repeat them." Countless historical figures, including Winston Churchill, have publicly emphasized the idea that not learning from history leads to its repetition. Moreover, I'm reminded of a succinct and simple African proverb: "Fools fail to learn."

Well, I was a fool on a highway of repetition, racing at a thousand miles per hour, once again neglecting myself to heal another damaged soul with my love or so I believed. I used to hold the conviction that my love possessed an unparalleled, transformative power, capable of healing and rejuvenating even the most tormented souls, even bringing them back from the brink of death. Yet, I've come to a profound realization: not everyone desires salvation. aptly put, " don't save them, if they don't want to be saved.

My soul cries, and I cringe at stories I've heard in my lifetime about some of the traumas women experience. The Butterfly was no different. At 15 years of age, she experienced her first intimate encounter with the man who should have been her first love but not her first adult experience—her estranged yet biological father who she had been reunited with as a pre-teen. These perversions would go on for a season, to the extent that she eventually welcomed them. He was a Jamaican Don Dada, who in those days lived a cash infused, fast and flashy life.

Subsequently, she grew up dancing at the same popular Atlanta Gentlemen's Club where my former romantic partner, AJ, had also danced during her young adult years, surprisingly, a place I have never visited. Many intriguing stories beg to be told, but some remain too personal to reveal. I hold profound respect for both my own privacy and that of the Butterfly. Nevertheless, I will endeavor to provide relevant background information to offer you, the reader, a glimpse into a paradigm that once was.

To provide some context, our relationship began as I sought a career change, driven by a desire for a fresh experience. After weighing the advantages and disadvantages, I made the decision to become a long-haul truck driver and embrace a life on the open road. The plan was to accumulate experience in the trucking industry before venturing into a limited liability logistics company, eventually owning a small fleet of my own trucks. I had recently enrolled in trucking school when I crossed paths with Butterfly. At the time, I was living out of my BMW or occasionally squatting in the upscale homes and condos where I subcontracted remodeling work. Though I remained unaware of Butterfly's living situation, I had a sensed that her time there was drawing to a close.

Fortunately for both of us, I discovered a loophole in my training contract that allowed my sponsors to provide additional funds to cover the cost of a hotel since there was no dormitory available while I attended the trucking program. I extended an invitation to her to come and live with me at the extended-stay hotel because, by that point, it was evident that we were undeniably addicted to each other. Our sexual connection was intense and charged with primal energy. We were as open as the sky, and our passion ran as deep as the ocean.

Regrettably, my studies fell by the wayside, and I was eventually dismissed from the training program, consequently concluding the hotel arrangement. I had no qualms about it because, to be honest, there was no way I was going over the road and leaving this hot young thing to the mercy of the streets. This was literally my mentality at the time. So full of **simp**le minded **symp**athy, my name could have been, "**Simp**Nation."

Fast-forward, I once again tapped into my creative ingenuity and orchestrated a scenario where I could secure the equivalent of three months' rent in exchange for installing hardwood flooring. A friend's father had a home in need of renovation. The home was fully furnished, as my friend had previously resided there before being welcomed back into his wife's residence following a separation of about a year. Interestingly, this friend is the same individual who introduced me to AJ several years prior. Talk about reincarnating with the same cast of characters throughout lifetimes.

Note: From a "Souls Eye View, here a divergence appears on my timeline. Influenced by choices steered by a twin elemental force, a notable shift occurs that can be likened to the butterfly effect, significantly altering the trajectory of my life's path. Further details on these subtle phenomena will be revealed in the later sections of the book.

Another notable moment transpired when Ms. Butterfly confided in me about her deep desire to have her two young children living with her once more. At that time, they resided with their father, who was temporarily staying with his sister. When the flooring for rent barter deal came through, I, captain savior, again to the resthaven rescue, invited Butterfly and her children to live with me. One of the rooms, conveniently, already featured a bunk bed. This arrangement couldn't have been more fitting. She could now care for her children, and we formed a small, makeshift family. I vividly recall her 10-year-old son during a family group hug, exclaiming in a full Disney character voice, "I like this new family."

We were content.

I had several meetings with her children's father, and in these encounters, the three of us engaged in intense discussions where he consistently tried to undermine our connection. It became apparent to me that, despite their separation, both of them remained emotionally attached and sexually involved. Initially, I considered that their connection was held together by their shared responsibility for their children, and he served as her safety net, so his presence didn't initially perturb me. After all, I was the newcomer, and she assured me she would communicate to him that they should no longer remain intimately involved.

The reality was that they had been officially separated for a considerable period, and yet he continued to be a thorn in my side. On one occasion, he shouted, "It's like you're under a spell with this guy," before rushing away with tears in his eyes. We all considered ourselves highly evolved and spiritual individuals. Nevertheless, I can't help but think that if we were super low vibrational beings and possessed less maturity and wisdom, things might have escalated into violence. It was a precarious situation, to say the least.

At times, her children's father would engage in stalking behavior, and there was even an unsettling incident where he positioned himself outside by our window early one morning, eavesdropping on her passionate expressions. You can only imagine our shock when we heard a male voice uttering explicit language through the open window. I'd sometimes encounter him at the children's school while dropping off or picking them up. He would eagerly await their arrival, wearing an enormous smile, only to have it fade when he realized it was me delivering the children in her vehicle. In those moments, I often recalled the lyrics from Outkast's Antwon Patton, where he recites, "Choose the right one or pick the kiddies up." I'm raising my hand now. It's me. I'm the one who picked the kiddies up. (S.M.H.)

A few months into our shared journey, I made a significant gesture by purchasing a ring and proposing marriage to her. This was a substantial step for me. However, earlier that evening, she surreptitiously accessed my emails and stumbled upon a message from the first week we met, which she perceived as passively flirtatious, leading to feelings of lingering insecurity. In her disillusionment, she reluctantly accepted the ring, only to return it multiple times, then accept it again when we'd reconcile. If my relationship with the Butterfly were a circus, our emotional rollercoaster would be the main attraction.

A memorable incident unfolded when we made the decision to embark on a road trip, journeying to the salt plains in Oklahoma for quartz crystal digging and then to the hot springs to collect well water. An argument erupted, and it led to the Butterfly occupying the back seat for the entire eight-hour drive. I can't recall the specific trigger, but at some point during our highly volatile ride, she struck me in the back of the head with a closed fist. Shocked and surprised, I instinctively raised my hand—either to reach into the back seat or to shield myself from further blows. This reaction caused me to lose control of the vehicle. The car spun around in a full 360-degree turn, spiraling into a cornfield before swerving back onto the road, only to end up in the cornfield again as if an unseen hand had pushed us. Fortunately, the semi-trucks on the road were at least a quarter-mile behind us, preventing a potentially catastrophic collision.

Shellshocked, We drove for the following 15 minutes in dead silence. I stepped out of the vehicle after finally stopping at a gas station and slowly walked around to her side of the rental car as she sat frozen in fear, I casually opened the door, pulled her out, and picked her petite frame straight up into the air. With her legs straddling my body, we kissed each other most passionately, like two people who had just escaped death. Were it not for the rule of law, we may have made love right there at the gas pump for all to see. We were certainly the type. At this juncture in our lives, our relationship was becoming increasingly volatile. I mention these incidents to illustrate how our relationship was becoming "intoxicatingly more toxic" with each passing day.

Once, at the suggestion of a shared mentor and friend who was also secretly in love with her, I made the decision to take her on a trip to Miami, hoping to mend our relationship, which endured but was marred by confusion and instability. I believed that a change of scenery might help heal our unpredictable connection. During the trip, we enjoyed riding scooters along South Beach and indulged in unmentionable intimate moments on Ferris wheels hundreds of feet above the ground. We visited aquariums and took smiling pictures with aquatic animals. We explored the piers by the beach on bicycles, went shopping, and experienced the nightlife by club-hopping. We even ventured to a nude beach together for the first time and captured artistic moments through photographs .

Despite the multitude of thrilling experiences, it may come as a surprise that our trip was punctuated by conflicts from start to finish. It began with an argument on the flight there, which then led to a passionate reconciliation the moment we touched down. This cycle continued with another breakup during a night out clubbing, quickly followed by yet another episode of passionate lovemaking. Again after the scooter rides and the nude beach excursion. Ultimately, we parted ways once more on the flight home, ending the trip on a rather sour note.

I would often ask myself, who does that? Who breaks up with someone when presented with a free vacation to South Beach? Our relationship mirrored the dynamic nature of the sun's bipolar solar cycle. Like the sun's oscillation between the North and South Poles every eleven years at its solar maximum, we experienced drastic shifts—from alignment to dissonance—but within the span of a single day. Although the trip was disappointing at times, the trip was pronounced with magical moments that appeared to eclipse the tumultuous ones.This is the same woman who appeared like a magical fairy at our first meeting, with whom I spent over an hour nuzzling heads in blissful silence, surrounded by a high aura of energy. And yet, here she was, standing as my polar opposite, and paradoxically, also as my inverted mirror reflection.

Our bond felt karmic, and we both often agreed that we must have shared past lives to be so intrinsically connected both spiritually and emotionally. Our energy was captivating, and our passion blazed as intensely as solar flares. It had the power to set a room ablaze or create a cozy atmosphere akin to sipping hot chocolate by a warm fireplace while watching the movie "Heat." In restaurants, we often caught the attention of strangers who would approach us, drawn to our radiant presence, expressing admiration. Similarly, in grocery stores, passersby would smile and join in our excitement as I juggled tangerines—like a clown—to amuse her, sparking her joyous clapping and genuine laughter.

I radiated a love so brilliantly illuminating that it compelled her to mirror and reflect it back to me. Yet, with all the magnetic, spellbinding, loving energy she absorbed, the inner turmoil gradually bred discontent within her, conflicting with the peace, order, and devotion she now experienced. It was as if she waged a war within herself, struggling to trust it because, in her eyes, it was too perfect.

These thoughts bring to mind the fable of the scorpion and the frog. In the story, the scorpion pleads with the frog for a ride across the river, but the frog is wary due to the scorpion's inherent tendency to sting. Despite the frog's reservations, the scorpion convinces him to provide the ride by pointing out the shared peril of both drowning if he were to sting the frog.

Reluctantly, the frog acquiesces. However, in the middle of the journey, the scorpion indeed stings the frog, sealing both their fates to drown. Baffled, the drowning frog asks the scorpion why he would commit such an act, to which the scorpion simply responds, 'I couldn't help myself, it's in my nature.' The moral of this story is that one cannot battle their innate nature yet they can integrate it. To resist it is to fuel it, while accepting it opens the door to transformation. when one denies the truth of themselves, it only grows stronger in the darkness to their disillusionment.

The saying goes that love is to pain as life is to death, and in the realm of coinage, though opposite, heads inevitably accompany tails. I share with you multiple instances of love's magnetic force to illustrate the dual aspects of the esoteric nature in attraction and repulsion regarding soul ties. For the second time in less than one orbit of our planet around the sun, I found myself descending into the sunken place of relationships, super-prompting intense shadow integration through the influence of a twin elemental.

During these trying times, a friend named Tai, My guy Sio's wife in fact," offered me some great advice. She shared a perspective that resonated deeply with me, saying, "Our demons are sometimes drawn to the demons in our partners, almost as if, against our better judgment, we unconsciously gravitate toward certain individuals to our own detriment." Upon introspection, her words felt like a raw and undeniable truth. *Her actual words, dipped in a southern drawl, were, "sometimes, our demons are attracted to their demons."*

By now, the whimsical madam butterfly and I had broken up so many times that I was unfazed when our relationship reached its definitive end. Instead, it was as if a weight had been lifted, and a sense that I had graduated from the cosmic karmic school I seemed to have attended for the past year. Unlike the portrayal in popular movies, It felt like a true school for wizards, instructed by the cosmos themselves, with me as the sole student—as most psychic classes for alchemists tend to be.

I don't mean to imply that during a couple of our disengagements, I wasn't a total mess, but all in all, the sporadic emotional rollercoaster that we experienced left me somewhat numb. During one of our breakups, I took up gardening, a hobby that quickly blossomed into a lifelong passion. It's fascinating to reflect on how this love for arboriculture inspired the creation of the Sacred Sunfood Society. Although still in its early stages of development, the organization is poised to effect meaningful change in the lives of many. Remarkably, its very foundation can be traced back to an unlikely source: the cause and effect principles sparked by a past heartbreak, ignited by a twin elemental flame.

Is it possible that such a path, one that is bound to create a ripple effect impacting the lives of others, was orchestrated from a fifth-dimensional space during pre-life planning? This transformation marked a significant shift in the trajectory of my life, undoubtedly triggered by a twin elemental. Engaging in self-imposed therapies like gardening played a pivotal role in healing my spirit and preserving emotional clarity, thereby keeping my heart open.

Shifting back to our primary subject, during butterfly girls "frustration-provoked rebellion," even her children, whom I deeply cared for, became increasingly frustrated and unhappy, which was evident in their behaviors. Consequently, they moved back in with their father while she and I endeavored to part amicably. We mutually agreed that she would find new accommodations within the month after securing the necessary resources. We no longer slept in the same bed and hardly talked, it was like walking on eggshells.

As we approach the culmination, it is important to note that I conducted myself with utmost propriety during these challenging times. Shortly thereafter, I secured a fairly substantial contract cleaning dorm rooms at a college campus before the semester started. This environment would set the stage for our final hoorah. I assembled a labor team and thought this would be an excellent opportunity for the butterfly to earn some extra income, expediting her move-out. I also believed this gesture might mend our relationship to some degree.

The ultimate drama during our time at the college was preceded by mounting tension. A jealous incident ensued after the project director, an attractive and composed young woman in a power suit, provided me with instructions for the day's tasks. The Butterfly evidently believed she should be present in all interactions between the director and I. Her insecurities would get the best of her during each meeting and her behavior didn't hide it.

The palpable tension lingered throughout the day, and our team members could sense it. The day culminated in a heated argument on the way home, a competition to deliver the deepest and most hurtful verbal blows. From my perspective, it became a battle of ice-cold logic versus irrational emotion. The Butterfly reached her limit and, in a moment of drama, demanded that I stop the car right in the middle of the street as I was driving home. She insisted on getting out then and there. I obliged without hesitation and from that moment on, did not see her again for several months. When our paths finally crossed again, we behaved as strangers, effectively closing the chapter on the Butterfly in my life.

In a whirlwind year, I opened my heart to more ecstasy and turmoil than in years of prior relationships. When all was said and done, I stood at the crossroads of my own narrative, facing the pivotal decision to either ascend to a higher version of myself or continue the all-too-familiar pattern of repeating old mistakes. In essence, I confronted two simple choices: evolve or repeat. This now is the simple question I pose for many students. Evolve, or Repeat!

I couldn't endure this again; I simply lacked the emotional capacity for it. Why would anyone willingly subject themselves to the kind of emotional turmoil I experienced over the past year? In my efforts to love someone else, the fundamental question I overlooked was, 'Do I even love myself? I mean, don't I deserve the same level of care and affection that I was so readily offering to others?

Since that time, while living in what seemed like a scripted simulation similar to a Broadway stage play viewed on an apple vision pro, I have come to wholeheartedly believe in emotionally intelligent, non-judgmental, non-attached and unconditional, freedom based love when romantically relating. This new perspective has evolved from the profoundly transformative lessons I learned in both relationships. These lessons set me on a journey toward transcendent self-discovery. Along this path, I gained a profound awareness of my true worth and recognized my all encompassing one true soulmate—myself.

Upon introspection, I realized that for the purest, most divine, and perfect love imaginable, I alone possess the capacity to love myself authentically and completely. To elaborate, this understanding led me to a fundamental truth: my soul is my eternal companion, making it my ultimate mate—I am my primary soulmate.

The ultimate purpose of life lies in serving one's own soul. It stands as the paramount relationship, foundational and sovereign, unmatched by any other in the universe. These two interconnected relationships played a pivotal role in my embodiment of this timeless wisdom. While I may have heard it a thousand times, feeling it penetrate my core was undeniably transformative, setting the course for the remainder of my natural life.

Regarding this pure and divine love that I speak of, regrettably, many individuals invest such a level of attention and devotion to others, including those they may have encountered just 24 hours prior, without ever contemplating granting even a fraction of this devotion to themselves. Loving someone you've known for just a week or even a year more intensely than someone you've known your entire life being yourself is asinin at best.

Furthermore, when I am able to love myself unconditionally and fully, my cup overflows with an abundance of that love, even if that love comes from me alone. This self-love becomes so profoundly abundant that I can generously extend it to others. Is it not a universal truth, that loved people, love people, just as hurt people, can hurt people, and healed people, usually heal people, denoting the law of psychological reflection and projection. Through nurturing love within myself, I become a generous source of it to share with others.

I discovered that one cannot genuinely love others unless they possess a deep understanding of what love is and experience it in their daily lives. Like extracting orange juice from an orange; you can only get from the orange what is within it, and it is certainly not apple juice. The same principle applies to human beings. If your inner essence is brimming with love, it will naturally radiate outward by default, whether you intend it or not.

Conversely, if you are filled with pain or trauma, similar to the orange's contents providing only orange juice, pain and trauma are what you will project. The lesson here is that when no one else extends love to you but you genuinely love yourself abundantly, you become saturated with love, and love becomes your essence, radiating from you. Keep in mind, when you fall in love, you can fall out of love, but when you've become love, filled with it in fact, it becomes your perpetual aura, whether you are in or out of a relationship.

In the quest for love, it's futile to expect a flawlessly tailored version of love and all the things that it entails, based on another person's distorted experiences or projected ideals and skewed notions of what love ought to be. Their individual and cultural backgrounds, coupled with their biases, subtly shape their judgments on a daily basis. A myriad of triggers, forming a complex spectrum, lurk deep within the subconscious, molding their belief systems and perspectives.

As a consequence, it's evident that individuals may perceive and react to the same things differently. For instance, you may interpret love as gifts and flowers, and your partner may see love as hugs and kisses, while your other partner may experience love as lots of sex and 'stunting' on others in your social circle for the validation purposes of being, "bae goals" for others. The book titled "The 5 Love Languages" by Gary Chapman offers a comprehensive framework for delving deeper into this concept.

The Indian mystic OSHO once remarked, "Nobody is Superior, Nobody is Inferior, Nobody is Equal Either. People are simply Unique, Incomparable. You are you, I am I." End quote.

The undeniable reality is that we are in a constant state of growth, and even I cannot precisely define what perfect love entails from day to day. Thus, it would be unreasonable to expect you to love me flawlessly, burdening you with such an immense responsibility. If I've formed my idealized concept of love from Disney movies while you've drawn yours from your grandparents' relationships, how can I anticipate you to fulfill my perfect love fantasy based on your experiences and not mine? This unrealistic expectation often leads to disappointment, a pattern observed in many, which then fuels disillusionment and contributes to a cycle of hurt people hurting others.

In the realm of love, all I can do is endeavor to discern what I believe I might require on a daily basis and adapt to provide it for myself as circumstances shift. The ever-changing nature of my needs depends on the day, season, and surrounding circumstances. What I should never do is assume that you must love me in one specific, flawless way. I literally won't even be the same person, consciously or cellularly in the next couple years.

I certainly won't remember the random conversation we had last thursday. Both of us are in a perpetual state of growth and transformation with every passing moment and thought, My most realistic hope is to connect with someone who can gracefully embrace this understanding with patience, compassion, and wisdom. I acknowledge that this might pose a significant intellectual challenge for some.

Regarding my personal journey, when it comes to both AJ and Butterfly, I can now discern that I was overlooking the crucial act of self-love. Instead, I was striving to love others wholeheartedly based on my preconceived ideas and often in pursuit of receiving endless selfless altruistic reciprocation—a paradoxical notion. It's possible I was attempting to fill a void within myself, perhaps due to a deficiency in self-love or potentially because of the cultural teachings that shaped my perceptions.

Contemplating the loss of my mother as an infant, I was brought to the profound realization that I may have been on a lifelong quest for unconditional love. As a young adult who left home prematurely and became a parent while in high school, I was compelled to navigate the complexities of love through a process of trial and error. I was devoid of any how-to manuals or guidance from my elders to illuminate a path of healthy and ethical relationships. I had placed unwarranted expectations on every relationship, hoping each one would be, "The One," only to be met with repeated disappointments.

Similar to many, I inadvertently fell into the pattern of serial monogamy. As I journeyed through the realms of attraction, passion, and love, my ignorance led to causing pain to some and experiencing it from others. I made a solemn commitment to myself: I would never wish the emotional pain I endured upon even my worst enemy, and consequently, I would never deliberately inflict such pain on others. Henceforth, I am dedicated to embracing 100% openness and ethical relating as my guiding principles. A freedom-centered approach to relationships, as opposed to an insecure slave-based approach, serves as the most nurturing path for my soul. Reflecting on my journey, I've learned through heartache and pain. Fortunately, my path didn't demand as many repetitions as some individuals still navigating similar lessons well into their 50s and 60s.

Life can often feel like a journey marked by repetitive patterns, echoing the Latin proverb *'Repetitio—est—mater studiorum'* — *Repetition is the mother of learning.* This complex process involves our subconscious replaying past traumas, a phenomenon known as repetition compulsion or trauma reenactment. To provide a contextual reference, imagine the mind as a playwright, crafting recurring dreams that echo the unresolved stories of our past. However, in reality, these reenactments extend beyond our dreams, subtly influencing our waking relationships and reactions. Experts in the field continue to explore and theorize about the intricate factors that drive this persistent dance of repetition.

The media mogul Oprah Winfrey once shared, "A lesson will keep repeating itself until it is learned. Life first sends the lesson to you in the size of a pebble; if you ignore the pebble, then life will send you a brick; if you ignore the brick, life will send you a brick wall; if you ignore the brick wall, life will send you a demolition truck."

In the realm of psychological exploration, Sigmund Freud sheds light on repetition compulsion, where individuals are unable to discuss or remember past traumatic events. The silence surrounding these experiences gives rise to a powerful unconscious force, compelling individuals to repeatedly act out or reenact these traumas. The underlying idea is that the secret or key to understanding this behavior lies within the intricate patterns of unconscious repetitions. I call these unconscious patterns, " Wash, Rinse, Repeat."

Moreover, there is something called the learning paradox, which emerges as a guiding light in human development. It beckons us to embrace **discomfort, challenge, and struggle** as our companions on the journey to genuine growth. When stepping beyond comfort zones, we grapple with new concepts and skills, creating a symphony where **dissonance births profound learning**. The paradox lies in acknowledging that true growth sprouts from navigating the tension between the yearning for comfort and the necessity of facing challenges. The past becomes a classroom for learned lessons, and the future serves as a canvas where these insights are applied.

Mastery in fields like music, art, athletics, surgery, or software development arises from repetition. Neural plasticity, the brain's ability to adapt and reorganize itself in response to new information, is key in learning. It strengthens neural connections, enhancing memory and skill development. This adaptability allows for continuous learning and improvement, enabling mastery. These same ideas align with the mastery of yoga, breathwork and states of Samadhi among other high vibrational practices.

Additionally, the learning paradox highlights the value of experiential learning and discomfort as catalysts for significant growth and understanding, emphasizing the transformative power of hands-on experiences across various disciplines. The objective, however, is to avoid spending a lifetime relearning the same lesson, lest you prepare yourself to spend several incarnations mastering that same daunting lesson.

Perceiving reality through a three-dimensional consciousness, we wear our flesh and its companion, the ego, much like a Halloween costume for the roles we are performing. Immersed in these characters, we act out our narratives with unwavering conviction, often serving as each other's teachers through experiences that include pain and suffering. It is through knowing pain that one can understand compassion, just as the contrast of suffering allows one to appreciate bliss and vice versa. I am forever grateful for the negative ad positive transformative traumas, and the teachers who helped me to channel the lessons learned and insights remembered.

My heart sympathizes with the countless individuals including my peers who persistently overlook the warning signs and neglect the red flags presented by various characters they encounter daily. Some are aware that they are being tested and consciously acknowledge their repeated failures with each new challenge. Regrettably, they continue to attract similar energies for decades, thereby hindering their own progress. I hope the wisdom in this book will contribute to their overall spiritual evolution because they deserve to manifest everything their hearts desire. It's vital to understand, however, that leading someone to water doesn't ensure they'll drink; until the student is ready, the teacher will not appear, and wisdom may fall on deaf ears.

After emerging from the adverse circumstances outlined throughout this chapter, there was a compelling need to craft a model to elucidate a dimension of shadow work within the twin elemental framework, which i've termed the Chemistry/Compatibility Index (CCI). Occasionally, referred to as the Chemistry/Compatibility Deficit or (CCD). The CCD model characterizes a phenomenon marked by a blend of intense attraction and limited compatibility, or conversely, a significant degree of compatibility with a lack of mutual attraction. In essence, it encapsulates scenarios where positive chemistry coexists with negative compatibility, and vice versa.

In a later chapter of this book, we'll delve deeply into the construct of and science of attraction. For now, it's crucial to acknowledge the existence of connections formed by encountering someone you find overwhelmingly attractive. They trigger all your attraction cues and attachment styles. You might go as far as saying, "I think I'm in Love", only to later realize you have absolutely nothing in common. In fact, you may low-key despise them, and end up resenting them, possibly because of the imperceptible things within yourself that they reflect. The same things that initially attracted you. Unhealthy loyalties are developed, emotional addictions are nurtured, trauma bonding ensues and ripple effects are abound, birthing entire civilizations in the astral realms while the blinded remain completely unaware.

Unfortunately, by this stage, it's often too late. The two of you are deeply entangled, deriving immense pleasure from one another. It's a full-blown addiction, one you detest. Recognize that sexual compatibility isn't a sustainable long-term foundation. You'll need more than physical attraction to sustain a holistically and mutually beneficial connection. Sexuality is hormonally regulated, and those hormones are in constant flux, especially as we age. The goal is to achieve magnetic sustainability. If you can't sustain magnetism and an overall equilibrium of soul attraction in alignment with your absolute highest reality, what is the purpose?

Becoming addicted to the chemistry while loathing the incompatibility sets the stage for a one-way journey into the realm of twin elemental shadow work for personal evolution. And all because you fell in love with an idea. The goal of the Chemistry-Compatibility Index is to strike a balance between the two. Excessive compatibility with too little chemistry can also lead to a shortfall, resulting in a purely platonic relationship and the potential for infidelity. Magnetic attraction isn't always an innate gift; it often demands conscious effort and maintenance to preserve equilibrium and uphold the CCD balance.

In my present-day interactions with potential partners or companions, I refrain from latching onto a fantasy. Instead, I embrace a person's soul and revel in their spirit from an "egoically" detached standpoint. I see them and appreciate them for exactly who they are. If who they are is a great person but not my lover, i do not resist that by moving forward as lovers. I love them fiercely, and accept that they are not meant to be my lover still. I acknowledge that maintaining a mutually fulfilling connection may require intention, effort and commitment from both parties involved.

This is not to be confused with romantic or sexual energy exchange but altruistic expressions of source love without attachment. In the interim however, I no longer have the energy to shame or blame a person for being themselves. The life coach, inspirational speaker, and TV personality Iyanla Vanzant encapsulates it perfectly with a statement made during a broadcast where she says **"I don't get to tell people how to love me. I get to see how they love and then choose if I want to participate."** #Bars — #Micdrop

This statement exemplifies the ownership of personal power and the assumption of responsibility for one's decisions in selecting a romantic partner. It empowers individuals to assert control over their lives and relationships, moving away from a passive role that sustains victim-centered psychology with blame as its sustenance. Such agency and self-awareness are pivotal in consciously co-creating alignment with one's needs and desires in love and life.

In the realm of self awareness, I've come to realize that while not all, a considerable portion of romantic connections are founded upon transient attractions molded by idealized perceptions and societal influences. It is more empowering to wholeheartedly embrace the present reality of our circumstances, irrespective of their permanence or impermanence, instead of retreating into escapist fantasies. In my perspective, placing belief in the genuineness of a relationship is a primary element in its success. Conversely, indulging in fleeting dreams and romantic illusions can ensnare you in a chemistry trap, where sustainable compatibility is notably absent.

A relationship founded on illusion simply cannot endure. This may explain the high rate of separation and divorce in modern society. This instability provides fertile ground for betrayal, commonly referred to as cheating. However, I contend that the notion of cheating applies only within the confines of a game. Relationships, in their truest sense, are not games. It is crucial to adopt this perspective to foster genuine, lasting connections, steering clear of game-like dynamics.

Despite considerable efforts invested in building enduring partnerships and cultivating legacies, the concept of emotional or sexual infidelity often takes precedence over the possibility of sustained growth or progress. This implies that the notion of cheating is generally considered more powerful than the idea of love or the establishment of wealth and legacy. Cheating trumps love, and cancels love for most. While it is commonly believed that God is Love, and love is the creative and most powerful force in the universe, real-world behaviors and actions often suggest that cheating is perceived as more powerful than love as it cancels and defeats love A.K.A. god energy. It's important to note that this statement is presented in a sarcastic tone and could be a topic for another conversation.

Furthermore, for the sake of this conversation, it is preferable that a lover's motivations are pure and honest when engaging in the relationship. Avoiding betrayal or cheating should not stem from mere compliance with requests. If someone refrains from betrayal solely due to external requests, it suggests a suppression of their true nature, increasing the risk of eventually succumbing to infidelity or unconsciously destabilizing the relationship. It is better for one to abstain from such actions not because of outside influence or relationship rules, but because it contradicts their intrinsic nature and values. Additionally, shaming someone into action often sets the stage for inauthentic behavior.

Drawing from my own experience, I am open to offering someone I'm dating the opportunity to explore non-monogamous options if they feel the need for greater variety in the relationship. If I genuinely love them and appreciate their company, creativity, and inspiration, among other things, I see no reason to throw the baby out with the bathwater, as the saying goes.

I am open to discussing it, without shame blame and hurt. My perspective is simple: There is no need to live a lie and betray not only your partner but yourself. If you desire more attention—as parents advise their toddlers— use your words and communicate like an adult; there's no need for concealment; live authentically! In the words of Iyanla, I will see how you love me and choose to deal or peal.

One cannot cheat on me as I do not engage in games or plays. The only betrayal occurs when they are not living authentically. They betray themselves by living a guilt-ridden lie, resembling an adolescent caught with their hands in the cookie jar, with telltale chocolate crumbs smeared across their guilty face while crying in denial. My relationships are so intuitively open that concealing a strong attraction would be more challenging than hiding lactose-induced flatulence in an elevator.

This marks the distinction between genuinely understanding your partner and embracing open, honest, and freedom-centered relationships from the start. Sometimes, you learn and know them better than they know themselves as you are their reflection. If it's not on that level then you my friend aren't really in a relationship. You are dating, and as the saying goes, if you aint married, then you're single.

Feeling that other human beings are attractive is entirely natural. However, suppressing your thoughts and emotions can lead to an unnatural buildup of pressure that can eventually reach a breaking point, similar to how pressure can cause pipes to burst. Honesty, authenticity, and integrity are some of the most alluring qualities for a mature adult.

Jada Pinkett Smith, as quoted on social media, shared a sentiment that I find both mature and inspiring. She asks, "Should we be married to individuals who cannot be responsible for themselves and their families within their freedom? Should we be in relationships with individuals who we cannot entrust to their own values, integrity, and LOVE?" Jada suggests that we should not be in relationships with people who are incapable of managing their own lives and responsibilities within their realm of emotional intelligence. She underscores the significance of finding a partner who comprehends that both individuals in a relationship must embrace their authentic selves, trusting and accepting each other for who they are.

This entails acknowledging that a person is just that—a person, not a storybook character—and will act in accordance with the reality of what we, as human beings, are. Exercising integrity and responsibility is something You would hope to expect.. Approaching relationships with integrity, trust, and a lack of judgment creates the potential for unconditional love to flourish.

The concept of "unconditional love" implies that this acceptance and trust do not rely on external circumstances, conditions, or prescribed rules. Instead, they are fundamental aspects of a natural relationship. By affording each other the "freedom to be themselves," individuals can responsibly pursue their unique paths and journeys without the pressure to conform to societal or partner expectations. This creates a safe space devoid of blame, shame, guilt, envy, or resentment. Such a supportive and accepting relationship plays a pivotal role in forging a robust and enduring connection with a soulmate.

There's no need to pretend to be someone you're not or conceal your genuine desires from another person, for there's someone out there for everyone. You might be surprised to discover that some individuals value a celibate or even a promiscuous partner. In fact, there are entire communities, such as the BDSM community, where your personal fetishes might be met with enthusiasm.

My outlook is, I wholeheartedly embrace being true to myself, and wouldn't want to change you for anything in the world. So, go ahead and be true to yourself and let's celebrate our unique and authentic identities together. Imagine me trying to change you into what I think you should be, through demands and ultimatums, even compelling you to love me according to my evolving, ever-shifting, and mutable expectations based on my daily moods and emotional fluctuations. This would be an arduous task, as my concept of love can transform from one day to the next.

It becomes problematic when someone attempts to enforce rules or expectations on how another person should manifest their love, rather than permitting a natural and authentic expression of that affection. Adding the threat of gaslighting if a partner doesn't comply makes it even more complicated. This does not align with a healthy love experience. I share these insights because I encountered them personally during my dating phase, particularly in my interactions with the two young ladies I discussed earlier in this chapter.

It's not unusual for partners in a relationship to resort to gaslighting, a practice that entails manipulating and distorting the other person's reality to retain control. This manipulation can happen when one partner attempts to coerce the other into complying with their compelling ideas and beliefs, constituting a form of psychological abuse. Could this be you? Do you abuse others through manipulation? You can not control the actions of others, only your own which gives you the power to choose if its a good fit or not before kindly exiting stage left, with no hard feelings.

When we love someone in an emotionally healthy way, we embrace and support them for who they are without attempting to change or exert control. We honor their individuality, acknowledging their distinct life path, which may diverge from our own. We engage in the relationship with not only passion, but compassion while establishing healthy boundaries to foster mutual growth and flourishing. This approach stands in stark contrast to the relationships I previously engaged in, as illustrated by the small portions of my life shared in this chapter.

Though it may all sound simple, the profound impact of these newly discovered thought processes and life-altering ideologies on every aspect of my life cannot be overstated. Originating from just two pivotal relationships—with one spirit and a transformative assignment—these experiences have been instrumental in reshaping my perspectives and my approach to human interactions. Consequently, they have redirected the trajectory of my life along my ensouled timeline, fundamentally altering my personality. In essence, this journey has led to the emergence of a new version of myself, marking a significant evolution in my existence resulting from a powerfully esoteric and enigmatic twin elemental effect.

These days I only seek freedom-centered connections where the space held for one another allows for all involved to be their authentic selves irrespective of the dynamics in play. In this space, the expectation and understanding is that I certainly am going to be my authentic self and so should you. If my presence doesn't bring an individual any value, then it may not be a good fit and there are no hard feelings. I believe in not obstructing another person's path to what's meant for them, just as I value that same consideration. I've come to understand that what's meant for me will naturally find me.

My voyage into the passionate depths of twin flames, with both AJ and Butterfly, taught me profound lessons and led me to an esoteric insight into how the mirrored essence of another soul can trigger profound transformations through elemental polarization in one's life journey. In hindsight, Twin Elementals represent the juxtaposition of two souls inhabiting human ego, seeking evolution through intimacy and love or in spite of it.

Twin elemental archetypes are among the most effective catalysts for initiating shadow work, as outlined in the psychoanalytic theory of Carl Jung. Jung theorized that the 'shadow' encompasses the darker aspects of our psyche. Twin Elemental Soulmates, in particular, are adept at triggering the introspective processes necessary for delving into and comprehending these hidden parts of ourselves.

The profound bond of Twin Elementals sparks a transformative metamorphosis, unfolding in diverse ways, both positive and negative. Whether it takes the form of a Twin Flame, Twin Flood, Twin Wind, or Twin Planet, the involvement will inevitably mirror a cosmic dance. This intricate choreography can either propel you towards profound transformation akin to the dark night of the soul or entangle you in a repetitive nightmare, seemingly impossible to escape.

The decision is yours: either rise to the occasion, embracing profound growth, or stay entangled in the cycle of suffering. Ultimately, the engagement of "Twin Elementals" presents a substantial opportunity for deepened consciousness and soul evolution, with each soul forging its distinct path toward higher sentience.

Today, I find myself fortunate to be in a conscious and enriching partnership with a life companion. Occasionally, I contemplate whether I truly merit this profound love and happiness. When we first came together, there was no resistance, just a wholehearted embrace—an unfamiliar experience for me and a tough act to follow. It was a sign that this connection was meant to be. She is an invaluable gift from the universe. In the words of a lyric from a song I penned, "If she is my reflection, then I must be beautiful!"

I am fully cognizant that the only constant is change, signifying that nothing remains permanent, and I wholeheartedly embrace this truth. We will treasure our time together, treating it as sacred. We will endeavor to remain fully present in the NOW until the universe guides us into the next dimension of our lives, and our souls embark on their respective after-futures.

My journey, which has unfolded along a seemingly predestined path, has been profoundly shaped by the insights of a mystical Ethiopian tarot reader and characterized by deeply moving relationships and experiences. It has been an amalgam of cathartic releases and cosmic revelations, culminating in the channeling of a divinely inspired yet inherently natural framework. This model elucidates the intricate duality between the enlightened and shadowed facets of the soul, as well as its relational counterparts. It serves as an essential guide for navigating one's personal timeline, steering towards the pinnacle of spiritual evolution.

Note: While the science of twin elementals encompasses various aspects extending far beyond romantic soul bonds, I will primarily utilize romantic relationships as the exemplar relational dynamic due to its universality.

Before we immerse ourselves in the pan-dimensional realm of Twin Elemental understanding, it is essential to start with a grounded examination of human relationships. To begin, we will trace our journey from the earliest beginnings of human interaction to the current dynamics of connection, encompassing the spiritual, emotional, and psychological sciences that underpin these relationships. This exploration will unfold in the chapters that follow.

Chapter Two

Love, Lust & Attraction

Demystifying the Forces that Drive Connection

Quote: "Your naked body should only belong to those who fall in love with your naked soul." — Charlie Chaplin

This chapter, along with the others, is essential for grasping the idea of twin elementals and their link to soulmates. However, before we delve deeper into the core of this book's theme, it's important to explore a key element that plays a significant role in influencing the dynamics of most relationships. That primal and animalistic drive within us all, which can be likened to a wolf in sheep's clothing on the one hand or the elephant in the room on the other, perhaps even the Trojan Horse in the room. It's rarely discussed, even when staring us in the face, and if acknowledged at all, it's often underestimated in its influence. I refer to it as the Trojan Horse because, by the time you realize its presence, the battle may already be lost. This powerful force often masquerades as the divine and wondrous emotion we call love, but it's a far cry from it. I'm talking about **"Attraction."**

It's vital to grasp this concept and comprehend its impact on people's lives and decision-making. Attraction is the spark that ignites the flames of passion, but mistaking it for love can lead to catastrophic choices. Many men have married, moved halfway across the globe, and started entire families with strangers, based on world-class attraction, only to later regret their choices. They soon come to realize the irreversible damage they've caused to their life paths, living out their days with resentment, affecting those around them, including their own children. For some, all the great things and or terrible things happening in their lives right now can be traced back to a simple attraction long ago that had a trickle effect they never imagined would land them in a alternate future be it a prison cell or head of a fortune five hundred company. A woman who is raising children alone can likely relate, having ended a long attraction based connection that was once mistaken for love.

It's important to understand that a powerfully compelling attraction can induce an altered state due to the transcendent chemistry it generates. This sets the stage for a potentially disruptive shift in an individual's life path. The subsequent integration of these imperceptible conditions can lead to subtle changes in one's living trajectory, appearing as a seamless sequence of events to the unaware observer.

It's worth noting that throughout one's lifetime, several highly magnetic encounters with twin elementals, each carrying the potential for these chemically disruptive attractions, can influence an individual's cognitive awareness daily. Over time, these cumulative experiences crystallize into what can be described as a "continuity of consciousness." This ongoing process offers numerous opportunities to exercise free will within the realm of duality, potentially leading to significant soul evolution.

In simple terms, this means as we go through life, we encounter people who have a big impact on us and influence how we behave—no matter how small. These interactions play a role in shaping our identity through the many choices we make. Through these experiences, we set the stage to, as the saying goes, "grow through what we go through," ultimately leading to spiritual polarization and soul awareness. The realization of twin elemental magnetism allows you to align yourself with either harnessing its powerful energy or being enveloped by it.

Imagine for a moment having a bird's eye view of life's entire battlefield—seeing it from a fifth-dimensional perspective outside of time, pinpointing every small decision that influenced the seemingly imperceptible causes and effects shaping your reality. The Twin Elemental Model is designed to train you to see with that perspective naturally, enabling you to make decisions from a higher plane of consciousness. Each chapter leading up to immersion in the concept is akin to Mr. Miyagi's 'wax on, wax off' method of training in The Karate Kid. Attraction is often the culprit in many of these decisions and it is not always a sexual attraction. Attraction to one's charisma can lead to joining a cult; attraction to wealth can lead to unethical choices; attraction to power can lead to compromising one's values.

Take note that to gain a deeper understanding of the complex nature of human coupling, it will be essential to eventually establish a historical context as a blueprint. However, to truly grasp the captivating essence that underlies and sustains these fundamental aspects of our connections, we must first delve into the mechanics governing the shadowed formation of relational bonds. This involves appreciating the magnetic attractions that unites two souls and initiates the transformative process characterized by the energetic exchange of what we are learning are twin elementals.

Please be aware that the term "human coupling i.e. a couple of humans," refers to the interaction between two individuals, encompassing a range of relationship dynamics including romantic, platonic, transactional, or commercial as individuals may be drawn to one another's spirit due to shared objectives or a mutual cause. For the purpose of this section on soul attraction, however, I will refer to romantic attractions for a broader impact.

There is a common saying that goes, "people who fall in love with the flowers and not the roots, do not know what to do when winter comes." This saying highlights the importance of not only appreciating the surface beauty of someone but to also understand and value the deeper, underlying qualities and characteristics that give them their resilience. In the context of relationships, this means taking the time to truly get to know and appreciate your partner beyond the initial attraction so that when challenging times arise, you are better equipped to navigate all aspects of them.

Let explore: What does it mean to be attracted to someone? Have you ever heard of the phrase "falling in love at first sight"? Despite its cliché nature, many relationships do begin this way. While it's not the case for everyone, the initial attraction is often the first step in the emotional process of falling in love. It's not surprising that "attraction vs. love" is what the protagonist in most people's love stories experiences.

That "N.R.E. or New Relationship Energy" is always filled with a surge of electrical impulses and **action potential**. This can lead to finding ourselves trapped in a never-ending loop of seeking temporary validation or pleasure, resembling the proverbial "Geek Monster," which I assure you, differs greatly from the, Geek-Squad. While some may argue that "geeking" on love at first sight is a paradox, or an oxymoron, there's no denying the powerfully magnetic pull it can have on two people.

For many individuals, as the initial attraction and chemistry fades, the stereotypical lens in their rose-colored glasses gains clarity. People begin noticing things they overlooked initially, realizing that their counterparts, aren't as likable as they first believed. This serves as a reminder that what you'll eventually see, doesn't always align with your first sight impressions.

What is an attraction as it relates to love? For starters, attraction transcends mere visual perception. Pheromones detected by the nose, appealing sounds, beautiful aesthetics, personal beliefs, and more exert influence over the mind and the senses, subconsciously persuading the brain that an attraction is unfolding. Simplified, physical attraction is broadly characterized as the sensation that arises when one finds another person appealing. It stems from the actual glandular chemistry shared between two individuals and can span a spectrum of intensities. It initiates with primary attractions rooted in appearance, then follows up with a secondary personality-based attraction, and then finally, self-projected beliefs begin to play a significant role.

I recently read somewhere that comedian Eddie Murphy allegedly once jokingly told his accountant, upon first seeing his Ex-Wife, Nicole, "she's so beautiful, I'd marry her today, without a prenup." Upon further investigation, I can certainly understand where that humor came from.

A personality-based and/or an emotional attraction is predicated upon the way a person makes us feel. It is either influenced by our own emotions or the emotions projected by the other person for us to mirror. It is usually a reflective cycle, meaning I project a smile at you, if your receptive, you reflect the smile back to me. I then immediately reflect a slightly bigger smile right back to you, and so on. With each cycle, the attraction's momentum grows stronger, resembling "parallel mirrors" facing each other to reflect infinite light until a secondary force disrupts the reflection. Most of time the attraction is immediate and on site without immediate need for validation from the other person.

One thing to remember in the realm of attraction is that physical attraction doesn't necessarily lead to a good or compatible relationship. That powerful sexual attraction you sometimes feel for a person most certainly can be misleading. It can lead to frustration later on because the initial physical connection didn't actually mean anything long-term, according to Dr. Margaret Paul, who's appeared on Oprah and holds her doctorate in psychology.

Dr. Paul says that the guy's many women find themselves attracted to often turn out to be sexually promiscuous, etc., and even insensitive, to say the least. This behavior is not what you would necessarily want in your partner if you've got plans to establish an actual relationship! Initial physical attraction is a very poor indicator of how well a relationship will work out, which in turn can lead to the feeling of abandonment or being played, among many things. What many women say they are looking for in a long-term partner are, in fact, all the opposite qualities of the average alpha male. Examples of this might be:

- **Sensitivity and Emotional Intelligence:** While the alpha male stereotype often emphasizes toughness and emotional stoicism, the opposite of this would be someone who is in touch with their emotions with a high level of emotional intelligence. They may be more attuned to the feelings of others and be more willing to express vulnerability.

- **Humility and Modesty:** Alpha males are often associated with a sense of entitlement and an inflated sense of self-importance. colored as confidence. The opposite of this would be someone who is humble and modest, with a healthy sense of self-awareness and a willingness to learn from others. They may not feel the need to constantly assert their dominance or prove themselves to others.

People are generally drawn to their romantic partners for a multitude of reasons, and it's not always straightforward. The meaning of attraction can vary greatly among individuals, with different interpretations of what it entails. A person can find themselves captivated by another individual, often without a clear understanding of why they feel this way.

Numerous factors can influence the type of attraction we experience towards another person, including our personal preferences. The circumstances under which we meet someone can lead to connections as well; for example, the combination of alcohol intoxication and a great DJ can set the stage for a bonding experience that may ultimately result in the birth of a child. People may also have preferences for particular personality traits, such as charisma or humor. Discovering that this charismatic and humorous personality also harbors insecurities and abusive tendencies may come later in the process.

Deliberate selection is sometimes called "sweet spotting." An example is when two people share the same fetishes, such as considering themselves to be "Furries" who happen to enjoy speaking to each other in intimate cat meows—yeah, that's a thing. Or perhaps a couple who are into Fae expressions or who enjoy gaming and playing Dungeons and Dragons. I-for-one, am not into D&D. I am; however, a nature spirit who is sometimes known to leave offerings for the trans-dimensional "Fae" who visit my garden or the lake nearby, and thus a fairy woman who can relate and occasionally expresses herself as a pixie, nymph or mami-wata mermaid might be ideal for attraction—look it up!

Intellectual attractions can be either a positive or a negative force. They are influenced not only by our own intellect but also by the intellect of the object of our affection, creating an intriguing dynamic. Have you ever met someone and instantly felt a profound connection with them, as though you had known them in a past life Alternatively, you may have encountered someone you just can't seem to shake, even though they repulse you on every level. When we find ourselves subconsciously drawn to another person's spiritual or intellectual qualities, the nature of these attractions is usually esoteric and can influence us positively or negatively based on where we are on our spiritual or intellectual paths.

It's a situation many of us can relate to – that inexplicable pull we feel toward someone that leads to a relationship. Initially, everything appears wonderful, but then a sense of déjà vu creeps in. We find ourselves facing the same issues and arguments, making us question if we're fated to repeat the same mistakes time and time again. According to the concept of karmic debt, this might indeed be the scenario.

The Recording Artist Jhene Aiko famously recites in her song Stanger's, the following lyrics, which illustrates the scenario perfectly:

Similar ways, similar game, Starting to feel the similar pain
Are you sure we haven't met before . . . You said you were different
But you're the same, stranger, I can not tell you
How many there have been, That were just like you . . .

Karmic debt refers to actions or events from the past that you're presently addressing. When you recognize recurring patterns in your current life that you find difficult to break, take into consideration that they may be unresolved issues from a former life. This would encourage you to explore appropriate avenues to seek healing.

Note: A former life can also mean A former time in your current life, as in the idiomatic expression, "A lifetime ago."

When we find ourselves drawn to someone who is kind, compassionate, and loving, it signifies a positive spiritual attraction. On the other hand, if we feel an attraction toward someone who is egotistical, self-centered, and critical, it's a negative spiritual attraction. These qualities may not be immediately evident in how they treat you, but if you observe how they interact with others, you may notice some of these patterns. Being attracted to negative habits such as smoking and drinking together etc, is not a positive attraction and can be a form of trauma bonding.

Awareness of our spiritual beliefs and values is key to setting healthy boundaries in relationships. Attraction to someone spiritually compatible can create a deep bond, while a lack of compatibility can cause conflict. In biblical terms, this is being equally or unequally yoked.

Freewill dictates that we will always have the power to choose our relationships, discerning between true connections and mere attractions. By understanding our spiritual and intellectual needs, we can attract fulfilling relationships. I believe the mind influences the body, and the spirit influences the mind. Many underestimate the spirit's role in attraction and relationships however. Attraction is like a kaleidoscope, revealing a wide array of colors and shapes, each possessing its unique characteristics. Just as the patterns within are intricate, attraction is a complex and multifaceted phenomenon shaped by numerous factors.

Some may be drawn to bold and vibrant hues, while others may prefer soft pastels. The beauty of attraction resides in its diversity, and it's essential to recognize that there is no single "correct" form of attraction. Understanding the existence of different types of attractions and their impact on our lives is vital. Consider your attraction to someone; it may be due to their physical appearance, common interests and values, or how they evoke your emotions. They can bring you great joy, energize your spirit, and make you feel more alive than anyone else. In essence, many elements influence the feelings we develop for others.

Developing what I term **"Attraction Awareness"** can foster a deeper understanding regarding the genuine sources of your **"Attraction Triggers,"** helping you to avoid entering relationships blindly and preventing future regret. Failing to understand how certain traits in others can trigger your attraction can have long-term negative consequences, particularly if those traits merely serve to fill unhealthy voids.

By taking the time to develop your attraction awareness—and I mean a deep dive—you can empower yourself to make conscious and intentional choices about who you welcome into your unique spheres of partnership. In doing so, this enables you to put your own well-being first and pave the way for more robust, rewarding partnership dynamics and relationships.

In recent times, there's been a growing awareness of diverse sexual orientations, such as Demi-sexual and Sapiosexual. Demisexuality entails finding someone sexually appealing only after fostering a profound emotional connection, while sapiosexuality pertains to sexual attraction to highly intelligent individuals. There exist additional attraction-based orientations, including, *A—sexual, Pan-sexual, Omnisexual, Auto-sexual, Androgeno-sexual,* and more.

These labels serve as a starting point, offering individuals insights into their attraction styles for a heightened awareness. It's crucial to acknowledge that one's attractions are not fixed and can transform over time. Therefore, it's important to be aware that what appeals to you today may not be the same to what captivates you tomorrow. Regarding attraction, remember that emotions, like the weather, can change quickly. It's not always wise to base lifelong decisions on temporary feelings, as they can lead to regret. Before making significant decisions, pause and consider if they align with your long-term goals and values.

Rational thought and introspection will always endure the test of time. Keep this in mind and grant yourself sufficient time to genuinely process each attraction. It's common to underestimate an individual's most remarkable traits or disregard red flags when captivated by their dazzle and allure. As the age-old saying goes, sometimes, all that glitters not gold.

Naturally, attraction often leads to the desire for romance. Romance, as a cultural construct, has evolved into various forms over the centuries. From the days of "romance" to the artistic movement of Europe, we've witnessed the progression of behaviors shaping our perception of romantic partnerships in love.

As our passions are increasingly ignited by compulsive attractions and influenced by direct or indirect social engineering, it's not surprising that attraction can sometimes overshadow authentic love. In fact, our relentless pursuit of attraction can become so overwhelming that it undermines and even supplants genuine love. Just like a Trojan Horse can infiltrate a stronghold, attraction, when masked as love, can infiltrate the heart and mind.

Years of scientific studies have shown that love is more than just feeling butterflies or passion. Brain scans reveal differences between love and lust. Lust activates the brain's pleasure centers, but love stimulates deeper, primal reward centers, similar to satisfying thirst with water. Imagine being extremely thirsty in the desert; when you finally drink water, your reaction would be intense gratitude and affection, not just "this feels good." You might even say, "I love water! Thank God!"

Love endures as a force that offers lasting comfort and stability. In contrast, lust is fleeting and tends to wane over time. While love provides solace, lust stirs excitement and thrills. Depending on the fuel source, lust typically fades away within a few hours, a few months, and sometimes a few years. It's crucial not to conflate lust with passion. Over time, passion can indeed evolve into love, but it's a misconception to blur the lines between these distinct responses.

If you're seeking a spring fling, summer romance, or winter cuffing, regardless of how infatuated you may become, try and refrain from declaring it as love. While deceiving and misleading others may be one thing, self-delusion is an entirely different matter. Unfortunately, it's not uncommon for people to lie to others, yet lying to oneself seems foolish, illogical, and negligent—downright derelict to be honest. In many cases, what lot's of people mistake for genuine love these days is primarily lust.

Contemplation: Sexual orientations like sapio-sexuality, despite being associated with an intellectual attraction, still contain the term "sexuality" within the language. Thus, even when an intellectual connection sparks a sexual relationship, it can be argued that the desire for physical intimacy ultimately drives the bond's formation. In other words, the primal urge of sexual desire may still underlie the force that brings individuals together, even when the attraction is not solely rooted in physical appearance but intelligence instead. Anything otherwise would result in a platonic relationship.

To clarify, I'm not saying lust is bad. What's important is knowing the difference between love and lust and being acutely aware of what's happening when engaged with either. This awareness helps you avoid falling in love without thinking and allows you to grow in love consciously. Especially in cases of sapiosexual attraction, where intellect is key, being mindful can prevent future regrets when infatuation evolves into lust and affects your choices.

One of the most vital life lessons is learning that falling in love automatically creates a parallel where you can just as easily fall out of Love. To grow in and as love, you also create a parallel, where you are simultaneously becoming love. Consequently, when you become a walkin breathing example of love, you will relate with others as such because you can only project what you authentically are. In essence, you literally transform into love itself!

Frequently, individuals who experience strong attraction develop a profound attachment to their perception of another person. They construct an idealized fantasy and, based on this fantasy, navigate a series of dilemmas, culminating in a conflict between the notion of a relationship and its reality. It is not uncommon to enter full worship mode and revel in its intoxication. Intriguingly, the entire essence of what is being described can be succinctly captured in a single word —Limerence.

REGARDING LIMERENCE

Psychologist **Dr. Dorothy Tennov** originally introduced the theory of limerence in her 1979 book "Love and Limerence: *The Experience Of Being In Love.*" This term describes a profound feeling that emerged from her analysis of over 500 interviews she conducted on love during the 1960s. Although not fully understood, there are numerous theories about the experiences falling under this concept. For instance, one theory suggests that individuals can become so captivated by their lover's smile or actions that they overlook any potential negative consequences for themselves. This happens because any attention received from someone you're infatuated with can seem positive, even if it leads to unhealthy behavior.

Dr. Tennov coined the term "limerence" to describe the falling in love experience and the associated symptoms commonly observed in her interviewees. These symptoms encompass intrusive thinking about the limerent object, a preoccupation with ascertaining whether the feeling is reciprocated, emotional dependence on the limerent object, and anxiety when limerence is not reciprocated.

Limerence can also bring about physiological changes, like an increased heart rate and the familiar sensation of "butterflies in the stomach" – something many of us have likely experienced. While limerence is often linked with romantic love, it can also manifest in non-romantic relationships, whether with a close friend, mentor, or even a celebrity, for instance.

To understand limerence better, here is the short form breakdown:

- Limerence is an emotional state of uncontrollable obsession and infatuation for a particular person, called the Limerent object.

- Limerence is usually experienced extensively, before a relationship. However, in some cases, it can happen during a relationship or even after a breakup.

- Limerence is characterized by intrusive thinking about the Limerent object and intense longing for reciprocation. It is also characterized by fear of rejection and anxiety over the outcome of the relationship.

- Limerent people can often feel that they are not good enough for the object of their limerence and worry that their feelings are not reciprocated.

- Limerence can lead to both positive and negative outcomes. On the positive side, it can result in a passionate and fulfilling relationship. On the negative side, it can be overwhelming and lead to obsessive and unhealthy behaviors.

- Limerence and infatuation mirror each other, share many similarities and are closely aligned.

It should be clear by now that, even though it may feel like love, limerence is distinct from love. Love is founded on trust, mutual respect, and unconditional regard, whereas limerence is rooted in intense desire and emotional neediness.

Limerence tends to be all-consuming, driving the limerent individual to behave in ways that deviate from their usual character. They may become obsessed with the object of their limerence, going to great lengths to get closer to them. Such behavior can include stalking, both in person and online, and weaving elaborate stories about a non-existent relationship, akin to the innocent infatuation of a young person who adorns their space with posters and screensavers of a beloved celebrity.

In certain cases, limerence is short-lived when the person you desire is also experiencing limerence for you. This occurs because familiarity can breed contempt or, at the very least, it breeds commonality and conformity. Consequently, a relationship can often form after reaching the climax of an exhilarating new attraction. It's typically after this stage that a more grounded and practical form of attraction can develop.

In other instances, limerence can be one-sided because the limerent person is unaware of the other person's feelings. This situation can cause the limerent individual to feel rejected and hurt when their advances are not reciprocated. After facing setbacks or disappointments, some people may become emotionally guarded and learn to switch off their feelings like a light switch, while others may lose confidence or lower their standards. It's worth noting that some individuals never experience limerence at all. Understanding how it works can assist you in dealing with it if you find yourself in the throes of limerence.

In many relationships, when two mutually limerent individuals are attracted to each other and even decide to marry, it is commonly believed that limerence typically lasts from three to thirty-six months (equivalent to three months to three years). During this period, in many marriages, the transition from the honeymoon phase to a more neutral phase of relating typically occurs.

You might remember falling in love with someone, but after three to six weeks or a couple of months, a switch flips, and old memories of past love stories start replaying in your mind, prompting your usual coping mechanisms. Could you have begun to settle into a new phase of relating that would have required a genuine attachment, devoid of limerence?

The fleeting aspect of one's limerence is not intended to endure indefinitely. When the limerent state has run its course, you are faced with a decision that unfolds in a predictable manner. You have essentially become like the characters from the 90s TV sitcom "Seinfeld" where you'd typically feed a torrent of short-lived relationships, naturally making you a serial monogamous. In the case of the characters Jerry, George, and Elaine, they frequently start each episode dating someone new, and initially on a high note. However, as the episode progresses, they invariably find faults with their partners, leading to a loss of attraction by the end of the episode.

Without a doubt, there are numerous instances and circumstances where passion-fueled, infatuated states of limerence evolve into enduring, authentic love grounded in regard rather than self-interest. However, before reaching that point, you will probably progress through the three essential stages of limerence which according to Dr. Tennov are as follows:

Stage 1 of Limerence: Attachment / Infatuation

Stage 2: Crystallization / Intensification

Stage 3: Deterioration / de-Intensification

The infatuation stage, "Attachment" is all about pleasurable attachment. It's when you become obsessed with the person you are limerent for, creatively conjuring feelings from your wonderful imagination. In extreme cases, you may start to stalk them or make up stories in your head about a relationship that doesn't exist and may never. Some people can see the whole wedding play out in their heads, with kids and all. I always say, "creative visualization is the mother of manifestation." but I digress.

During limerence, your interest in their life intensifies, and the desire to learn everything about them grows. While getting to know someone is an exhilarating aspect of courtship, it typically thrives on mutual engagement rather than creepy social media stalking.

There is a saying that goes; (and I'm paraphrasing) you don't fall in love while in the presence of a person; instead, you fall in love in the holographic space between your ears. This is to say that when you are not with them, the stories you fantasize about in your head are what make you fall in love. It's all about the mystery at this point which intensifies the attraction. The hunt is on. The chase gives you an adrenaline rush when attempting to secure the prize. It's a whole game, and playing it can be exciting as long as you're not losing.

For some, after engaging in sexual activity for the first time, the limerence either immediately diminishes or gradually begins a slow decline. To add a touch of humorous insight, the popular American rapper Dwayne Carter, also known as Lil Wayne, Lil Tunechi, or Young Tuna Fish, once said, *"As soon as, I cum,—I come to my senses."* This clever wordplay captures the sentiment of many individuals who experience limerence as their initial attraction starts to dwindle into the fading realms of oblivion.

The second stage, known as "Crystallization," revolves around the intensification process. During this phase, the obsession deepens, and you might find yourself growing possessive of the person you're limerent for or believe you're in love with. When limerence is mutual, you become deeply invested, and a sense of ownership towards your relationship may arise, sometimes blurring the line between possessing the person.

This is the stage where the concept of possessing or owning someone, with phrases like 'you are mine' or 'you belong to me,' takes on the form of subjugation and unnatural submission. This pleasurable attachment can morph into a codependent bond, sometimes seen as endearing or even perceived as cute somehow. It's common to desire to spend all your time with the limerent person and experience jealousy when they interact with others. It may even lead to distancing yourself from friends and family as limerence consumes your life.

Country and R&B songs are particularly known for expressing and promoting intense limerent behaviors like this through their lyrics. Common phrases in these songs include "you are my everything" and "you are the sun, moon, and stars." Many of these songs also contain lines such as "I would do anything for you" and "I'm crazy in love with you." Others convey deep longing, like "it's been an hour since you've been gone, and I can't live without you."

These lyrics can give the impression of an exclusive love, such as "only you, and no one else from the pool of eight billion humans can love me," while others express a desire for a fairytale relationship with lines like "I hope we feel this way forever, forever-ever, forever-ever." The list is endless. Consider how often you or someone you know has felt this way about someone, only to experience the same feelings repeatedly in several subsequent relationships.

This is the phase where we've often been conditioned to perceive it as endearing to own or possess our lover, thus romanticizing this unhealthy behavior. A more profound examination reveals an eerie similarity between these notions and behaviors reminiscent of Jeffrey Dahmer. The only distinction lies in the fact that, instead of being coerced, you must willingly sacrifice or arrest your social development, as it becomes a prerequisite for this possessive love to thrive. Yes it is true, the process of arrested development is often present in these ownership relationships.

When we objectively evaluate these behaviors, do they truly enhance our overall well-being? The response may differ based on one's individual circumstances and life experiences. Someone who has endured a profound absence of love and never felt valued might consider these behaviors acceptable. Yet, an individual who has recently escaped an abusive, excessively needy, extremely jealous, overprotective, and possessive partner who now lives in a shelter for battered women may hold a different viewpoint.

In these types of relationships, genuine love for other humans, socializing with anyone from the opposite sex at all, or even finding anything about any other person on the planet earth attractive is not at all tolerated—effective immediately. The gospel of this mentality dictates—Thou shalt not admire their unique hairstyle, or their humor, nor their sense of fashion and creativity, not even their intelligence, can ever be admired. Everyone must be unequivocally unattractive and unadmirable from here on out for the rest of your days on earth - Because, apparently, arrested development should naturally feel good. (sarcastically written) Somehow, on a planet filled with insecure individuals, this is supposed to all make sense.

Take note that while I playfully tease about the constraints one may encounter during this stage of limerence, It is essential to emphasize that delving into the intricacies of open social dynamics while in a committed partnership, particularly when individuals lack self-control, personal integrity, or respect for boundaries, is much like unlocking Pandora's box. This act can unleash potentially adverse consequences, and I strongly advise against engaging in such scenarios, as the ensuing repercussions can be truly detrimental for individuals who lack the maturity to handle such complex social dynamics.

The third and final stage of Dr. Tennov's theory called Limerence, is referred to as "Deterioration," representing a De-Intensification. This is when the obsession begins to wane, and you might start to perceive the person you're limerent for in a more realistic light. Your interest in their life may decrease while your focus shifts back to your own. Around this point, you may feel like you've lost yourself in this new role and are no longer your true self. Despite the initial allure of becoming one with the limerent object, reality sets in, and the once-fading fantasy begins to reveal its worn edges more prominently.

Like a child growing tired of a once-beloved toy, you might contemplate discarding this old fascination that no longer entertains you as it once did. If life, in general, isn't going well, you may even begin to blame your former limerent object for your personal unhappiness, perhaps lashing out and shaming them over trivial matters seeing as proximity could result in you unfairly directing your frustrations at them. It's common to vent our own stress or problems on those close to us, as they are often the easiest targets for our emotional reactions.

After investing so much in the once intoxicating feelings, you could find yourself resenting the limerent object for no longer providing the same emotional high, subconsciously seeking to punish them. This is a common scenario involving projecting one's personal issues onto others. If this has happened to you, it's important to remember that a person's issues have more to do with themselves than with you.

Often, in cases of shame and blame-oriented coping, it is said that you are not what they think you are; instead, they, are what they think you are. An insecure ego often tends to self project internal dissatisfaction. There are cases where one partner is cheating, and they wonder if and why the other partner is or isn't cheating, accusing them either way. This projection may serve as a release valve for the pressure and guilt they feel for their own betrayal, displaying full-on self-projection.

In situations like these, self-sabotage is in full effect, and unless both parties demonstrate maturity in pursuing a mutual understanding and engaging in effective communication to kickstart the processes of forgiveness, healing, or even an amicable separation, they are pretty much screwed, to put it bluntly. To experience this multiple times during one's life is like living in a loop from which it is difficult to escape.

Frequently, separations unfold amidst stress and emotional turmoil, making it challenging for the individuals involved to sustain a friendship. This immature conduct can exacerbate the pain, particularly in cases where children are a part of the equation. If you've played a role in raising stepchildren and subsequently forfeit the chance to keep actively nurturing those bonds after a toxic breakup, the wounds run even deeper.

Needless to say, over time, the fervor of limerence has a tendency to fade. Consequently, you're left with one of two scenarios: either the complications described earlier or, in the most favorable scenario, after all things considered, you find yourself in possession of something precious, a transparent, authentic and secure connection, abundant with compatibility. Within this space lies the most remarkable groundwork for nurturing a love that endures.

So, the pivotal question emerges: Can limerence truly pave the path to a long-lasting and deeply satisfying connection? This question hinges on two fundamental factors—understanding the difference between feelings of limerent attraction versus endearing affection and regard.

Moreover, you can empower yourself by understanding the intricate process initiated when the chemical concoction responsible for attraction affect your brain and body. This chemical elixir propels you through discrete stages of attraction, potentially guiding you towards the prospect of enduring love with a significant other. These brain-imbued chemicals play a significant role in shaping what we universally recognize as classic attraction, foundational limerence, and the overarching sensation of falling head over heels in love.

Let's shift gears for a moment to explore a different line of thought. My first encounter with the term "triggered" occurred within the pages of Daniel Goleman's book, Emotional Intelligence. While the concept of being "triggered" goes back to the early studies of post-traumatic stress disorder (PTSD) after World War I, it gained much wider recognition in the years following the publication of Goleman's influential book.

Oddly enough, while Mr. Goleman's book may have embedded the term "triggered" into the public consciousness, it leaves me wondering why another equally vital term from his work didn't enjoy the same widespread recognition. This term is none other than **"flooding,"** specifically emotional flooding. I witness individuals use the term triggered all the time and think, I wish they also championed awareness to the concept of flooding with the same enthusiasm. To fully grasp the concept of flooding, you need to first consider what triggers the emotions to flood. In a nutshell, when an emotion is triggered, its intensity can potentially overwhelm the brain's chemistry, diluting all other thoughts, emotions, and chemicals, to varying degrees.

At this stage, it's important to understand that when I mention "emotion," I am talking about the chemical and hormonal responses that lead to our feelings.

Take, for example, studies showing that depression often stems from a chemical imbalance, specifically low serotonin levels. On the other hand, some suggest that microdosing psilocybin mushrooms, which contain DMT, might help reduce depression.

While I haven't witnessed conclusive evidence for either viewpoint, it's abundantly clear that an excess or deficiency of any brain chemistry can significantly impact one's mood, attitude, and emotional expression. Consequently, when the brain's chemistry becomes saturated with substances like Adrenaline, Serotonin, THC, or DMT, " all considered to be chemical compounds," it triggers profound changes in mood and behavior, leading to various emotional expressions. Though we all have the ability to naturally induce these compounds via brain chemistry, an example of chemical flooding can be seen as the act of overwhelming the system by flooding it with an external source of chemical stimulants such as synthetic drugs or designer herbs to create a synthetic mood or high. For instance, a blunt of marijuana is the trigger that floods the brain with THC.

A similar scenario often unfolds when someone behaves in a manner that's out of character, or as some people put it, "doing the most." For example, if you see someone in public losing their composure, shouting, or acting erratically, they are likely experiencing emotional flooding. This state happens when a person is triggered, leading to overwhelming emotions that disrupt their brain chemistry and neural pathways, making self-control difficult.

In some instances, emotional flooding can reach a point where it leads to a blackout, causing individuals to forget the events that transpired. This occurs because the overwhelming emotions effectively shut down or deactivate other parts of their brain. In earlier times, this phenomenon might have been perceived as a spirit taking control, sometimes referred to as a "walk-in." Perhaps this is why the phenomena of blacking out when over indulging in flooding the blood with the chemical compounds found in alcohol spirits is common.

Having said all of that, when we return to the topic of limerence, we see that intense emotions flood the brain's chemistry in a similar way, making other brain chemicals appear inactive. This mirrors the chemical effects of drugs, where the molecules produced by emotions from love to anger have addictive properties, also akin to those in substances like coffee or cigarettes.

In moments of anger, your body's muscles become tense, and it releases neurotransmitter chemicals, called catecholamines, which surge into the brain, unleashing a brief yet intense burst of energy. However, as the flooding subsides, the brain's chemical equilibrium is restored. Regrettably, the exhilaration stemming from this chemical rush often drives individuals to pursue that sensation further, regardless of the unhealthy consequences.

An inexperienced and immature mind will attempt to prolong the experience by convincing itself with narratives for justifying toxic behaviors such as jealous rage or envious shaming while being fully aware that the behavior is unnecessary. If one is not mindful, emotional flooding can occur anytime an individual is triggered, leading to sudden shifts in attitude or emotional expression and potentially causing unpredictable behavior. The next time you experience a full grown adult having a temper tantrum and meltdown, you now know that they are flooding.

Note: It's intriguing that the chemical response to anger mirrors the chemical reaction to fear, which can be equally habit-forming. Consider haunted houses, horror films, or the perpetual stream of negative news programming, and how people willingly seek these experiences despite the potential psychological toll.

From a subjective standpoint, limerence shares similarities with the natural release of dopamine experienced during a runner's high after a vigorous workout. It also bears resemblances to the more potent chemical addictions associated with fear, anger, and authentic love, all triggered by the chemicals within our brain. Essentially when our attraction triggers induce the limerent feeling of falling in love, the addictive chemicals we experience are akin to a powerful emotional flooding.

When strong attraction sets off a surge of endorphins and dopamine, a person can become deeply limerent, starting the journey of falling in love without any safeguards. We've been instructed, conditioned, and influenced by sources like romance novels and TV shows to view this state as charming and healthy. We aspire to emulate the romantic couples we see on screen, yet, deep down, we recognize the disparity between fictional narratives and real life.

Is it not lost on us, however, that when we see Keanu Reeves or Denzel Washington in an action-packed film as essentially a badass and serial killer, no matter how much we admire their characters, we know this can not be our real life? So why attempt to imitate some of the fictional and impossible scenarios we see in the movies regarding love when deep down, we know this most likely can not be our real life. A two-hour feel-good film edit couldn't possibly encompass a two-year or two-decade relationship.

The boundaries between love and limerence have become so normalized that you might say, "I don't see a difference. What's the fuss? Aren't they essentially the same?" Allow me to define the distinction in simple terms. When misunderstood, limerence can subtly morph into a toxic form of perceived love, wherein our focus narrows to how the object of our affection gratifies our desires and makes us feel good, all while unknowingly attempting to fill voids within ourselves.

It's a transient, ego-driven and selfish state of mind that prioritizes maintaining our perpetual emotional high. This mindset inevitably leads to contemplation of what the other person does for us rather than nurturing a sense of unconditional service and regard. An element of attachment prevails because we don't just see the other person as an individual; it can feel as though they owe us something. Their role becomes one of loving us in a specific and exclusive manner, no matter the circumstances, and we hope they embrace the task of being the savior of our hearts.

On the flip side, limerent expressions might take the form of "I need you," strategically designed to elicit a sense of guilt driven obligation from the other party. In this type of relationship, your self-concept becomes inseparable from the other person, as the primary focus revolves around seeking attention and having your needs constantly affirmed, in contrast to fostering a sense of shared freedom and individual expression.

Moving into the next phase, limerents often hold the belief that their partners should consistently reciprocate their feelings, if not surpass them, without any expectations or conditions. Worship me with no questions asked is the ideal yet unlikely situation. When the same level of intensity isn't mirrored, feelings of insecurity can foster the illusion of rejection, paving the way for potentially harmful gaslighting or abandoning the investment all together. In some cases, those who frequently quits may be described as lacking perseverance or commitment. They may be seen as unreliable, inconsistent, or easily discouraged. This behavior suggests a tendency to give up when faced with challenges or when immediate success isn't achieved.

In contrast, genuine love constitutes a selfless gesture primarily centered on others. It's not solely about how this person makes you feel but, rather, about how you can positively impact their emotions. Love is propelled by the aspiration to comprehend, connect, and serve freely, akin to a new parent's lack of expectations regarding their infant. While a smile here and there is appreciated, love is devoid of transactional demands, and nothing is mandated from the infant to receive a parent's love. Parental love isn't contingent on specific conditions; it's unconditionally given. A very different type of love shared between lovers.

Similarly, consider the scenario where an emotionally whole individual seeks to offer assistance while visiting a grandparent. The usual intent is not to seek anything in return when expressing love to your MeMaw or PawPaw. Genuine love forges a connection between two individuals who deeply care, and their actions are driven by the desire to give without anticipating any reciprocity, apart from acts of kindness.

Achieving this level of understanding necessitates some degree of enlightenment. Co-dependent relationships, when attempting to embody this kind of love, will inevitably encounter frustration. It's challenging to love others if we haven't first cultivated self-love. It's like the blind leading the blind.

Moreover, susceptibility to limerence is heightened if you're infatuated with the very concept of love, meaning, you are in love with the idea of being in love. Insecurities within individuals can frequently trigger intense attraction during the initial phases of dating, as they yearn for validation and reassurance from their prospective partners. Limerence has the power to obscure your judgment, leading you to make choices you wouldn't ordinarily make, such as overwhelming your romantic interest with excessive affection, i.e. Love Bombing them to death.

Numerous individuals react with discomfort when faced with upfront love bombing and may deem it unsettling, thereby undermining any limerence they may have felt themselves. Another unfavorable consequence can compel the limerent to intensify their efforts and commence to making sacrifices they wouldn't typically consider, ultimately diminishing their own value.

If you ever find yourself entangled in such a situation, it's imperative to step back and reevaluate your circumstances. Limerence is a powerful feeling that holds the potential to guide us toward love, respect, and trust. Yet, if we're not vigilant, it can inadvertently lead us down a protracted and shadowed path.

Exploring attachment styles along with limerence offers valuable insights into the complex dynamics of attraction. These styles greatly affect what triggers attraction in an individual and significantly influence their behavior in relationships. Understanding a person's attachment style is key to how they experience limerence and interact in their relationships.

Attachment theory is the collaborative masterpiece crafted by **John Bowlby and Mary Ainsworth**. Together, they laid the groundwork for what we now comprehend as attachment styles, and their pioneering work has established itself as one of the most influential theories in psychology. This visionary duo provided us with a framework for comprehending the development of attachment styles and their profound implications for our interpersonal connections. It is postulated that attachment styles take root during our formative years of early childhood. As you engage with this material, take a moment to introspect and contemplate whether any of the information strikes a chord with your own life experiences, particularly those rooted in your childhood.

The four main attachment styles are :

1. Secure/Insecure Attachment Style: People with a secure attachment style feel comfortable with intimacy and are usually willing to express their feelings, needs, and desires openly. They're not afraid of commitment and generally have positive views of themselves and their partners.

People with a secure attachment style tend to be more trusting, loving, and supportive in relationships. They're also more likely to forgive their partner's mistakes and feel confident in their ability to work through challenges together. A person is less likely to be attached to superficial and trivial things when they are secure. All other attachment styles that are not secure are known as insecure attachment styles.

People with an insecure attachment style might have more difficulty with intimacy and emotional closeness. They might fear commitment, worry about being rejected or abandoned, and have negative views of themselves and their partners.

2. Anxious attachment: People with an anxious attachment style tend to be clingy, need constant reassurance, and become easily jealous. They might also have difficulty trusting their partner and feel like they're always on the lookout for signs that their partner will leave them. In many cases, they may be considered co-dependent and possibly even have low self-esteem.

3. Avoidant attachment: People with an avoidant attachment style tend to be more distant and independent in relationships. They might have trouble expressing their needs and feelings and seem emotionally disconnected from their partner. They may generally fear commitment and harbor a subconscious overall fear-based outlook on relationships in general, colored as independence. When engaged in a relationship, they may come off as selfish and a separatist. This avoidant style fears abandonment, and thus they make sure not to ever put themselves in a situation that can cause them to be abandoned. High-frequency, short-term flings are their preferred relationships.

4. Disorganized attachment is a mix between the two other types. People with disorganized attachments may feel secure and insecure in their attachments, or they may fluctuate between both, sometimes appearing bipolar. They may say they seek to be more independent and yet cling to dependency patterns or vice versa in a very unorganized way.

Disorganized attachment can be linked to experiences from early childhood. When a child's caregiver proves to be unpredictable or absent, it often fosters a sense of insecurity and fear. Consequently, the child may develop coping strategies centered around avoidance or emotional numbness. These coping mechanisms can subsequently pose challenges in adult relationships.

An unhealed individual with a disorganized attachment style can introduce unnecessary turbulence into an otherwise harmonious and smooth-sailing relationship. This attachment type and personality remind me of the character Joan Clayton from the popular TV show "Girlfriends," for those who are familiar with the series.

It comes as no shock that numerous individuals have turned to social drinking, marijuana and other substances as coping mechanisms for the daily challenges of social interactions, especially when they've grappled with disorganized attachment styles in their early development. Nevertheless, it's crucial to recognize that substance use may not represent the most viable long-term solution.

As individuals progress through life, they construct a psychological framework that extends from the womb to the tomb. Our character is significantly molded by our environment, encompassing our social, communal, and familial background. It's not unusual for more recent generations, the so-called digital natives, to occasionally resort to technology as a surrogate babysitter. Profound neglect during one's formative years can leave an enduring and profound impact on their emotional development.

If a child's basic needs for love, attention, and security are not met, they might grow up feeling unloved, unworthy, and insecure. This sense of inadequacy can lead to problems in self-esteem and other aspects of life. Most attachment styles develop from these early experiences and continue to influence and shape their adult relationships. It's intriguing to note that the words "parent" and "partner" bear a remarkable resemblance in spelling, differing by the placement of just a single letter.

We each have unique attachment styles that can change through our life experiences. When we're attracted to someone who triggers our basic, nonverbal cues for connection and survival, it creates a profound feeling. This attraction is partly driven by our attachment system, which includes our nervous system and limbic brain, and is influenced by the hormones and neurochemicals they produce. Not being aware of these factors can result in behaviors that might not align with our best interests.

In Eastern philosophy, a key teaching from the Buddha highlights that attachment leads to suffering. This is because attachment fosters a strong desire for things to remain constant, despite change being the only constant. The shackles of attachment can frequently bind us to the pain of loss, stemming from our attachment to the very things we fear losing. Yet, there exists an alternative path – one that encourages us to release our grip and savor the present moment for all its worth. "In the moment" is not a terrible place to nurture authentic love. In fact, it's a great state of mind to share with another person when traversing the path of love. Not judging the past or worrying about the future but instead loving tremendously right now in real-time.

In a platonic context, like friendships, team mates or business partnerships, the influence of attachment styles becomes clear. For instance, in a friendship, an anxiously attached individual might constantly fear abandonment, leading to clinginess or misinterpreting minor issues as signs of a waning bond. This can strain the relationship, as their need for reassurance might overwhelm their friend. Conversely, in a business partnership, if one partner has an avoidant attachment style, they might shy away from close collaboration or emotional investment in team efforts, potentially hindering trust and open communication. Understanding and balancing these attachment styles can help maintain healthy, supportive platonic relationships, allowing each person to cherish the present interactions without undue stress about the relationship's future.

The Chemical Cocktail.
From the ancient wisdom of Buddha to the groundbreaking work of Dr. Dorothy Tennov, John Bowlby, and Mary Ainsworth, brilliant minds have continuously enriched the ongoing conversation. An exceptional thinker whose approach I truly admire is Dr. Daniel G. Ayman, a New York Times best-selling author renowned for his book, "The Brain in Love."

Much like attachment theories, Dr. Ayman's theories outline **four phases of attraction**, each characterized by a vital chemical interplay. Considering the profound emotions that love evokes, one could argue that a distinct chemistry underpins it. I find the breakdown of Dr. Ayman's four attraction phases to be fascinating as they offer a blueprint for the intricate chemistry, that when triggered, floods the brain to initiate what we can now refer to as limerence.

The initial two phases of attraction can fall under the realm of limerence theory, which includes infatuation and attraction. The inaugural phase, as Dr. Ayman dubs it, is "The Look of Love." During this stage, one's attraction is primarily based on the physical appearance of the person in question or, as mentioned earlier, on the image one might have of them. It's a time when you find yourself utterly captivated by someone, unable to free your mind from their allure. You might even find yourself doing things you wouldn't ordinarily do in your pursuit to impress or capture their attention. At this juncture, your attraction can give rise to an insatiable desire to be with this person, akin to an eager drug enthusiast geeking for their next fix. Your longing knows no bounds.

These feelings are mostly translated into a desire for sexual gratification and are predominantly driven by the male and female hormones **Testosterone and Estroge**n. It's no surprise that men are driven by visual stimulation and how a woman looks. A visually appealing woman is what essentially dominates a man's desires. Men are believed to appreciate big butts or big breasts because of a subconscious desire and genetic disposition to find a fertile, healthy woman who can reproduce quickly and easily. Possibly a trait leftover from our primate days. Studies have shown when men are exposed to images of beautiful women, the system responsible for regulating emotion and motivation, known as the Limbic System, lights up like a Christmas tree. #Science

In contrast, the Prefrontal Cortex, which is responsible for controlling judgment and reason, begins to shut down, leaving one to believe that a beautiful woman can turn a man into a temporary imbecile who acts impulsively and without reason. On the flip side, it is quite the opposite for women. When exposed to images of attractive men, their brain activity shows no changes in judgment, even if they reported an equal level of interest. This reaction is because women are more concerned with how a man thinks and acts as it displays his ability to provide stability and security.

So, despite the prevailing notion that the fairer sex is "overly romantic" or excessively emotional, Dr. Ayman's research suggests that men are more prone to experiencing love at first sight compared to women. Women, on the other hand, exhibit a higher propensity for commitment. If you've been following closely, you might have already deduced this pattern. It's essential to understand that when a man showers you with affection and attention, it doesn't necessarily indicate his readiness to walk down the aisle in the near future. While professing such intentions might be part of his love-bombing strategy, the true test lies in whether he is willing to back up his words with action when the time comes.

Within Dr. Ayman's four attraction phases, the second phase is aptly named "The Honeymoon Phase." It's the stage where you find yourself utterly infatuated with your partner, seeing perfection in every little detail about them. Everything feels fresh, and you're viewing your partner through those delightful rose-colored glasses. In this phase, they can do no wrong, and even red flags are forgiven. Kirlian aura goggles might might be a better example for seeing these wonderful things not normally seen by the eyes.

Infatuation isn't merely an emotion; it's a potent "motivational drive" powered by the brain's reward system, fueled by a cocktail of chemicals including **Epinephrine, Norepinephrine, Dopamine, Serotonin, and Phenylethylamine or P.E.A.** Epinephrine and Norepinephrine are produced in the adrenal glands, spinal cord, and brain, functioning as excitatory neurotransmitters that deliver an exhilarating **"adrenaline rush"** following the initial attraction.

Dopamine is the neurochemical closely linked to pleasure, motivation, and concentration. It's responsible for those persistent thoughts like, "Why can't I get them out of my head?"—a common experience in the realm of psychology. On the other hand, Serotonin, often dubbed the "feel good" chemical, generates feelings of contentment in a partnership. And then there's P.E.A., an adrenaline-like substance referred to as the "love molecule," which kickstarts the release of these various chemicals, culminating in that euphoric sensation.

The **third phase** of attraction is often termed "the Power Struggle Phase." It's a pivotal juncture where you're confronted with the decision to either deepen your connection or disengage. Dr. Ayman suggests this phase typically spans a period ranging from six months to three years. During this stage, the brain transitions from the initial infatuation mode into a desire for a committed relationship, provided you've reached that point. In retrospect, the alternative is that you would deplete yourself from an incessant and chronic state of lust.

Somewhere in this transitional period, you begin to realize that your lover is not perfect and you have different views on things. **Oxytocin and Vasopressin** are the chemicals involved in this drop-off. They begin to take the place of the more "hot and heavy" chemicals. Oxytocin is related to feelings of closeness and being "in love." Elevated levels of Oxytocin are also associated with increased feelings of trust. Vasopressin is involved in regulating sexual persistence, assertiveness, dominance, and territorial markings.

Notably, while men might be attracted to and fall in love more quickly than women, the chemical switch-over into committed feelings is more likely to occur first in women. As you grow more comfortable with your partner and feel a sense of security in the relationship, you might find yourself less inclined to continuously seek their approval. At times, you might even unintentionally begin to take them for granted.

The "mystery" that once fueled those fantasies, giving rise to that hot to trot brain chemistry, gradually loses its mystique. The fuel for our fantasies may begin to wane, resulting in the depletion of certain other chemical reservoirs as well. In retrospect, the flooding begins to drain like the hoover dam. If there is no balancing of compatibility with chemistry, a deficit could spell out disaster— i.e., the C.C.D. or chemistry-compatibility deficit.

At this point, many relationships start to fizzle out as the initial excitement has worn off, and we're left with the reality of our not-so-perfect human partner. You begin to look at them like, been there - done that, or like, I've seen this show already. You think to yourself, this person bores me; they no longer entertain my ego as they once did, and so season two of your personal romantic dramedy comes to be officially canceled.

At times, as the intensity of infatuation chemicals diminishes, individuals may erroneously interpret the waning intensity and euphoria as a sign of falling out of love. Moreover, prompted by the withdrawal from these infatuation-inducing chemicals, some may seek out other partners or engage in novel experiences, such as swinging or S&M, in an attempt to recapture that natural high. Alternatively, they may resort to stimulants like ecstasy, alcohol, or marijuana to reignite those sensations of excitement or, at the very least, to endure and cope with the loss of fervor. Nevertheless, relying on such substances to recreate these emotions can be detrimental and may result in enduring consequences.

But on the contrary, when the intense attraction associated with limerence triggers the flooding of love chemistry in our brains, it can lead us to fall hard. These limerent attraction chemicals colored as love can crystalize and become embedded in the limbic part of our brains, which is responsible for our emotions, memories, and arousal. It can influence our entire reality. When we find ourselves unable to engage with our beloved as we once did, it's commonplace to encounter withdrawal symptoms. This can result in inflammation of that limbic region, which translates into tangible physical discomfort. The anguish can be all-encompassing, and it might feel as though a literal piece of ourselves is missing.

The yearning to be in the proximity of the object of our affection can completely dominate our thoughts, making it a formidable challenge to focus on anything else. Managing emotional distress can be a tough endeavor, making self-care imperative during these moments. Reaching out to loved ones or professionals can provide valuable support in navigating these intense emotions and discovering healthy coping strategies.

On the Pink Matter project by the talented recording artist Frank Ocean, the masterful poet Andre Benjamin eloquently recites words that vividly illustrate this phenomenon of limbic embedding. As he aptly puts it,

"Since you've been gone, I've been having withdrawals,
You were such a habit to call
I ain't myself at all, had to tell myself, "Nawl"
She better with some fella with a regular job."
I didn't wanna get her involved.
By dinner, Mr. Benjamin was sitting in awe..."

When the chemistry between you and a love interest has solidified in your limbic system, it creates a powerful physical and emotional connection. This connection is neurologically encoded in, not surprisingly, the pink matter of your brain—and heart so to speak, subsequently leading to a deep attachment to the object of your desire. As a result, your lover becomes a holographic extension of your physical being and embedded in your psychology. When your loved one is no longer around, it can feel like you've been robbed of a literal piece of your soul. This feeling can be overwhelming and can impact your well-being in profound ways.

This is equivalent to when you've been in a long-term relationship with someone, you may have shared many experiences and created memories together. These shared experiences become an integral part of your identity shaping who you are as a person and the very core of your being. Like the pollination or genetic fertilization process, they have become finely integrated into your physical and astral person. When such a relationship comes to an abrupt end, relinquishing those memories and the person who had been an integral part of your life can be an exceptionally arduous task. The pain of separation can be so profound that it manifests as a genuine physical aching. In both romantic and platonic relationships, the shame associated with pain can lead some individuals to transform it into anger, eliciting emotions similar to those expressed in the *"Haters Anthem"* record by the dynamic group *Infinity Song*. Opting for healing over harboring resentment is invariably a healthier choice.

While love is often considered an intangible emotion, the chemicals it invokes exert a very tangible influence on the mind and body. This influence may manifest as depression, sleep disturbances, obsessive thoughts, decreased appetite, and an inclination to isolate oneself. Do any of these experiences sound familiar to you? Such a state of emotional turbulence can be attributed to low Serotonin levels, which can trigger all these symptoms. Additionally, a shortage of Endorphins, the regulators of pain and pleasure, might explain why we can genuinely experience physical pain during a breakup. Yes, as mentioned previously, your heart can literally ache and actually feel broken.

The good news is that the relationship can blossom into something more special and esoteric, even for those who make it through this phase. Regarding Dr. Ayman's theory on the four phases of attraction, **the fourth** and final attraction phase is "the Consummation or mature love phase."

This phase materializes, naturally, when you make the resolute decision to commit wholeheartedly. You begin to relax into a more routine and stable sense of normalcy. You feel more deeply attached and bonded and start to trust the consistency of the relationship. In this stage, you accept the person for who they are and love them unconditionally. We decide here to commit to our partner and our relationship fully. We become more intentional and are finally ready to make things official, whether it's moving in together, getting married, or having children.

During this phase, we become wholeheartedly devoted to our partner, fully dedicated to nurturing the relationship. When you've weathered the trials of time and found yourselves to be compatible enough for a lasting partnership, you'll know that you've reached this stage. It either happens organically, because playing the field has grown tiring and you're at a place of peace in your life, or it happens after doing the work it takes to create and maintain a deep, meaningful connection for a responsible, loving relationship. It doesn't feel forced and generally flows and feels easy.

Additionally, Dr. Ayman emphasizes that while bonding chemicals play a pivotal role in the development of a relationship, effective communication and mutual support are vital for elevating the initial phases of attraction and infatuation to the level of committed love. In essence, building and savoring a fulfilling relationship necessitates effort and dedication. In the event that you find yourself with a partner who becomes detached, it's crucial to maintain emotional well-being and refrain from idealizing that individual.

Up to this point, we've uncovered that love, for many, might not be love in the conventional sense but rather a fleeting chemical euphoria camouflaged as romance and limerence, intricately influenced by our attachment styles. We've also delved into the revelation that heightened dopamine levels, coupled with the release of the related hormone Norepinephrine, occur during the attraction phase. These chemicals engender a sense of elation, vitality, and euphoria, to the extent that they can result in reduced appetite and insomnia. In essence, one can become so "in love" or adversely, so heart broken, that they can't eat or sleep, closely resembling a drug addict.

Furthermore, we've come to understand that the brain can cement the bond through the release of Oxytocin, frequently referred to as "the love hormone." This neuropeptide originates in the hypothalamus and is discharged by the pituitary gland during moments of intimacy, encompassing various activities such as hugging, breast massage, and even orgasm. These are just a few of the components in this addictive cocktail.

- **Serotonin.**

- **Dopamine.**

- **Endorphins.**

- **Oxytocin. Etc.**

Love exerts an influence on Serotonin, a neurotransmitter that plays a pivotal role in behavior and mood regulation. What's intriguing is that the impact of love on Serotonin varies significantly depending on gender. In men, romantic relationships tend to lead to a decrease in serotonin levels, while women experience a substantial increase in Serotonin.

Activities such as hugging, kissing, cuddling, and sexual intimacy can all trigger the production of oxytocin, fortifying the emotional bonds between adults. These effects have resulted in Oxytocin being categorized among the other "happy hormones" renowned for their ability to positively affect mood and emotions, making human connections a delightful experience.

When it comes to attraction, we have frameworks that help us understand it, highlighting the complex ways we fall deeply for someone, sometimes even losing our sense of reason. Each type of attraction is marked by its own set of hormones produced by the brain.

Lust: Pheromone - Testosterone / Estrogen

Attraction: Dopamine - Norepinephrine - Serotonin

Attachment: Oxytocin - Vasopressin

Much like the little bio-robotic avatars we were designed to be, we find ourselves constantly being programmed by a never-ending dance of seductions, peacocking, and the alluring pull of sexual marketing campaigns as well readily accessible soft porn on our daily socials. These elements have us perpetually captivated, prepped, spellbound, and wholly immersed in the ever-present cravings for attraction and the exhilarating rush of chemicals abound in N.R.E, or New Relationship Energy, 24/7.

As a side note: "Peacocking" a term first made popular by the legendary pickup artist "Mystery," and is what dating expert and coach James Preece describes as "something men do to highlight their strong points to stand out from their competition. It's typically employed to attract women, much like peacocks flaunt their feathers to woo a mate or a pigeon might puff out its chest to appear more virile or strong. Neil Strauss, author of 'The Game' says that the equivalent to the fanned peacock tail is a shiny shirt, a garish hat, and jewelry that lights up in the dark—basically all the things he previously dismissed as cheesy but soon learned, if you don't stand out, you fit in.

Notably, women have their own versions of this behavior. In today's world, seductions are just a click away, with social media models indulging in daily bouts of thirst-trapping, courtesy of digital filters, transformative make-up, seductive yoga, and flashy twerking. Add trendy digital filters and they are off to the races as if they've been anointed by divine decree. The age-old adage that "sex sells" requires no elaborate explanation. We inhabit a realm of perpetual fantasy, both dishing it out and eagerly consuming it, leaving many constantly revved up, yearning for the next dopamine-infused hit of attraction or limerence.

The avenues through which people can encounter attraction, limerence, and love are remarkably diverse. The manner in which each individual's epigenetic profile, psychology, personality, and attachment style interplay will shape their unique response and experience of these phenomena. While these experiences can be immensely rewarding, they can also be intricate and occasionally overwhelming.

As we've seen, there are an array of attraction dynamics that can be influenced by our brain chemistry and the circumstances we find ourselves in. It's crucial to bear in mind that no two individuals are identical. Our attachment styles and attraction triggers come in diverse variations, meaning what resonates with one person may not necessarily resonate with another. Gaining an understanding of your relationship preferences and how they may manifest in the context of enduring commitments can significantly enhance your journey toward a more enriching and enlightening romantic partnership as well as platonic and transactional ones.

Throughout our history and into the limitless expanse of our future, it remains paramount to comprehend the underlying purpose and rationale of our connections with others. It is imperative to know that when we tread this path unaware, we risk confusing the fiery flames of lust for the enduring warmth of love. In a non-romantic context, it's crucial to distinguish between the intense zeal of ambition and the sincere motivation aimed at collective achievement.

It's possible to stake our entire existence on a lifelong quest for compatibility, only to realize that what initially appeared as a dazzling peacock or a rare unicorn had merely triggered a cascade of chemicals, which, with time, might lack the necessary elements to develop into a lasting lifetime of unwavering, unconditional support.

In exploring the science of attraction and soon the history of human relationships, we will possess a blueprint for unraveling the forensic mysteries that bring us into contact with our soulmates. These significant individuals have the potential to fundamentally influence our identity through the mirrored reflections and experiences we share with them ultimately polarizing the elemental nature of our spirit.

Chapter Three

The Timeline

Back down memory lane: A History of Relationship Models

Quote: Important encounters are planned by the souls long before the bodies see each other. — Paulo Coelho

Have you ever reflected on your relationships and felt uncertain about how they became so serious or complex? Maybe you're in the early stages of a relationship, be it romantic, platonic, or otherwise, and wondering where it's headed. Given the many ups and downs that relating with others bring, you might question why we involve ourselves with people at all.

Have you ever considered the reasons, purposes, and processes that has shaped our current relationship culture as a species, given that most of our social behaviors are inherited? It's a valid question that many people have contemplated over time. You might also have wondered how our society evolved to its current social state and who first conceived the relationship models we practice, as well as when and where it all took place. Why do I crave love, or why am I deeply in love? Why do I choose to engage with and entertain the company I keep, or why do I hang around the types of people I hang around? With so many questions persistently swirling in the background of our thoughts, it's easy to become overwhelmed or even confused. However, gaining clarity on these questions by exploring their possible origins can help us make sense of our interactions. To truly comprehend twin elemental alignments and the purpose of karmic soul ties, it's essential to first understand the foundational principles that govern basic relationship dynamics.

Indeed, today is but a tapestry woven from the threads of yesterday. We are the living embodiment of our past. We are, quite literally, the sum of all that has come before us—a continuous narrative shaped by the choices we've made and the paths we've laid. Just as the food consumed earlier lays the foundation for the cells that will sustain us in the days to come, so too has our actions shaped the collective paths of our future. Each choice made and morsel consumed contributes to the construction of our present selves, like bricks laid one upon another in the architecture of time.

The upcoming chapters aim to bridge the gap between ancient and contemporary timelines, offering insights into the foundations of your personal relationship culture, including romantic dynamics and socio-political structures. In these chapters, you'll gain a comprehensive perspective on the development and evolution of relationship structures over time, exploring their origins, progressions, and underlying influences that have shaped the modern relationship culture you are undoubtedly a part of. While various approaches can describe the construction of relationship culture, these next two chapters provide a concise and interconnected timeline overview for contemplation.

As you get into this chapter, you'll notice a shift in writing style. It may, at times, resemble a history lesson, which is different from the story telling style of the previous chapters. While this may not be everyone's reading preference, it's crucial to establish a practical understanding of the topic before diving into more complex ideas. By establishing these basics, we'll construct a solid framework to guide us when exploring more intricate and thought-provoking concepts.

In truth, it might help to envision yourself as a dedicated and enthusiastic history buff who enjoys the intellectual empowerment and expertise gained from learning about historical events. With that in mind, take a deep breath, and let's begin.

Human relationships can be complex and or challenging to navigate. The progression of human relationships throughout millennia has been significantly influenced by cultural, social, and historical factors. Consequently, a diverse spectrum of relationship styles has emerged, reflecting the intricate development and adaptation that has transpired over time. From the traditional roles and expectations placed on individuals in various societies to the changing attitudes towards marriage and family dynamics, the history of human relationships is rich and complex, continually evolving as society changes.

In our exploration of the origins and complex dynamics surrounding human coupling, we'll first examine how various archetypes interact psychologically. This encompasses romantic partnerships, platonic acquaintances, and transactional-only associations. As we delve into the past to uncover clues about our present state, we'll also explore how different archetypical characters can profoundly influence and shape the destinies of entire civilizations through the impact of their interpersonal relationships. By scrutinizing the intricacies of human relationships, we can gain insights into how these interactions continue to impact our lives today, including our individual psyches. Without a doubt, the actions of your ancestors eons ago have a direct impact on how you function in the present.

What if the Kellogg Company had never launched its marketing campaign touting the slogan, "Breakfast is the most important meal of the day," to sell more cereal boxes? What if the decline in the use of slaves and indentured servants to cook meals hadn't sparked the processed food and fast food revolutions? Would we still eat just one meal a day instead of three? Would there be an obesity epidemic? Consider another scenario: What if the advertising genius Claude Hopkins had never convinced Americans—and ultimately the world—to brush their teeth daily because a company wanted to profit from a flawed product? Would you and your community still walk around every day with unbrushed teeth and bad breath? The actions of individuals in the past, regardless of the intention, affect our collective lifestyles and daily decisions today.

Imagine if Cleopatra had never influenced Julius Caesar to adopt a more advanced system for calculating time, thus changing the calendar to what we currently use. Would Monday have been Monday? Would Caesar have ever been assassinated at all had he never crossed paths with his twin elemental soul tie? Would Rome have become the Rome we know, and would its predecessor, America, even exist as it does today? Furthermore, would the world be the world we know now?

This is the power of origins and how they affect and influence who you think you are at this very moment.

Question: Did you know that your ancestors set a course in how you would relate to others before you were born? This course may have exerted a profound influence, potentially even epigenetically shaping your personality, thereby contributing to the formation of your present belief system regarding love and relationships. After all, are we not beneficiaries and products of our cultural environment?

Consider this: Insects and animals have established systems to ensure their administration, copulation, and propagation. Similarly, civilizations across various realms, whether on Jupiter or within the Orion constellation, have their systems in place for the administration of copulation, and propagation. Regarding interpersonal and social structures, humanity is no different.

While gaining a clear understanding about the evolution of systematic social structures, including love and marriage on planet Earth, one can vividly imagine a flowing timeline from antiquity to the present day. This journey would feature numerous stops highlighting how various cultures have approached love, courtship, and marriage throughout history.

To enhance our understanding, allow me to provide evidence in support of our objective. First, I'd like to take you on a journey back in time to illustrate the fascinating nature of human companionship. To begin this exercise, imagine, if you will, that we are entering a physical time machine. It could resemble a bright orb, a flying saucer, or the DeLorean with butterfly doors from the "Back to the Future" film. The details are not crucial; it's all within your imagination.

During our journey through time together, think of it as akin to boarding a scenic bus or train ride, with each subsection and contemplation within the chapter acting as a stop along the way. Picture each scene as if you're viewing it from a bird's-eye view, like a futuristic observer looking down. Envision that you're strolling the streets of that era incognito, draped in an invisibility cloak. Engage fully in this mentally immersive experience, as if you're a living participant in an interactive documentary. Imagine immersing yourself in the ambient sounds of daily life, observing the vivid expressions on people's faces, and catching the scents that evoke the sensory experiences of different times and cultures.

Throughout our journey, we will travel as far back as the prehistoric era and the Neolithic period. From there, we'll move on to the ancient Alkebulan, Sumerian and Egyptian civilizations of antiquity. Next, we'll venture through the Middle Ages, exploring Greco-Roman and Medieval European cultures, before arriving at the Romanticism and Renaissance eras. Finally, we will delve into the contemporary era of modernized living, where the influence of advanced media and technology can instantaneously impact the collective consciousness of our global community, bringing forth both altruistic as well as nefarious consequences.

The purpose of this virtual journey is to provide an objective exploration of the history of Attraction, Romance, and Love, as well as Kinships, Friendships, Relationships, and Marriage—as they relate to esoteric soul pairings. We will traverse time, from the prehistoric era to the modern age, gaining a deeper understanding of humanity's emotional evolution. Throughout this voyage, we'll delve into the influence of cultural revolutions and on how we engage regarding companionship.

You will soon realize that the preoccupation with these inherent and essential ideas about our relationship models is among the most critical aspects of our human development. Our position on the human timeline is shaped by our relationship models, and these models incorporate a technological element with systemic implications. To grasp these concepts from a broader, macro perspective establishes the groundwork for recognizing the significance of acknowledging a twin elemental's power to instigate disruptions, both on a macro and micro level of your personal timeline and spiritual trajectory.

The intricate ideas about these models have been transmitted through the centuries, with records dating back thousands, and even tens, or hundreds of thousands of years. Whether conveyed through primitive cave paintings, Sumerian cuneiform on stone tablets, Egyptian hieroglyphics on pyramid walls and papyrus, or even inked penmanship and typography on modern paper, our ancestors have left us clues as to what they were up to. It's evident that these concepts remain relevant, persisting as constants throughout the ages, underlining their enduring significance in the human experience.

The wealth of information left by our ancestors, encompassing their rituals, patterns, and records that detail their way of life, vividly demonstrates how their interactions and expressions have influenced and molded our own unique and inherent characteristics today. That first boyfriend who exhibited overprotective or jealous tendencies or that college girlfriend who expected to be treated like the Queen of England may have inherited those personality traits based on preexisting behavioral inclinations intricately connected to the various milestones of human development.

These insights from around the world, spanning centuries, will serve as our golden tickets to the past. Let us wholeheartedly embrace the spirit of Sankofa, a term from the Twi language of the Akan people in Ghana, which conveys the idea that it is not taboo to return and retrieve what is at risk of being left behind or lost. This profound concept will lead us on our journey and inspire us as we embark on this brief odyssey together.

The question lingers: How did it all begin? Let's unpack that.

PRIMATES

By starting with the most fundamental and primal illustration of relationships in the natural world, we can establish a bedrock for basic comprehension. Investigating the dynamics of relationships in nature sets the stage for a more comprehensive grasp of human interaction. Apes, in particular, serve as a valuable and alternative model to glean insights into human behavior.

Primates first appeared in the fossil record around 55 million years ago and may have originated as far back as the Cretaceous Period. Apes, which evolved from catarrhines, emerged in Alkebulan-Africa approximately 25 million years ago during the middle of the Cenozoic Era. The catarrhines are a group of anthropoid primates comprising the Old World monkeys, apes, and humans.

Being one of our closest evolutionary relatives, though a distinctly different species, apes share significant genetic similarity with humans, rendering them an ideal subject for preliminary research on human behavior and evolution. Both apes and humans exhibit complex social behaviors, tool use, and communication systems. Within the spectrum of ape behavior, their ability to express love and affection is especially noteworthy and provides a valuable lens for the study of human social behavior.

Researchers have specifically noted a wide array of affectionate behaviors in apes, including embracing, kissing, and grooming. These captivating behaviors underscore the importance of social bonds and emotional connections within the ape social structure, particularly within familial and close friendships.

Moreover, apes offer a unique case study of how social hierarchy and order can be upheld through expressions of affection, rather than relying on aggression or violence. In ape communities, the alpha male occupies a dominant position, yet they frequently employ grooming and other acts of affection to foster loyalty and preserve social harmony. This mirrors how a spouse or parent may employ kindness and favor to promote harmony in the household or how certain politicians may compromise to achieve their goals. This underscores the significance of positive social interactions and emotional connections in maintaining order within a hierarchical structure. Use the potty, get an organic lollipop or help me move my armoire for a beer and I'll owe you a favor is how that generally could look in a modern household.

The study of apes and their behavior furnishes valuable insights into the origins of human social behavior and the pivotal role of affection in upholding social stability. Through this brief examination, we can gain a deeper understanding of the evolutionary underpinnings of our social conduct and how love and emotional connections contribute to social order and stability. Ultimately, apes offer a captivating and instructive framework for exploring human behavior and impart crucial lessons on nurturing healthy and interconnected communities.

If you've ever pondered why many of us crave affection and attention, consider the parallels with apes. It's likely that such inclinations may be ingrained in us genetically, shaped by millennia of epigenetic and habitual neuroplastic programming. Furthermore, when your loved one tells you to stop acting like a monkey, well, you get the picture!

REGARDING PREHISTORIC MAN *~2.5 million years ago to 1,200 B.C.*
Allow me to transport you back to an era predating modern humans—a time not entwined with primordial ooze or ethereal realms, but distinct from the ape species. I'm referring to an epoch anterior to the current epigenetic code of Homo Sapiens, an era when the ensouled roamed the Earth, inhabiting Homo Erectus and Neanderthal avatars. Redirect your imagination across the expansive Alkebulanic or African plains, all the way to the grand Caucasus Mountains and other regions across the Asiatic continents, prior to continental drift.

Undoubtedly, Homo Erectus and Neanderthal civilizations stand as some of the most captivating and enigmatic subjects in the realm of anthropology. Despite the temporal and biological chasm that separates us, pondering the experiences and lives of our ancient forebears, the Homo Erectus and Neanderthals, are indeed intriguing. What lessons can their cultures impart about our own development, especially regarding our interactions within contemporary human groups? An examination of their communication methods, division of labor, and social norms can grant us deeper insight into the evolution of our modern political and social systems, not to mention our romantic tendencies.

THE TIMELINE

Researchers have been unearthing fresh revelations about these two ancient cultures and their resonance with our own. While we once conceived of prehistoric and early humanity as simplistic brutes, a more nuanced portrait has emerged. Although our ancestors lacked the sophisticated, reverse-engineered electro-tech of today, they possessed unique attributes that set them apart. Notably, Homo erectus residing on the African plains, with their larger skulls and potentially enlarged pineal glands, may have fostered a profound spiritual connection to the Earth and even higher dimensions of psychic consciousness.

This newfound perception of our ancient forebears as sophisticated and spiritually attuned beings challenges the longstanding notion of their primitiveness and intellectual inferiority. Instead, it unveils a fresh perspective on their intellectual and spiritual capacities, unveiling the intricate and multifaceted nature of prehistoric cultures. In today's era, as humanity proudly advances towards a transhumanist technocracy, science increasingly supplants spirituality. In the future, we might forget that spirituality ever existed. However, for those who do remember, it may be fascinating to learn that its origins trace back to prehistoric ancestry.

One of the most remarkable aspects of early human culture is their profound love and affection for their families and companions. Unlike many other species, they displayed an extraordinary lack of discrimination between members of their own group and those from other groups. Moreover, they exhibited remarkable tenderness and care for their children, a rarity in the animal kingdom. These observations collectively suggest a deep-seated sense of empathy, compassion, and nurturing among these ancient people.

Recent scientific journals and publications including the Smithsonian National Museum of Natural History have cast a fresh light on the Homo Erectus species. In stark contrast to earlier beliefs, Homo Erectus was an exceptionally sophisticated species with adaptations that enabled them to thrive across a range of environments. For instance, Homo Erectus became the first hominin to migrate out of Africa and into Eurasia, marking a pivotal moment in human evolution. They also possessed a notably larger brain, with an average cranial capacity ranging from 950 to 1000cc, surpassing their predecessors. Additionally, their anatomy was finely tuned for long-distance travel, featuring elongated legs and a narrow pelvis.

Evidence indicates that Homo Erectus demonstrated advanced tool-making skills and the ability to control fire, which served as a crucial tool for cooking, warmth, and illumination. This mastery of fire—the forebearer to electricity—played a substantial role in their survival and paved the way for the eventual development of larger human societies.

Regarding their social organization, it is believed that Homo Erectus groups were relatively simple, with a limited division of labor and a minimal social hierarchy. They likely inhabited small settlements, camps or villages, engaging in various activities such as hunting and gathering for sustenance—a social work culture very different from office spaces but not much different from warehouse and field work. One can only wonder about the potential impact on their daily lives if they indeed had command over resources like the cannabis plant or psilocybin mushrooms. We know that the oldest known written record of cannabis use comes from the Chinese Emperor Shen Nung in 2727 B.C. However, this does not exclude the possibility that it may have been used even earlier. For some, a brief internal, introspective trance might conjure up memories of past lives as Homo Erectus personalities traversing the cosmic mycelial network.

Furthermore, some researchers speculate that Homo Erectus might have been the first hominin to employ language, given the discovery of a gene associated with speech and language in their DNA. Fossils of Homo Erectus have been unearthed across vast regions, spanning from Africa to Asia, providing a treasure trove of information regarding their range, distribution, and evolutionary history.

Through ongoing research and discoveries, we continue to gain valuable insights into this climacteric species and its role in our social evolution. By examining evidence from our hominid ancestors, it becomes apparent that networking and community building are not new phenomena, but rather practices passed down by those who came before us. The ability of prehistoric humans to connect and interact as souls embodied in flesh surely set the course for our current path, excluding any external (i.e. extra terrestrial) influences that may have diverted our collective evolutionary trajectories.

Additionally, recent findings suggest Neanderthals pioneered the concept of "home," fundamentally changing perceptions of their civilization. According to an archaeologist from University College London, recognizing a permanent residence marked a significant evolutionary step in human development, influencing social interactions and cognitive processes.

Neanderthals, who also mastered fire use around a hundred thousands of years ago, constructed early forms of shelter using stones and wood for protection against the elements. Further research reveals that these shelters, used sporadically over tens of thousands of years by groups of up to 20 individuals, evolved to include windbreaks made from wood and bones. This adaptation highlights their transition to more settled, sophisticated communities long before modern humans arrived in Europe.

These represent just a few examples of how the culture of prehistoric humanity can offer valuable lessons about our own development and predispositions for family bonding. By delving into their customs and way of life, we can glean a wealth of knowledge about our evolutionary origins and our place in the world, particularly our enduring fascination with interpersonal relationships and or why it is that we can't seem to get enough of each other? Having evolved over centuries of conditioning and development, and considering the attitudes of prehistoric humans, it becomes apparent why modern people have a deep-seated inclination for intimacy with their counterparts. Basically, it's in our nature.

THE NEOLITHIC PERIOD: Stone Age | Bronze Age | Iron Age

Throughout human history, our ancient ancestors have granted us a wealth of evidence that provides insight into their existence and way of life. From the Paleolithic era, which dates back 2.5 million years ago, also known as the Stone Age, on to the Neolithic period, spanning 10,000 years ago and known as the Bronze Age, we find evidence of their creativity, craftsmanship, and cultural practices.

This evidence encompasses a wide range, from ancient tools to beautifully adorned stories painted on cave walls and timeless carvings etched into stones. While many may associate cave paintings with prehistoric depictions of hunting and warfare scenes, recent archaeological findings in central Turkey have unveiled cave paintings offering a captivating glimpse into the social dynamics of the time. These paintings offer a peak into an era still shrouded in mystery.

One particular image, which I find especially intriguing, was a cave painting unearthed in what is believed to be an 8000-year-old shrine. It portrays men and women dancing together, possibly participating in a ritual celebrating anything from marriage to the spring harvest. If you were to close your eyes and take a deep breath, you could almost transport yourself to such a festive gathering amongst friends. You might wonder who among them would have been inclined to leave behind the symbolic "We Were Here" graffiti.

Despite its primitiveness compared to our contemporary standards, the inherent drive to encapsulate and convey our culture through art has always been, and will remain, a fundamental facet of human expression. In places where culture thrives, where celebration abounds, and where art flourishes, you'll also find the undercurrents of attraction, the nuances of sexual behavior, and the intricate politics of relationship dynamics at play. Parties and gatherings in Neolithic and Paleolithic times reveal much about the social structure and community of ancient humans. These events demonstrate a deep sense of cohesion and cooperation, reflecting the organization of early societies. Rituals and beliefs, often intertwined with these gatherings, provide insights into their customs and traditions. The presence of rituals, artistic expressions, and symbolic objects at these events suggests a rich array of cultural practices.

From a psychological perspective, these gatherings indicate that early humans valued celebration and leisure, pointing to a stable and secure existence. They also highlight the importance of socialization, helping individuals form bonds, establish norms, and create a shared cultural identity. Interestingly, some people today claim to have experienced past life regressions, recounting memories of love interests from these ancient times and recognizing those endeared souls in their current lives. These narratives evoke the enduring importance of social dynamics, suggesting that soul pairings, karmic connections, and soul contracts have been significant across the ages.

Such tales add a fascinating layer to our understanding, intertwining the historical with the spiritual, and reinforcing the notion that the social interactions of our ancestors continue to resonate in profound ways. Neolithic and Paleolithic gatherings thus offer a profound glimpse into the intricate social dynamics, cultural practices, and psychological well-being of our ancient ancestors, as well as the timeless nature of human connections. The sole distinction between the dramas of your neolithic ancestors and those of your current social circle is the passage of time.

BASIC ORIGIN THEORIES

Let's take a brief detour for a moment. Numerous theories have emerged concerning the origins of organized human coupling models, i.e., marriage etc.

Some suggest their inception within smaller prehistoric groups, while others propose larger tribes as the initiators. Nonetheless, the precise details of this process remain a mystery. Ongoing research and discoveries are shedding light on the complex evolution of human relations regarding social influence.

There are various beliefs about the origins of marriage itself. Some argue it began with the invention of writing, while others link it to the creation of money. Some contend that marriage is a product of the rule of law, which, in turn, circles back to the management of property and material resources. Beyond organized marriage, comprehending the forces driving the attractions leading to human coupling—one need look no further than the influence of hormones. Yet regarding the organized social rituals surrounding marriage, as humanity became more sophisticated and civilized, civil unions would also grow in sophistication.

Scholars and experts would likely argue that the development of a structured society was catalyzed by the advent of writing, ultimately giving rise to the field of accounting. This paved the way for engagements where family elders provided financial backing, often showcasing their wealth through jewelry, livestock, or land and property (all defined as "money" in Black's Law Dictionary).

These elders would presumably institute the rituals of courting and marriage to align and consolidate personal resources ensuring the future interest of both bloodlines—potentially the idealistic birth of legacy. These perspectives are vastly different compared to the current idealized perceptions and romanticized views of marriage and personal choice. Marriage would have been an expectation and more in alignment with greater family obligation or duty, similar to doing chores or attending college. Marriage can be compared to the original social tax to ensure the collective survived and thrived in abundance.

Naturally, like any business arrangement, the rule of law was crucial to safeguard these agreements, necessitating an organized social structure. This structure could be represented by a family matriarch or patriarch who commanded respect, or a tribal chieftain. The emergence of this societal framework signifies the origin of social and civic technology, instrumental in driving the evolution of our current human condition. These technologies, by weaving themselves into the fabric of various societal aspects, have profoundly reshaped and influenced our collective human experience, molding contemporary societies in significant ways.

Thus, the eternal question arises: which came first, coupling or contract? It resembles the age-old puzzle of whether the chicken or the egg preceded the other. I surmise that coupling and contract were initially intertwined, with consummation serving as the concluding act. Throughout history, within diverse cultural and social norms, the response to nature's call, be it through verbal agreement or unopposed actions, has consistently marked the commencement of a mutual understanding. This understanding is essential to establish connections and foster group dynamics. Naturally, these acts would evolve to secure the agreements and enforce them for the benefit of all parties involved.

QURANIC & BIBLICAL ORIGINS

From a broader perspective, we are naturally led to consider the influence of religion on early civilizations for context. This brings us to the spiritual narratives that shaped ancient societies and their relationship structures. Regarding origins, the Quran, for instance, portrays Allah as the mastermind behind the heavens and the earth's creation. It fervently underscores the universe's formation, encompassing the vastness of space and the earth, as a magnificent testament to the divine will and power of Allah.

Regarding the creation of man, the Quran states that Allah created Adam and his progeny, emphasizing the unique status of humans as the vicegerents on earth. It imparts the profound insight that humans are molded from humble origins, comprising clay and a mere drop of fluid. The creation of man and woman is depicted as a unified act by Allah, who fashioned them from a single soul, underscoring their intrinsic equality and shared origin. This holy text highlights the role of humans as stewards on earth, entrusted with mutual duties of support, respect, and kindness towards one another, akin to garments that offer protection and comfort.

It emphasizes a balanced partnership in marriage, advocating for equity and compassion, principles echoed in the broader context of other religious teachings that celebrate divine craftsmanship in the universe's creation and human life. Through these narratives, the Quran, along with other religious texts, presents a vision of a morally and spiritually accountable humanity, called to fulfill its duties under the gaze of a singular, all-knowing deity.

While the Quran emphasizes equality between genders, the interpretation and application of its teachings can vary significantly across different Islamic cultures.

This divergence often leads to perceptions of disparity in gender dynamics when compared to contemporary global standards. Such variations underscore the complex interplay between religious texts, cultural interpretations, and modern values, highlighting the ongoing dialogue within communities about aligning traditional practices with current ideologies on gender equality.

Alongside the Quran, biblical origins also persist. In the Bible, the Book of Genesis unfolds the tale of creation, meticulously describing the emergence of everything, from the depths of the seas to the diversity of animals, ultimately culminating in the genesis of Adam. Specifically, in Chapter 2, Verse 7, the narrative portrays the Lord God's artistry in forming man from the very dust of the ground, infusing life through a breath into his nostrils.

The divine act continues as God plants an eastward garden in Eden, establishing Adam's dwelling. Eve's creation takes a fascinating twist, emerging from one of Adam's ribs. According to Genesis 5:4, Adam's legacy extends to sons and daughters, his life spanning a remarkable 800 years following Seth's birth. The intriguing saga diverges as some accounts suggest Adam's sons sought wives from distant tribes and unmentioned corners of the world, while others contend that their unions occurred through incest within their own lineage.

The venerable Book of Genesis, among the world's most "contemporarily" ancient religious texts, weaves a narrative encompassing the birth of the world, the inception of humanity, and the cultural milieu of the earliest humans. However, the text leaves many questions unanswered, and the interpretation of the story concerning Adam and Eve and their descendants varies greatly among different religious and cultural traditions. The text's interpretation diverges significantly from what some deem as a more original and non politically influenced bible with versions such as the Ethiopian coptic bible: Some treat the more popular King James biblical text as an unequivocal historical record, while others find metaphor, allegory, code and parable within its pages.

The narrative of Adam and Eve's tale has been deeply influenced by a multitude of forces, thus evolving religious and philosophical ideologies. Between scientific discoveries, prevailing cultural norms, and the revelation of concealed biblical volumes, including the Gospel of Thomas, the Book of Mary, the Book of Jubilees, and the more widely recognized Book of Enoch, among others, we gain more insight into the dynamic interplay between religion, culture, and knowledge throughout history.

For a more unabridged or original outlook of early christian doctrine, outside of the gnostic essenes, the ancient Ethio-Coptic biblical account is by far one of the best sources. The Ethiopian Bible, also referred to as the "Ge'ez Bible" or "Ethiopic Bible," holds a profound significance deeply rooted in Ethiopia's cultural and religious legacy. Its origins intertwine with the legendary narrative of Queen Sheba, celebrated for her historic visit to King Solomon in Jerusalem, which reputedly resulted in the birth of Menelik I, the progenitor of Ethiopia's royal dynasty.

Returning to Ethiopia, Menelik I ascended to become its first emperor, establishing a dynasty that endured for centuries. This royal lineage, alongside Ethiopia's early embrace of Christianity in the 4th century, forms the bedrock of the Ethiopian Orthodox Church and provides a unique historical and spiritual foundation for the Ethiopian Bible. With its extensive collection of 88 books versus the 73 books in the catholic bible, including scrolls predating the famed King James Version, the Ethiopian Bible stands as one of the oldest and most comprehensive Christian scriptures.

Offering insights into a lineage of Christian worship predating the conversion of many other nations, the Ethiopian Bible remains relatively obscure beyond Ethiopia's borders. Unfortunately, in the tradition of supremacy ideology, many believe, if it's not Roman, it's not christianity. For those seeking more accurate and original accounts of the origins of mankind, marriage, and civilization according to Christian traditions, the Ethiopic Bible—which includes the Books of Mary, Enoch, and others—offers a rich source of material. These texts provide detailed narratives on the stories of Adam and Eve, among other foundational tales about the origin of humanity and how they should conduct themselves. Many of our current traditions are a continuation from beliefs inherited from the pages of these books.

THE ANNUNAQI

Amid the many theories about the genesis of humanity's inclination toward love, marriage, companionship, and family bonds, one origin story that piques my fascination traces back to ancient Sumer, nestled in the heart of Mesopotamia. Here, diligent archaeologists have unearthed stone tablets with cuneiform inscriptions offering epic tales of creation and other remarkable narratives.

These ancient records, uncovered through the relentless efforts of luminaries like Zecharia Sitchin, and more contemporary scholars such as Billy Carson, present sagas of unparalleled richness. Here, one encounters the epic narratives of the likes of Gilgamesh, the mystical Emerald Tablets, and the grandeur of the Enuma Elish. Within these scrolls lie accounts of humanity's primordial inception, a tale intricately linked to celestial Nephilim or Deities known as the Annunaki.

These records describe the galactic wanderings of these gods, voyaging through the Milky Way aboard the colossal, Jupiter-sized mothership known as Nibiru. Their cosmic mission? To sow the seeds of life on our Earth, thereby engaging in the collaborative design and genetic coding of humankind to further their ambitions, most notably, the quest for precious gold.

Numerous scholars entertain the notion that this theory might elucidate the remarkable leap in evolution, transforming primates into the modern humans we recognize today, all transpiring within a comparatively concise timeline. The veracity of these accounts, it must be acknowledged, fuels spirited debate. They form part of the diverse array of theories and convictions that individuals contemplate concerning the genesis of humanity and its intricate ties to higher entities or extraterrestrial deities.

To encapsulate, this narrative implies that the extraordinary leap in human genetics and technology finds its roots in the sway of advanced extraterrestrial intellect, akin to the archangelic order depicted in biblical lore. As per this hypothesis, these celestial beings bestowed upon humanity the foundations of a refined civilization.

This encompassed **the wisdom of marital rituals,** the establishment of societal and physical infrastructure, encompassing law, agricultural cultivation, livestock husbandry, and the formation of central settlements. Notably, these principles harken back to ancient Stone Age encampments discovered in the expansive landscapes of South Africa, and pygmies of central Africa, legacy stretching back countless millennia.

Admittedly, this theory remains enigmatic and a subject of fervent discourse. It stands among a myriad of conjectures, all striving to illuminate the enigma of human civilization's inception. It's worth noting that the biblical phrase "let us make man in our image" can be traced to Genesis 1:26, where it portrays God in dialogue with other exalted divine beings, orchestrating the birth of humanity.

In some interpretations, these sacred words bear the imprint of earlier texts, suggesting the influence or translation from sources like the Enuma Elish.

Perhaps some heavenly host of angelic alien visitors did give us a more advanced program to copulate and populate with each other and thank goodness for that because, as common knowledge would have it (thanks to countless hours of television), the archetypal alpha caveman might have resorted to a rather rudimentary approach: clubbing their intended partner on the head, tossing them unceremoniously over their shoulder, and deeming the task complete. Hence, I extend my gratitude to culture, civilization, and the institution of marriage for fostering a refined and sociable atmosphere, even if it was initiated by ancient beings resembling archangels, such as the Anunnaki. Note: It's worth mentioning that many of these identical narratives found their way into the Dead Sea Scrolls and eventually became integral components of what we recognize as the Bible today. Numerous themes, storylines, and characters within the Hebrew Bible exhibit striking parallels with the more ancient Epic of Gilgamesh, none more so than the narratives revolving around the Garden of Eden and the Genesis flood.

Indeed, books such as **"The World's Sixteen Crucified Saviors: Christianity Before Christ"** by *Kersey Graves*, among many, provide valuable insights into various but virtually identical creation stories and mythologies from different cultures, that shed light on the commonalities and shared themes in these tales. They help us understand the rich tapestry of human beliefs and traditions that have shaped our cultural heritage.

Irrespective of whether a race of advanced beings known as the Annunaki, akin to fallen or archangels, interceded in the human timeline, catalyzing an augmentation in our natural evolutionary path, one fact remains undeniable: the pursuit of companionship has been and will forever be ingrained in our very essence. And where companionship thrives, so too do emotions and beliefs, shaping the manner in which we connect and govern ourselves. It is not lost on us, however, that everything from our awkward idiosyncrasies to our hormonal sex drives could indeed have been influenced by a hierarchy of angels, better known as the extraterrestrial race called the Anunaqi.

THOTH THE ATLANTEAN and the DOGON MYTHOS.

Another theory that ignites the imagination and stirs the depths of historical curiosity suggests that the roots of civilization were not merely sown by human endeavor but were bestowed by a figure of profound wisdom and ancient lineage. This figure, Thoth the Atlantean, emerges from the mists of time, bearing gifts of knowledge and enlightenment. According to legend, Thoth hailed from the enigmatic land of Atlantis, traversing the boundaries of realms to become a pivotal architect in the foundation of civilization, as chronicled in the mystical Emerald Tablets.

These Tablets are revered as artifacts of esoteric wisdom, which speak of Thoth's unparalleled intellect and his role in guiding humanity towards the dawn of enlightened existence. Through these tablets, Thoth is alleged to have imparted the sacred art of writing, transforming mere symbols into the bearers of history, culture, and law. His teachings on mathematics laid the geometric groundwork for society's infrastructure, enabling the construction of monumental edifices and the precise charting of celestial bodies.

But Thoth's contributions were not confined to the intellectual and the structural; he also instilled the societal fabric with the virtues of marriage and communal harmony, fostering bonds that are the bedrock of civilization. As the guardian of the moon and the inventor of the calendar, Thoth marked the passage of time, facilitating the alignment of human activity with the cosmic rhythm, essential for agriculture and ceremonial observances. Among the most intriguing of Thoth's legacies, as detailed in the Emerald Tablets, is his endeavor to civilize the "black inhabitants," of the land he entered—believed to be Khemet

This echoes the narratives of the Dogon tribes in central Africa, who recount tales of celestial visitors bestowing cosmic knowledge upon them as well —a legacy meticulously preserved through their records to this day.

According to Dogon, the space visitors known as the Nommo played a significant role in the creation and shaping of the world. In some versions of Dogon history, the Nommo are described as amphibious beings who descended from the sky in a vessel that landed in the waters near the Dogon region. They are often depicted as teachers who shared wisdom and knowledge with the Dogon people, including agricultural techniques, social organization, and spiritual practices. Overall, while the Dogon mythos does include elements of divine beings shaping humanity and civilization, interpretations of these stories can vary, and they are subject to cultural context and individual beliefs within the Dogon community.

Whether it be stories of the Dogon, the Anunnaqi, or the passages in the emerald tablets regarding the Atlantean, Thoth, history hints at beings, superior to man passing along the instructions for civilization.

Furthermore, according to the emerald tablets, Thoth's far-reaching influence, suggests he shared his boundless wisdom with peoples across the ancient world, guiding them from the shadows of prehistory into the light of structured society. This narrative paints Thoth not only as a teacher of the Egyptians but as a global civilizer, whose knowledge was a beacon to all corners of the earth. For ancient Egyptians, the named Djehuti, often referenced as Tehuti, which was eventually translated to Thoth (from Koine Greek: Θώθ Thṓth, borrowed from Coptic: ⲑⲱⲟⲩⲧ Thōout) resonates as a symbol of divine intellect and authority.

While some may dismiss the tales of Thoth and the Emerald Tablets or recorded Dogon history as mere myths, the enduring symbols of their wisdom found in the cornerstones of ancient civilizations hint at a deeper truth. For those who believe, Thoth the Atlantean stands not just as a mythological figure but as the very father of civilization itself—a divine emissary who, through his teachings on the Emerald Tablets and his interactions with diverse peoples, laid down the framework upon which the world was built. *Contextual notes for further reference:* The origins of the Dogon people trace back to the enigmatic Tellem—predecessors who once thrived in Dogon Country. These early inhabitants, often referred to as Pygmies due to their diminutive stature, have been known by various names including the Bana or the red people. Their descent is believed to be from the most archaic hunter-gatherer populations of the central African rainforest. Expansion to Central Africa by the ancestors of African Pygmies most likely took place before 130,000 years ago, and certainly before 60,000 years ago. This lineage suggests an unbroken chain of knowledge and tradition, passed through generations long before the advent of structured civilization.

Interestingly, genetic studies reveal that the Pygmies exhibit a remarkable genetic diversity, indicating a deep, indigenous connection to their land and an evolutionary lineage distinct from other human populations. Their genetic markers show them as a group that diverged significantly from other humans, with only the Khoisan peoples showing an older genetic divergence. Thus, the longstanding knowledge of the Pygmies and the Dogon about the cosmos is not a myth but a testament to their ancient and profound connection to the universe.

This knowledge concerning far away star systems, now validated by modern science, dispels any misconceptions and underscores their place as custodians of ancient truths in a modern world. This profound historical understanding serves as compelling evidence to dispel any notions that their knowledge of our solar system and beyond is mere myth. Considering that the Great Pyramid of Giza, constructed for Pharaoh Khufu, is roughly 5,000 years old as determined by Western scientists, it is astonishing that the traditions of the Dogon people extend even further back—surpassing Egypt's first dynastic culture by over 60,000 years.

It is believed by some that these are the tribes and peoples that Adam and Eves children mated with. One might speculate whether the stories passed down by the Dogon share a common origin with the stories of Thoth's Emerald Tablets or the Enuma Elish and or the Epics of Gilgamesh—interpretations perhaps obscured or altered through translations throughout the millennia. This impressive historical depth highlights the ancient and rich heritage of the Dogon people. Their detailed cosmology and traditions provide a continuous link back to the very origins of civil human thought and behavior including companionship modalities.

CONTEMPLATION ONE

Everything has an origin, and many relationship models throughout history have originated via religious beliefs and traditions. Across cultures, marriage assumes the mantle of a hallowed institution sanctified by a higher authority. Here, religious convictions preside over the landscape, delineating the roles, responsibilities, and the very bedrock upon which fidelity, loyalty, and unwavering commitment between partners are built.

When considering the evolution of our shared relationship models, it is critical to acknowledge the significant role of religion in shaping the interplay between our emotional instincts—or heart-centered drives—and our cognitive processes—i.e., intellectual drives. In simpler terms, looking at how religious beliefs and teachings shape the way we feel about and understand relationships, can be better understood if we can comprehend how integrated emotions and thoughts are influenced by the traditions of the particular religious model.

However, In the contemporary realm of spiritual awakening, an undeniable shift unfolds. There exist a growing number of individuals who are moving away from conventional religion, yearning for a direct communion with the divine, free from intermediaries or the middle man. Yet, for the majority, tradition remains an indomitable force that most people will inherently uphold.

This alternative spirituality shift is driven by the belief that old-time religion is outdated or primitive and that humanity, as a species, is maturing and outgrowing unfounded rituals and practices such as slavery, religious crusades, human sacrifices, and Salem-like witch hunts among many oxymoronic practices. Many people feel as if, in the age of information, ignorance is a choice.

Even amid this sweeping shift from the trappings of old time religion, a remarkable constancy persists. Most individuals, ensnared within the web of this transition, continue to employ the original religious relationship models as the blueprint for their amorous unions. The influence wielded by these models retains its remarkable significance, resilient as individuals continue to move away from the broader tapestry of organized religions.

Research has shown that many non-religious yet spiritual individuals still highly prioritize these values and romantic belief systems, even though they may dismiss all of the other practices. While the universality of this phenomenon is arguable, it bears emphasizing that those with alternative belief systems, whether they be practitioners of Wicca, Hoodoo, Atheist, or even Luciferianism, often perpetuate romantic relationship models mirroring the traditions of mainstream religious origins.

Those with Middle Eastern heritage will often shape their relationships in accordance with the principles outlined in the Quran, while Hindus and other cultures maintain their unique romantic traditions as well, even when living within new cultural paradigms that offer alternative models compared to those of the past.

In essence, even as some extricate themselves from the embrace of traditional religion, these inherited dynamics continue to exert an indelible influence on their lives, relationships, and decisions. They hold in high regard relationship paradigms deeply entrenched in their religious ancestry, whether this reverence occurs consciously or resides within the subconscious.

As incongruent as it may seem, It is not implausible to envision that an Atheist, an Ifa Orisha practitioner or an adherent of the witchcraft faith can exhibit a possessiveness or jealousy akin to a Catholic lover. This resonance emerges from the shared origins of their emotional and romantic relational styles, despite the divergence in their contemporary beliefs and chosen lifestyles.

A striking illustration of this concept is the case of a Western individual who converts to the Yoruba religion, known for endorsing polygyny as a relationship model. Even though this individual might fully embrace the tenets of their new faith, they often retain their original Christian-influenced views on relationships. This indicates a selective adaptation of beliefs, where one's foundational relationship model, shaped by earlier Christian principles, persists despite adopting a new religious framework.

In essence, an individual may accept every other practice, including altar work, ancestral veneration, and even animal sacrifice, but the one thing they wouldn't dream of giving up is the tradition and inheritance of their relationship models. Regarding the practice of polygamy and monogamy, these divergent beliefs could possibly originate from the deeply ingrained psychological impact of one tradition that worships a self-proclaimed jealous god, while the other venerates multiple deities. This fundamental difference in theological perspectives is only one example that may explain the varied cultural narratives inherent within practiced relationship models and the influence of religious origins.

Note: It is important to remain aware of the boundaries that uphold a safe and responsible outlook on relationship models for collective sustainability. We must avoid becoming so liberal that these boundaries are completely erased, which could lead to the exploitation of children and the fostering of destructive behaviors that destabilize healthy communities.

CONTEMPLATION II : Demystifying Partnership

As we press forward, it becomes increasingly evident that the realm of compatibility and embarking on a romantic partnership can be complex. There is no one-size-fits-all approach. Thus, we must take into consideration a multitude of factors, including but not limited to social status, sexual desire, personal economics, and a diverse set of skills, encompassing the ability to provide for, secure and even please. These factors merely represent a fraction of many factors to consider when exploring the intricate dynamics of coupling, copulation, and connection.

Crucially, one must recognize that the realm of compatibility is inherently subjective, liable to fluctuate not only from person to person but also from one moment to the next. Amidst this intricate interplay, an abundance of factors, spanning from genetic predispositions to environmental influences and personal life experiences, converge to shape the vast spectrum of elements that sway our romantic leanings and their exact origins.

In all candor, it remains an enigma to pinpoint with certainty the absolute beginning of love, dating, or the institution of marriage, especially when one considers that even the microscopic entities that make up the building blocks of our material existence, such as bacteria and mitochondria, engage in copulation. Nonetheless, it stands to reason that, as a gregarious species, an innate and profoundly ingrained longing for companionship and partnership runs deep within us. Essentially, the quest for an affectionate and steadfast partner lies at the core of our prime directive: **Self-Preservation.**

In the context of self-preservation, it's crucial to recognize that many individuals are, often unknowingly, hypergamous or guided by hypergamous tendencies. (To provide some background:) Hypergamy is the drive to seek a partner with higher social, economic, or educational status—a desire to "marry up," so to speak. Historically, this behavior was more visible among women, shaped by societal structures that limited their access to advancement. For many, marriage into a higher social status became one of the few pathways to upward mobility.

However, hypergamy is not constrained by gender today; it reflects a broader human impulse to connect with what we perceive as aspirational. Whether consciously acknowledged or not, hypergamy often influences our partnership choices, highlighting our intrinsic pull towards status, security, growth, and self-preservation. Recognizing this can deepen our understanding of relational dynamics, illuminating the subtle ways we seek alignment between our personal lives and our broader attractions.

Although this drive may manifest uniquely in each individual, the fundamental impulse to pursue a compatible partner stands as a universal and compelling force in the hodgepodge of human existence. Bearing this in mind, it is crucial to recognize that no solitary individual can fully cater to the entirety of our needs or exceed our every expectation. Does that make sense to you? One person simply can not where every hat needed for your fulfilment. One person can not be your mailman, milkman, minister, mechanic, moviestar and marital spouse. Only an immature and childlike mind will nurture this sort of unrealistic fantasy. Being mindful of this realization, allows us to clearly delineate our objectives in the pursuit of a romantic partnership, thus accepting the truth of who, and what we actually are to each other.

Before we proceed with this contemplation, allow me to elucidate my usage of the term _"Partner, and Partnership!"_ This term assumes diverse meanings contingent upon the context in which it is employed. Some conceivable definitions include:

A person who collaborates in a venture, business, or undertaking with another individual or group, typically characterized by a cooperative nature, with shared profits and losses. A person's spouse or significant other, with whom they share romantic or intimate involvement. A person or entity that engages in collaborative efforts with another individual or group on a project or initiative, typically entailing shared responsibilities and objectives. A member of a sports team who participates alongside another player as a unit, frequently in doubles or tandem events. When I allude to a "partner," I signify an individual with whom you have mutually agreed to embark on an intimate partnership, for a span that may encompass weeks, months, several years or extend over a few decades. These partnerships and collaborations span a broad spectrum, encompassing romantic and platonic connections, as well as sexual or domestic unions, and even extend to those formed for security's sake.

Individuals unite to forge partnerships for a multitude of purposes. It becomes clear that a variety of partnership models, particularly in the context of intimate relationships, are widespread and are not to be confused with *sexual connection and partnership*. In clarifying intimacy and intimate partnerships, gestures such as holding hands with your best friend or bestowing a kiss on your grandmother's forehead exemplify acts of intimacy.

Certain individuals establish domestic partnerships, enduring the journey due to financial obligations or for the sake of their children, culminating in what one might may term a transactional partnership. Others engage in brief sexual or romantic partnerships driven by mutual pleasure. While the fantasy they share is of eternal love, the reality often proves temporary. Consider how many times you've dated someone and imagined it would never end. It's unlikely that a relationship would have endured if you had started by acknowledging that it wouldn't last forever. Emotional solace and camaraderie represent motives for certain individuals to partner without embarking on marriage or long-term commitments.

Furthermore, some individuals opt to share living spaces and expenses, akin to roommates with added benefits denoting a domestic partnership. It's noteworthy that some individuals engage in polyamorous relationships, forming connections with multiple partners simultaneously for whatever needs they imagine they have. This phenomenon is illustrated through the example of polyamorous throuples, with each member having their unique motivations for participating in these romantic partnerships. Though not all, these partnerships are generally temporary as well.

Beyond holistic relationships, there are formal non-romantic partnerships, such as business and commercial collaborations, where individuals may share the title of co-founder to a business venture subsequently spending more time co-creating together than with their actual families. The passion they share for their venture is quite an intimate exchange. Additionally, some individuals are both romantic and business partners.

Various types of partnerships can fulfill specific needs, the ultimate goal in a romantically whole relationship, however, is to consolidate multiple partnership roles into a life partner who possesses all the necessary qualities for a healthy and sustainable symbiotic relationship. Such an intentional partnership can offer much more than the average paper—meaning married on paper—when both parties are fully committed and spiritually aligned. While no one partner can where all the hats created in the vast cosmos, they can cover the essentials and then some, seeing as you can have anything, but you cant have everything.

Intentional relating within a partnership is akin to the spirit of a contract: it's a transparent undertaking where both parties clearly understand and agree to their roles and responsibilities. This approach promotes open communication and mutual understanding, mirroring the clear, explicit expectations set forth in contractual agreements. This notion becomes clear when we understand that choosing a life partner is a deeply intentional and deliberate process, in contrast to paper marriages i.e. state contracted, which may sometimes be more symbolic and lack well-defined strategies beyond the pursuit of domestic living and endless romance. However, paper marriages should certainly be considered for their legal benefits and other practical advantages. In hindsight, a fully invested life partner can cover many aspects, effectively fulfilling diverse partnership purposes across multiple facets of one's personal and professional life, bringing immense value to both individuals. While no one person can fulfill every need in life, a good life partner can cover a broad spectrum of basic necessities.

Unfortunately, many legal marriages today, particularly among younger couples, emphasize the romantic and imaginative aspects of a partnership, often overlooking its essential purposes. These purposes can range from long-term financial responsibilities to legal trusts and securities, among others. Although marriage ceremonies can occasionally overlook these elements, conscious life partners place a high priority on making intentional and thoughtful choices, united in their commitment to creating a meaningful and fulfilling life together. Ask yourself, are you willing to share account numbers, debt and children with the one your currently sleeping with in real time. If not, consider, contemplating the definition of your partnership dynamic.

Conscious and intentional life partners understand the importance of the partnership as it relates to planning for the future together, including ensuring their estates are in order. Having legal documents such as power of attorney or a legal trust in place to carry out wishes in case of illness or death, as well as considerations for whole life insurance, medical insurance, and offspring planning, including college tuition and a well thought out strategy for land ownership and other holdings are all imperative considerations. The establishment of family credit should always be considered as an essential priority in the long-term planning of a life partnership. Not only are family trusts important but land trusts are also critical components to consider.

These elements are important for those in the position to seek a successful and enduring life partnership. If the purpose of long-term coupling and cohabitation is not to establish a family cooperative, then what is its purpose? Anything else is not a life partnership. One could simply date "randoms" throughout their life or enjoy a romantic companion without the added commitment if romance is the only objective. Consider the value of honesty and intentionality with both yourself and your partner regarding what it is you're actually doing or partnering up on. This line of thinking has the potential to prevent significant issues down the road. This, of course, is just one perspective and contemplation among many.

When it comes to partnerships and companionship, the concept of having a helpmate is found in various religious doctrines, as most relationship models originate from religious teachings as discussed in the first contemplation. In Genesis 2:18, it is written, "Then the Lord God said, 'It is not good that the man should be alone; I will make him a helper fit for him." This passage implies that God recognized that Adam needed a companion and partner.

The idea of a helpmate is not limited to one religion; it can be found in various faiths. For instance, the Quran portrays a spouse as a "garment," offering comfort and protection. The Talmud, a pivotal text in Jewish law and tradition, delves into marriage laws and obligations, addressing the responsibilities of both partners.

Additional Jewish texts, like the Midrash, the Zohar, and writings by medieval Jewish philosophers, delve into the significance of marriage and the role of a spouse as a helpmate in creating a family and a meaningful life. Within these contexts, it becomes evident that family is the primary concern, with romance taking a secondary role to the business of Family.

The foremost focus is on family trust and estate, ensuring a lifestyle that goes beyond mere surviving to thriving. One might speculate that civilizations in the Orion and Andromeda constellations don't merely survive but instead thrive under their social systems, relationship models and civic technologies. Are we, as humans, so constrained or neglectful in our endeavors to advance our relationship systems for the sake of thriving? This last statement is a contemplation all unto itself!

Yes, it is indeed true, romance can enhance and sweeten life's circumstances, much like icing on a cake. However, it's essential to have authentic and intelligent relationship systems to cement a union, ensuring the longevity and sustainability of intentional life partners.

While love is boundless and ideally unconditional, it's important to note that marriage, romance, and most relationships do not always align. Actual love transcends these constructs, while the concept of family requires a structured framework to function harmoniously, with specific conditions being met. In simple terms, **love may be unconditional, but relationships are not.** #Facts

Building a robust and functional family unit necessitates effort and dedication to meet the required conditions for its purpose, ensuring a smoothly functioning and fulfilling life for all parties involved. This clarifies why even though some individuals still love you, they cannot be with you and must love you from a distance to maintain an overall healthy lifestyle.

In essence, depending on an individual's stage in life, they may not be ready for such responsibilities or commitments, even though their natural inclination may lead them to seek a partner for various reasons. In such situations, it is advisable to maintain a keen awareness of the nature of your partnership with a significant other, allowing you to discern whether you're simply "playing house" or "establishing a home." This serves as the core of this particular contemplation—being intentional, knowing the difference and and accepting the reality of your desires and decisions.

With this awareness, consider that your relationship might be confined to a sexual and or domestic partnership alone, devoid of genuine friendship or a financial trust that extends to sharing a bank account. Some married couples or long-term relationships lack the financial intimacy to share commercial trust and interests beyond splitting the rent—*and they call themselves married.*

Alternatively, you might be part of a co-parenting and transactional partnership, enriched by genuine companionship because you both truly enjoy each other's company. Perhaps you're solely engaged in an emotional partnership upheld as a long-distance, phone and facetime relationship. Maybe you derive satisfaction from the companionship of a "work husband" or "work wife," making the workday more enjoyable. Either way, one should not become upset if they are not being honest with themselves about the type of dynamic they are engaging within when they partner up with another for the exchange of energy, especially when the partnership dynamic hasn't been expressly commutated and agreed upon.

The partnership spectrum is diverse and intricate, shaped by cultural norms, personal preferences, and individual needs. It's possible to have significant compatibility in a sexual partnership while not experiencing the same level of compatibility in the domestic side of the partnership, even if deeply committed to love. The same can be said about a transactional partnership lack genuine love. In such situations, it's vital to avoid pressuring or shaming a partner for their limited enthusiasm in less-connected dynamics.

To prevent disappointment, it's crucial to establish and honestly acknowledge the true nature of your partnership, rather than making unspoken assumptions about its type. Merging all your desired partnerships into a homogenous mixture when no single partner can fulfill every role is a recipe for disappointment.

While some individuals claim to be in a love partnership, they might actually be in a highly pleasurable sexual partnership, where their affection is primarily directed at the intoxicating pleasure. In light of this, an individual may experience feelings of betrayal upon discovering the true nature of their union, realizing it is more centered around intense physical pleasure than genuine emotional connection or intentions to cohabitate indefinitely, under the dynamics of a domestic partnership.

Notably, as social creatures, humans seek relationships and partnerships not only for companionship but also for personal growth and mutual assistance in navigating life's challenges. While securing basic needs and survival is the most critical challenge in life, having a loving partner who is also a supportive helpmate can significantly enhance our journey toward meeting our needs and achieving personal growth.

The Hierarchy of needs Theory by American psychologist *Abraham Maslow* illuminates the fundamental human needs motivating behavior, including the need for safety, love, esteem, and self-actualization. Analyzing this theory provides insights into how the quest for a helpmate is rooted in these fundamental human needs. Abraham Maslow proposed the five fundamental human needs that drive our behavior in 1943. His theory arranges human needs in a hierarchical structure, with the most basic and fundamental needs at the bottom and higher-level needs at the top.

These are the five levels of Maslow's hierarchy of needs:

1. Physiological needs - These are the most fundamental human needs for survival, including food, water, shelter, and sleep.

2. Safety needs - These needs revolve around our sense of security and safety, encompassing protection from physical harm, stability, and order.

3. Love and belonging needs - These needs are linked to our social interactions and relationships, including the need for love, affection, and a sense of belonging.

4. Esteem needs - These needs are tied to our self-worth, achievement, and recognition from others.

5. Self-actualization needs - These needs involve the desire for personal growth, self-fulfillment, and realizing our full potential.

In line with Maslow's theory, individuals usually address their fundamental physiological and safety needs before progressing up the hierarchy to fulfill higher-level needs for love, belonging, esteem, and self-actualization. Maslow's hierarchy of needs aligns with the various types of romantic partnerships people engage in, as individuals often seek partners who can assist in meeting their needs at different levels of the hierarchy.

For example, individuals with unmet physiological and safety needs may look for a partner who can offer stability and security, emphasizing basic necessities like food, shelter, and safety. Those who have satisfied their physiological and safety needs may seek partners to fulfill their love and belonging needs, focusing on emotional support, companionship, and a sense of belonging. Individuals who have met their love and belonging needs may search for partners who can help meet their esteem needs, valuing recognition, respect, and a sense of achievement.

Finally, those who have addressed their esteem needs may seek partners who can assist them in satisfying their self-actualization needs. These individuals prioritize partners who can intellectually challenge them, support personal growth, and help them realize their full potential. Consequently, people's progress through Maslow's hierarchy influences the types of partnerships they pursue and their priorities in relationships.

Understanding the dynamics of your partnership without self delusion is essential for a successful union. Many people struggle to identify the type of partnership they're in, often having high expectations for a specific dynamic while actually being in another. For instance, someone may be in a simple sexual partnership driven by attraction but treating their partner as a full-fledged life partner, only to become infuriated when their expectations aren't met.

In certain instances, boyfriends and girlfriends may take on the roles and privileges typically associated with husbands and wives without properly discussing or genuinely earning such privileges. For example, if an eighteen-year-old expects their similarly aged partner to behave like a seasoned and mature life partner, disappointment may ensue when the partner fails to meet these expectations, potentially leading to volatile scenarios. This gap often arises in fundamental relationship models, stemming from underdeveloped emotional intelligence, flawed mindsets and misguided perceptions.

It's perplexing when a late teenager or someone in their early twenties feels hurt because of their partner's immaturity, especially considering that their partner is likely just starting their independent life journey, or may even still be in their formative stages at home with no real world experiences to draw from. They are expected to think and operate with the wisdom of someone who has earned that wisdom through trial and error spanning decades.

It is certainly a reality faced by many young people. It's crucial to approach these situations with empathy and understanding, while also acknowledging that certain partnership dynamics, such as life partnerships, shouldn't be expected if both individuals aren't ready for such commitments. In this context, maturity and genuine self-honesty become most evident and valuable, exemplifying a deep sense of self-esteem rooted in authenticity.

Though some individuals may struggle to adapt their perspectives, these clear descriptions aim to provide greater clarity about who you are, why you're together, and the purpose of your intimate relationship. Regardless of your chosen partnership model, it's essential to enter into it with full awareness rather than through overly optimistic assumptions. Remember that not every partnership needs to encompass the full range of responsibilities found in a life partnership.

In the realm of relating with great life partners however, you'll ultimately want what I consider an LLC—a long-term lifestyle companion. Just like a limited liability company, having an LLC helps you limit your life's liabilities when in the company of a trusted long-term lifestyle companion—or, for some, a long-term lifestyle commitment.

It's perfectly fine to enter into a limited liability partnership; however, If you find yourself in a sexual partnership without having established a life partnership, it's important not to become disillusioned upon realizing that a life partnership may not be forthcoming. Similarly, if you are in a financial partnership expecting it to lead to a sexual partnership or in a domestic partnership hoping for it to fulfill emotional needs, do not lose heart when you recognize the discrepancy between your expectations and your current situation.

Understanding your partnership dynamic and not assuming it is something that doesn't align with your expectations is the first step to fostering a healthier, more productive, and fulfilling relationship. This approach can eliminate much of the drama and chaos often experienced in contemporary relationships. Going forward, please consult the previous section whenever the term "partner" is used.

CONTEMPLATION III : Demystifying symbolic representations

In our previous discussion, we explored the multifaceted responsibilities of intimate partnerships. While the term "life partner" is commonly associated with traditional marital roles of husband and wife, this manuscript views it as a purposeful and deliberate alliance.

Chasing fairytale notions about marriage might lead people to underestimate the fundamental effort needed to maintain stability in an intentional life partnership. For example, some women might initially find contentment in receiving a ring and a proposal alone to become a wife, only to later regret their choice if it was not carefully contemplated and genuinely inspired.

In contemporary culture, the mere symbolism often suffices, eliminating the need for further training or development beyond the initial symbolic gesture. This reflects a broader trend where individuals may want to get married but learn they never wanted to be a spouse, similar to how some want to have a baby, but never desired to raise actual children. Ultimately, babies grow into children, and marriage entails the complexities of living as a spouse.

In contemporary times, the traditional notion of becoming a wife and receiving a ring, along with all the fairytale elements it entails, has been reimagined and modified from its original roots. Yes, reimagined and modified. Yet, it's essential to recognize that delving into the origins of common concepts or beliefs can enhance our comprehension of their evolution over time and the diverse influences that have molded them, as the roots can profoundly impact the fruits.

Origins can also offer us insights into the cultural and historical context in which a concept or belief took shape, shedding light on the motivations and beliefs of its originators and promoters. This, in essence, is the overarching goal of this chapter. By comprehending the origins of a concept or belief, we can assess its pertinence and applicability in the present day. We can scrutinize its strengths and weaknesses, potential advantages and disadvantages, and contemplate whether it should be adjusted or refined to align more effectively with contemporary needs and values.

For example, the tradition of wearing wedding rings dates back to ancient Egypt, around 6,000 years ago, symbolizing eternal love with the circle's endless nature and the gateway to the unknown through its center. The tradition of wearing wedding rings was later embraced by the Romans, who infused it with the notion of possession. Placing the ring on the fourth finger of the left hand, believed to connect directly to the heart, the Rome saw the ring not just as a symbol of commitment but as a symbol of ownership over one's spouse.

The adoption of durable materials like iron further emphasized the strength and permanence of this bond. Over the centuries, the Christian church imbued the ring with spiritual significance, emphasizing fidelity and commitment under divine advocacy. The symbolism of wedding rings evolved through the Renaissance with increasingly elaborate designs, culminating in the 20th-century adoption of the double-ring ceremony (where both partners exchange rings) following world war two.

In addition, the tradition of women assuming their husband's last name upon marriage has deep historical roots as well and spans several centuries. One theory suggests its commencement in medieval Europe, where a woman's legal identity became intertwined with her husband's upon marriage, and adopting his last name signified this transition. Another theory traces its origins to 16th-century England, where common law mandated surnames for everyone, and women adopted their husband's last names to comply with this requirement.

A more credible explanation for the adoption of surnames is the similarity to how slaves assumed their masters' last names as a method of marking property. Last names were used as a form of branding or identification, akin to the branding of cattle. Speaking of cattle, in certain cultures, it's not unusual to gauge a woman's value in terms of a few heads of cattle, exchanged for her marriage to a groom and his family.

Historically, in specific African and Indian cultures, as well as medieval European countries, dowries were comprised of cattle presented by the groom's family to the bride's family. In these societies, cattle and sometimes horses, held immense value, functioning as both assets and currency, thus becoming customary. The quantity of cattle exchanged varied depending on the economic circumstances of both families and the social standing of the groom.

Dowry practices frequently served to forge social alliances and foster stability among families, which ad nothing to do with romance or love. Nevertheless, in modern times, the practice of dowry has faced censure for its role in perpetuating gender disparities and contributing to violence against women. It is often perceived as a transaction wherein women are regarded as commodities, subject to purchase and sale in contemporary times.

Bride dowry continues to be a prevalent tradition in the Middle East, as well as numerous Asian countries, and parts of the Pacific Islands, particularly in Melanesia. The exchanged amounts can range from symbolic sums to thousands of U.S. dollars, with certain Thai marriages involving as much as $100,000 in dowry. This practice has its origins in medieval Europe and is documented in the ancient Babylonian Code of Hammurabi as an established custom.

The Torah addresses the payment of a bride price to the father of a virgin, with Jewish law mandating a formal contract, known as a ketubah, to be signed by the betrothed couple, replacing the tradition of a "bride price" paid by the groom at the time of marriage.

Regarding the notion of women being regarded as property, it's crucial to acknowledge that this concept has manifested in various cultures throughout history. In ancient Greece and Rome, for instance, women were seen as the property of their husbands or fathers, with severely limited legal rights. In medieval Europe, women were often considered inferior to men and were subjected to laws that curtailed their autonomy and control over their own possessions.

In terms of legal precedents, the idea of women being owned by men has been ingrained in numerous legal systems across history, including the English common law tradition. For instance, under common law, a woman's legal identity fused with her husband's upon marriage, stripping her of distinct legal existence and rights. This legal doctrine, referred to as "coverture," persisted in England and many of its former colonies, including the United States, until the 19th century.

Possessing this information is not intended to undermine or invalidate current practices based on their historical origins, but rather to dispel any misconceptions. Modern women still merit a ritualistic display that honors the recognition and acknowledgment of their value and their sought-after contribution to a marital union.

Regrettably, it is neither uncommon nor a well-kept secret that women have been regarded as property by individuals who lag in their evolution. Throughout human history, there have been numerous instances where people sought to assert ownership over others based on gender, status, or race. The practice of enslaving and possessing fellow humans has left its mark on many historical civilizations.

Archaeological findings suggest that slavery dates back as far as four to ten thousand years ago in ancient Sumeria, where slaves were engaged in various tasks, including farming and household labor. In societies that embraced such practices, women, like slaves, bore the last names of those who implemented these systems of human ownership.

In ancient Egypt, it is believed that indentured servitude was a common practice, with slaves employed in construction, mining, and agriculture, not to be confused with chattel slavery. Surprisingly, some estimates indicate that at certain periods in Egypt's history, up to a third of the population may have been either slaves or indentured servants, most likely, the working class. Similarly, slavery was prevalent in ancient Greece, where slaves fulfilled roles as domestic servants, agricultural laborers, and even soldiers. In Athens, owning slaves was indicative of wealth and status, with some households possessing dozens of them. A labor-intensive lifestyle can significantly influence the customs of dating, marriage, attraction, and the broader romantic social order, thereby establishing traditions that persist across multiple generations, long after the original conditions have transformed. Note: It's crucial to clarify, particularly for those less familiar with the concept, that the term "slave" does not refer exclusively to individuals of African descent or any specific racial group. Furthermore, wouldn't it be intriguing if we discovered that the term "slave" was merely an interpretation of the word "employee" when referring to pre-inflation ancient civilizations seeing as slaves were generally seen as the help and sometimes recognized as family to many.

Despite the prevalence of aggressive censorship campaigns, such as critical race theory, it remains evident to many that sadistic slavery endured as recently as a century ago and persists in various modern forms. This includes illegal human trafficking and subtler manifestations like systemic racism models that advance hidden agendas imperceptible to the untrained eye.

It is evident that the world's major economies continue to reap the benefits of the wealth, status, and power acquired through the transatlantic slave trade, even in contemporary times. Furthermore, various institutions established as a result of the slave trade's legacy continue to operate to this day. All of this implies that the inclination of humans to enslave or possess one another is not a recent phenomenon. Moreover, the idea of owning women as wives is not a novel concept seeing as though the practice can be traced back to enduring cultural practices, such as dowries and the tradition of women adopting their husband's last names.

To conclude, although the concept of a wife has evolved and been reimagined and redefined through the ages, its origins are marked by a complex history. From metallic rings, cattle, cash and diamonds as dowries to secure our property, we have come a long way. In this reflection, I propose that a more promising approach to partnerships lies in prioritizing purpose and connection in the sustainability of our species and spiritual evolution over mere constructs and fairy-tale rituals.

This contemplation may pose challenges for some, especially those who approach it primarily from an emotional, rather than a historical, perspective. It's crucial to bear in mind that as we evolve and transform, our customs and their interpretations change as well. While something may have had a particular origin, we possess the capacity to reimagine and adapt it to assume new significance.

Through a "cultural consensus," these adaptations can gain widespread acceptance and prove advantageous for society.

Today, showing off a big diamond ring, emphasizing its authenticity, and adopting a different last name may convey one message, whereas in the past, it held an entirely different, possibly nefarious, meaning. Yet, we possess the ability to attribute whatever meaning we prefer in today's ever changing world. With this contemplation, we gain a more nuanced understanding of certain power dynamics and relationship behaviors in modern-day interactions, tracing their origins and historical context as it relates to our own personal experiences.

CONTEMPLATION IV

In moving forward with a final Contemplation -

Another inescapable reality is the perpetual evolution of our social and cultural surroundings, often beyond our sphere of control or influence with regard to our interpersonal interactions. As social beings, humans, primates, packs, and even certain insects are intrinsically interconnected and depend on their social frameworks and core operational mechanisms for their well-being and prosperity. These conditions underlie their existence and play a pivotal role in their overall welfare.

Consider, for example, a socially interdependent hive of bees or a colony of ants, where an abundance of food can trigger subtle modifications in their systemic routines. In such a scenario, the queen might increase her mating rate, resulting in a threefold population increase. Conversely, a six-month drought during a scorching 100-degree Texas summer might prompt an insect queen to conserve water and food resources, temporarily curtailing insect reproduction until more favorable external conditions prevail. These instances underscore the profound influence of environmental and social conditions on the adaptation of behavioral patterns for coupling, copulation, and flourishing, encompassing not only humans but a spectrum of social creatures.

The dynamics surrounding resources, among other considerations, hold the potential to exert a substantial influence on the foundational systems that govern collective behavior. This influence may lead to disturbances in the social frameworks employed for both copulation and population growth. In turn, these shifts in social models influence the interrelations of individuals within a group, as well as their interactions with those outside the group. For instance, the development of primates in a tropical climate will vary significantly from that of primates in an ice age.

A prevailing belief holds that we are products of our environments, suggesting that the observable behaviors of a group and the prevailing social order are inherently molded by a confluence of internal and external factors. This underscores the degree to which social creatures are interconnected and dependent on their social and environmental contexts for their individual and collective prosperity—a central thesis and underlying theme to this entire chapter.

With these insights, imagine a propagandized campaign backed by the budget of a wealthy industrial complex, with a single agenda to influence a population through technology, or a planetary-level event, such as a global pole shift. Such scenarios would inevitably alter the trajectory of a species, leading to significant transformations.

Imagine waking up one morning to discover that a meteor made entirely of gold has shattered in the atmosphere, scattering billions of precious fragments onto the lawns of every citizen, instantly granting vast wealth to all. How would such a monumental event reshape our social fabric? This scenario invites us to consider the potential shifts in our perceptions of attraction, the trajectories of our relationships, and the foundational structures of family building in a society where wealth is suddenly universal. How would our values change when financial status is rendered moot?

This thought experiment challenges us to reflect on the intrinsic qualities that attract us to others and the underpinnings of the families we choose to build based on environmental influence. Despite the captivating insights into the origins of relationships and how relationship culture can be altered with time, it's essential to recognize that these ideas remain theoretical in nature.

One striking example of how courtship rituals can be profoundly affected by circumstances is when a nation's men depart for war, leading to an upheaval in the balance of male-female dynamics. This historical imbalance ripples through time, leaving a lasting imprint on how individuals of that era approach relationships and how subsequent generations perceive courting dynamics and the significance of repopulation.

Regarding the cultural shifts prompted by war, it is notable that throughout history, certain cultures have adopted practices such as polygyny to restore balance during post-conflict periods. This approach was often employed to protect widows and orphans, providing them with stability, security, companionship, economic support, and opportunities for reproduction and affection. Such practices were seen as essential measures to ensure the continuity and resilience of societies ravaged by war.

Natural disasters, ranging from tsunamis and hurricanes to the specter of nuclear fallout, have the potential to disrupt the regular operation of society, encompassing the established norms concerning romance and relationships. This is particularly evident in less-prepared communities, where such cataclysms can induce a transformation in cultural perceptions of bonding, companionship, or their scarcity.

Let's now redirect our attention to the historical events that illuminate the evolution of contemporary relationships. Picking up where we left off, our "time machine" exploration will commence with an examination of family dynamics, marriage culture and interpersonal dynamics in Ancient Egypt, along with the societal gender roles, expectations, and social hierarchies that prevailed during that era.

As we embark on this imaginative journey through history, visiting various waypoints along the timeline, we will gather further empirical evidence to either substantiate or challenge the multitude of theories believed to have shaped our current landscape concerning love, intimacy, drama, and transformative relationships. While taking into account the limitations of ancient records, my aim is to provide a balanced and nuanced perspective, distinguishing between what is known and what remains open to interpretation.

ANCIENT EGYPT: *4000 BCE – 600 BCE*

Before delving into the four mid-chapter contemplations, we explored diverse origins and social systems on our historical timeline, spanning from primate and neolithic to even the possibility of archangelic and extraterrestrial origins. However, the ancient Egyptians stand out as a significant example of early social frameworks that continue to exert a profound influence on our current state. Later in this book, you will discover how establishing a foundation on human interaction from its inception offers a behavioral blueprint explaining why we engage as soulmates in various dynamics. Ancient Egypt represents a rich and diverse civilization that endured for several millennia, marked by the ascent and decline of numerous dynasties, each with its unique culture and traditions. Stretching from the Early Dynastic Period, commencing around 3100 BCE, to the conclusion of the Ptolemaic Kingdom in 30 BCE, Egypt crafted a multifaceted social, political, and religious system that left an enduring legacy to human history.

The Nile River stood as a source of immense wealth for the inhabitants of Ancient Egypt. Not only did it offer sustenance through fishing and transportation, but it also played a pivotal role during floods, enriching the land with nutrients from its extensive black silt deposits. The fertile floodplain of the Nile held paramount significance for Ancient Egyptian agriculture, consequently influencing their social development. This natural abundance played a fundamental role in sustaining civilization for millennia, setting it apart from other regions where scarcity might have provoked struggle.

This invaluable resource stood as one of the most apparent external factors influencing the entirety of Egyptian culture, encompassing not only intimate relationships directly but also indirectly. Looking back, a flourishing infrastructure hinges on a thriving social framework, and a robust social structure finds its underpinning in strong family units, cascading all the way down to individual relationship structures.

Domestic relationships held pivotal importance in Ancient Egypt. Love and marriage were esteemed, fostering close-knit families. This robust familial bond played a pivotal role in shaping a flourishing society that would ultimately wield a profound influence on global culture. The ancient Egyptians were pioneers in developing a writing system, early medicine, architectural innovations, and brewing beer. Their impact resonates in various facets of modern life, evident in the design of 21st-century Ankh and Djed-styled electric transformers, as well as architectural motifs adorning strip malls, and even capitals or commercial buildings.

Across numerous societies throughout history, women have served as the nucleus of the family, offering care, nurturing, and the gift of new life. Yet, in many of these societies, the status of women has been recurrently marginalized and undervalued. Ancient Egypt, however, stood as a remarkable anomaly to this trend, where women occupied a position of high esteem within their culture.

In stark contrast to numerous contemporary cultures, the ancient Egyptians held a profound belief in the intrinsic power and wisdom of women. This belief was substantiated by the frequent allocation of women to positions of authority and leadership. Astonishingly, a number of female pharaohs governed over Egypt during its extensive and illustrious history, including Queen Tiye, Hatshepsut,

Nefertiti, and Cleopatra. Such a phenomenon stood as a remarkable achievement in an era when patriarchy prevailed as the norm in most cultures, seldom affording women the opportunity to hold positions of political power. Modern women who lead in industry may draw inspiration from their ancient Egyptian ancestors.

While beauty standards have evolved throughout history, the ancient Egyptian ideals of beauty undeniably continue to shape contemporary standards, leaving an indelible mark. It is undeniable that beauty has perennially played a pivotal role in matters of attraction and relationships. One of the most conspicuous manifestations of ancient Egypt's influence on modern standards is the way we perceive makeup.

Even in antiquity, makeup held a significant place in Egyptian beauty culture and continues to be a cornerstone of our contemporary beauty industry, thereby leaving an enduring impact on the evolution of attraction dynamics. While the styles and products have evolved over time, from Nefertiti's alluring influences to Rihanna's Fenty brand, the fundamental concept of using makeup to enhance one's natural beauty can be traced back to ancient Egypt.

Another aspect in which ancient Egypt's beauty ideals have left an imprint on modern standards is in our perception of hair. In ancient Egypt, long and lustrous hair was revered as a symbol of beauty and was adorned with intricate styles which includes braiding. This notion of long, exquisite hair continues to hold sway in our contemporary culture, evident in how celebrities and ordinary individuals choose to style their hair.

The utilization of wigs in Ancient Egypt remains a subject of profound fascination for historians and archaeologists. Back in 3400 BC, wigs were predominantly donned by the privileged members of Egyptian society. These wigs served a dual purpose in ancient Egypt: they symbolized high social status within the rigid hierarchy and offered protection from the sun for shaven scalps, signifying nobility. Beyond their symbolic import, wigs also served a pragmatic function by promoting hygiene and diminishing the occurrence of head lice.

In the Amarna period, ancient Egyptians cultivated an infatuation with Nubian wigs, meticulously crafted to emulate the short, curly hair of Nubian tribal individuals. It is believed that Queen Nefertiti embraced the Nubian wig after witnessing it worn by Nubians in the Pharaoh's army. This led to the widespread adoption of Nubian wigs among Egyptian elites during that era, underscoring the profound influence of Nubian culture on ancient Egyptian fashion, as recorded by historians. Certainly, trends that could possibly be deemed as "ratchet" in modern high society which has spawned the implementation of civil rights laws such as the "Crown Act."

In sum, the practice of wearing wigs in Ancient Egypt stands as a testament to the paramount significance of appearance and social status within this civilization. The import of wigs transcended the boundaries of Ancient Egypt, as their utilization as symbols of power and status was similarly witnessed in other ancient societies, including their adoption by the Greeks and Romans. Who would have thought that five thousand years later, the Egyptian customs of wearing wigs would still be trending.

Although civil unions in ancient Egypt frequently stemmed from arranged marriages, they nonetheless attributed significance to the concept of attraction and the quest for partners who possessed physical desirability. Ancient Egyptians held the belief that physical attraction was indicative of good fortune and a harbinger of a joyful and prosperous marriage. From the realm of makeup to that of hair, the ancient Egyptians laid the groundwork for numerous beauty standards that remain profoundly relevant in contemporary times.

In addition to the importance of making yourself up to be attractive for your potential lover, using oils, hennas, clays and minerals, Ancient Egypt was also one of humanity's earliest known cultures to record the nuances of charm, flirtation, and physical affection as a dynamic in relating with a lover. Poetry from thousands of years ago about love from ancient Egypt is well-documented in numerous records. Poetry was an important genre in ancient Egyptian literature, and it was often used to express feelings of passion and desire between two people.

One example of ancient Egyptian love poetry is the **"Poem of the Righteous Sufferer,"** which was written in the Middle Kingdom period (between 2040 and 1782 BCE). This poem tells the story of a man who is deeply in love with a woman but is unable to be with her due to societal constraints. In the poem, the man laments his situation and expresses his love for the woman in poignant and heartfelt terms:

> quote: *"She is more beautiful than any woman, Her hair cascades like the rays of the sun. I desire her more than anything in the world, But alas, she is not mine to possess."*

Another example of ancient Egyptian love poetry is the **"Love Song of the Harper,"** which was written in the New Kingdom period (between 1550 and

1070 BCE). This poem is a dialogue between a man and a woman, in which the man expresses his love and desire for the woman, and the woman responds with words of love and affection. The poem is notable for its depiction of the deep and enduring bond between the two lovers, as well as its celebration of love as a powerful and transformative force:

> quote: *"Your love is a flame that consumes me, Your kisses are sweeter than honey. I am yours forever, my love, My heart is yours to keep."*

These examples of ancient Egyptian love poetry offer a window into the emotions and experiences of love within ancient Egyptian society illustrating the lasting influence of love and desire in inspiring and uplifting the human spirit. They also serve as evidence that art forms like poetry were vibrant cultural expressions that shaped their era, consequently impacting the dynamics of their interpersonal relationships. Be it Taylor Swift singing, 'Love Story" or Beyonce singing, 'Crazy in Love', or even LL cool J singing , "I need Love", poetic inclinations regarding our sentimental expressions are as old as the pyramids.

The manner in which the ancient Egyptians perceived relationships and family has left a profound imprint on our contemporary outlook on 21st-century relationships. While arranged marriages are less common in many Western cultures today, we still attach great significance to finding a healthy and physically attractive partner, often going to great lengths to showcase our attractiveness in the hopes of winning the affection and commitment of potential partners. Perhaps we, too, share the belief that the more attractive our partner, the greater our fortune and prosperity in the relationship—akin to our Egyptian forebears. Regardless, the legacy of this remarkable civilization directly informs our choices in selecting partners today and will continue to influence us for generations to come.

EGYPT to ROME: 300 B.C.E.

Following the reign of several dynasties, the power structure in ancient Egypt eventually yielded, paving the way for its ultimate conquest by Greece. The culmination of Ancient Egyptian civilization, as we recognize it, transpired in 332 BC. The decline of ancient Egypt coincided strategically with a time that allowed for the exploration and settlement of new lands, particularly in Europe.

The initial occupants of the region were the Greeks, who established their own Egyptian state, the Ptolemaic Dynasty, which endured for nearly three centuries until 30 B.C. It was in that year that Rome assumed control, in part due to its proximity to Alexandria and the intricate drama involving Cleopatra, Caesar, and Mark Antony. This transition in leadership and culture consequently reshaped the dynamics of how individuals in that region would relate to one another within various forms of companionship.

While the foreign puppet regimes and Pharaohs of the Ptolemaic kingdom endeavored to govern Egypt using traditional Egyptian methods, the advent of Roman rule heralded a cultural shift. This transformation ultimately ushered in a new religion known as Christianity, thanks to the influence of Emperor Constantine and the Councils of Nicaea. Over time, these developments exerted a profound impact on the social fabric of the entire region, reshaping how people interacted with one another and even how they structured their familial relationships.

NOTE: The Council of Nicaea represented the inaugural of the seven Ecumenical councils that laid the foundation for what we now recognize as Christianity. Subsequently, the Council of Trent emerged as the 19th Ecumenical council, introducing revisions for political advantage. King James I played a pivotal role in this process, selecting the most esteemed versions of the Bible of his time, democratizing and rendering them more accessible to the public—effectively solidifying the current incarnation of Christianity as an organized religion with influence over numerous relationship models worldwide. This represented a significant departure from the original Gnostic practices that served as a guiding light for the world's spiritual adepts, providing a more crystallized buffer between humanity and the divine.

Throughout history, spiritual belief, mediated through organized religion, effectively constituted the governing principle, also known as 'The Law.' Religious law and spiritual devotion, while incorporating fundamental mysticism, significantly molded the way of life for its adherents, impacting their daily rituals, customary ceremonies, and the broader day-to-day culture—ultimately influencing how individuals related to one another.

This implies that if your way of loving, behaving, and expressing love were analogous to a computer program, the culture and religion of your region would serve as the operating system or software guiding your functions. This is similar to how contemporary society is significantly influenced by music, film, and media when it comes to our perceptions of romantic relationships. Even though it's an artificial light, we cannot deny the media's influence as our guiding light regarding how we relate to one another.

INTERJECTION:

While our current exploration of the timeline predominantly centers on the mainstream cultures that have impacted Western thought, it is imperative to underscore the substantial contributions of a multitude of diverse cultures throughout history. From ancient era's to the medieval period, these societies have played a pivotal role in shaping our comprehension of emotions, relationships, and the concept of committing to a life partner. Recognizing and valuing these varied cultural influences is essential in shaping our perspectives on love and companionship.

Early Hindu culture and the prehistoric and pre-colonial San people of South Africa serve as particularly notable examples for contemplation due to their profound influence on the evolution of human emotions, relationships, and the concept of coupling. Additionally, genetic evidence hints at the San people's ancestral origins of the Mongoloid races.

Furthermore, the Malian Empire stands as one of the most intriguing and potent empires in recorded history. At its zenith between the 13th and 16th centuries, a distinctly captivating element of this culture was the presence of the divine feminine spiritual aspect, which endures to this day and maintains a profound impact on the region. This is exemplified by the veneration of the great mother and other akin deities.

Without a doubt, this influence exerted a substantial role in shaping their comprehension of family structures and companionship, especially when juxtaposed with many Western cultures of the same era. The prominence of the divine feminine and the associated nurturing attributes undoubtedly contributed to a heightened recognition of the role of women within the family and community, subsequently nurturing stronger bonds and more egalitarian relationships between partners.

It is also imperative to acknowledge the significance of Timbuktu in Mali, renowned worldwide for its myriad schools and illustrious libraries. The intellectual and cultural opulence of Timbuktu drew scholars and students from across the globe, establishing it as a nexus of learning and a vital hub for the exchange of knowledge. Mansa Musa, who reigned over Mali from 1312 C.E. to 1337 C.E., left an indelible mark on the cultural and religious landscape of the region. Following his conversion to Islam and a pilgrimage to Mecca, he proclaimed Islam as the national religion, enacting a law that mandated all subsequent Mansas—or kings of Mali—to embrace it.

This transition was hardly unexpected, given the widespread influence of original Islamic culture along the North African trade routes, enabling the flow of commodities, concepts, and religious convictions. The embrace of Islam by Mali undeniably contributed to the shaping and or shifting of their cultural identity, influencing their perspectives on family structures, relationships, and gender roles.

Mansa Musa is celebrated for his role in erecting numerous public edifices in urban centers, including the renowned Djing'uere'ber Mosque and the esteemed Sankore University. These remarkable civilizations, akin in magnitude to ancient Egypt, have left an indelible imprint on world culture and have significantly influenced the manner in which we approach companionship and coupling.

The predominant Islamic influence during that epoch leaned towards a patriarchal outlook, a perspective that would undoubtedly exert a substantial impact on how individuals formed partnerships when juxtaposed with the indigenous cultures of the region. These multifaceted cultural influences would have played a pivotal role in shaping attitudes towards relationships and the concept of partnering over the course of time.

In retrospect, when contemplating some of the ancient cultures with a proclivity for arranged marriages, it is intriguing to observe that many individuals often recount their experiences in comparable terms. Although they may not have initially chosen their partners, they frequently narrate the journey of growing to love and appreciate their chosen companions over time. This phenomenon is in part attributable to the recognition that having a life partner to establish a home, rear children, and secure a comfortable life is a value that many people eventually come to cherish and rely upon. The consistent proximity that fosters trust and familiarity can culminate in a profound and enduring love that transcends initial uncertainties or reservations. Additionally, the significance assigned to companionship throughout life's daily trials cannot be overstated.

I recollect the story of how my father and stepmother were introduced by their parents in rural Georgia during the 1980s. Both found themselves in search of a life partner and spouse to assist in raising their respective children, and the wise grandparents from both sides played a pivotal role in facilitating their meeting. As fate would have it, they discovered compatibility (at that particular time), leading to their eventual marriage. This union provided my siblings and I with a stable environment during our relatively brief upbringing. It's worth noting that many blind dates, orchestrated by mutual acquaintances, share similarities with arranged marriages, particularly after saying "I do."

ROME-ANTICS 600 B.C.E. to 475 A.D.

Beyond ancient Egypt, the practice of arranged marriages continued in various forms throughout history. In Rome, for example, while the higher echelons of society often practiced arranged political couplings, it was not uncommon for commoners to marry for love rather than political reasons. As time passed and cultures' evolved, the idea of romance would soon manifest in full force, but not before going through some growing pains.

The word **"Romance"** and or Romantic, which can be described as '*Rome's-Antics*' or '*Rome-Mancy*' —similar to '*Necro-Mancy*,' reminiscent to the death of love by Rome-antic divination—is French vernacular derived from *the vulgar Latin adverb,* **Romaníce**. A slang word for acts that were likely taboo behavior—much like passionate P.D.A., or "Public Displays of Affection," today.

The original Latin adverb from which the word ***Romaníce*** derived was "**Ro-manicus**" and meant ***"of the Roman style."*** Some scholars believe that this term originally referred to certain cultural practices, including some forms of homosexual behavior that were common taboo in ancient Rome. Over time, the colloquial slang "**ro-manicus**" emerged as "**romaníce**," which eventually evolved into the word "**Romance**."

Instances of '**Romaníce**' behavior in ancient Rome are depicted in various works of art, such as Michelangelo's homo erotic Sistine Chapel painting, as well as stone sculptures featuring naked young boys under the robes of older men which would have been very **romanicus or romaníce** in nature due to their intimate posturing. These depictions, marked by their intimate postures, exemplify the "romanice" and aesthetically distinctive nature of some Roman art. Some might argue that these depictions were purely innocent, yet these same voices may also contend that the inclusion of perverted adult-oriented humor in popular children's shows are also all in good fun and harmless.

Nonetheless, such practices extended beyond the realm of art and were reportedly widespread among soldiers, sailors, explorers, and even politicians who embarked on lengthy sea voyages accompanied solely by young servants. Ancient Rome was a patriarchal society that imposed significant restrictions on the roles and opportunities available to women. Consequently, it was exceptionally rare to encounter women engaging in maritime ventures for trade or conquest, as these activities were typically regarded as the exclusive domain of men. Instead, the prevailing expectation for most women was to remain at home, tending to domestic responsibilities and child-rearing.

Imagine being 400 miles out at sea, enduring subpar conditions on a wooden vessel, far from home. It becomes apparent how one might yearn for affection, the comfort of family, and the simple pleasures often taken for granted. Engaging in excessive drinking and licentious behavior could distort one's perception of gender, blurring the line between male and female identities. In essence, debauchery and depravity resulting from late-night drunken indulgences could lead corrupt minds to start transforming young servants into convenient bedmates.

This seemingly carefree, unaccountable lifestyle may have felt like a matter of choice and not obligation. However, the submissive parties, acting from a place of servitude, might have had a different perspective. Yet, when one is courted consistently with favor or tantalizing promises of freedom, wealth, and status, especially when groomed since childhood, the prospect of a better life can inspire a more agreeable attitude.

In reality, Roman men could engage in homosexual relations without facing serious repercussions, provided they assumed the dominant role rather than the submissive one. Permissible partners included active slaves, individuals who had been enslaved in the past, servants, prostitutes, and entertainers. Those living in infamia, associated with infamy, were fair game. These individuals were typically second-class citizens, lacking the same legal safeguards as most citizens. Romaníce, which would later evolve into Romance, likely originated within the gray areas where cultural influences and power dynamics intersected. Who would have ever thought that the romance individuals covet today may have been born from alternative lifestyles?

The process of grooming the youth is reminiscent of the case involving 14-year-old Sally Hemmings and the third U.S. President, Thomas Jefferson. Young minds are highly impressionable, which is why laws exist to protect underage individuals from predatory adults. However, history reveals that the powerful often operate by a different set of rules than the commoners.

Similar to prison politics in today's penal systems, where dominating another inmate through sexual acts could establish one's reputation as a formidable alpha male, provided they were the aggressor and not the victim, some men in ancient Rome also embraced a comparable conquest mentality. In this context, individuals who initiated sexual acts were frequently perceived as figures of power, a notion that resonates across various fields, including the music industry.

Regarding the parallels of military and prison power dynamics, I'm reminded of the infamous, Fleece Johnson's chilling declaration: "I likes' ya, and I wants ya, so we can do this the easy way, or we can do this the hard way." Indeed, there appear to be numerous parallels between certain aspects of ancient Rome's military structure and today's Prison Industrial Complex concerning power dynamics among men.

A scene from the movie 300 also comes to mind where King Leonidas alludes to the Athenian boy lovers who defied the fictional God King Xerxes of Persia. Homosexuality in ancient Rome is well documented and far from a secret. Some individuals speculate that its influence may persist within the Roman Catholic Church today, particularly among some priests and their choir boys.

It's essential to recognize that the concept of romaníce taboo extended far beyond homosexual relationships alone and could encompass any and every forbidden attraction. This included affairs with married individuals, instances of incest, Pedo or Ephebophilia, and even relationships across different social classes. The literary masterpiece of "Romeo and Juliet" vividly exemplifies these enduring themes as a prototypical example. Though their tale is marked by tragedy, it stands as a symbol of the forbidden nature of romantic ardor. A more contemporary narrative fitting this archetypic attraction is the 1990 romantic film featuring Richard Gere and Julia Roberts, known as "Pretty Woman," where attraction between classes flourished.

One could make the argument that escapism and fantasy, often seen in stories of forbidden love, form the very foundation of today's fairytale-inspired relationship culture. It's no wonder that many individuals partake in serial dating, which can provide a continuous flow of dopamine and may bear a resemblance to polyamory. It's believed that the pleasurable, dopamine-fueled fantasies in romaníce became so profound that they assumed an almost divine nature, and they were even regarded as one of the purest expressions of the seven Greek love styles, known as Aga'pe.

Cultural evidence found in popular artwork, such as Michelangelo's Sistine Chapel, and in literary creations like poetry and plays, where characters are willing to risk everything for their forbidden love, as seen in Romeo and Juliet, provides valuable insights into the perspectives on love and relationships of a particular kind during specific eras. These works offer glimpses into the historical and cultural context of romance, delivering a nuanced understanding of the development of romantic ideals across time.

If we consider that the taboo aspects of "Roman-Antics" contributed to the emergence of the concept of "Romance" as we know it today, it becomes easier to grasp why the duties, obligations, and daily trials of marriage did not inherently spark the creation of Romance as a concept. Unlike the unrestrained romaníce behavior fueled by the allure of forbidden fruit, it may surprise many to learn that the concept of romance originated from taboo behavior. Additionally, modern relationships rooted solely in romance have their foundation in this unconventional origin.

It's worth noting that participating in forbidden taboos can generate a sense of thrill and danger, heightening feelings of excitement and passion. Moreover, the element of secrecy and clandestine behavior linked to such actions can enhance their allure and excitement, creating the perfect recipe for falling in love. Many marriages were traditionally arranged by families to advance their own interests, often disregarding the excitement and desires of the individuals involved. Thus, the concept of romance and the emergence of the notion of a "side chick" or side dic. — tator, — of the heart that is —never mind —moving on.

Such relationships continue to be common in contemporary society and significantly influence popular trends, contributing to the diversity of today's cultural landscape. These diverse viewpoints on love and relationships provide a nuanced comprehension of romance and its role in human connections.

Contrary to popular belief, numerous romanicus or romaníce relationships in ancient Rome were infused with a profound capacity for love. This love may have encompassed the affection for perverse pleasure and shamelessness or the love of freedom that accompanied the libertinism of romanice interactions. By some accounts, these relationships were considered a form of escapism, free from the burden of responsibility and accountability, given that Roman law did not acknowledge same-sex marriages at that time.

In retrospection, marriages were initially formed to secure livelihoods and ensure survival for self-preservation. Nonetheless, somewhere along the way, these priorities shifted, and romantic love became the primary focus in attracting and choosing a partner. The focus transitioned to excitement and the indulgence of each other's fantasies, leading to a change in priorities. This transition might help elucidate the psychology behind the popularity of books like "Why Men Love Bitches" and "Why Pretty Girls Love Bad Boys." These polarizing dynamics can provide an exhilarating surge of brain chemistry, resulting in a fluctuation between excitement, romance and indifference, all in pursuit of feeling truly alive. Other dynamics might be perceived as mundane, or, frankly, quite boring thus lacking the fuel to drive attraction.

The Freedoms and Philosophies of Love.

The adage "Freedom ain't free!" has long resonated in American culture, encapsulated by Crosby, Stills & Nash in their 1971 song, highlighting the costs of freedom. quote: Find the cost of freedom buried in the ground - Mother Earth will swallow you and lay your body down.' This concept was not foreign to the Greco-Roman world, where pursuit of dominance for peace and power was underpinned by formidable military might, enabling societies to flourish in wealth and freedom. This era celebrated the freedom to explore love, innovation, and philosophy, echoing Thomas Hobbes' notion that leisure is the Mother of Philosophy.

The roots of Western philosophy, aimed at understanding life and the universe, trace back to the 6th century B.C.E. with the Pre-Socratics, who explored natural wonders and human-divine relations. Thales, Heraclitus, and Parmenides, among others, laid foundational theories about reality and change, paving the way for philosophical exploration of love and existence.

During this pivotal era, a philosophy developed that provided a deeper understanding of love, encapsulated by the seven Greek love styles. These styles offered profound insights into emotional and relational dynamics, shaping cultural perceptions and interactions at the time. They not only influenced personal relationships but also extended their reach into the arts, governance, and daily social practices, giving the culture a framework through which to explore the complexity of human connections. This philosophical evolution contributed significantly to the ideological and ethical fabric of the society, weaving through its collective consciousness and laying the groundwork for future discourse on love and relationships. Note: If you are listening to this publication through digitally enhanced dictation, please excuse any inaccuracies in pronunciation. The seven philosophical love styles include:

Eros

Eros embodies passionate, romantic love, marked by an intense longing and attraction. Frequently depicted in cinema and literature, it is synonymous with a profound physical and emotional connection.

Philia

Philia signifies a deep, genuine friendship rooted in trust, mutual respect, and a solid connection. It thrives among close friends and family members, who share common values and offer unwavering support.

Ludus

Ludus captures the essence of playful, flirtatious love often seen in the early stages of a relationship. Characterized by light-heartedness and amusement, it sets the stage for a deeper, more committed bond.

Storge

Storge represents the unconditional love that springs from familial ties, characterized by loyalty, nurturing, and a deep sense of security among family members and close friends.

Philautia

Philautia promotes a compassionate form of self-love that encourages self-acceptance, respect, and personal growth, highlighting the importance of recognizing one's own value and achievements.

Pragma

Pragma is dedicated to enduring, practical love built on mutual commitment and understanding, typical of long-standing relationships that blend romantic affection with deep friendship.

Mania

Mania denotes an obsessive type of love, often accompanied by jealousy and a fear of abandonment, which can lead to possessiveness and controlling behavior within relationships.

Aga'pe pronounced A-gha-pay

Agape expresses selfless, universal love, characterized by empathy, altruism, and a boundless desire to share and reflect love unconditionally, reminiscent of global compassion or spiritual awakening.

These seven philosophical concepts of love were among the first widespread cultural ideologies to permeate Western civilization. Their dissemination inevitably spurred growth, which in turn precipitated change. Traditional customs were slowly being replaced, ushering in a new era that highlighted the ability of both partners to leverage power dynamics in relationships. This shift was not all-encompassing but evident within specific circles.

With the spread of romantic courtship and new philosophical ideas, the golden age of the ancient Greco-Roman culture emerged. Love was beginning to be considered a divine force that transcended human understanding. For the upper class, marriage still revolved more around property and politics than emotions, as it did in most cultures that recognized the paramount importance of wealth preservation.

Still, as the centuries progressed, attitudes toward love as a requirement for marriage and the significance of status began to shift. For example, mirroring the trend of courting, the concept of dating began to gain popularity, especially among the middle and upper classes. The word "courting" originates from the Middle English word "corten," which means to court or woo. This, in turn, comes from the Old French word "cort," meaning court or king's court. The term originally referred to the behavior and etiquette expected in a royal court, including the respectful attention and service to someone, often of higher status. Over time, it evolved to refer to the process of seeking someone's favor or affection, especially in a romantic context.

Perhaps these were the modest origins of the 'boyfriend-girlfriend' culture. While "mistress" and "beau" were precursors to "boyfriend" and "girlfriend," historical sources date the first usage of these terms to around the mid-1800s, with some variation of a decade or two. This marked a significant departure from the still-common practice of arranged marriages in many other social orders. Only in more recent history has the idea of dating and then marrying for love become widely accepted across most cultures.

If you've been following along, you're likely to discover that all this discussion leads to a fresh and enlightened comprehension of why people enter into relationships in the first place. Regardless of our backgrounds, the language we employ, or our origins, we are inherently shaped by today's prevailing romantic culture, merely due to our proximity to it.

As Western culture continues to spread globally, with English as a dominant language, understanding the historical underpinnings that influence the ways in which many couples relate to each other becomes increasingly important. By delving into the cultural, philosophical, and literary traditions that shape contemporary romantic ideals, we can gain a deeper comprehension of the complexities of love and human connection as they pertain to us.

Throughout the Middle Ages and into the Renaissance era, the popularity of using romance and dating as means to cultivate attraction and fall in love continued to rise, despite marriages still being viewed as a way of forming alliances between noble families. During this time, the younger generation had some influence in choosing their potential partners, as long as their families held equal status. Nevertheless, it's essential to recognize that multiple choice isn't much of a choice when your choices belong to a small, select group, especially among nobles and royalty.

At the end of the day, what many experience as romance is, at its core, romantic entertainment. Much like the drama of reality TV, the stage-play events that make up our temporary lives as human avatars lead us to entertain each other's egos with passion, humor, or indifference. Romance, in this sense, serves as a powerful catalyst for building character and shaping identity. Long before television or the internet, romance—and the drama it brings—was our most vivid source of entertainment, revealing life's lessons through every passionate entanglement and heartache. In this way, romantic connections act as mirrors, reflecting the masks we wear and the authentic selves we might aspire to become.

RENAISSANCE to VICTORIAN

In the Victorian era, men and women aspired to establish ideal relationships that would meet the exacting standards of a demanding society. Those who fell short in exhibiting the desirable qualities deemed important by Victorian society faced the risk of being dismissed by potential partners as unsuitable mates. However, before these times, with arranged marriages, one may not have had a choice. Today, while not officially a formal practice, we subconsciously continue to adhere to the standards established during that era.

By the 18th century, change was afoot once more. The dawn of the Industrial Revolution resulted in a more mobile workforce, making it increasingly challenging for people to find strong partnerships or enduring love within their immediate and sometimes temporary communities. As society grappled with disruptions, it led to a surge in marriages of convenience. These unions hinged on financial stability or social status, dependent on the location and aspirations of the individuals involved.

Given the survival-based nature of these unions, rooted in self-preservation and existence rather than romantic love, one could argue that they exemplify what can be referred to as existential love. Philosophers might conclude that existential love, being the initial form of love that prioritizes self-preservation and survival, is more profound or divine than romantic love. Marrying for convenience or survival, rather than a lasting love, could possibly offer a partnership that provides a sense of security, rendering it more appealing than other trivial options during challenging times.

As the industrial revolution found equilibrium, these trends eventually gave way to much more romantic notions of love and marriage between the late 18th and early 20th centuries. Unbeknownst to the populace, a novel microcosm of ideas was brewing amongst smaller upper-class circles, ready to make a global impact. You may have observed, when culture-shifting revolutions in collective thought occur, our ideas about companionship shift as well. Whether we relate for love, survival, or as a means of advancement, the choices we make are almost always influenced by our vast social conditions and external environment, often in ways that are imperceptible.

As one moves along the historical timeline, it becomes increasingly evident that for centuries, relationship dynamics and everything associated with love have consistently undergone dramatic transformations in response to fluctuations in our shared reality. Contemporary love is no exception; the subtleties of modern day love are a relatively recent development, undoubtedly influenced by the advancements humanity has made over the past century or so.

It was only during the early 20th century, with the emergence of Hollywood's golden age, that love and romance began to be widely portrayed as an idealized emotional concept on the big screen, rather than a construct centered on family, community, and legacy-building. This shift in popular culture mirrored broader societal changes, including an increasing emphasis on individualism and the rise of new forms of media that facilitated the widespread dissemination of romantic ideals. These evolving attitudes toward love and relationships would continue to evolve over the course of the 20th century, as new technologies and cultural trends transformed the ways in which people engaged with each other and the broader world.

As artistic mediums became more accessible and affordable, it was only a matter of time before these ideas rapidly disseminated through the collective consciousness and reached the masses. Popular forms of entertainment, such as grand theatrical productions, playwrights following the lines of Shakespeare, popular orchestras, romantic novels, radio shows, and films, made these progressive and modern ideas about romantic love more widely accessible than ever before. This cultural shift reflected larger societal changes, including the rise of mass media and the growing importance of individualism and personal fulfillment.

RECAP.

Prior to this golden age of Hollywood, we've recognized that from the Neolithic age to Ancient Mesopotamian and Egyptian cultures, marriages were primarily business transactions, and relationships were typically seen as a means of acquisition, cementing alliances between families and gaining social status. Community leaders also arranged marriages to solidify relationships between different tribes or clans. They were usually devoid of romantic love but likely developed into existential familial love over time. While not quite the culture of romance we would eventually see take shape, expressions of amorous attractions were still abundant as seen in ancient Egyptian poetry such as, Love song of the Harper."

Upon further examination, we would find that in Medieval Europe, marriages were often arranged by families to increase their social standing or land holdings. Romance was not initially a priority. However, in contrast, as humanity continued to evolve, we can observe that a conquest-obsessed yet powerful Greco-Roman culture could afford to explore doctrines, philosophy, and unconventional coupling styles as humankind expanded its social and technical capabilities into the new age. With the growth of these philosophical doctrines, they began to place a significant emphasis on attraction and romance in companionship.

Now that we're all up to speed, it's worth noting that as romantic thought evolved, it eventually blossomed into a full-blown movement. This movement gave birth to those progressive new ideas projected early in the 20th century via Hollywood. This movement was the Romanticism Movement of the 19th century, also known as the Romantic Era. Officially commencing in the late 18th century, The Romanticism Era could be seen as comparable to the psychedelic-induced, hippie-charged rock-n-roll movement of the late 1960s and early 70s—if it were on steroids. Instead of L.S.D., red wine was the substance of choice. Rather than listening to Jimi Hendrix and the Grateful Dead, individuals favored the works of Bach and Brahms. And instead of tie-dye or psychedelic posters, art by the likes of Van Gogh was in vogue.

Romanticism Era late 1700s -mid 1800s B.C.E.

In the late 18th century, a profound intellectual shift began to sweep through Western civilization. This transformation bore the name "Romanticism" and would go on to imbue countless works of literature, painting, music, and architecture over the following half century. In a manner reminiscent of the origins of romance, "Romanticism" represented a rejection of the principles of order and rationality that had long defined classicism and neoclassicism.

Instead, it celebrated the individual, emotional, and visionary facets of human experience, contrasting with the dated conventionalism of the 17th and 18th centuries. In a nutshell, Romanticism represented free expression. The Romanticism era, left an indelible mark on the arts of the time, profoundly influencing society as a whole. So, why did Beethoven choose to name his most beloved sonata after the moonlight? When reflecting on Beethoven's Moonlight Sonata, it's pivotal to recognize its birth in a period marked by a profound artistic upheaval. This era was characterized by a vibrant spirit of romance and freedom that captivated the youth, much like a natural mystic blowing through the air. The Romanticism movement spread rapidly across the globe, leaving its mark on every continent in various ways. Germany, often considered its official starting point, was among the most profoundly affected nations. Writers and artists embarked on a rebellion against the rigid rules of classism. In France, Romanticism coincided with the onset of the French Revolution, giving birth to a new generation of poets and writers who fervently championed freedom and democracy, alongside the continued influence of iconic fashion houses that remain relevant today. Think of French fashion houses like Hermes or Louis Vuitton, and classical composers such as Joseph Bologne, Chevalier de Saint-Georges, Johannes Brahms, or Frédéric Chopin.

In England, Romanticism rekindled an appreciation for nature, the outdoors, and a return to traditional values and customs. Wherever it found a foothold, Romanticism cast a profound influence on the world, thereby shaping the styles of companionship among all those it touched.

The Victorian era bore witness to seismic shifts in society, politics, and the economy, all fueled by the industrial revolution. Writers responded to this transformative era with an outpouring of essays, novels, poems, plays, autobiographies, and journalism. Even today, Romanticism remains an influential presence in the arts, leaving its indelible mark on our daily lives. The rise of social media, for instance, can be traced back to the Romantic ideal of unbridled self-expression.

In many respects, we still inhabit the world fashioned by Romanticism. The Enlightenment era marked the ascendancy of reason and logic over tradition and religious dogma, propelling advances in science, medicine, and philosophy. The Romantics emerged as passionate counterforces to the Enlightenment's reign, valuing emotions, intuition, and imagination above reason. They birthed numerous masterpieces in literature, art, music, and even politics. It's akin to spirituality eclipsing organized religion.

In everyday existence, the Romantic movement left its imprint on fashion, architecture, and even the very fabric of self-perception. The individual ego acquired unprecedented significance. To grasp the significance of individuality in the Romantic movement's discourse, one might draw parallels with the foundational tenets of democracy, where every voice holds sway.

For more than two centuries, Romanticism has exerted a profound influence on Western civilization. Its cultural impact extended to daily life, religion, art, literature, and politics. Romanticism and the ideals of liberalism share historical roots, with both movements championing individual liberty and self-expression, and challenging established authority and hierarchies.

The Catholic Church's response to the Romantics was varied, yet predominantly negative. The Church perceived the Romantic movement as a challenge to its authority and influence, leading to measures aimed at its suppression. These measures encompassed the censorship of books and artworks, as well as the exile or imprisonment of those who dared to express dissent. In some tragic instances, the Church even resorted to executing individuals for their beliefs.

Nevertheless, within the Church, not all members stood in opposition to the Romantics; some embraced their ideas and played a role in disseminating their message. However, the Romantic Movement fundamentally contradicted the principles upheld by the Catholic Church. Therefore, its initial quest for universal acceptance as a way of life was likely destined to falter. It's probable that the establishment saw it as a threat to order and control.

For background reference The History of Romanticism is often traced back to the publication of the Lyrical Ballads in 1798, which was a collection of poems by William Wordsworth and Samuel Taylor Coleridge. In the "Preface" to the second edition of Lyrical Ballads, Wordsworth described poetry as the "spontaneous overflow of powerful feelings." This became the manifesto of the English Romantic movement in poetry. Other important figures in the early phase of the Romantic movement in England include William Blake and Percy Bysshe Shelley. Innovations marked the first phase of the Romantic movement in Germany in both content and literary style. German Romantics were also preoccupied with the mysteries of nature and religion

The Romanticism Era marked an era of profound transformation. At its zenith, it upended the very fabric of mainstream society and set the foundation for our contemporary culture, reshaping how we approach dating. This pivotal epoch, born out of discontent with the established order, left an indelible mark on history, influencing the way we perceive and process our thoughts.

Your existence serves as living testimony to the enduring impact of Romanticism. The cultural movements of Rock and Roll, Jazz, R&B, and Hip Hop, alongside abstract art, comic books, and short films at festivals, all trace their roots to the broader cultural thrust of free expression. These diverse forms of artistic expression share a common objective: uniting people through the allure of each other's creativity and individuality. From prehistoric displays of tenderness to Egyptian adornment, and Rome's "Antics", the yearning for connection has remained constant. These influences have all played a part in shaping our inherent drive to seek potential partners, long before our birth.

The Romanticism Era ushered in the dawn of individual creative thinking among the masses, sparking a prolific and ceaseless flow of ideas and concepts related to love and relationships. Without this era of artistic and intellectual exploration, the diverse spectrum of ideas and viewpoints on love and relationships that we have today might never have come to fruition. When a notion gains currency, it often spreads swiftly through the population, eventually becoming an integral part of the cultural fabric.

Today, we are presented with an almost limitless array of individual perspectives and insights on how to love and navigate relationships, thanks to the multitude of viewpoints that have evolved over time. A quick glance at social media attests to the overwhelming evidence of this phenomenon. Social media has evolved into a platform for individuals to express their unique viewpoints on love and relationships, contributing to the ever-expanding landscape of ideas and opinions in this domain. For instance, Facebook serves as a hub for finding random counsel on love and relationships. There's absolutely no shortage of self-proclaimed experts eager to dispense profound wisdom on the subject, guiding you on when, where, why, and how to love within a relationship.

It's worth remembering that the next time you defy the established order in protest, immerse yourself in classical music, or contemplate the profound layers of a Van Gogh or Basquiat painting, you are participating in a tradition that commenced over two centuries ago. This tradition traces its roots to a band of individuals who had grown weary of the lackluster, monochromatic ambiance of their surroundings, which extended to prevailing perspectives on love and relationships. Their mission was to infuse vitality and ardor into every facet of existence, sparking a fresh surge of creative expression and individuality that endures to the present day.

To put it in relatable terms, think of it this way: Many people tend to overlook the significant struggles for basic inclusion or human rights experienced by marginalized groups, whos struggles ultimately paved the way for the liberties most groups take for granted today. Basic rights such as riding on buses, dining in restaurants, and participating in the political process of voting were not readily available to many in the West without the relentless efforts of said marginalized groups. Sadly, many of these groups, despite their contributions, continue to be treated as second-class citizens in many cases. Yet it does not diminish the fact that our culture of freedom is built upon the sacrifices and struggles of those that came before us and laid a path so that all could enjoy the liberties afforded to many.

It's easy to take our modern liberties for granted, as if they have perpetually been in place, seamlessly integrated from the beginning of time. Yet, it is imperative to remember that our species has frequently displayed a propensity for stigmatizing dissenting viewpoints and stifling independent thinking, particularly during more rudimentary periods. The cultural freedoms we presently relish were diligently secured through centuries of struggle, championed by individuals and movements that contested conventional norms and championed the causes of enhanced equality, personal liberty, and self-expression.

When scrutinizing the spectrum of human emotions in the context of relationships across different eras, it becomes evident that the approaches to love employed by populations, experience cyclical shifts and modifications. These transformations are often reactions to the predominant circumstances of the time, encompassing enduring political or geographical upheavals, natural calamities, and even comprehensive cultural movements. As we approach the end of this timeline journey, we gain a deeper understanding of how the dynamics of human relationships resemble the shifting patterns of a kaleidoscope. Just as each turn of the kaleidoscope reveals a new, intricate design, our interactions and connections continuously evolve, reflecting the complexity and beauty of our shared experiences.

In modern cultures, love has evolved into a remarkably intricate pursuit. Given the myriad cultural influences, dynamics, and values in play, it's unsurprising that discovering a harmonious partner can pose a formidable challenge. Nevertheless, billions of individuals worldwide persist in the quest for that extraordinary connection, holding onto the hope of encountering their true love, firmly believing their soulmate is out there, awaiting the serendipitous moment when their paths will inevitably intersect.

Chapter Four

Generations

The Current Timeline Re: Baby Boomers, Generation-X Millennials, Gen Z & Gen Alpha

Quote: "We are not the same people this year as last; nor are those we love. It is a happy chance if we, changing, continue to love a changed person."
— William Somerset Maugham

MODERN-DAY LOVE PROGRAM

As chapter two provided us with a broad historical timeline spanning several millennia, let's now shift our focus to a shorter timeline, zooming in on the last century. We have reviewed a vast expanse of time from a bird's eye view and our exploration on the history of human connection will culminate to its final destination, the contemporary era, specifically the 20th and 21st centuries.

Rest assured, the history lesson is almost over. As we near the conclusion of our historical exploration, let's not lose momentum. Our objective remains to lay a solid groundwork for grasping the complexities of human nature and our deep-seated yearning for meaningful relationships. With this in mind, we shall forge ahead on our investigative journey, committing ourselves to take a forensic look at the behaviors and tendencies we exhibit in contrast to our predecessors. This chapter provides a thorough investigation into the psychology and behaviors of current generations, with a close examination of their habits and patterns in forming connections. It also explores the intriguing aspect of generational proximity.

Peering into the tendencies of a central population for over the course of a century is like glimpsing into a matrix of the world's relationships, offering a comprehensive view of how people now interact and connect. Readers are likely to find both entertainment and valuable insights within these pages. As we move into the present century and beyond, a greater diversity in how love is expressed and deep connections are formed is anticipated. The interconnected nature of our world now offers unparalleled opportunities to meet and interact with people from various backgrounds. This contemporary era of love, relationships, and social connections presents new predicaments, making it more challenging than ever to navigate contemporary relationships effectively.

From authentic soulful connections to hook up culture and the blurring of gender roles as well as trauma bonds masquerading as love, and now even virtual marriages, we find ourselves in an entirely new arena where old rules no longer hold the same weight. The shifting landscape of modern relationships also introduces a plethora of innovative ways to meet potential partners, from social media to online dating. With such a vast array of options available, determining where to begin can be a daunting task.

As we confront the challenges of modern times, we encounter not only the traditional obstacles but also novel difficulties arising from modern technology. In the past, relationships adhered to traditional roles and expectations, but in the modern age, they have become far more fluid and at times, may lack accountability and consequences. We are no longer bound by the same norms and expectations as our forebears, which can be both liberating and confusing.

In the old days, social interactions were governed by a much more rigid structure, and deviating from these norms often led to consequences like isolation or ostracization. In contrast, contemporary interactions are marked by a flexible, unrestricted, and liberal approach, akin to a "free-for-all" with "no holds barred." While this provides individuals with greater autonomy and choice, it can also lead to uncertainty and ambiguity regarding the expectations and boundaries of social interactions.

The modern approach to falling in love seems to involve a sense of free-fall, characterized by unaccountable emotions, often in pursuit of fleeting infatuations that trigger temporary rushes of dopamine. Occasionally, a few fortunate souls may serendipitously stumble upon true and enduring love. Congratulations to those who are favored, or simply lucky in matters of the heart.

I am deeply fascinated by the journey that has led us to this point in time. What path did we follow to arrive at this specific spot in our collective journey? Together, we've traversed the ages, time traveling through the chronicles of history, spanning centuries. Now, we find ourselves in an era dominated by a media culture, where timelines overflow with live stories, selfies, quick videos, and constant updates.

Regrettably, our current social landscape can at times resemble a voyeuristic bazaar or an auction block, designed to attract the insatiable and the eager. This situation echoes the allure of the sirens in Homer's Greek Odyssey, whose bewitching melodies lured unsuspecting sailors to their tragic demise.

Nonetheless, it is important to recognize that by immersing ourselves in the study of relationship culture throughout history, especially in the climate of the present era, we open our minds to a wider terrain, shedding light on previously obscure concepts and structures underlying our relationship ideologies and principles. This process of discovery is a form of enlightenment, broadening our understanding and perspective.

For context, consider Plato's Allegory of the Cave. In this philosophical narrative, prisoners are confined to a cave, only ever perceiving the reality of shadows on the wall, cast by objects behind them. This limited view forms their entire understanding of the world. When one prisoner is released and experiences the world outside the cave, he is initially overwhelmed but gradually comes to recognize a much richer and more complex reality than he ever knew existed.

Similarly, as we explore the historical progression of relationship culture, we are resemblant to Plato's freed individuals. Stepping out of the confines of our prior understanding—or misunderstanding, we encounter a more nuanced and comprehensive view of how relationships have evolved over time. Like Plato's characters, who become enlightened upon exposure to previously unknown realities, we too gain enlightenment as we delve into the depths of relationship history, uncovering layers of social and cultural dynamics that have shaped the way we connect and relate in the present day.

With that said, let's dig deeper and streamline our millennium-long journey into a centauric perspective, starting at the beginning of the 20th century. We will examine each era, leading us to our current position on the relationship continuum. This analysis will provide us with a better understanding of the social, cultural, and technological shifts that have occurred and how they've influenced the way we relate to one another in real time.

While these generational insights may not capture every individual within the group, they strive to offer a comprehensive overview of the majority's experiences and perspectives. It's been suggested that there could be eight generations coexisting today, I'll be focusing on the four most recognized, which I've listed below.

The 8 generations are generally:

- The Lost Generation: born between 1883-1900

- The Greatest Generation: (born between 1901 & 1927

- The Silent Generation: born between 1928 & 1945

- **Baby Boomers:** born between 1946 & 1964

- **Generation X:** born between 1965 & 1980

- **Millennials a.k.a. Gen Y** born between 1981 & 1995

- **Generation Zeta:** born between 1996 & 2010

- Generation Alpha: born between 2011 & 2025

Again, I'll only focus on the current top four being Boomers, Gen X, Gen Y, and Gen Z.

Baby Boomer

An old African proverb says, "When an elder dies, a library burns to the ground." In writing this book, I've discovered that individuals born around the 1900s are scarce, yet occasionally, we come across someone who was. Often, they may not have documentation to prove their age, but there is typically compelling evidence supporting their claim.

Interestingly, I recently came across a social media post showcasing a large family of siblings from South Georgia, known as the Relaford siblings, who were all in their 90s, with one who has recently celebrated their 100th birthday. They all glowed with vitality, and I couldn't help but think of how the elder generations are the last of a much simpler time.

Essentially, the first three generations of the 20th century were predominantly marked by war, economic depression, racial inequalities and various hardships. The mid to late 19th century bore witness to the first industrial revolution, ushering in significant technological advancements in manufacturing and production. These innovations facilitated the expansion of telegraph networks and railroads, speeding up the transportation of goods across the country. Moreover, the improvements in manufacturing and production technology allowed for the installation of telegraph networks, once restricted to larger cities.

These developments were akin to the arrival of the internet, revolutionizing communication and paving the way for modern dating conveniences. Much like texting today, the telegraph network empowered individuals to rapidly send messages across great distances, a significant leap in connectivity for the common person. Take a moment to consider how the absence of texting would alter the development of your relationships today. How would this change your approach to dating and maintaining connections? Without telegraphs or text how do you imagine the human species would propagate their relationships and soul bonds today.

The transformations of those times further promoted the urbanization of smaller towns, transforming them into thriving cities and granting rural residents the opportunity to travel and work, leading to improved lifestyles. Telegraphs served as precursors to telephones, which, in turn, paved the way for cell phones, ultimately laying the groundwork for the internet, and the subsequent progression to A.R., V.R., and Neural Link technology. In essence, a technological boom leading to a relationship boom has the potential to alter the trajectory of the entire species, potentially paving the way for an alternate future, much how twin elementals disrupt the living timelines of their mirrored counterparts.

The second wave of industrialization unfolded from the late 19th to early 20th centuries, marked by rapid advancements in the steel, electric, and automobile industries. One can't help but wonder if the artistic freedom of expression spawned by the Romantic Era had anything to do with the innovations taking place. It appeared that the stage was set for substantial economic growth and cultural progress. However, the advent of the first two world wars, along with the Great Depression, intervened, halting or neutralizing this promising future.

As you might anticipate, these events had a significant impact on how men and women related to each other, loved, and married. Considering what you've learned thus far, contemplate how these prevailing circumstances may have shaped views on love, dating, courtship, and marriage during that era."

Nonetheless, as things gradually stabilized towards the end of the Silent Generation's era, we witnessed a remarkable surge in population growth in the West. This increase meant more connections and consequently, more births. Here enters the Baby Boomer era. Between 1946 and 1964, around 76 million babies were born in the United States, almost as if the nation were making up for lost time and opportunities following the return of over 10 million soldiers from World War II. In a manner akin to prisoners released after a long sentence, these soldiers had a profound craving for love and a peaceful, less traumatic lifestyle, which in turn fostered a desire for family living and the pursuit of the American Dream.

That term gained prominence during the Roaring Twenties, an era characterized by economic growth and significant cultural transformation in the United States. It rose to greater recognition through literature, including F. Scott Fitzgerald's novel "The Great Gatsby," which portrayed the pursuit of wealth and success as an integral aspect of the American Dream.

Emerging on the heels of this prosperity, the baby boomer generation claimed the title of the largest generation in U.S. history, constituting approximately 40% of the population until, eventually, they yielded the throne to the Millennials. However, with their substantial numbers, baby boomers wielded a profound influence on the future culture of love and relationships. To this day, many modern relationships still carry forward the ideologies that emerged during their era. If you thoroughly examine what you believe the principles of a relationship should be, you'll likely find that, for you and many of your peers, the ideologies shaping your views on courtship, relationships, and marriage are predominantly rooted in the beliefs that emerged during the baby boomer era.

Furthermore, one may also consider the factors that contributed to the endurance of relationships within the Baby Boomer generation. Was it propelled by passion, love, the need for survival, propaganda, or perhaps a blend of all these elements, enhanced by a touch of romanticism or Egyptian-style seduction? Reflecting on the seven philosophical concepts of love that permeated ancient Greek culture, one may ponder the core motivations for love within those relationships. I would venture to say that one of the primary influences stems from the fact that the Baby Boomer generation, or "Gen B for Boomers," came of age during the pinnacle of American prosperity, granting them a level of health, security, and comforts previously unmatched. Couple this with a genetic propensity for forming enduring family structures stemming as far back as our days as primates and you've got the recipe for a boom in baby making.

In the Baby Boomer era, people relished a wide range of recreational activities and dating adventures. This entailed attending dances and parties, visiting drive-in theaters, frequenting diners and soda fountains, and partaking in traditional dating customs such as going out on dates and engaging in heartfelt conversations before making out in the backseat of a 57 Chevy at lookout point. Love letters and phone calls served as commonplace forms of communication, particularly for nurturing long-distance relationships. Joining social clubs, community church's and organizations presented opportunities to encounter new individuals and foster romantic bonds. These pursuits and traditions left an indelible mark on the social lives of baby boomers and influenced their experiences of fun and dating during that period.

Television shows like "I Love Lucy" and "Father Knows Best" established the tone of the time, and the introduction of microwaved dinners streamlined meal preparation, making life more convenient. It also provided a compelling excuse to put the children to bed early, possibly with the intention of adding to the family. This was the prevailing social and cultural climate of the era, laying the foundation for the concepts that molded the romantic landscape that would follow.

It's worth mentioning that the G.I. Bill, which extended various benefits to returning veterans following World War II, provided a significant boost, offering some extra cushioning to the socioeconomic status of specific segments within the Baby Boomer generation to prosper and accumulate wealth. Imagine if the veterans of World War I had also had access to a GI Bill. In this alternate scenario, it's conceivable that the United States might have avoided the Great Depression altogether, potentially leading to a different trajectory in the development of romantic relationships among Americans. Perhaps that generation would not have been silent and the baby making boom would have commenced a little earlier.

"Well, you live and learn. What can you do?" The lesson was learned, and those Bills arrived just in time for the second depression and the military veterans, of a certain class, of the Baby Boomer generation.

Contemplating the points raised above, regarding alternate timelines, one might also ponder the potential repercussions on specific disenfranchised classes within the Baby Boomer generation of America and the subsequent generations that followed. What would the timeline look like if these disenfranchised and excluded segments of the population had received the same government benefits and support, devoid of legal fraud, following their loyal military service. How might such support have shaped the outlooks and behaviors of these individuals concerning the future of love, stability, and family structures, in contrast to the evident impact on their current timeline, which subsequently affects the whole of society? Those responsible for much of the covert appropriation at the time often overlook how their nefarious actions will eventually affect their own interests or well-being.

The course of the country's history could have taken a drastically different trajectory if those disenfranchised, tax-paying citizens had received the same legal benefits as their peers, which may have facilitated greater progress in their families, personal relationships, and overall financial well-being. This is just one illustration of how nefarious disruptions to society or a particular social class can shape an entire generations capacity for social interactions including how they relate romantically and build families with their soulmates.

It's no mystery that the cultural legacy of the Baby Boomer generation has exerted a profound and enduring influence on American culture. This generation has made indelible contributions, spanning civil rights, politics, women's liberation, music, and fashion. When it comes to love and relationships, the Baby Boomers have left an indelible mark.

Many notable figures emerged from this generation, making outstanding contributions in the realm of arts. Icons like John Lennon (the founder of the Beatles), the brilliant Jimi Hendrix, Jerry Garcia of the Grateful Dead, and reggae legend Bob Marley exemplify the diversity and impact of those born during this period. As the Baby Boomers reached maturity in the 1960s and 1970s, they boldly challenged numerous long-standing societal norms and traditional values that had persisted for generations, even in the face of institutionalized discrimination, corporate-backed bias, and municipality-supported prejudice.

The forward-thinking Baby Boomers who paved the way into the future exhibited a greater openness to exploring various forms of relationships. They were also enthusiastic about dismantling barriers rooted in race and ethnicity. This generation would then pass the baton to Generation X, who proved even more receptive to change and more willing to challenge conventional values. Undoubtedly, the influence of the Baby Boomer generation has left an indelible mark on how we love and connect with others in America today, extending its reach even to the most recent generations entering the world. In the ongoing narrative of cultural evolution, the Baby Boomer generation stands as a testament to the power of collective action and progressive ideals, shaping not just their own era but continuing to influence the fabric of society for generations to come.

Generation X

I could start from a thousand different entry points, but I choose to dive headfirst into the heart of the storm. Did you know that during the 60s and 70s, right after the baby boom and the surge in family formation, divorce rates skyrocketed? Enter the latchkey kids—also known as Generation X.

Stranger things were indeed on the rise, and I'm not referring to the likes of Michael Jackson's "Thriller," but even stranger phenomena. Not quite the realm of the Upside Down or Demogorgons, but undeniably reminiscent of "Back to the Future," Skeletor, and the "Goonies." I'd like to believe this strangeness is a good thing, considering this generation gave birth to the author of the book you're currently immersing yourself in.

If rock and roll was the defining sound of the Baby Boomer generation, hip-hop and heavy metal would eventually emerge as the equivalent for Generation X. From The Sugar Hill Gang, The Beastie Boys, Rakim, Metallica and Guns & Roses through to Nirvana, Smashing Pumpkins, Eminem and the Wu-Tang Clan, Gen X is, was, and always will be, a special breed.

According to a Stanford University study, the youth of Generation X, appeared more cynical, disillusioned, and disenchanted than previous—somewhat akin to an 80s hip-hop song—influenced by the global culture of the time of course. I would advise you not to push a Gen Xer because they're most likely close to the edge and certainly trying not to lose their head – Aha —Ha-Haa... [Apologies, moving forward]

Though this latchkey generation, who practically raised themselves (possibly due to the rise in single working moms by way of inclusion movements), was considered the lazy slacker generation who lacked discipline, they did eventually get it together. Life has a funny way of setting you on the right path—provided you survive your twenties without falling victim to unfortunate social traps like drugs, fatal STDs, or prison—or general Reaganomics culture.

Perhaps this latchkey mentality fostered a profound sense of independence within this generation. While their technology might seem rudimentary compared to what today's youth enjoy, it was Generation X that pioneered the first home computers, internet connections, video games, cellular phones, and even Walkmans—all precursors to iPods and other mobile music devices. Of course, these elements would eventually be consolidated and integrated into your current smartphones, yet, they are all undoubtedly the innovative spawns of Generation X.

Before the era of constant digital content, Generation X pioneered the trend of binge-watching television through reruns, syndication, and marathon viewing. Iconic shows from MTV's lineup and beloved TV families became a significant part of our lives. Series ranging from "Family Ties, Punky Brewster, Facts of Life and "The Cosby Show" to "Different Strokes" Family Matters and "The Fresh Prince of Bel-Air" influenced our perceptions of family dynamics, as well as love, attraction, and dating. These shows played a crucial role in shaping our understanding of family structures and social interactions, making them an important aspect to consider in a detailed analysis of the factors that have molded our current collective reality, especially in terms of social interaction programming.

The idea that television families shaped society's view of romantic relationships differs significantly from the influence of ancient Egyptian, Greco-Roman, religious, or Romantic-era ideals on human relationships. Along with television, numerous studies have examined the sociological impact of music. For instance, R&B and hair band rock greatly influenced the youth's hormones at the time, potentially leading to the birth of many of today's adults.

Consider the impact of Sir Mix-a-Lot's "I like big butts and I cannot lie" – the famous "Baby Got Back" song. The catchy and influential nature of such songs likely played a role in sparking many short-lived romances, which, in turn, contributed to the rise of latchkey kids in our society. It's interesting to think that you might be dating someone now who was born as a result of these phenomena. Between television, radio, and cultural traditions, these generations were heavily influenced, which shaped their perceptions and responses to human relationships, creating a ripple effect and a lasting impact on future generations.

From the artistic movement of romanticism to the creation of Hollywood films and television programming, coupled with the widespread availability of lyrical and musical content, humanity has never before experienced such a rapid and significant disruption in how we experience and process the culture of love and interpersonal relationships. It's unfortunate that some individuals may experience a soul connection, but their social programming can lead to misjudgment and miscalculations in decision-making, causing them to miss out on what could potentially be a transformative experience or even the love of their life.

Consider the depictions of Disney princesses, opulent weddings in grand ballrooms, and Valentine's Day celebrations replete with roses, chocolates, and diamond rings, along with other acts portrayed as chivalrous gestures. These have significantly influenced how we approach courtship and relationships and what is considered valuable material exchanges for establishing deep soul connections.

It's astonishing to hear stories of couples divorcing over a lack of Valentine's Day gifts - a concept rooted in fiction with echoes of real-life occurrences. However, these representations merely scratch the surface. The ascendancy of advanced technologies, driven by corporations with substantial marketing budgets and agendas, has unquestionably molded our attitudes toward human mating and coupling.

Technology is essentially transdimensional as it can transcend the boundaries of time and space, simultaneously disseminating sound and images to influence thought and emotion across the entire globe in an instant. This is an immensely potent tool for shaping the human mind and the population concerning courtship, dating, falling in love, and starting families. It's important to consider that your significant other might be deeply influenced by someone elses marketing strategies, prejudices, objectives, opinions and agendas, which can affect how you and others relate to one another.

In earlier generations, young people primarily sought entertainment in each other during dates. Generation X, on the other hand, sought supplementary alternatives to complement the traditional romantic pastimes. While it did not differ significantly from the preceding boomer generation with their record players, diners, and cinemas, it laid the foundation for what the subsequent generations would experience.

Furthermore, Generation X, often labeled as the 'lost generation,' by there predecessors is frequently perceived as cynical and, as previously mentioned, somewhat jaded. This viewpoint can be understood by considering iconic artists from that era, like Kurt Cobain of Nirvana or Tupac Shakur. Their perspectives are reflective of the significant events experienced during their time on Earth.

Gen X'ers have observed the world go through a few major wars, witnessed the effects of communism, and the emergence of Silicon Valley. They've been present for assassinations and both natural and less natural disasters, including the devastation of premeditated drug epidemics on entire communities. They've even played a role in influencing the rest of the world unlike any other time or generation in history.

Hip-hop and rock music alone have reshaped humanity and how individuals perceive themselves and those they desire. And let's not forget boy bands and blockbuster movies; the list goes on. They've witnessed it all, and it's apparent. What's most intriguing is that they're still here, sometimes even at the forefront of contemporary trends.

Despite the negativity often attributed to this generation, they are, in fact, quite affectionate. However, they tend to approach relationships with a more pragmatic perspective than their forerunners. Love is a complex matter, and Generation X is well aware of this fact. They've witnessed their parents' marriages dissolve and experienced the failures of their own relationships.

They've witnessed the heartbreak and agony that accompany love gone awry. Consequently, they approach love and social interaction with a measure of caution and skepticism. They understand that love isn't always a smooth journey, but they also recognize its inherent value. Interestingly, in many instances, they are even more inclined to divorce than their parents, yet this isn't necessarily a negative phenomenon. It signifies their willingness to extricate themselves from unfavorable circumstances and their determination to persevere until they discover what they seek.

Despite being the generation most prone to wearing their hearts on their sleeves and sometimes diving headfirst into situations fraught with redflags, Gen Xers have demonstrated loyalty and commitment. Their focus in relationships often leans more towards quality than quantity.

Even though Generation X may not be the most outwardly romantic group, they have a notable capacity for forming lasting connections. In a world that's increasingly turbulent and unpredictable, this skill is perhaps more important than ever. Generation X has reshaped what it means to be in a relationship. While they don't always get it right, they are actively seeking new and better ways to experience social and romantic connection, perhaps one of the last generations to cultivate interpersonal relationships in some of the traditional ways of times bygone.

This section offers insight into the unique contributions Generation X has made to the relational landscape, setting them apart from the behaviors and cultures of their predecessors. Next, we will delve into the generation that Generation X holds in the highest regard, their offspring - the Millennial Generation.

Millennials

Millennials in love! What a fascinating sight. If you're not sure what that entails, no worries; I'm here to provide insights. My goal is to present various perspectives by shedding light on facts, truths, and widely accepted beliefs about millennial behaviors gathered from multiple sources. With over 75 million strong, this is the largest generation, surpassing the baby Boomer generation. Millennials in America constitute the most diverse and vibrant group one could imagine.

Drawing from my observations and research, Millennials (also known as Gen Y) exhibit a distinct approach to interpersonal relationships, love, and social interactions with other souls, shaped by their upbringing and worldviews. Firstly, they have come of age in a world where technology is ever-present, making them more comfortable with online communication and connections, sometimes even surpassing face-to-face interactions.

Additionally, they frequently relocate, providing them with a broader global outlook on relationships. Unlike previous generations, Millennials are more inclined to believe in soulmates and genuine love, potentially influenced by their upbringing at the core of the media world. Before we delve into the perspectives on love and relationships as they relate to the millennial generation, let's briefly explore the overall psychological composition of the Milli-Gen, a.k.a. Gen Y.

It's no secret that millennials have gotten a bad rap regarding their work ethic. They're often accused of being entitled and expecting things to be handed to them without putting in the effort. You often hear the stories from the grandparents of how they had to walk 100 miles to get to school and how having a school bus is a privilege.

According to the elder generation, going to college and the mall or eating out everyday versus cooking is all a privilege. You have it easy, they say, and still don't appreciate it. Some millennials may indeed have been raised with an entitlement mindset, but that doesn't mean that the entire generation is lazy or unwilling to work hard. In fact, many millennials are highly driven, motivated and willing to put in the extra work to get ahead.

Over the past two decades, millennials have taken the reins of global culture and generated the largest number of millionaires worldwide. Their innovation and assertion have spurred the rise of the on-demand lifestyle we all relish today. Concepts like Uber or Netflix would have been alien to the baby boomers and Gen X'ers. Summoning a ride to someone's apartment whom you just connected with on social media, to Netflix & chill, while snapping selfies labeled "#BaeLife" might be something your grandfather would deem idle, eccentric, imprudent, or even sinful.

Although your Gen X father might have given it a fleeting look, he likely preferred the spontaneity and vibrancy of heading to the mall, skating rink, club or even south Beach's Spring Bling and Atlanta's Freaknik for an unpredictable and thrilling experience—Though in his older years, he might opt for the simplicity of swiping left to find a date, as it undoubtedly requires less energy.

Contrary to popular belief, among older generations, The Millennial Lifestyle revolves around creating an impact. In their professional lives, millennials are resolute in seeking solutions that are aligned with the current era while also acknowledging and respecting the past. They reject the notion that tradition is the only way things should be done and are committed to effecting change at every level.

Socially, millennials are more engaged and connected than any generation before them. They harness technology to stay connected with friends and family across the globe. Politically, millennials are well-informed and actively engage in the "democratic" process. They are dedicated citizens who deeply care about the world and strive to enhance it.

As the world grows more intricate, employers now seek employees possessing more than just technical skills. They yearn for individuals capable of critical thinking, problem-solving, and effective communication. Unfortunately, many colleges tend to emphasize the development of technical skills as the primary goal for graduates to secure meaningful employment. The economic mindset is closely aligned with the societal mindset, which in turn is in sync with the interpersonal mindset. This profoundly influences interpersonal relationships—more than anything else—and these dynamics are the lifeblood of soulmate expressions. It is all interconnected.

Consequently, a significant number of millennials find themselves lacking the vital soft skills—often synonymous with people skills—crucial for success in the modern workplace or in thriving social environments. This could be a contributing factor to why many individuals are dissatisfied with their jobs and even personal relationships at times. The lack of self control and solution oriented problem solving skills in social situations can make it hard for individuals to get along with others which can also affect the cultivation of soft skills. A glimpse into almost any prank reel in the social media space will reveal the lack of self control, problem solving skills and social adaptation.

Economically, Millennials exhibit a strong entrepreneurial spirit and resourcefulness. They continuously seek innovative ways to both save and generate income. While the search and seizure of coin for some might differ from the actual outcome, they navigate it adeptly. The Millennial lifestyle, on the whole, revolves around active engagement, staying informed, and a resolute commitment to contributing value to the world in which ever way best serves them.

In 2017, the Institute for Public Policy Research released a report titled "15 Economic Facts About Millennials." This report highlighted the millennial generation's remarkable achievement with one of the highest rates of higher education completion. The report unveiled that over 47% of millennials aged 25 to 34 hold a post-secondary degree.

~ I imagine the boomers might have achieved similar numbers if they hadn't had to walk a hundred miles to school every morning or toil in the cornfields after school - but I digress.

While this statistic highlights millennials' remarkable educational achievements compared to previous generations, employers often express concerns about the shortage of soft skills, such as interpersonal communication and teamwork. A significant number of millennials enter the workforce without the necessary readiness to navigate office dynamics or manage complex customer service interactions.

I mention these facts to emphasize their overall personality and social intelligence. The data on millennial work ethics is a mirror to their general behavior, offering clues about their social abilities in areas like dating and romance. Furthermore, this information sheds light on how they interact in long-term relationships, including with life partners and soulmates.

Recognizing the importance of soft skills in relation to social relationships, including dating, prompts questions about millennials' ability to establish effective romantic connections. Do millennials possess the essential soft skills required for nurturing enduring romantic relationships? The lack of soft skills can negatively impact social relationships.

Individuals facing challenges in communication, empathy, and emotional intelligence may encounter difficulties in connecting with others and cultivating strong interpersonal relationships. These difficulties may include issues with initiating and maintaining conversations, interpreting social cues, and understanding others' perspectives, ultimately leading to misunderstandings and conflicts. This can make forging social, professional, platonic, and romantic connections more challenging, **ultimately contributing to a world filled with introverts and socially awkward individuals.**

Various reports indicate that millennials experience higher levels of anxiety and depression than their predecessors, a phenomenon partly attributed to the accelerated pace of life driven by technology. They find themselves perpetually inundated with news concerning imminent environmental crises, income disparities, and a job market growing progressively uncertain. Amplify this with the ceaseless pressure to attain perfection—courtesy of the ever-present influence of social media—and it becomes unsurprising that many millennials encounter challenges in safeguarding their mental well-being.

One study found that 31% of millennials say their partner's mental health problems have negatively impacted their relationship. This study, conducted by researchers at the University of Missouri, concluded that millennials who registered elevated levels of anxiety and depression exhibited a heightened probability of experiencing dissatisfaction within their relationships. Self-projection is likely the culprit.

It's evident that mental health challenges can have far-reaching consequences on your interpersonal relationships, occasionally triggering dysfunction in other aspects of your life. This prompts the question of what these observations signify for romantic relationships involving millennials. To shed light on this matter, if you're in a relationship with a millennial, it becomes pivotal to foster understanding of their potential struggles with anxiety and depression. It's worth noting that exercising patience, compassion, and providing support can wield a profound and positive impact. It's also important to remember that these statistics merely reflect a segment of this diverse demographic.

There's no doubt about it: Millennials are profoundly reshaping our norms and traditions. From their consumption of media to their approach to life and work, this generation is unmistakably making its indelible mark on the world. And when it comes to family life, Millennials are once again challenging the established norms.

Prior research has unveiled that Millennials are opting to delay marriage and parenthood more than their predecessors did. This means no more 18-year-old weddings the day after graduation. A fresh analysis of government data by the Pew Research Center underscores that Millennials are embarking on a different journey when it comes to shaping—or perhaps not shaping—families in contrast to the generations that came before.

In their postponement of marriage, western Millennials exhibit a higher likelihood of having children without the bonds of wedlock while cohabiting with their partners. The data also illuminates that a significant portion of Millennials is more inclined to reside with their parents rather than owning their own residences. These insights suggest that Millennials tread a path in family formation that starkly deviates from those traversed by all prior generations, including the ones rooted in antiquity.

While some may misconstrue this as an indication of Millennial indolence or irresponsibility, it fundamentally mirrors the shifting social norms and the mounting economic obstacles they face. Within an era marked by astronomical housing costs and ballooning student debts, it's hardly surprising that young adults are reassessing the conventional ideals of family life.

Tales have been told about how the inhabitants of other nations cast shame on Western practices—while simultaneously rushing to integrate with the West as quickly as possible. With this in mind, it's wise to be cautious, as many might find themselves adopting these same behaviors sooner than expected due to their cultural trajectories.

Furthermore, armed with the above data, it becomes evident that many millennials are grappling to secure their place in today's economy. The weight of student debt and the scarcity of promising job opportunities have a knack for complicating aspirations of marriage and family initiation. Yet, according to marriage and family therapist Jennifer Behnke, this merely forms a fragment of the narrative. A considerable number of millennials uphold exceedingly stringent criteria for what a marriage ought to encompass, rendering any notion of settling, entirely inconceivable. "They're not in pursuit of a carbon copy of their parents' marriages," she noted.

Behnke, whose primary practice revolves around millennials in Juno Beach, Florida, emphasizes that numerous clients in her care have accumulated a wealth of unfavorable experiences within their relationships. Whether through witnessing their parents and grandparents' divorces or having endured the wounds inflicted by former partners, they've grown wary of embracing anything short of the perfect relationship. While this may initially seem like a commendable stance, Behnke sounds a cautionary note, highlighting the potential perils of such an approach. "The crux of the issue is that perfection remains an elusive ideal," she emphasized. "No relationship is impervious to imperfection."

Furthermore, Behnke imparts valuable advice to Millennials, stating, "If you're grappling with discouragement regarding your prospects of encountering genuine love, consider adopting greater flexibility in your criteria for a partner. After all, marriage encompasses more than merely discovering an impeccable individual." She aptly remarks, "It entails encountering someone imperfect and embarking on the journey of loving them, flaws and all."

In a world where social media reigns supreme and it often appears that everyone is engrossed in their digital devices, it comes as no surprise that millennials approach dating differently compared to their parents. With a simple swipe of a finger, one can instantly access potential companions from across the globe.

While this might appear advantageous, it has also instilled impatience in us and rendered us less inclined to commit.

In the past, individuals would embark on initial dates, and unless an absolute lack of connection became evident, they typically continued seeing each other. However, in the present era, where a myriad of alternatives is readily available at our fingertips, the inclination to search for someone better becomes a constant temptation. This profusion of choices has made us more discerning and less likely to grant people a chance. So, while dating may be more accessible than ever, it has created some unique challenges for millennials.

In the digital age, little love tests project from smartphone screens in the palms of your hand while proof of people's affection through social media posts, relationship statuses, and "bae" selfies are constantly required. Couples always run the risk of disagreements stemming from oversharing or under-sharing on social media. It's undeniable that dating and relationships have undergone a profound transformation in the 20th and 21st centuries, particularly in the post-pandemic era. Although every generation has its issues, the truth is, certain dating issues are unique to millennials.

Here are the three most common ones:

1. Social Media and Smartphone Addiction: It's no secret that millennials can become inseparable from their phones. However, in the realm of dating, this addiction can pose a significant challenge. Continuously checking your phone or social media notifications can hinder your ability to give your date your undivided attention, potentially making you appear disinterested or distracted. To leave a positive impression, stow your phone away and focus entirely on your date.

2. Commitment Fears: Millennials, thanks to Tinder and other dating apps, have grown accustomed to casual dating and hookups. Consequently, they often struggle with committing to a single person. A popular escape route these days is the polysexual lifestyle, sometimes mistaken for polyamory.

3. Over-Reliance on Technology: Even when the potential partner is promising, millennials often lean too heavily on technology.

In this digital age, it's effortless to become absorbed in your phone and lose touch with the real world. This technological dependency can pose a significant issue when it comes to dating. Millennials have become so accustomed to text and social media communication that they frequently struggle with face-to-face interactions and essential interpersonal skills. While they may not be true digital natives like other generations, they have undoubtedly settled into the digital realm.

Here's a universal piece of advice from Gen X: To create a favorable impression, tuck away your phone and devote your full attention to the person before you. Face-to-face communication for couples tends to foster stronger relationships. Often, couples invest an excessive amount of time in texting, resulting in their discomfort with in-person conversations and an inability to engage in constructive, respectful disagreements, particularly when addressing sensitive matters. Such circumstances frequently lead to emotional distress for couples. Maintaining open communication to address and resolve issues is key to nurturing healthy, joyful relationships.

With millennials leading the charge, we now live in a world where we have more choices than ever before regarding our love lives. The multitude of options and avenues for connection understandably places significant stress on committed relationships, as they endeavor to fulfill our ideals and dreams of love. We can opt for online dating, engage in casual encounters, or commit to monogamous partnerships.

Now-a-days, You can also explore polyamory, celibacy and even pan sexuality without judgment, depending on your preferences in today's romantic climate. There are many different paths to take, and it can be overwhelming when trying to figure out which one is right. Yet, a constant belief persists: the enduring allure of the fairytale notion of true love. People yearn to discover their soulmates and aspire to have all their dreams and desires fulfilled upon finding them. Regrettably, this idealistic pursuit frequently culminates in disillusionment.

Many people hold excessively high expectations that are simply unattainable, a sentiment shared by Millennials and the various generations they date. These lofty standards often lead to the selection of incompatible partners and an undue burden on relationships, resulting in their eventual strain. It's crucial to bear in mind that love can be both intricate and chaotic, particularly in today's society. There is no single prescribed method for discovering it, and it seldom adheres to our preconceived notions.

While the internet has introduced new challenges in the realm of modern love, it has also made it easier to access a plethora of potential partners. An intriguing aspect of this abundance of options is the difficulty in maintaining enduring trust among romantic partners, given the constant temptation of infidelity. In an era where exquisitely filtered photos constantly saturate the subconscious with fantasy-driven micro-doses of dopamine, the adage "out of sight, out of mind" holds little relevance.

As millennials grow older, they are taking a different approach to love and relationships than previous generations. They are inclined to perceive love as an integral aspect of their lives, yet they are also more receptive to the notion that love may not be everlasting, and relationships often fall short of the idealized expectations. They recognize that "happily ever after" is not a guaranteed outcome, and love doesn't invariably overcome all obstacles. This shift in attitude can be ascribed to various aforementioned factors, including the heightened emphasis on career and lifestyle choices among millennials.

Furthermore, as previously mentioned, millennials have come of age in an era of heightened social media usage. Consequently, the heightened awareness of diverse relationship options renders them less inclined to settle for anything less than their genuine desires, even if that entails only finding value in contrived personas reminiscent of anime characters or pop singer imitations. Dare I remind you, some of these egoic characters call themselves literal Barbie dolls and sometimes even Bad Bee's—which is somehow a good thing.

Ultimately, millennials are primarily concerned with ensuring their well-being and are prepared to take any necessary steps to achieve it. One certainty remains: millennials are redefining the dynamics of 21st-century relationships and imparting to the world the intricate subtleties of entanglements and situationships like never before.

Generation Z

Should you ever find yourself attempting to take a quick nap at the airport during a flight delay, and you overhear a group of young adults settling into your section, using phrases like "that drip was litty," with another emphatically shouting "Facts," or perhaps someone remarking, "Fam took an L with those Jay's, no cap, that flex was 'hella' weird!" chances are, your section has been infiltrated by a lively group of Gen Z individuals. You might even catch the term "Ops" being thrown around, as anyone who's "not a part of the gang" is considered the OP-position. And when I say "gang," I'm referring to groups such as the chess club, football team, fashion crew, or Dungeons and Dragons enthusiasts.

If you thought millennials were a force to be reckoned with, wait until you experience the impact of the Gen Z population. Millennials played a pivotal role in the digital revolution, sowing the seeds initially planted by Gen X. If Gen X laid the foundation and millennials cultivated it, Gen Z is unquestionably the generation that's reaping the harvest. This post-millennial cohort, often humorously referred to as Gen Z—for "Zombie" by some—represents the newest wave of American adults.

The Pew Research Center classifies anyone born after 1996 as part of Gen Z, and they already constitute a significant portion of the U.S. population. Considering that Gen Z are the young adults currently at the forefront of shaping culture, it may be beneficial to extend our focus on this generation a bit longer.

When delving into the psychology of Gen Z, particularly in terms of social connections, it's crucial to understand that each new generation not only inherits the traits of its predecessors and compound them, but it also adds its own unique twist – think of it as a 'mutated' version. For instance, if Gen X were the original latchkey kids, then Millennials are like an upgraded, 2.0 version of that. Similarly, while Millennials struggle with anxiety, Gen Z has become the very symbol of this issue. This means we need to layer our understanding of each past generation to fully grasp the next. With this in mind, we'll continue to delve deeper into our analysis, building upon what we've learned from those who came before.

Regarding the temporal and temperamental nuances of Gen Zeta, consider the following. The year 1995 marked the commercialization and widespread introduction of the internet to the general population. Consequently, the first wave of Gen Z individuals began incarnating into earthly existence the following year. They truly cannot fathom a world devoid of the internet, setting them apart from any preceding generation. They represent the most interconnected, informed, and diverse generation in history. While earlier generations were busy downloading emails on AOL, Gen Z souls were also "downloading" into human avatars, coexisting in the same digital realm—true digital natives indeed! An even more mystifying aspect reveals itself when we consider that seven years after the initial wave of Gen Z members incarnated, Myspace made its entrance into the digital landscape.

Here's why! Around the age of seven, children typically traverse several pivotal developmental stages. These stages fall under the umbrella of middle childhood—according to *Erik Erikson's* psychosocial development model—and is a period marked by substantial growth and change across various aspects of development. This phase is also commonly referred to as "school age," where children typically embark on their first-grade journey. During middle childhood, children typically experience a number of physical, cognitive, social, and emotional changes. Some of the key developmental milestones that children may experience during this time include:

1. *Physical development:* Children in middle childhood continue to grow and gain strength, coordination, and physical skills. They may become more agile, athletic, and coordinated and may also develop greater endurance and physical stamina—as opposed to a newborn.

2. *Cognitive development:* Children in middle childhood continue to develop their ability to think, reason, and solve problems. They may become more proficient at tasks such as reading, writing, and doing math and may also develop greater logical thinking and problem-solving skills.

3. *Social and emotional development:* Children in middle childhood continue to develop their social skills and emotional intelligence. They may become more adept at forming and maintaining friendships and may also begin to understand and express a wider range of emotions.

Among the Seven Stages of Life, middle childhood is closely associated with the Concrete Operational Stage—according to the psychologist *Jean Piaget's* theory of cognitive development. This stage is characterized by the emergence of logical, systematic thinking and the capacity to manipulate and transform mental representations.

If you've wondered, yes, it is generally true that children blend fantasy and reality before the age of seven. This occurs during Dr. Piaget's, " **Preoperational Stage,**"of cognitive development, which spans from approximately 2 to 7 years of age. During this stage, children engage in symbolic play and are often unable to distinguish between fantasy and reality. They might believe in imaginary friends, magical thinking, and fantastical stories as if they are real. Their thinking is also characterized by egocentrism, meaning they have difficulty seeing things from perspectives other than their own.

As they progress into the Concrete Operational Stage (around age 7 and lasts until about eleven or twelve), they begin to develop a clearer distinction between fantasy and reality and gain the ability to think more logically about concrete events. During this period, children develop the ability to think logically and systematically about concrete, observable phenomena. They improve their skills in manipulating and transforming mental representations and can perform operations like classification, ordering, and seriation.

Simultaneously, children in the Concrete Operational Stage often grapple with abstract and hypothetical concepts, encountering challenges in comprehending perspectives other than their own. They may also find it challenging to grasp the concept of conservation, which posits that certain physical properties remain constant despite changes in appearance. All in all, the Concrete Operational Stage represents a critical period of cognitive development, as children start to cultivate more advanced thinking skills and become more proficient in reasoning and problem-solving. When considering that the Concrete Operational Stage was preceded by the Preoperational Stage, and in a world where social media emerged, Generation Zeta and social media are not just contemporaries; I.e., 'twin's', they were raised together, inevitably sharing traits.

This parallel development invites us to ponder the implications, reminiscent of the "Rhesus Monkey and Human Child" study conducted in the 1960s by psychologist Harry Harlow and his colleagues. In this experiment, a rhesus monkey and a human infant were raised together until the study had to be abruptly stopped. The intertwined growth of Generation Zeta and social media raises intriguing questions about their shared influences and future impact on society, much like the insights gained from Harlow's research into attachment and development.

The fact that Gen Z entered egoic consciousness around the same time that Myspace—Facebook's precursor—became prominent in the public's consciousness, holds profound significance. The fact that Generation Zeta's Preoperational Stage coincided with the rise of the internet adds a fascinating dimension, prompting us to explore how their early cognitive development was influenced by the digital age, in contrast to previous generations. They are the true digital natives, growing up in a world characterized by constant change and uncertainty unfolding right before their eyes. This environment has imparted to them a global perspective and an insatiable desire for vanity and instant gratification, especially in the realm of social connections with others.

The silver lining in it all is that they are remarkably entrepreneurial, with a significant number of them enthusiastic about launching their own businesses. Never before in history have a group of 12-year-olds became millionaires through the creation of YouTube videos and then leveraged that capital to become multi millionaires by the age of twenty one,—just ask Mr. Beast. Another noteworthy fact is that Gen Z is the most racially and ethnically diverse generation in history, with 44% of Gen Zeta's in America identifying as something other than white. The increased number of Asian and Hispanic children, alongside foundational black Americans, has played a significant role in this diversity. Additionally, Gen Z stands out as the most educated generation, surpassing even the Millennials.

A recent report from the Pew Research Center reveals that 34% of Gen Zeta's have completed some college, with 15% earning a four-year degree. Despite these advantages, Gen Z faces significant challenges as the first generation to grow up entirely in the post-9/11 world, coming of age during times of economic turmoil and political polarization. Yet, they continue to fearlessly challenge the status quo while maintaining an optimistic outlook.

Those who are handing the baton to this generation play a pivotal role in shaping their attitudes toward lifestyle and relationships. Parenting significantly influences future beliefs, behaviors, and worldviews. Gen Z's parents are primarily from Generation X and older Millennials, and they are raising their children much differently from how Baby Boomers raised theirs. From their perspectives on work and education to managing debt and saving, parenting shapes everything, including the outlook on future relationships and behaviors.

Gen Z's parents are more likely to experience divorce compared to previous generations—if married at all—and many of them juggle multiple jobs. Consequently, they have less time to spend with their children, much like their own parents did. They also tend to rely on technology to entertain and educate their kids. It's not unusual to see a millennial or older Gen Z parent handing a cell phone or tablet to their toddlers for distraction. All these factors are poised to exert a significant influence on the future of Gen Z and how they relate.

Considering all these variables, one might assume that these young individuals don't stand a chance in the ever-changing world. However, when we look at older Gen Z'ers, we observe a trajectory distinct from the generations that preceded them, particularly in terms of education. They are rapidly establishing themselves as the most educated generation yet, and it's not surprising, given that previous generations have persistently stressed the importance of education.

A recent study indicates that 57% of Gen Z's are currently enrolled in college, surpassing the 52% of Millennials in 2003 and the 43% of Gen X'ers in 1987. This upward trend is partly due to Gen Z's lower likelihood of dropping out of high school compared to previous generations. Speaking candidly, if I had to take the equivalent of the B train from the Bronx to get to HS18 in Brooklyn every day in the late '90s, I might have considered dropping out or exploring homeschooling as well.

Fortunately for Gen Z's, they are increasingly inclined to pursue higher education compared to earlier generations, benefiting from online education options and a higher likelihood of living with college-educated parents. Many of them choose to enroll in four-year colleges and universities. It's evident that this generation places a strong emphasis on crafting successful futures for themselves.

Having instant access to tools that can ease the challenges of education provides valuable reinforcement. Additionally, listening to podcasts such as "The Ed Mylett Show," Tom Bilyeu's "Impact Theory," David Shand's "Social Proof," or any content from Eric Thomas or Earn Your Leisure, with your millenial and Gen X parents, fosters an educational and inspirational environment by default.

In the mid-2020s, the majority of Gen Z members fall between middle school age and their mid to late twenties, highlighting the significance of education in their life experience. Notably, a recent study reveals that 78% of Gen Zeta's identify themselves as "lifelong learners." These metrics bode well for educators, as they indicate that Gen Z is receptive to new concepts and open to the investment in their education.

Nonetheless, it also implies that educators must be attuned to the distinctive challenges confronting this generation. For instance, Gen Zeta's frequently exhibit a greater comfort with online learning compared to traditional classrooms, which is not surprising since they are digital natives. They also favor shorter, more focused learning experiences over extended lectures or textbook assignments. Consequently, educators aiming to captivate Gen Z must be flexible and open to experimenting with innovative teaching methods, including modules and similar approaches. This raises an important question: how can one capture their attention long enough to engage them in the soulful art of true love?

To be successful in today's world, wherever you are in the cashflow quadrant, having a solid educational foundation is essential. For these reasons, Gen Z will likely continue to place a high value on scholastic education as we move into the future. Despite their numerous academic achievements, there are high concerns that essential common sense and general perceptiveness may face challenges in the years ahead, particularly in terms of social, emotional, and, most importantly, romantic intelligence.

Regarding education, there is an ongoing argument that public schools have traditionally concentrated on readying students for the work & labor force vs. wealth and independence, while promoting specific values and principles like patriotism, nationalism, and conformity. However, a growing number of schools are now dedicated to establishing a more inclusive, diverse, and fair learning environment that equips students for triumph in an ever-evolving world.

Nevertheless, there are areas where the public education system lags. Essential life skills such as financial literacy, taxes, budgeting, and banking are often overlooked in the curriculum. All very necessary for attaining social achievement and acquiring optimal partnership opportunities. Moreover, crucial social skills necessary for adult success, like effective communication, conflict resolution, and problem-solving, are not always adequately emphasized in the classroom. This oversight can leave young adults without key skills needed for successful adulting.

This has led to the emergence of many new independent platforms like the Ms. Rachel Youtube channel and SunChildrenSeries.com or its companion Youtube channel among many others. They are gaining traction because of their commitment to diversity and fairness in educational resources, particularly in the teaching of essential soft skills required for positive socialization.

What implications does all of this have for Generation Zeta in their perceptions of the world concerning social interactions and forming romantic bonds? Given the emphasis on training, programming, and education compared to hands-on social encounters, is Gen Z at risk of evolving into a generation of adults characterized by linear thinking and excessive analysis versus soulful consciousness and spiritual intuition?

When individuals describe someone as having "linear" thinking, they typically imply that the person tends to think logically, analytically, and sequentially. This is occasionally linked with left-brained thinking, which is commonly perceived as more analytical and detail-oriented. The central question is whether linear and logical thinking could influence an individual's capacity to establish emotional connections, especially in the context of forming romantic relationships.

While linear and logical thinking can sometimes affect a person's ability to emotionally connect in romantic relationships, it's not always the case. Many factors are involved. For instance, individuals who favor logical thinking might sometimes depend too much on reasoning and analysis in romantic situations. This neurotic tendency can lead to overthinking and might even cause anxiety over relatively straightforward decisions.

This approach can pose challenges to their ability to forge emotional connections with potential partners or soulmates, as they might prioritize intellectual compatibility over emotional chemistry which can lead to CCD or chemistry-compatibility deficits. Secondly, individuals with a strong inclination toward logical thinking may encounter difficulties in authentically and genuinely expressing their emotions. This can hinder their capacity to establish emotional bonds with others since emotional openness and vulnerability are pivotal aspects of intimacy.

Another aspect of concern for the future of social and emotional connections among Gen Z and forthcoming generations is the increasing incidence of disruptive neurological conditions, like ADHD and anxiety disorders. These conditions may exert a substantial influence on how individuals interact with one another, encompassing their romantic relationships.

Take autism, for example, a developmental disorder impacting social interaction, communication, and behavior. Individuals with autism, even on the lite end of the spectrum, may encounter challenges in grasping social cues and articulating their emotions, which can complicate their capacity to establish intimate relationships. Likewise, individuals with ADHD may contend with issues of impulsivity and distractibility, resulting in difficulties sustaining focus and attention during interactions and conversations. Anxiety disorders may further affect social functioning, potentially prompting individuals to shun or disengage from social situations all together.

Recent years have witnessed a plethora of studies focusing on autism and ADHD, with researchers making substantial strides in comprehending the consequences of these conditions on children and forthcoming generations. This reflects an increase of over 130%. However, recent CDC data shows an even greater rise in autism spectrum disorder prevalence in the U.S. The latest report reveals that in 2020, one in every 36 children in America was diagnosed with autism, marking an increase of nearly 250%. It's probable that this prevalence has continued to grow since then.

While researchers are still trying to determine the exact causes of this increase, some experts posit that alterations in diagnostic criteria, heightened awareness, and improved screening methods could be contributory factors. It's worth noting that some studies have identified a connection between elevated levels of specific heavy metals, such as lead and mercury. Nonetheless, other studies have reported no "substantial" link between heavy metal exposure and these conditions.

ADHD, on the other hand, is a neurodevelopmental disorder characterized by inattention, hyperactivity, and impulsivity. According to the Centers for Disease Control and Prevention (CDC), the prevalence of ADHD in children aged 2-17 increased from 6.1% in 1997 to 10.2% in 2016. It's important to recognize that both autism and ADHD can bear substantial ramifications on children's future growth and achievements.

Additionally, A study featured in JAMA Pediatrics in 2020 presented a projection that by 2030, the prevalence of autism in the United States might reach levels as significant as 1 in 33 children. Given the remarkable upsurge within a relatively brief span, the future trajectory of this phenomenon remains uncertain.

The question remains: how will this impact future human relationships, whether platonic, transactional, romantic, or otherwise? As previously mentioned, a common trait among many individuals in this generation is a tendency to overthink. This can lead to anxiety, indecisiveness, and other negative outcomes. Contributing factors to this trend include increased access to information, higher expectations for productivity, and a greater focus on Self-criticism.

With many individuals being low on the spectrum and almost undetectable, these conditions can have an impact on how individuals approach romantic relationships, encompassing their aptitude to initiate and sustain intimate bonds with others. To illustrate, individuals with autism may encounter challenges in interpreting and reacting to social cues, thus facing hurdles in the realms of dating and cultivating romantic relationships. Similarly, individuals with ADHD may find it taxing to maintain focus and enthusiasm toward a romantic partner and becoming bored easily, while those grappling with anxiety disorders may contend with sentiments of insecurity and self-doubt in their romantic involvements.

Consider this: Human behavior is often influenced by those around us due to proximity. Even individuals who do not inherently display the aforementioned traits can find themselves affected by them as our lifestyles intersect. This is similar to the principle of sympathetic resonance, where striking a bell or glass causes others to emit the same sound because the vibration from the first object triggers vibration in others with similar natural frequencies.

When groups mirror traits due to proximity, it is often referred to as "social convergence" or "social mirroring." This phenomenon occurs when individuals or groups that are in close contact or share similar environments develop similar behaviors, attitudes, or traits over time. Social convergence reflects how shared experiences and environments can lead to similarities in characteristics and behaviors among people or groups.

In essence, as these traits become more prevalent in the overall culture, it becomes likely that your own social behaviors will start to reflect them, almost involuntarily, influenced by the dominant trends in relationships and social interactions. Ultimately, the way we connect and interact as ensouled humans on a predestined path for soul evolution will be collectively influenced by our shared histories and environments. Who knows? Much like selecting specific training programs, perhaps the very challenges and diversity presented by these environmental conditions are precisely why our souls choose to incarnate into them in the first place.

Considering the intricate interplay of numerous elements, it's beyond doubt that Gen Z embodies a remarkably individualistic and charismatic generation. Their yearning for freedom and adventure is evident, forever seeking novel means of self-expression. Consequently, it comes as no shock that their generation has thrown out the values upheld by earlier generations, instead forging their own love guidelines tailored to the digital era.

Furthermore, Gen Z has departed from conventional societal gender norms within relationships and is shaping new guidelines as love extends its reach to embrace the LGBTQNB+ community. This encourages contemplation about the differences between their generation and Millennials, particularly in the context of discovering and perpetuating soulmate relationships and their role in the preservation of the human species. With over 72 new genders according to medicinenet.com, Gen Z and beyond are certainly blazing their own trails.

Gen Z stands out from Millennials in profound ways, especially in the realm of interpersonal relationships. Their remarkable acceptance of diverse identities and fluid gender roles is a defining trait. Growing up in the digital age grants them access to a wealth of media and information resources, enabling a nuanced understanding of gender and sexuality. What truly sets them apart is their strong individualism, as they hold their autonomy and personal freedom above all else.

Today, a wave of gender fluidity sweeps through society, with Generation Z at its forefront. Six out of ten Gen Z individuals advocate for official forms to expand gender options beyond the binary, and a remarkable 35% personally knows someone who prefers gender-neutral pronouns. These statistics represent a seismic shift from prior generations, marking a significant rise compared to the 25% of Millennials, 16% of Gen X'ers, and a mere 12% among Boomers. Traditional gender roles, rooted in a bygone era when hunting for food was the norm, no longer hold sway. Due to the efforts of political lobbies and well-funded special interest groups, newer generations are now more motivated to embrace tolerance and accommodation.

In numerous cases, the economic landscape has shifted dramatically; women have the potential to earn significantly more than their male counterparts, and men increasingly choose to become stay-at-home dads when they have children. As members of this generation contemplate marriage, nontraditional weddings are on the rise, and some may even forego ceremonies altogether.

It's undeniable that we've come a long way from the days when our ancestors arranged marriages. Wouldn't you agree? Traditional gender roles have undergone constant evolution over the years, with recent decades serving as a clear testament to this transformation. The Z generation, having grown up in a world that embraces nontraditional family structures and relationship dynamics, epitomizes this shift.

One significant outcome of the rejection of traditional gender roles is an intensified emphasis on financial independence. Historically, marriage often entailed a financial transaction, with women assuming the lion's share of domestic responsibilities such as chores and childcare while men served as the primary breadwinners. However, as traditional gender roles recede, couples increasingly view marriage as an equal partnership.

Change in perspective has ignited a fervent emphasis on personal financial independence. Both partners now share the responsibility of contributing to household finances. Consequently, Gen Z prioritizes financial autonomy over traditional goals like homeownership or family building. In their worldview, work and intimacy share equal importance, and they won't compromise one for the other. It's worth noting that modern television shows are increasingly showcasing a trend where career is depicted as more important than family life for this generation.

This generation displays remarkable open-mindedness when it comes to love and relationships. They are enthusiastic about exploring different kinds of connections without being restricted by traditional societal expectations. With the abundance of options available through social media, finding would-be love has become easier than in the past. This generation is always connected, whether they are talking to friends or potential partners, thanks to the constant presence of the internet. While this continuous connectivity has its benefits, such as easier communication and staying in touch with loved ones, it also reveals the negative aspects, including the potential for increased anxiety and depression.

On one hand, anxiety can be triggered by seemingly normal sources, including basic interpersonal interactions. These traits become visible for example in roles like customer service, where individuals, such as the barista at your local coffee house, may struggle with maintaining eye contact or projecting confidence when greeting you, possibly traits inherited from a previous generation where grunge birthed the emo personality and so on to the current presentation of personality. Despite projecting confidence with gender fluid presentations, adorned with vibrant colored hair, piercings, and anime tattoos, some Gen Zeta's may exhibit a hesitancy to engage fully. Conversely, interactions with those outside of their familiar circles might invoke anxiety and social awkwardness.

Adding to the mix of depression and other social challenges, a grave yet often overlooked phenomenon is the scourge of cyberbullying, a matter of profound concern. This issue frequently culminates in tragic outcomes. Recent years have witnessed a surge in suicide cases among young adults victimized by cyberbullying. While the internet serves as a powerful tool for connecting people, it can also be weaponized to inflict pain and humiliation. Heartbreak, neglect, a lack of validation, or downright cruel comments push many young souls into isolation and despair, where they believe that ending their lives is the only option and sole escape route. [SHOULD YOU OR SOMEONE YOU EVER FEEL THIS WAY , TEXT 988 FROM YOUR SMARTPHONE]

Based on the Harris Poll, a staggering 81% of teenagers deem mental health a major concern in the United States. Amid constant news headlines about mass shootings, emerging geopolitical tensions, and evolving virus variants, not to mention the emotional pressures posed by the virtual realm of social media, it's hardly surprising that Gen Z is now widely regarded as the most stress-ridden generation. Remarkably, this is transpiring without the burden of mortgages, juggling multiple college tuitions, grappling with child support, or navigating alimony payments.

In essence, this generation is relentlessly pushing the boundaries of the psychological intricacies of the social interaction and dating landscape, redefining what is possible and socially acceptable. In contrast to every preceding generation, Gen Z exhibits an extraordinary inclination toward pursuing a much different interpersonal connection experience.

Despite often being grouped with Millennials, Generation Z represents a distinct and diverse cohort. Unsurprisingly, much like the Milli-Gen, they also frequently employ technology to seek romantic connections. However, the surprising aspect lies in the manner in which they utilize dating apps. Unlike Millennials, who may have a greater predilection for committed relationships, Gen Z individuals appear to predominantly employ dating apps for casual hookups or brief encounters, particularly within the older segment of the Gen Z population. This trend is likely influenced by their experience and age, similar to the previous two generations when they were around that age, with the difference being increased access and technology.

Call it a hunch, but I would argue that if the music culture of today is any reflection of the hookup behavior of the youngest adult generation, then we may not have far to look for an explanation. During the first draft of this book, Doja Cat, Ariana Grande, Rihanna, Drake and Sexy Red, are some of the most downloaded musicians that currently influence Gen Z culture. All it takes is a simple lyric search to get an idea of the mentality many young people mimic these days.

In addition to pervasive music culture, this behavior might also be attributed to the fact that Gen Z members are less inclined to have secure jobs or established careers at this stage of their lives, making it challenging to embark on serious relationships. Alternatively, they may still be too young to fully comprehend or attach importance to something as intricate as a full-fledged adult relationship.

Certain Gen Z members employ technology to foster entirely digital "situationships." In such instances, the relationship exists exclusively in the online realm and may never culminate in an in-person encounter. It essentially resembles a simulated relationship existing primarily in the digital sphere. While this may initially appear as a recipe for trouble, some digital daters assert feeling more at ease expressing themselves online than they would in face-to-face encounters.

Furthermore, a plethora of new dating apps with a TikTok-like feel has emerged, targeting Gen Z individuals for the reasons mentioned previously. Research indicates that merely "1 in 10" Gen Ze'ers express a desire for committed relationships, while the remaining 9 out of 10 primarily employ dating apps and websites to explore casual romantic connections.

In simpler terms, they may use these apps and sites to flirt with multiple individuals or engage in several relationships without ever intending to meet their matches in person. When face-to-face meetings do occur, it often centers around the aim of casual encounters. However, this pattern is not entirely new concerning young people over the past five decades, yet, when a genuine connection forms, it can override all previous theories.

This form of dating can offer convenience and enjoyment, but it carries its share of risks. For instance, establishing a genuine connection with someone can prove challenging when communication solely transpires online. Furthermore, the absence of physical cues that accompany in-person interactions makes it easy to misinterpret someone's intentions even when on the Facetime or Marco Polo apps.

A study conducted by the research firm Swipe Right For Love revealed that a striking 91% of college students engage with dating apps. The research further highlighted that individuals of all genders primarily employ online dating for "entertainment" purposes over any other motive. While there's no harm in utilizing dating apps for amusement, it's crucial to remain mindful of the perils associated with fabricating fictitious relationships in the digital realm. The potential for undesirable consequences when emotions are at stake is consequential.

Social media has significantly transformed the dynamics of our interpersonal interactions. In yesteryears, friendships thrived on shared interests and face-to-face encounters. Today, with the emergence of the internet and social media, we have the capacity to connect with individuals worldwide who share our transient interests. Nonetheless, this contemporary model of friendship is not without its complications. As we are physically distant from our genuine friends, it becomes effortless to overlook them or to undervalue their presence.

Additionally, we are often only presented with the positive aspects of our friends' lives, leading to feelings of envy or jealousy. Consequently, it comes as no surprise that many individuals might assert that their social media connections aren't equivalent to real friends. While social media has undeniably enhanced our capacity to establish connections, it has concurrently facilitated the distancing of individuals who hold paramount significance in our lives, such as genuine friends and family, alongside our momentary digital acquaintances. Nowhere is cancel-culture more prolific than on social media.

Considering its widespread popularity, it's essential to acknowledge that Tinder has emerged as one of the world's most extensively utilized dating apps, amassing a user base exceeding 57 million and garnering 4.1 million subscribers for its premium services since its inception. Upon its 2012 debut, Tinder was originally crafted to facilitate college students in connecting with new acquaintances on their campuses. Nevertheless, the app promptly resonated with a broader demographic and now serves individuals of varying ages and backgrounds.

Tinder's immense popularity can be attributed, in part, to its user-friendly interface. With just a few clicks, users can effortlessly swipe left or right to indicate their interest in potential matches. However, this convenience is not without its drawbacks, as Tinder has faced censure for transforming dating into a superficial exercise, where users predominantly assess each other based on physical appearances.

One of Tinders drawbacks is the promotion of casual hookups over long-term relationships. For many users, it's more about bolstering self-esteem by accumulating as many matches as possible, almost similar to a computer game. Profiles have morphed into meticulously curated consumer products, and each match is perceived as a validation transaction. The pursuit of likes has grown to such an extent that even a self-assured individual might be lured into becoming an attention-seeking addict, constantly seeking the next like-induced dopamine high.

Given the substantial portion of our communication occurring online, it's unsurprising that an increasing number of relationships originate in the digital realm. However, the internet's anonymity can create a cold and impersonal environment. In contrast to online interactions, many individuals, even among the most recent generations, exhibit a preference for text-based communication or the utilization of apps like "MarcoPolo" over engaging in traditional phone conversations. This preference is a reflection of the contemporary communication landscape. When communication breaks down, we may essentially be heading towards the beginning of the end.

Occasionally, within hookup culture, despite our human nature, we may find ourselves catching genuine feelings for someone. However, accompanying the rise of the non-attachment dynamic prevalent in many of these "internet-tionships" is the phenomenon of ghosting. Ghosting occurs when an individual abruptly terminates all digital communication with another person without offering any explanation. It's akin to a breakup, but the absence of closure frequently intensifies the emotional distress.

In past eras, individuals might have terminated a relationship by relocating or ceasing all communication. Such actions were frequently motivated by societal stigma, apprehension of rejection, or a traditional inclination to distance oneself from painful recollections. Today, ghosting has gained prevalence, facilitated by the ease of digital disconnection. A mere click of the mouse allows us to block a person's number or remove them from our social media accounts.

Though ghosting may appear as an expedient means to terminate a relationship, it can inflict significant emotional distress. In layman's terms, it can hurt quite a bit. The individual subjected to ghosting is deprived of any explanation or closure, left in a state of perplexity regarding their actions and plagued by self-doubt. One moment, you're engaged in a continuous exchange of texts or messages, and the next, the other person vanishes into the digital void. The absence of closure can be profoundly exasperating, provoking questions about one's perceived wrongdoings or even the authenticity of the relationship. The person who ghosts may have valid reasons, yet it's crucial to remember that their actions aren't necessarily a reflection of you or your worth.

It is unfortunate, but with trends as mentioned in the previous paragraphs, the future of society could be on a trajectory towards a hodgepodge of antisociality. In other words, a confused and exceedingly awkward social landscape might be looming, if not already here. Ongoing studies are examining the emerging trends that define this generation. Research has confirmed that Generation Z encounters more challenges related to antisocial behaviors compared to previous generations. In fact, they face nearly double the rates of depression compared to the often-depressed Millennials.

Gen Z is particularly intriguing for researchers because they dedicate a significant portion of their time to sharing their lives, thoughts, and beliefs on social media. Research has confirmed that Generation Z encounters more challenges related to antisocial behaviors compared to previous generations. In fact, they face nearly double the rates of depression compared to the often-depressed Millennials.

Furthermore, they discovered that Generation Z is more inclined, for instance, to view themselves as overweight compared to previous generations at the same age, along with various other insecurities. Researchers postulate that this surge in depression, body image issues, and weight concerns may be attributed to the heightened pressure Gen Z faces to conform to societal norms. Given the significant role of media tech in their lives, the ease of comparing themselves to others often leads to feelings of inadequacy.

The paramount question becomes, how will these challenges influence their choices when seeking their cosmic counterparts and soulmates, ultimately benefiting the species as a whole and the evolution of their own souls? As humanity progresses through the ever-evolving journey of love and evolution, what unique contributions will Generation Z make to the human family as they navigate the intricacies of forming relationships, procreation, and survival as a species? These are the inquiries that increasingly preoccupy the minds of many as we observe contemporary dating trends.

Nevertheless, two decades down the road, a Gen Z reader could possibly pick up this book and come to the realization that, despite the formidable challenges they faced, they emerged as a remarkably resilient and inventive generation, perhaps murmuring to themselves, 'We managed quite well.' And who's to say, they might even chuckle in disbelief at the idiosyncrasies of the newly emerging Generation Alpha, Beta or Delta.

Gen Alpha & Beyond

At this point, we've laid the foundation for understanding the evolution of love in the human species over the past millennia. We've also briefly explored the psychology of peripheral human connections in our personal lives. Transitioning from this broader historical context, we have now delved into the intricacies of 21st-century behavior when it comes to human connections. Whether through genetic manipulation, epigenetic evolution, or purposeful social engineering, we've traversed a fascinating array of generational psychology and relationship models. Looking back, we can glean a vivid vision and an intuitive path toward where we might possibly go from here.

Now, if you're on your way home on an early flight with no layovers but the pair of youngsters sitting behind you are using words like Bussin, Riz, Drip, Sus, ATE and Delulu, then yes, you've guessed it, generation alpha is live and direct and there's nothing you can do about it because you're on a direct flight for the next 4 hours.

Following the Zeta Generation, often referred to as Gen Z (not to be confused with zombies), it appears we've exhausted our alphabet and must circle back to the starting point with Alpha, followed by Beta, Delta, and so forth. Alpha may signify a novel human generation deeply immersed in the realms of relationships. The concept of New Humans or Humans 2.0 doesn't seem far-fetched, especially considering the transhumanist future that our species is actively co-creating, particularly with the advancement of wearables such as neural interfaces, bio-enhancement devices, injectable nano tech meds and AI-assisted companions.

Some notable mentions are the increasingly popular wearables such as smartwatches, fitness trackers, smart glasses, fitness apparel, smart jewelry, head-mounted displays (HMDs), hearables, mRNA technology and e-textiles. These integrative technologies are revolutionizing our interactions and reshaping the world around us, poised to play a crucial role in defining future human relationships and connections. As we approach a world led by the Alpha Generation and beyond, their impact promises to be even more profound and transformative.

From wearables to injectables, Gen A is at the brink of a revolutionary genesis. Virtual Reality is also set to redefine the landscape of the 21st century. V.R. can be likened to "3D internet." Consider that, in the present day, we engage with 2D flat screens and are already entranced by the illusion of cutting-edge technology. Even the rudimentary versions of the V.R. we have today offers a tantalizing glimpse into the future.

Imagine contact lenses that not only immerse you in the vastness of the internet or a gaming environment but also provide an exceptionally clear, high-definition experience that outperforms current virtual reality (VR) technology by a factor of 100. Thanks to advancements in Artificial Intelligence software, avatar and image generators, as well as deepfake technology, it becomes conceivable that your potential partner could appear as a completely artificial companion, intricately tailored to match your psychological profile, perhaps even accompanied by another simulated companion providing digital polyamory.

Predicting the exact contours of the future remains a challenge, but when we examine the current path, it becomes evident that Generation Alpha will introduce a fresh perspective on how Earth's inhabitants experience love. They are poised to revolutionize the playbook while navigating an all-encompassing digital realm, and their relationships will mirror this transformation.

Although it's too early to compile comprehensive relationship data for them today, one can only extrapolate from existing trends. Here's another exercise, not dissimilar to the time machine visualization.

Take the current year you live in and add 50 years to it. Ask yourself how old you will be and what year it might be. Maybe 2075. Maybe 2099 or 2145. Maybe even the year 3000, and you, a newly enhanced cyborg living on Mars, have the task of researching literature from the early twenty-first century. Much like the poetry from ancient Egypt, you might find clues to how humans related to each other in the past. In this vision, whatever the year, after taking a deep breath, ask yourself, "what does love look like in this time?"

No matter how you envision love, the pervasive influence of technology will indubitably set Gen Alpha, Beta, Gamma, Delta and so on's love culture apart from that of their forebears. Gen Alphas are predisposed to making comparisons with others. In their quest to showcase individuality, they are increasingly inclined to present themselves using filters, avatars, and embellished personas.

As the current egocentric and narcissistic trend, characterized by seeking celebrity-like attention through hosting, posting, and going live for instantaneous feedback, prevails, there is potential for increased transparency regarding their relationship status and perspectives on love. However, this transparency may emanate from a potentially delusional standpoint. It's important to note that this might not be everyone's experience, yet the prevailing trends, trajectories, and forecasts indicate uncannily parallel directions.

While my initial intention was to concentrate solely on the most well-known generations, I'd like to make an exception and provide a brief overview of Generation Alpha in this special presentation. This generation will undoubtedly be characterized by a strong emphasis on individuality and a preference for personalization while simultaneously being immersed in a globalized world culture marked by elements of homogeneity and sameness. We will witness more Gen Alphas deviating from conventional relationships and venturing into uncharted territories in matters of love. They will boldly explore their sexuality and question established gender norms, reshaping the fundamental concept of what a relationship can encompass.

Each time I inquire with young individuals about their intentions of starting families in the future, namely my own children, they consistently express their disinclination to have children. This leads to the speculation that over time, marriage and the conventional nuclear family might lose favor.

Moreover, It's not inconceivable to envision the emergence of life-sized, silicon companions, akin to those available on RealDoll.com, equipped with advanced A.I. conversation technology. Consider, for instance, how individuals who are naturally reserved or plagued by social anxiety will have the opportunity to forge profound connections with avatars meticulously designed to be their ideal companions. Furthermore, the possibilities are boundless. Such a notion may not be as outlandish as it sounds and could, in the not-so-distant future, be presented as a thoughtful bar mitzvah gift, framed within the context of safety and security concerns in an ever-evolving world.

Anticipate a rise in open relationships, polyamory, and Solo Polyamory within the Gen Alpha cohort. After all, the question arises – is it genuinely infidelity when it involves an A.I. doll or an A.I.-generated computer bot/assistant (or three), brought to life through holographic projection from your smartphone or augmented contact lenses? Generation Alpha and those succeeding them will embrace diverse relationship models and forge their own paradigms concerning love and intimacy. Barbaric ownership rules will not find a place within the context of love and connection in the future, especially among the more spiritually evolved individuals who still seek human companionship. Instead, freedom-based relationships will take precedence.

The influence of social media will persist as a pivotal force shaping the interrelations of Gen Alphas, and we should anticipate witnessing ever more imaginative applications of technology in their efforts to connect with their loved ones including the emergence of esoteric sciences and technologies. Collectively, they will boldly venture into experiments that challenge the established norms, albeit within the confines of their heavily regulated digital domains or within their own minds. Those not completely immersed in technology will develop a distinctive approach to love and will evolve in tandem with the constantly shifting terrain of the digital and spiritual worlds. Some will favor traditional roles and as for the notion of real-time soulmates, only time will tell.

In all likelihood, as metaverse-like platforms become increasingly prevalent, the majority of our interactions will migrate to these digital realms that serve as substitutes for the physical world. While these spaces often imitate reality, they can never truly replicate it. Many individuals will find solace in virtual environments that, while not a perfect imitation, offer high-definition graphics as the norm. This provides an escape from the anxieties of real-world social interactions, similar to the way social media functions today.

However, there is a potential concern on the horizon. Individuals may start to experience virtual disassociation, struggling to distinguish between the virtual and real worlds. This issue could become increasingly problematic in the coming decades seeing as some individuals even today merge the two as one reality believing everything the experience in the social media sphere. Consider the serious implications of gang members on the south side of chicago who are very serious about the convergence of social media post, drill music and real life crime. For some of them, social media can be the difference between life and death.

As the technology becomes more accessible and prices drop, devices such as the currently available Vive, Valve, or Oculus V.R. (among others) can transform the ordinary confines of your living space into a captivating illusion resembling the most breathtaking natural wonders on Earth. Now, envision meeting an exceptionally attractive partner in such a setting and delving into an intimate connection. Yet, this partner is a fusion of the real and the digitally enhanced, modified with a new set of plugins and filters.

Indeed, this concept is a far cry from the application of ancient Egyptian makeup, yet at its core, the intent to enhance one's allure remains unchanged. Whether it's a beautifully simulated hologram or any other form, its appeal remains consistent, regardless of the energy or light source involved. However, delving deeper into this topic would require a separate discussion in another manuscript. In the future, it's plausible that you may never encounter your "twin flame" in the physical realm but could engage in a fully developed relationship with them via a hologram and their accompanying A.I. chat assistant. If this concept appears farfetched, consider how our ancestors from just a few hundred years ago would perceive our current methods of social interaction, especially in the context of forming romantic connections.

At present, as we contemplate the future's uncertainties, all we can do is appreciate the realization that the most recent generations are reshaping the very essence of what it means to be human. They have taken it upon themselves to redefine not only pronouns and genders but also orientations, ethnic identities, and racial backgrounds. In the simulated world accessible through your subscription to the most prominent digital platforms, your possibilities are boundless, enabling you to become anyone you desire. Here, you have the liberty to amass and expend as many digital coins and bit currency as necessary to adorn yourself with the latest creative enhancements.

As for the physical world, with options such as melanin shots and skin lightening, wigs and color eye contacts, individuals can transform from Greek to Sumerian or from South African to Asian on any given Sunday. It's an embodiment of the age-old adage, "when in Rome, do as the Romans," even if that includes looking like one for the winter.

These trends are already discernible in today's relatively rudimentary social media structures, where digital glamor has become the prevailing standard with fun filters. Whether it takes the form of a narrative akin to the love story of Cindi Mayweather and Sir Anthony Greendown or that of Lucy and Ricky Ricardo, one certainty remains: when souls are engaged, the presence of companionship for spiritual growth will endure.

The innate human tendency to be drawn to fantasy is undeniable. Whether it's in the realm of pornography, interactions with escorts, or the phenomenon of catfishing, our imaginations often lead us toward our desired destinations, reinforcing our beliefs as we move forward. With the collaboration of creative minds and well-funded companies, the prevalence of idealized fantasies is poised to grow. The scenario I described a few paragraphs earlier may become a tangible reality in the near future.

As technology continues its exponential advancement, with capabilities roughly doubling every eighteen months, and as artificial intelligence makes daily leaps and bounds, what was once mere imagination has become tangible reality. This transformative technology holds significant implications for how we interact and is set to reshape the landscape of our current understanding of relationships. However, as with any development, there are both positive and negative aspects. Those who control the narratives will influence them in line with their preferences, potentially creating disparities for some individuals.

Admittedly, this technology is still in its nascent stages, and extensive research is imperative before digital companions can achieve widespread availability. Nonetheless, the conceivable applications of this technology are boundless, and it is poised to revolutionize our perceptions of love and relationships. One thing remains indisputable: Generation Alpha and beyond will pioneer the evolution of how we engage in loving relationships, while the rest of us, the most recent "elderly", will inevitably follow the prevailing trends set by our Gen-A leaders. Yes indeed, Grandpa, the generations of the future, with their "literal" surgically implanted third eyes powered by Apple computers, will be the leaders of the free world and piloting the Amazon drones that deliver your pharmaceuticals.

Certain trends are already on the horizon and simply waiting for society to catch up. Consider the concept of "market fit." Market fit pertains to the degree to which a product or service aligns with the needs and desires of a particular market or target audience. Ultimately, achieving market fit with Gen Alpha will require a deep understanding of this generation's needs and preferences and a willingness to adapt and innovate to meet those needs.

Our grandparents couldn't utilize Uber or partake in social media until the market evolved to accommodate them, or, in other words, until the internet emerged to fit the market. Subsequently, Gen Alpha, rather than conforming to outdated models, will craft their own technological advancements when the time is ripe, ushering in an era of remarkable progress and transformation.

In essence, Gen Alpha's fearless nature will drive them to experiment and push boundaries, especially in the virtual realm. They may challenge the status quo, yet, primarily from the safety of their digital spaces. Their views on love and relationships will be shaped by the ever-evolving virtual landscape, leading to a distinct approach to matters of the heart. With the rise of metaverse-like platforms, it's likely that most human interactions will eventually shift to these digital domains, replacing traditional real-world engagements.

By reading the last two chapters, you have effectively peeked into the matrix - specifically the psychological blueprint of relationships matrix, that is. You've embarked on a journey to witness the fundamental building blocks of human interactions at a semi-forensic level. Taking into account everything discussed, coupled with the information that will be shared next, you'll soon develop a deeper understanding of why you feel drawn to or distant from certain people, especially in the context of destined soul connections.

The landscape of love and basic social interactions is constantly evolving, full of twists and turns for everyone. So, what comes next? Regardless of our generation or the type of relationship we pursue, the truth is clear: whether online or in the busy aisles of a local Walmart, we are all actively shaping and co-creating our lives together every day. This journey reveals even deeper layers as we delve into mystical destinies and intertwined fates that are woven into our love stories and social interactions.

Having navigated the intellectual challenges and absorbed academic perspectives, we now arrive at the perfect time to delve into the complex, layered world of predestined and interpersonal soul ties. This point invites us to deeply explore the nuances and varied viewpoints related to real-time soulmate connections.

Our journey includes analyzing psychological, emotional, social, and spiritual elements that influence attraction, attachment and even adversarial dynamics between rivals.

We'll also look at methods for enhancing communication, resolving conflicts, and maintaining healthy boundaries. This exploration will lead us to the revelation of the four twin elemental archetypes, unveiling the detailed nature and characteristics of every soul tie and soul mate you've ever met.

Through it all, we shall discern how these diverse elements coalesce to weave the intricate tapestry of predestined and karmic soul connections. While historical retrospectives and academic theories establish a robust framework for comprehending human behavior, it is essential to recognize the intricate interplay of human emotions and attractions that drive our inclination to unfold our lives and destinies in the company of others.

By scrutinizing various perspectives and experiences, we can glean valuable insights into the myriad factors that mold our relationships and enrich our comprehension of love, intimacy, and human connection regarding soulmates and the soul ties that manifest them. Keep in mind that when predestined karmic forces are understood, one can mitigate the unforeseen events that can either wreak havoc on one's life or open the floodgates of abundance.

Continue your journey, whether through reading or listening, and you will uncover some of the most enthralling revelations elucidating the intricacies of how and why every facet of your destiny regarding human interaction is certainly pre arranged within a programmed simulation and infinitely more captivating than you could have dared to imagine.

Chapter Five

Soulmate Psychology

A Collective Consensus

Quote: "I feel like a part of my soul has loved you since the beginning of everything. Maybe we are from the same star." — Emery Allen.

Having gathered and organized the practical yet essential elements, we are now ready to piece them together and make a case for the existence of the soul as it relates to living souls and their mates, i.e.—**Soulmates.**

Within these pages, we've meticulously uncovered a central theme: the deep interconnectedness of individuals throughout history, especially in the realms of love, attraction, and shared human aspirations. Although we've covered a broad spectrum of topics, this is merely the beginning. What you've read so far, has most likely been integrated into your subconscious, broadening your knowledge and establishing a foundation for understanding the myriad of concepts that await.

To master what I call your "emoverse" (your emotional universe), you need the grounding balance and reflective insights provided by others to achieve equilibrium. This isn't about seeking validation, though many people do crave it; rather, it's about recognizing that most people naturally seek feedback and interaction to navigate the landscapes of our reality effectively. After all, what better way to understand oneself than through a mirror, whether literal or metaphorical?

Without someone to mirror and reflect our deep emotional and psychic selves, our awareness of these aspects might be largely unrecognized making us quite awkward within a social species. As social beings, we engage in imitation, mirroring, and reflective interactions akin to call and response dynamics. These interactions not only validate our existence but also contribute to the formation of our narratives and memories. Through this ongoing engagement, we develop a continuity of consciousness, shaping our individual identities and egoic personalities.

Nonetheless, As individuals journey through life, they often find themselves in a carnival-like *"hall"* of mirrors, each mirror reflecting a different facet of their personality, unveiling diverse versions of themselves. This path, fueled by our innate drive for self-preservation, often leads to a compelling realization: if one is to seek a partner, why not set sights on the ultimate companion—the best of the best. In this context, the enchanting and elusive concept of a Soulmate emerges, introducing a fascinating layer to our quest for connection and companionship.

Should we regard the concept of soulmates merely as a myth, or can it be viewed through a practical lens? Can the idea of a soulmate truly reflect a deep connection with one's soul, or is it merely a comforting belief that arises organically from our experiences and desires? This inquiry is designed to provoke thought and examine whether the notion of soulmates holds any tangible significance in our lives.

Just as many of our convictions and beliefs are rooted in our emotions, the concept of Soulmates follows a similar pattern. History has shown how certain beliefs have triggered conflicts and violence, only to be debunked by evidence generations later. In the absence of evidence, individuals can become entangled in impassioned disputes, driven by unwavering convictions and intense emotions. It is worth noting that when beliefs are instilled from an early age, they can become deeply ingrained and difficult to question, exhibiting similar behavioral patterns to those observed in the "five-monkey" experiment.

For context—The five-monkey experiment is a psychological study illustrating the influence of ingrained beliefs due to social pressure. In this experiment, five monkeys are confined in a cage with a ladder leading to a basket of bananas. When one monkey attempts to climb the ladder, the experimenter sprays all the monkeys with cold water. To avoid getting sprayed, if a monkey tries to climb the ladder, the other monkeys attack the one attempting to reach the banana.

This process is repeated until the monkeys learn to avoid climbing the ladder altogether.

Over time, the researchers substituted the monkeys in the enclosure one by one with new monkeys. Remarkably, the new monkeys also learned to avoid the banana, even though they had never encountered the water spray. After several generations, none of the original monkeys remained, yet the behavior endured. This led to the conclusion that the monkeys' behavior was shaped not by their individual experiences but by the collective learned behavior of the group, which became ingrained and perpetuated among new members.

This experiment offers a captivating insight into the inheritance of behavior, particularly concerning our traumas and beliefs, with seriously significant implications for our shared relationship culture. A quick scroll through almost anyone's social media timeline exposes a generation of adults who appear disoriented, perplexed, and emotionally scarred by the way much of society interacts. The five-monkey experiment underscores how this behavior can manifest in various situations, from abusive relationships to the perpetuation of racist or sexist attitudes, suggesting that they may trace back to inherited emotional inclinations. This would include our ideas on soulmates along with many other ideologies.

The notion of soulmates maintains a consistent presence in most people's minds, shaped by a blend of collective awareness, enduring generational beliefs, and personal experiences. This is not to suggest that soulmates are a myth or unreal, but rather to highlight that our perspectives on them can vary widely, often introducing mythical attachments. To gain a deeper understanding, let's carefully examine the concept. By starting with an understanding of what a soul is, we can then explore the idea of a soul having a counterpart or mate. With this groundwork, we'll delve into the complexities and dynamics that provide insights into the overarching concept of the quintessential Soulmate paradigm.

Public Consciousness Regarding Soulmates:

The idea that there is one particular person out there who can make each one of us happy, whole, and complete is constantly presented through portrayals in books, plays, films, magazines, and television media. We see it in the fairytale of Cinderella, where a handsome prince saves a beautiful young woman from servitude and they live happily ever after. We see it in classic love stories like Romeo and Juliet, where two star-crossed lovers defy all odds to be together until death does them a part. And we see it in countless romantic comedies, where the protagonists finally finds happiness with each other after going through a series of awkward misadventures. The message is clear: If we could just find that one perfect person, all our problems would disappear, and we will live happily ever after—certainly a message deeply ingrained in the subconscious.

Yet, this notion can be both naïve and harmful. It's naïve because it creates unrealistic expectations in relationships, making people feel incomplete without a special partner. It's harmful as it can breed separation consciousness and trap individuals in unhappy or abusive relationships, under the belief that they've found their only match. Conversely, it might lead some to become serial monogamists, frequently leaving relationships in pursuit of a more 'magical' partner, believing the current good one isn't perfect enough.

The fundamental truth is that we are each responsible for our own happiness, and no one else no matter how perfect, can fill that void. While some may be burdened by religious dogma that suggests they were born as wretches, I would assert that your creator designed you as a perfect and complete being. Need evidence? Just glance at your baby pictures.

Nonetheless, as social beings, we undoubtedly rely on one another. While it is undeniable that you possess all that you'll ever require within, a brief stint living alone in the forest or the desert makes it abundantly clear why the adage "No man is an island" holds true. In general, we are interdependent, and an interpersonal partner adds significant value to our journey through life.

A self-realized sage may reach a point where such ideas diminish, it's important to remember that even they entered this world with the help of a divine partner—their mother. An old African proverb reminds us, "If you want to go fast, go alone; but if you want to go far, go with others." The wisdom of indigenous elders is unparalleled. Even the mystic sage has his guru and his disciples. While the quest for that one perfect person in the vast universe amongst countless souls might appear counterintuitive, there are certainly those who enter our lives for remarkable reasons.

In general psychology, a Soulmate is a term describing your ideal counterpart. Many believe in someone who completes you, giving life a unique purpose. However, when asked, opinions vary widely on the exact meaning of a soulmate and whether they truly exist. According to Dictionary.com, a soul mate is defined as "A person with whom one shares a strong affinity, common values and tastes, and often a romantic connection." By this definition, it's evident that soulmates do indeed exist, as we've all encountered individuals with whom we share these profound qualities at some point in our lives. In fact, everyone has at least one person with whom they share a solid bond, be it a parent, child, best friend, or even a beloved pet for some.

Going beyond contemporary definitions, and delving into the historical roots of this concept , we find an allegory in Plato's "Symposium." written almost twenty five hundred years ago. In this work, the philosopher quotes the poet Aristophanes, who proposes that all humans were once conjoined with their other half, only to be separated by Zeus out of fear and jealousy. Aristophanes vividly describes the profound experience of two soulmates reuniting in the following manner:

Quote: *"When they approach one another and unite, the thrill and joy is so intense that in their ecstasy they would not know how to contain themselves; and when they separate once more, the pain and distress is very great."*

In Plato's "Symposium," Aristophanes' speech contains an allegory about the origin of love. He proposes that human beings were initially created with four arms, four legs, and a single head with two faces. These original humans were so formidable that they dared to challenge the gods. As a consequence, the gods decided to punish them by splitting them in half. From that point forward, humans were condemned to seek out their other half to regain a sense of completeness.

For over two thousand years, this concept has become closely associated with the idea of finding one's Soulmate. The notion that we are all on a quest to reunite with our other half resonates profoundly, and the idea of being reunited with our lost love is incredibly compelling.

Yet another early instance of the term "soul mate" appearing in the public record can be traced back to the early American poet Samuel Coleridge. In 1822, he penned a letter in which he proclaimed, "To be happy in Married Life ... you must have a Soulmate." Coleridge firmly held that a thriving marriage demanded a spiritual bond and transcended mere economic or social compatibility.

Coleridge and Plato were by no means pioneers in utilizing erotic and marital metaphors to fathom the link between the human soul and a divine counterpart.

An array of religious traditions have harnessed such metaphors to illustrate the profound connection between the two. From Judaism to Christianity, mystics and theologians have for ages perceived an amorous union with the divine as the route to genuine selfhood, happiness, and wholeness.

In essence, many spiritual traditions liken our connection with God to that of a marriage. Hence, it's no wonder that their concepts exert a profound influence on our understanding of the soul and its connection to the divine. A mere listen to the fervor of contemporary gospel music (much like Country and R&B) reveals that the hymns dedicated to God capture the very essence of a profound and intimate relationship, resemblant of a fervent amorous bond, mirroring the deep connection of soulmates.

An intriguing viewpoint is offered by Dr. Michael Tobin, a seasoned family and marital psychologist with over 40 years of experience. He asserts that there exist various types of soul mates, and not all soulmates are destined for lifelong romance. I've incorporated Dr. Tobin's theories as contextual examples for vividly conveying the notion that individuals forge numerous insightful connections throughout their lives. These connections naturally propel them onto paths of growth, healing, and experiences that ultimately mold and define their journey.

Here, as outlined by Dr. Tobin, are six distinct types of soulmates to keep an eye out for in your own life.

Romantic Soulmates

Romantic soulmates spark each other's passion throughout their union," Dr. Tobin notes. "They possess the ability to elevate each other to peaks of both physical and emotional fulfillment." Yet, breakups are a common experience, even in relationships that check all the boxes for intensity and connection. "Passion may initially blaze intensely only to quickly fade away. In contrast, for those exceptional romantic soulmates, the passion endures over time, fueled by their mutual dedication to sustain the flame in their relationship.

Soul Partners

If it's been a long time since you've been in touch with an old elementary school friend, yet upon reconnection, everything clicks effortlessly, this phenomenon can be understood through the concept of a soul partner. "A soul partner is someone with whom you may not have interacted for years, yet upon meeting again, it feels as though neither time nor distance has impacted the connection's intensity," Dr. Tobin elaborates.

Karmic Soulmates

Recognizing a karmic soulmate comes from a deep alignment with shared goals. "Together, you aim to create positive change in the world, with your abilities enhancing each other's—making you perfect teammates for a common cause." Such connections transcend the need for romantic love or intimacy, focusing instead on leveraging individual strengths for a significant purpose.

Companion Soulmates

This is the perfect complement to you, much like how peanut butter complements jelly. "Friends play a crucial role in our life's journey, especially those soulmate friends who support us through every season of life. They share joy in our happiness, offer comfort in our struggles, celebrate with us in our victories, encourage authenticity, accept our flaws, and stand by us steadfastly, even in moments of disagreement," as described by Dr. Tobin.

Kindred Soulmates

Recognizing a kindred soulmate happens when you align on both minor and significant matters. "Your passions align, humor resonates together, and even in agreement or disagreement, it's handled with care and warmth; competition arises without envy or resentment. Such individuals walk alongside you on the path towards truth and love.

Soul Contracts

Dr. Tobin suggests that soul contracts are a fascinating aspect of soulmate connections, marked by mutual dedication to honesty, emotional transparency, accountability for dishonesty, and authenticity, among other goals. An example of a soul contract could be a marriage where infidelity occurred, yet the couple chooses to stay together—not for external reasons like children or societal expectations—but due to a deep, inherent pull within their agreement that binds them for life.

Irrespective of your perspective on Dr. Tobin's theories, it's impossible to deny the intriguing insights and valuable framework they provide for understanding the multifaceted nature of various soulmate relationships. When exploring the diverse manifestations of a soulmate in your life, several dynamics come into play.

Despite its widespread appeal, the notion of "Soul Mates" has been critically examined over time. While there have been some intriguing findings, most researchers are still skeptical about scientifically validating these ideas. It's important to recognize that personal experiences and beliefs about relationships significantly shape your views on the concept of soulmates.

Many people share similar beliefs however. For example, did you know that The Marist Institute for Public Opinion (MIPO), a prominent survey research center home to the Marist Poll, reports that nearly three out of four (73%) American residents believe in soulmates, with only 27% who do not? In a subsequent inquiry by Marist, 66% affirmed their belief that two people are destined to be together, while 34% held a different view.

Undoubtedly, these responses were influenced by their personal experiences, circumstances, public influence, and group dynamics. Have you ever wondered who tends to believe more in the concept of soulmates, men or women? According to the polls, 74% of the men surveyed believed, whereas 71% of the women surveyed shared this belief in finding the perfect partner.

How do different generations perceive the existence of soulmates? Younger Americans, those under 30, exhibited the highest belief. The younger generations appear more starry-eyed than ever, with 80% of those under the age of 30 and 78% of individuals in their 30s to mid-40s expressing their faith in soulmates. In comparison, people in their late 40s to early 60s stood at 72%, while those beyond 60 years old registered at 65%. Overall, regarding a collective consensus, each generation boasts a substantial percentage of individuals who believe in soulmates in various forms.

In this discussion, we will explore the diverse origins, approaches, and emerging themes surrounding the concept of soulmates. Additionally, we will delve into research concerning a specific set of theories coined as **"Destiny beliefs"** and **"Growth beliefs,"** formulated by **Dr. Raymond Knee**, a dedicated clinical psychologist who has devoted his career to assisting people in finding their soulmates. I believe Dr. Knee's work is of paramount importance regarding this conversation, as it allows you, the reader, to contemplate which belief resonates with you.

Through his research, Dr. Knee arrived at the conclusion that "Destiny belief" revolves around the stability of one's perceptions of romantic relationships and entails the belief that relationships are either destined or they are not. In essence, it proposes that either you experience immediate chemistry or it's not meant to be—a notion almost suggesting that it all hinges on universal chance.

His discovery unveiled that individuals holding "destiny beliefs" predominantly seek positive emotional reactions and initial compatibility with a partner without prior knowledge of their personality profile or what might influence them at that specific moment or stage of life. I've personally witnessed that the majority of interactions, whether from my own experiences or those of my peers, tend to conform to this pattern of falling versus growing into a dynamic.

Consequently, these beliefs propel individuals with destiny-oriented outlooks to experience intense passion and satisfaction in the initial stages of a relationship, especially when compatibility and fortunate timing align. However, when inevitable challenges surface, those embracing destiny beliefs may exclaim that things are moving too fast, struggling to cope effectively, ultimately opting for leaving the relationship as the sole solution. They seek out a more ideal and compatible match elsewhere.

Hence, their relationship pattern essentially reflects quantity over quality in the long run, resulting in numerous intense but brief connections. It's astonishing how many people unconsciously subscribe to this belief system when establishing connections with potential partners. A brief exploration of social media posts unveils the mindsets of many single individuals, including their embrace of cancel culture and **unreasonable demands for perfection in forging chemistry.** To understand the romantic rejection prevalent in today's cancel culture, one need only look at the "Pop the Red Balloon or Find Love" internet dating shows with host Arlette Amuli. These dating shows vividly illustrate the harsh realities and fleeting nature of modern relationships.

Conversely, according to Dr. Knee, individuals embracing "Growth Beliefs" primarily seek partners with whom they can grow with over time, addressing conflicts as they emerge. Growth belief centers on the perception of problems in a relationship as manageable challenges that can be surmounted, as opposed to the approach of discarding everything when difficulties arise. In essence, it emphasizes taking charge of your life and assuming responsibility for its outcomes. These underlying assumptions and beliefs regarding romantic relationships shape our behaviors and inform our ideals for how we cope with the challenges in a relationship..

Following a period of diverse relationship experiences, the accumulation of these encounters naturally leads one to ponder: do I believe in the existence of one utterly perfect person exclusively meant for me? Researcher Raymond Knee and his colleagues were eager to explore potential variations in people's responses to this question. Employing the destiny and growth belief model, they uncovered that holding firm to the concept of perfect soulmates can foster unrealistic expectations within individuals regarding their relationships. Consequently, when reality doesn't align with their lofty ideals, they may become disheartened or lose faith in the relationship.

Individuals of this mindset are prone to experiencing complex relationships if they don't choose to give-in and part ways early on. Those who lean toward destiny beliefs channel their mental energy and inner inquiries toward their partner, pondering questions like, "Is this my one and only? Can I find something better, or is this the extent of it?" These internal deliberations persist, even in situations where everything appeared perfect just weeks before, and their partner was deemed a potential soulmate.

On the other hand, those with growth beliefs engage in a slightly different internal dialogue, one that might revolve around questions such as, "What is our overall purpose? What accountability can I assume for my role, or what resources are at our disposal to grow closer?" Ask yourself, which of the two have you been more prone to acting as?

The notion that your happiness depends on finding and being with one individual out of the 8 billion inhabitants of Earth, who just so happen to reside in your charming hometown of Willacoochee, Georgia, with its modest population of 1,300, can unduly limit your opportunities to cultivate meaningful connections and savor life's most exquisite experiences. This perspective may lead you to invest an excessive amount of time in the pursuit of that elusive perfect partner, potentially diverting your focus from nurturing the relationships you already have.

We all say we understand that there is no such thing as perfect, yet we often find ourselves excessively critical and judgmental—again reminiscent of the characters George and Jerry in the Seinfeld sitcom. There always seems to be something off with the person they're dating. Repeating this pattern is like an intriguing but perpetual little game we play with ourselves throughout our lives, possibly without ever culminating in a formal life partnership.

With each passing year, some individuals console themselves with the belief that one day, the ideal partner will magically materialize, only to witness the accumulation of birthdays, marking the passage of time and the arrival of old age with no one but your regrets and bad habits to keep you company.

This isn't to imply that you should lower your standards, but if you are still in the process of healing and living in your car, it may be unfair to expect a potential partner to reside in a mansion as a condition of your affection. If you genuinely aspire to grow with a life partner, it's imperative to weigh the significance of other qualities that hold greater importance for a successful long-term relationship.

While you're entirely at liberty to prioritize as you see fit, rational thinking suggests that fixating on such superficial aspects may not lead to a fulfilling partnership and could potentially result in spending your later years in solitude, with only a hoard of cats for companionship. No judgment here, as I recognize that this arrangement holds tremendous appeal for some individuals. The scent of ammonia emanating from a cat family of 34 members can be less taxing than navigating human egos in some cases.

Some people engage in passionate, intense, short-lived relationships, but frequently find themselves disillusioned and frustrated when inevitably confronted with challenges. These people are what Dr. Knee would call Destiny believers. They place substantial faith in 'deal-breakers' and persistently seek the elusive 'perfect' partner. Although they may initially view compromise as a form of settling, they paradoxically anticipate their partner to compromise as a prerequisite for their love.

When difficulties arise within the relationship, their coping mechanism often revolve around the thought, "I should move on and find my one true love." which has the potential to happen several times a year. Since there is no one perfect individual, this quest resembles an endless pursuit, comparable to a puppy chasing its tail in never-ending circles.

Initially, they may perceive their partner as a beautiful reflection, igniting intense passion—kindred to Twin Flame energy—only to witness the gradual depletion of the flood of brain chemistry from their bodies. Consequently, disillusionment takes hold, shattering their idealized image of the perfect relationship. This leads them to place sole blame on their love interest, holding them entirely accountable for any issues. Despite experiencing this cycle repeatedly, individuals deeply committed to their belief in destiny and exhibiting these tendencies often struggle to recognize the recurring pattern.

On the other hand, there are those relationships where the individuals involved exhibit a tad more patience in relational matters compared to their counterparts. Dr. Knee would consider these types of relationships to fall under "Growth belief." These types of individuals generally take a bit longer to commit, driven by a keen interest in proactively addressing any potential challenges before making swift decisions.

They firmly hold the belief that any relationship can evolve and thrive through dedicated effort and compromise, even in the face of adversity. Their perspective frames the relationship as a long-term investment. When setbacks occur, Growth believers display a greater willingness to adapt, explore fresh perspectives, exercise patience, and seek harmonious resolutions. This approach is perceived as inherently growth-oriented.

This mindset stands in stark contrast to that of the Destiny believer, representing a proactive approach of taking one's destiny into their own hands. Romance with a Growth-oriented perspective may not experience the same intensity and euphoria on a daily basis. However, when challenges surface, they are driven to take the lead in resolving conflicts and maintaining their commitment to their partner. Consequently, they often revel in longer and more gratifying relationships over time, as opposed to abruptly parting ways over minor misunderstandings.

Research has shown that the perpetual quest for a one and only true soulmate diminishes the motivation to invest in making a relationship succeed. Essentially, the attitude becomes, "If it's broken, throw it away and find another one." In certain instances, a relationship might only have minor scuffs or scratches, but some might immediately opt for a refund. Yet, there are those who choose to buff out these imperfections with their sleeves. This isn't an act of giving up or settling; it's an embodiment of adaptability and a willingness to grow, recognizing that no one is flawless, possesses all the answers, or has life entirely figured out.

As one grows wiser with age, it becomes apparent that some individuals undergo a gradual transformation from a destiny belief like system of relating, to a growth belief like system, often driven by the experiences they gain through trial and error. This shift may occur after recognizing the substantial energy wasted by not selecting life's battles more judiciously. Many come to the realization that compromise and growth are not negative qualities. There's a saying that goes, "I'd rather have peace than to always be right." This adage applies to friendships, associations, and relationships alike.

It's important to note that this doesn't dismiss the beliefs of all destiny-like believers. Many enduring and joyful relationships exist where the involved partners genuinely attribute their union to destiny. In fact, I believe that most individuals possess a blend of both mindsets. The Universe can be viewed as a finely tuned machine, where almost everything appears to follow some preordained path.

However, I also believe that relationships like the ones mentioned have taken the time to become solution-oriented and to grow together. In 99% of cases, it's likely because they have genuinely developed deep love for each other. This love entails patience, understanding, and a willingness to make the necessary sacrifices to sustain a happy relationship.

Hence, while destiny may have justifiably initiated their connection, it's wisdom, patience, and love that have kept them together. It's worth emphasizing that most individuals tend to display a blend of both mindsets, although one will eventually often take a dominant role.

Your interpretation of a soulmate can vary considerably, depending on your life experiences and your personal connection to the concept. You might find alignment with the insights of Dr. Michael Tobin, Dr. Knee, or the philosophical musings of Plato and the poetic reflections of Samuel Taylor Coleridge, all enriching the collective understanding and belief in soulmate ideology. A quick Google search will reveal a multitude of concepts and perspectives related to the notion of soulmates. However, at its most fundamental level, the concept can be distilled into two main principles.

The first and more widely accepted principle is symbolic. It generally signifies that a soulmate is an exceptional partner in someone's life. However, in this context, it's crucial to note that this usage is entirely non-spiritual or mystical. The statement "they were made for each other" is not to be taken literally by those who employ the term in this manner. In other words, soulmates need not be seen as exclusive or as karmic twins or reincarnated lovers. They can simply be exceptionally wonderful romantic partners or friends. The second rationale is of a more spiritual and literal nature. This perspective entails a profound, pre-existing understanding of each other, even before two individuals come into contact. Concepts like reincarnation occasionally come into play in this context. This level delves into the esoteric and extends beyond linear thinking.

Delving deeper, the concept of us being intricately designed by some divine plan or purpose isn't new, but it hints at a deeper layer of existence. Soulmates, as the theory goes, come into existence when two people share an unbreakable bond. Publicly available information suggests that scientific instruments recorded evidence—from around 1900-1910—about fundamental energy patterns that reveal the source of existence which could offer foundational evidence for souls and their mates.

Walter John Kilner, a British physician from the late 19th and early 20th centuries, pioneered research into the human aura, notably through his works "The Human Atmosphere" and "The Human Aura," published in 1911. His experiments with dicyanin dye sought to improve the visibility of auras, positing that these could offer insights into an individual's health. Semyon Kirlian later contributed to this field with the invention of Kirlian photography, a method believed to capture the energy fields or auras of living organisms, thus expanding research into bioenergetics.

In the late 20th century, Guy Coggins introduced aura imaging technology, using biofeedback to create color representations of auras. While not recognized scientifically as a diagnostic tool, this technology has become popular in holistic and alternative health circles for aura visualization. These endeavors, while not conclusively proving the existence of a soul, suggest that there may be aspects of the human body that extend beyond conventional understanding.

Exploring the field of psychology, which undeniably displays characteristics of a scientific discipline, reveals a rich array of data and research supporting various theories about the enigmatic concept of soulmates. Whether through mathematics, science, psychology, astrology, transcendental phenomena, or simple reasoning, there is a substantial body of scientific evidence suggesting the existence of highly compatible partners, potentially with non-physical aspects, in a broader context.

This evidence becomes especially evident after nurturing a lasting, deep, and meaningful relationship where both individuals have conscientiously collaborated to nurture their best selves in love. Furthermore, astrological and psychological assessments can be harnessed to align practical qualities for overall compatibility.

Reflecting on it, one might wonder why the concept of a soulmate often seems linked to the past or a distant, almost mystical realm. Why can't a chosen partner, selected through social and emotional acumen in this lifetime, be the beginning of a love story where both cultivate a world-class love transcending the boundaries of time and space? Is it unimaginable for this to be the first lifetime together, or must it always trace back to a past life? Whether it does or doesn't, these are the types of inquiries that enable us to thoroughly understand the concept from a holistic perspective.

In a joyful and thriving relationship, love has the potential to cultivate all the multifaceted qualities found in a profoundly compatible soulmate connection. One that becomes so uniquely special that it's impossible for anyone to replicate, rendering your partner utterly irreplaceable. Just as your mother, your grandmother, and your spouse hold irreplaceable roles in your life. The same applies to your twin sister, your daughter, your dearest friend, and that twin flame from the past who reshaped your entire perspective on consciousness—they too are unique and irreplaceable.

In essence, when you elevate your inner divinity to its highest self-expression, every relationship you form becomes a one-of-a-kind, irreplaceable union of souls, as each connection mirrors your essence. More on this in the upcoming chapters.

With that, I want to express my firm belief in, and conviction of, both normal and paranormal, natural and supernatural concepts of soulmate sciences. I've witnessed firsthand normal, abnormal, and even paranormal events to the extent that despite my skepticism toward many things, I'm aware of the value in not throwing out the baby with the bathwater, regarding this subject.

Having provided a brief overview of widely accepted theories and introduced ideas from respected researchers, I am now keen to transition into a more esoteric yet practical viewpoint. It's time to distill this topic down to its fundamental elements, focusing on the very essence of the soul. Considering that mainstream science doesn't allocate significant resources to the study of the soul, one might find themselves drawn to explore this subject through mystical and esoteric terminology to attain a profound comprehension.

It's worth noting that there are no educational courses within the public school system that delve into the essence of the soul. Nor is there a public entity that officially endorses the concept of the soul other than various religious doctrines. This subject has yet to evolve into a publicly administered, pharmaceutically replicated, and controlled science and thus degrees and certificates hold no authority in this space. Drawing from history, one undeniable fact emerges: no matter how extraordinary a concept may be, without the official seal of approval from the mainstream media, it often remains hidden from the public's gaze.

There's a well known quote suggesting that history is written by the victors. This hints at a profound truth – history isn't always a strict account of facts but often a reflection of the victors' interpretation. The same lens can be applied to mainstream media. In the era before the internet's ubiquity, glimpses of information about the soul were relatively rare unless you delved deep into religion, spirituality, and occultism, or were a devoted reader, researcher and-or yogi practitioner.

Fast forward to today—where the Pew Research Center reveals a fascinating statistic—over two-thirds of U.S. adults embrace the existence of the soul and an afterlife. It's intriguing that the concept of the soul continues to captivate the western imagination, even in a time when religious beliefs across the world are waning. You might even argue that belief in the soul has transcended belief in the traditional anthropomorphic God, often depicted as a tall, bearded figure in mainstream culture.

In an evolving landscape, a growing number of Americans are distancing themselves from the divisions inherent in traditional, fixed religions. Instead, many are gravitating towards the universal principles that thread through all religions with concepts like love and goodwill. The phrase "I'm not religious, but

I'm spiritual" is a common refrain, reflecting a desire to connect with something supernatural and transcendent, even when the form of that connection remains uncertain. What is strikingly clear, though, is that the notion of "the soul" has etched itself deeply into the public consciousness, suggesting that people remain intrinsically connected to the idea of something greater and that there is more to existence than what meets the eye.

Venturing back in time to the cradle of Western thought, we find Greek philosophers discussing the soul. Plato, for instance, proposed that even after death, the soul endures and retains the capacity for thought. He postulated that as bodies fade away, the soul experiences a cycle of rebirth into new bodies, a concept known as metempsychosis. Aristotle, on the other hand, held a different perspective, contending that only a part of the soul, the intellect, possessed immortality.

Remarkably, Ancient Egypt laid the foundation for Western civilization, and delving into the intricate tapestry of that ancient culture reveals a wealth of references to the soul. Among these, the Papyrus of Ani, later known as the "Book of the Dead" stands out as an invaluable source, shedding light on Egyptian beliefs concerning the soul's post-mortem journey and its intricate connection to the physical body.

The ancient Egyptians possessed a profound comprehension of the soul, envisioning it as a complex entity with various facets known as the **Ren, Ba, Ka, She'ut,** and **Ib**. Imhotep, a polymath of ancient Egypt, conceptualized the Ka as one's double, the Ba as the very essence of the soul, and the Akh as its spirit. The Book of the Dead eloquently described the soul as eternal, with its journey extending beyond the realms of death. In the tapestry of Ancient Egyptian culture, the ultimate life's purpose was to prepare the soul for the afterlife, ensuring its passage through the judgment of **Ma'at,** the goddess of truth and justice.

The soul is a deeply rooted concept in modern culture, from soul music and soul searching to soul food and soul brother. Once a word takes hold, so does the idea it represents. Like NLP or (neuro-linguistic programming), these cultural habits in thought and language could be considered self-programming and passed down, much like many of our relationship models.

With this viewpoint in mind, and with an unwaveringly open and objective outlook, it becomes plausible that the concept of the soul could even be a construct intentionally embedded, rather than an empirical reality—unless you've experienced ensouled phenomena first hand such as P.L.R. or N.D.E.—It represents something that may not have any actual existence outside of our thoughts and imaginations. Nevertheless, the idea of the soul persists because it speaks to something deep within us - something that we can't fully explain but know exists.

For my history enthusiasts and those with keen intellects as well as those passionate about the art of storytelling, if you really want to know how and where our shared ideas of the soul **in the west**, beyond ancient Egypt, most likely emerged and spread, come, take a little trip with me. I will endeavor to present another short timeline as succinctly as possible. This trip down memory lane will explore the intricate forces that have subtly shaped our collective understanding and perceptions of the soul and spirit. I recommend that interested readers highlight names and passages that resonate with them for further study.

For Context:

> The origin of the Catholic Church is traditionally traced back to the teachings of Jesus Christ and the establishment of the Church by his apostles. Here's a concise overview:
>
> 1. **Historical Context**: The roots of the Catholic Church are found in the ministry of Jesus Christ, who lived in the 1st century CE in the Roman province of Judea. He is considered the central figure in Christianity.
>
> 2. **The Apostles and Early Church**: After Jesus's crucifixion and resurrection, his apostles, particularly Peter and Paul, played a crucial role in spreading his teachings. Peter is traditionally regarded as the first Pope, based on his role as the leader of the early Christian community in Rome.
>
> 3. **Formation and Early Development**: The early Christian community was initially <u>a sect within Judaism.</u> Over time, as followers of Jesus, known as Christians, spread across the Roman Empire, they formed distinct communities. The term "Catholic" (from the Greek *katholikos*, meaning "universal") began to be used to describe the universal Christian Church by the early 2nd century.
>
> 4. **Imperial Endorsement and Expansion**: In the early 4th century,

Emperor Constantine formally established The Catholic Church after the Edict of Milan in 313 CE, which granted religious tolerance to Christianity, leading to its gradual acceptance and integration into the Roman state. <u>The First Council of Nicaea in 325 CE</u> was significant in defining Christian doctrine and combating heresies. The Church's structure, including the papacy, which continued to develop through the centuries.

5. **Medieval and Modern Periods**: The Catholic Church played a central role in medieval Europe, <u>influencing</u> various aspects of <u>life and governance</u>. Over time, it expanded globally through <u>missions and colonization</u>. The Christian Crusades were a series of religious and military campaigns initiated by the Latin Church in the medieval period. The nine major Crusades took place over a period of approximately 176 years, from the First Crusade in 1096 to the Ninth Crusade, which ended in 1272.

The Reformation in the 16th century led to significant changes and the establishment of various Protestant denominations, but the Catholic Church continued to evolve and adapt. The Catholic Church considers itself to be the one, holy, catholic, and apostolic Church founded by Jesus Christ, with its spiritual and organizational lineage traced through the apostles and early Church Fathers.

Now;

- Let's begin our journey in the ancient city of Constantinople, today's Istanbul. From its establishment in 330 A.D. by Emperor Constantine until 1922, it was the bustling capital for the Roman, Byzantine, Latin, and Ottoman Empires. Its prime location between Europe and Asia made it a crucial cultural and trade center, setting the stage for decisions that still influence us today.

- Fast forward to 869 & 870 AD, the city hosted the Council of Constantinople, also known as the Fourth Council by the Catholic Church. This gathering was pivotal, focusing on serious theological disputes, **especially concerning the nature of the soul and spirit.** The council's Eleventh Canon made a bold statement: humans have a body and soul, but the idea of a spirit should only be considered in abstract or metaphorical terms. Thinking of the spirit as a real entity could get you ousted from the church community. Central to the council's debates was Photius, the Patriarch of Constantinople. His role in the Photian Schism highlighted the growing rift between the Eastern Orthodox and Western Catholic branches of Christianity. Photius was a controversial figure, particularly for his dual-soul theory, which, if believed, could lead to accusations of heresy and extreme punishments. The outcomes of these debates didn't just stir up local drama; they caused a permanent split between the Eastern and Western Churches. The East continued to delve into the concept of the spirit, while the West condemned such discussions as heretical. This division deeply influenced Christian theology and the dynamics between the two church branches for centuries.

- Jump to the 10th to 12th centuries, an era marked by a strong emphasis on dualism, not dismissing the Trinity but stirring nuanced debates and diverse beliefs within medieval Christianity. It was also a time when heretical movements like the Cathars, who embraced a dualistic worldview, emerged, contrasting sharply with mainstream Christian doctrine. These theological debates shaped how individuals viewed their spiritual journeys and concepts of salvation, wrestling with ideas of predestination, free will, and the nature of salvation. While some groups leaned towards a binary understanding of heaven and hell, the broader medieval doctrine upheld the Trinity. The drama of these historical events could rival any modern epic, with intrigue, conflict, and shifting allegiances as compelling as those found in the Game of Thrones series. Photius, for instance, a notable medieval scholar, was excommunicated due to his controversial theories on the soul, causing a rift within the Church that lasted until it was formally healed on December 7, 1965.

- By the 14th century, the focus shifted to Cartesian dualism, introduced by René Descartes, which separated the mental from the physical realms, suggesting the mind could exist independently of the body. This philosophical shift had a profound impact across various fields, from psychology to artificial intelligence, continuing to fuel debates about human nature.

- During the Venus transit from 1874 to 1882, a critical time in our understanding of human nature unfolded. Wilhelm Wundt stood out among key figures; he established the first experimental psychology laboratory and famously described humans as sophisticated animals. Concurrently, perspectives from France likened humanism to an exotic machine, and Pavlov criticized the nebulous concept of the soul for complicating scientific inquiry. Wundt's stance on the soul mirrored the council's treatment of the spirit centuries earlier, advocating for a theoretical, symbolic, or metaphorical engagement with the soul, if at all. Practical application became relegated to biofeedback experiments involving physiological measurements. This approach set the stage for a 20th-century perspective that largely marginalized and minimized the soul, leaving many within various religious and philosophical communities at a loss to articulate the essence of the soul or distinguish it from the spirit.

- The late 19th and early 20th centuries witnessed the rise of

New Age practices like séances, psychic phenomena, past life recall, and hypnotherapy, emerging as prominent models for exploring the soul. From the philosophies of Indian Yogis to the occultist teachings of Madame Blavatsky, C.W. Leadbeater, and Rudolf Steiner, along with organizations like the Theosophical Society and others, a new era of spiritual intellect was secretly emerging. This evolution brings us to the present spiritual trends of the 21st century, where such practices have not only gained mainstream acceptance but have also intertwined with various aspects of wellness and personal development.

- Today, these methodologies are part of a broader spiritual movement that embraces a holistic approach to understanding human consciousness and the essence of our being, reflecting the continuous human quest for deeper meaning and connection. You can find a million and one intuitive opinions regarding the subjects deep within the rabbit hole of twenty first century social media. Amidst the vast array of opinions on social media, the question remains: Do we transcend our physical existence to explore other dimensions? According to many near-death experience survivors, the answer is a resounding "Yes!"

My own curiosity about the soul was sparked by the 1907 "21-gram experiment" by Duncan MacDougall, who attempted to measure the soul's mass by weighing a human body at the moment of death. Despite skepticism, this experiment prompted further exploration into the potential existence of the soul, continuing to captivate those intrigued by the mysteries of human existence.

When I stumbled upon security camera footage on YouTube, which seemed to capture the moment a soul departed a mouse caught in a trap, I couldn't resist delving deeper into this intriguing enigma. These incidents ignited my imagination, opening the door to countless "what-ifs." I've come across countless photographs portraying ethereal figures near accident scenes, and even witnessed a Tesla Automobile detecting a presence through radar in a graveyard, where the human eye saw nothing. There are numerous accounts of young children who appear to see deceased grandparents, elders, and other ancestors present in rooms, even as the family continues with their daily activities.

The true turning point, however, was my experience at a home rehab site. From the corner of my eye, I would often glimpse a little girl and a man in overalls watching me from across the room. Yet, every time I turned to look, they vanished. It wasn't a source of fear, just a curiosity, as the mind's capacity to play tricks on us is well documented, just ask Willie D, Scarface or Bushwick Bill.

As fate would have it, one day, in the presence of the realtor, the homeowner, and fellow contractors engaged in a conversation, one of my machines - a floor sander - inexplicably roared to life and began rolling toward me. I stood perilously close to a long wooden staircase, and had I been knocked down, the outcome could have been far from pleasant. However, I managed to intercept it without any trouble. In a playful jest, I suggested that perhaps it was the mischievous little ghost girl playing pranks. What followed was a collective gasp, a sudden paleness washing over the faces of those present, and, one by one, they recounted their own encounters with the little girl and the man in overalls.

This wasn't a tale from the boundless realm of the internet; it unfolded in the tangible world, affirmed through the consensus of a group. It was an experience that left no room for doubt about the existence of souls and disembodied spirits. Had only I saw the ghostly figures without the validating consensus, doubt would have always lived rent free somewhere in my mind. These experiences, coupled with a series of esoteric encounters dating back to my early childhood and teenage years, laid the groundwork for the discussions that will follow.

To truly grasp the life and purpose of a soulmate, we must first recognize that souls and spirits transcend the boundaries of mere imagination and engage in meaningful exchanges and interactions. This understanding allows us to comprehend the subconscious motivations behind attracting a soulmate. By doing so, we can unravel the significant roles various soulmates play in our life narratives, serving as catalysts for change and agents of transformation throughout our journey.

Furthermore, beyond the realm of suspected ghosts and apparitions, some may wonder about the existence of alternate dimensions, multiverses, and otherworldly realms mentioned by near-death experience (NDE) survivors, or the Terence McKenna-like explorations of remote viewers traversing the mycelium networks of time and space. In the forthcoming chapters, we'll explore various religious studies and practical scientific accounts that present replicable evidence achieved through systematic experimentation and observation.

These findings allude to the existence of a supernatural world beyond the veil. In the forthcoming chapters, we will establish a compelling foundation, affirming the existence of the soul and exploring its mysterious purpose and tangible impact in daily life, including the soul's communal aspects. The following chapter will site various traditional references for the living soul and delve into aspects of reincarnation.

Chapter Six

Religion & Reincarnation

The Gospel According to Several Belief Systems regarding the Soul

Quote: "Life and death are like inhalation and exhalation. They always exist together." — Sadhguru

To embark on a genuine exploration of soulmates, we must delve into the very essence of souls. When we truly immerse ourselves in the profound concept of souls, it becomes inevitable to traverse the intriguing realm of reincarnation. While some may dismiss reincarnation as a mere superstition, this enduring concept has been zealously debated across diverse cultures and religions for centuries.

In this chapter, we'll provide a backdrop to the intricate subject of reincarnation. This will enable us to grasp the evolution of the idea over time and its diverse interpretations across the globe. The term "reincarnation" has its roots in Latin, loosely translating to "Entering the Flesh Again." This belief, dating back centuries, supposes that the soul of a departed individual can, in time, inhabit a new physical form—a doctrine echoing beyond the boundaries of the Egyptian and Greco-Roman empires.

In the last chapter, we briefly touched on the compelling instance of this belief that emerges in the Book of the Dead, a compilation of funerary texts guiding the departed through the afterlife. These texts describe the soul's journey through various afterlife stages, culminating in its rebirth into a new body.

Beyond the Book of the Dead, ancient Egyptian tombs depict scenes through drawings and carvings. In these images, the deceased are guided by the god Anubis into the underworld, where their souls face judgment by the god Osiris. This judgment, known as the Weighing of the Heart, takes place in Duat, also referred to as the Underworld. Anubis uses a feather as a symbol of Ma'at—the goddess of truth and justice, crucial for cosmic order. The judgment determines the fate of the soul in the afterlife, potentially leading to a new physical form through reincarnation.

Furthermore, the Egyptians believed that certain individuals, such as pharaohs and other high-ranking officials, could become gods after death and that their spirits could continue to intervene in the affairs of the living. It's worth noting that several ancient civilizations, which have received relatively less attention from Western scholarship, including the Kingdom of Kush, the Kingdom of Axum, as well as civilizations like Wagadu and the Songhai and Mali Empires, also held distinct beliefs pertaining to reincarnation.

The ancient Greek philosopher Pythagoras, residing in the 6th century BCE, is also recognized for his belief in reincarnation. He imparted the teaching that the soul, eternal and unbounded, could undergo rebirth in a new body after death. Plato, spanning the years 428–348 BCE, also hints at reincarnation in a compilation of his essays. In Book X of Laws, he references the spiritual principle of cause and effect, commonly known as karma, stating:

"Know that if you become worse, you will go to the worst souls, or if better, to the better; and in every succession of life and death, you will do and suffer what like may fitly suffer at the hands of like."

Similarly, in his Second Ennead, Plotinus writes that reincarnation is a dogma recognized throughout antiquity. He goes on to say that souls expiate their sins in the darkness of the infernal regions before being reborn into new bodies to face new trials. These texts make it clear that the idea of reincarnation was not foreign to the ancient philosophers and that it was a belief held by many people in antiquity.

The major religions that hold a belief in reincarnation are generally found on the continent of Asia, notably Hinduism, Jainism, Buddhism, and Sikhism, all of which arose in India. The reason for this is that the concept of reincarnation is central to the Asiatic worldview. Many cultures in Asia believe that the soul is reborn into another body after death. This cycle of birth and death continues until the soul reaches liberation from the material world.

These beliefs provides a framework for understanding the cycle of life and death and help to explain the suffering in the world. It also offers hope for a better life in the next incarnation. For these reasons, reincarnation is a crucial belief in many Asiatic religions. The world's major religions (Hinduism, Buddhism, Christianity, Islam, and Judaism) all have different rules and beliefs, but they all hold in common a doctrine of karma or the law of cause and effect, even after death. This law states that what one does in this present life will affect the next life. Simply put, one cannot experience anything after death unless, on some level, they remain alive. The following sections highlight the origins of the various ideas that surround the concept of reincarnation.

In **Hinduism**, the process of birth and rebirth—i.e., transmigration of souls—is endless until one achieves moksha or liberation (meaning "release") from that process. Moksha is achieved when one realizes that the eternal core of the individual "atman" and the Absolute reality "brahman" is one. This means that one can escape from the process of death and rebirth also known as samsara.

All major religions teach some version of this same fundamental doctrine of karma. It is a central tenet of these religions that one's actions have consequences, both in this life and in the next. As such, it provides a moral framework for living and motivates people to act ethically. The doctrine of karma also helps to explain why things happen as they do, both good and bad. It is a way of understanding cause and effect in the world.

Jainism is a religion that reflects a belief in an eternal and transmigrating life principle known as Jiva. Jiva is defined as an individual soul. This means that Jainism believes in karma, which is the burden of old deeds that a person does. As a result, the new karma that is acquired during the next existence is added to the old karma. However, the Jiva can free itself through religious disciplines, such as ahimsa, translated to mean nonviolence. By rising to the place of liberated "Jivas" at the top of the universe, the "Jiva" can end the cycle of reincarnation.

Orphism, a mystery religion prominent in the ancient Greek world, held that the soul was preexistent and would survive bodily death to be later reincarnated. This belief was shared by Plato. More specifically, Plato believed that the soul participated in frequent incarnations and that through these experiences, it could eventually regain its former pure state. The Orphic mystery religion and Plato's philosophy provide interesting insights into the ancient Greek views on life after death and the nature of the soul.

Sikhism is a religion that originated in the 15th century in the Punjab region of India. It is a monotheistic faith that teaches that there is only one God and that people can achieve salvation through meditation, good deeds, and devotion to God. One of the central beliefs of Sikhism is reincarnation, which is based on the Hindu concept of rebirth. Sikhism teaches that after a person dies, their soul is reborn into another body and goes through multiple existences before eventually being united with God.

The Sikh holy book, the Guru Granth Sahib, also describes a final judgment where all souls will be weighed according to their good and bad deeds. Those who have lived lives of righteousness and service will be rewarded with eternal life in paradise, while those who have sinned will be punished in Hell. Ultimately, however, even the sinners will be granted salvation and absorbed into God. Thus, reincarnation and the Last Judgment are both important aspects of Sikh theology.

In **Buddhism**, it is believed that there is no such thing as an unchanging, substantial soul or self. Instead, what we think of as our individual selves is just a composition of five ever-changing psycho-physical elements known as Skandhas. These skandhas are forms, sensations, perceptions, impulses, and consciousness, and they all come to an end when we die. However, the karma we accumulate in life does not die with us. It becomes a Vijnana, or germ of consciousness, in the womb of our next mother. In other words, our karma is reborn in a new individual.

Through discipline and meditation, it is possible to achieve a state of complete passiveness known as Nirvana. In Nirvana, birth and rebirth cycles are broken, and we are freed from the suffering that comes with it. So while Buddhism denies the existence of a soul or self in the traditional sense, it does believe in the transmigration of karma, which gives each of us our unique individual experiences to *come as you are or as you were* for that matter.

As you can see, the idea of reincarnation has been around for centuries and is found in many different cultures. While the concept is not an accepted doctrine in orthodox Christianity, Islam, or Judaism, there are some sects within these religions that do believe in reincarnation. In addition, there are certain mystical sects within Judaism and Islam that also believe in the cycle of rebirth.

Although most denominations within Christianity and Islam do not believe that individuals reincarnate—in the traditional since which is back in physical form—particular groups within these religions do refer to reincarnation; these groups include the mainstream historical and contemporary followers of Cathars, Alawites, the Druze, and the Rosicrucians. Some Christian groups that support the idea of Reincarnated individuals include the Cathars and Alawites.

The Cathars were a group that originated in the 12th century. They believed in dualism, which is the belief that there are two Gods; one good and one evil, similar to modern Christians' belief in Jesus and Satan, the two opposing super beings that lord over humanity. The Cathars also believed in reincarnation and that the soul was trapped in the body until it was purified through good deeds.

The Alawites are a religious group that originated in Syria in the 9th century. They, too, believe in reincarnation, and they also believe in metempsychosis, which is the belief that the soul can be reborn into another person or animal.

The Druze are a religious sect that originated in Egypt in the 11th century. They believe in absolute predestination, meaning that everything that happens to a person is determined by God. They also believe in reincarnation and that the soul is reborn into another person or animal after death.

Islam teaches that there is life after death, known as Akhirah. In Islam, it is Allah who decides when a person dies, and most Muslims believe that when they die, they will stay in their graves until Yawm al-din, the Day of Judgement. All people will be resurrected and judged by Allah according to their deeds on that day. Those who have led good lives will be rewarded with paradise, while those who have committed evil acts will be punished in Hell.

Akhirah is an important belief in Islam as it motivates people to lead good lives and do good deeds. It also helps to comfort Muslims in times of grief, knowing that their loved ones are not truly gone but are simply waiting to be reunited with them on the Day of Judgment. The concept of judgment after death is central to Islamic doctrine and is mentioned frequently in the Qur'an, the holy book of Islam.

Although the Qur'an, the holy book received by the prophet Muhammed, doesn't really address the concept of past lives and rebirth, **Sufism**, a mystical sect of Islam, accepts the transmigration of souls as a reality. In the words of the Sufi teacher, Sharf-U'D Din-Maneri: *"O Brother, know for certain that this work has been before thee and me in "bygone" ages.... No one has begun this work for the first time."*

The idea that we have all lived before and will continue to live again after death is a concept found in many different cultures and religions. For the Sufis, this cycle of birth and death is an opportunity to purify the soul and to become closer to God. In each life, we have the opportunity to learn from our mistakes and to become better people. The Sufi belief in transmigration provides hope that we can make progress on our spiritual journey, even if it takes many lifetimes.

Similarly, the great Sufi poet Rumi wrote: *"I died as mineral and became a plant, I died as plant and rose to animal, I died as an animal, and I was Man.... Why should I fear? When was I less by dying?"* For the Sufis, then, the idea of reincarnation is not something to be feared but rather a natural process that we have all undergone many times before. Only through repeated lifetimes can we hope to achieve union with the Divine.

Though **Orthodox Judaism** officially rejects the belief in reincarnation, some sects within Judaism accept it as truth. **The Hasidic sect** and those who follow the **Kabbalah**, a collection of mystical texts first published in 1280, both believe in the transmigration of souls. Rabbi Manasseh ben Israel (1604-1657), a theologian and English statesman, said that reincarnation was a fundamental point of their religion. He cites **the Zohar**, a book of Jewish mysticism, as evidence for this claim. Interestingly, even within one religion, there can be conflicting belief systems about an afterlife. This goes to show how complex the topic of reincarnation can be.

Christianity is much the same as Islam, with similar heaven and Hell, dualistic, good place and bad place scenarios concerning what happens to the soul after death. Today Christianity teaches resurrection instead of reincarnation. Some people would argue that Jesus spoke of reincarnation when he spoke of John the Baptist as the prophet Elijah's reincarnation. There are those that would debate them to no end, but that is a conversation for Sunday school.

The conventional Judaeo-Christian narrative of life after death unfolds like this: You were born. You lived. You died. Following a judgment, you went to heaven or Hell for eternity. However, data from the Pew Forum on Religion and Public Life (2009 survey) reveals a surprising trend— not only do a quarter of Americans believe in reincarnation, but 24% of American Christians also express a belief in it. These statistics mark a notable departure from the traditional narrative ingrained in the baby-boomer generation. I would encourage you to explore "NDE or Near Death Experience videos on the internet, shared by many devout Christians, to encounter some truly incredible and uplifting stories.

Christianity is often viewed as a reimagining of ancient Egyptian religions, introduced to Rome by Emperor Constantine and solidified during the early councils of Nicea. Given this historical context, it follows logically that early gnostic Christianity may have endorsed reincarnation rather than resurrection, akin to their predecessors in Egypt. It is speculated that these two concepts were initially intertwined and later separated over time, possibly due to translation losses. A wealth of evidence, both from ancient and more recent times, underscores the use of religion as a manipulative political tool to govern and control the masses for societal order. As explored earlier with "King James the 1st" in preceding chapters, this aspect of religious manipulation has deep historical roots.

In 553 A.D., during the Second Council of Constantinople, the idea of reincarnation was deemed incompatible with the Christian church. The notion of reincarnation stirred intense debate among early church fathers. Seeking reconciliation between the leaders of the Eastern and Western branches of the Christian church, the Second Council of Constantinople addressed reincarnation. Though not formally rejected, the work of early church fathers accused of teaching reincarnation were banned. Consequently, 553 A.D. marked the conclusion of the reincarnation debate within the dominant Christian community.

The primary reason for the rejection of reincarnation by the mainstream Christian Church throughout history is its contradiction with the doctrine of corporeal resurrection. Furthermore, the doctrine of reincarnation challenges the necessity of Christ's redemptive sacrifices. If individuals can be reincarnated with multiple chances to rectify their actions, the rationale for Christ's sacrifice diminishes, and the fear of death, a powerful tool for fear-based rulership, loses its grip. NDE survivors consistently express that life continues beyond death.

Early Christian leaders vehemently opposed this belief, staunchly advocating the doctrines of bodily resurrection and redemption through Christ alone. Controlling the narrative of Christ, not as a consciousness but as an entity, afforded dominion over the minds of the people, serving as the gatekeeper to the afterlife—effectively wielding control over the living through hell based psycho-spiritual technology.

Nevertheless, reincarnation retained popularity among certain Christians, especially in the Eastern Orthodox tradition of that era. Amid the opposition, many early Church fathers adhered to the idea of reincarnation, deeming it compatible with original scripture and offering an explanation for certain human experiences. This belief found resonance among early Christian theologians like Valentinus and Basilides of Alexandria.

Theologians who embraced reincarnation drew significant inspiration from the philosophical ideas of Plato, who, in turn, derived insights from earlier Greek philosophers. Figures such as Basilides, Valentinus, and Origen, situated in or near Alexandria, Egypt, were not only geographically but also intellectually interconnected. The endorsement of reincarnation among early Christian clergymen finds easy understanding in this context of geographical proximity and the profound influence of all the early clergymen and philosophers.

Plato, asserting that the human body was a punishment for souls and that knowledge could not be acquired in a single lifetime, subscribed to the belief in reincarnation. His location in Alexandria placed him at the epicenter of a diverse golden- to dark brown population, encompassing various doctrines and cultural influences.

According to Plato, the soul is immortal, traversing different bodies throughout its existence, with the ultimate aim of accumulating enough knowledge to break free from the cycle of rebirth. To acquire this knowledge, the soul must undergo a process of forgetting, allowing it to start afresh in each life and learn anew. Although reincarnation is not widely accepted today, Plato's rationale offers a thought-provoking perspective on why some individuals choose to believe in it.

It's essential to note that Plato's mentor and teacher was Socrates, the philosopher primarily known for the philosophical maxim, 'Know Thyself.' This quote, also the first of three Delphic maxims inscribed in the forecourt of the Temple of Apollo at Delphi, has deeper roots, initially borrowed from the walls of Egypt's Luxor Temple. In Egypt, it stood as one of the cardinal concepts in ancient African sacred wisdom.

One could contend that for a soul to genuinely know itself, it must undergo a multitude of lifetimes. This concept suggests that a soul can achieve a profound and comprehensive understanding of itself only by facing diverse situations and circumstances in various lifetimes, much like a painter requiring different colors and techniques to craft a masterpiece. Each life presents distinctive opportunities for growth, learning, and self-discovery, contributing to the soul's evolution and progress toward cosmic self-awareness, ultimately becoming a universal phenomenon.

Socrates asserted the immortality of the soul, contending that death is not the culmination of existence but a mere separation of the soul from the body. Discussing the soul's pre-existence and its divine connection, he implied its eternal nature and knowledge derived from past experiences. If Socrates, who is revered as the father of Western philosophy, embraced reincarnation, contemporary culture would inherently share a consciousness or, at the very least, a subconscious consensus about life after death. This would be intertwined with religious doctrines and dogmas, despite the many councils that attempted to erase the ideology from the records.

However, truthfully, we don't require their validation, as most of us inherently believe in the soul as the animating force within our physical bodies—an electricity propelling us forward. Our physical bodies are akin to a spotted yellow bananas' peel, with the true self residing within not only as the soft banana flesh but the photonic electric life force hidden within the electrons of what appears as a banana to the eyes. When all else fades, what endures is a genuine and living soul. If this holds true, I must ask: Are you really just Jacob, john, Jamal, Mary, or Makeba, or is your true self something else altogether?

Like wearing a costume which will inherently come off, should I recognize you the character of the costume or the one wearing the costume? Is your body simply a vehicle, much like your automobile, carrying precious cargo within and guided by a GPS programmed with a destination and purpose? Many people behave as if the outfits they wear are their identity. Others see their career as their entire identity, believing they hold no intrinsic value outside of their job title. Instead of saying, "I am a soul," "I am a man," or "I am Joe," they declare, "I am a doctor," "I am a lawyer," or "I am a police officer." Could it be that beyond the identity seen by others, the true essence of who you are exists and functions in another realm altogether?

As time unfolds and cultures undergo transformations, we can anticipate numerous variations and shifts in humanity's belief systems, encompassing fundamental concepts like those related to life and death. Following the age-old adage, the more things change, the more they stay the same.

Given that the majority of the world population adheres to religious beliefs, with Pew Research Center (2019) estimating that about 16% globally are religiously unaffiliated and WIN-Gallup International (2017) reporting that around 13% identify as atheist or agnostic, it becomes essential to explore the religious origins of these various beliefs to understand their broader impact.

Elements inherent to our nature may persist but manifest in more vibrant patterns, exemplified by the recorded accounts and tireless research that have led us to the subject of our upcoming chapter. In the next chapter, we will elevate the discussion and dive into a phenomenon known as spontaneous past-life recall. By examining these phenomena, we will gain real-world insights from the many cases of our contemporary peers, offering us an in-depth look at the living soul and its role in our waking lives.

Chapter Seven

A Case for Past Life Recall

Exploring the Macro Conscious Mind

Quote: *"People can only meet you as deeply as they have met themselves."*
—*Matt Khan.*

Have you ever met your true self—the all-pervasive self realized version of you, often described by the sage of Arunachala, 'Bhagavan Ramana Maharshi?' If not, have you at least dreamed of or experienced yourself in trance from past lives? What if you could see several stories unfold from various lifetimes where you were dressed in the flesh of another human being. It would still be essentially you, just with a different name, body, and backstory. Much like an actor deeply immersed in a role on stage or a personality you assume while asleep and dreaming, the question remains: how deeply do you know who you truly are?

In this chapter, we aim to gently explore the vast nature of the soul, utilizing peer-reviewed scientific methods in relation to accessing the subconscious and superconscious mind. To provide perspective on how the immeasurable mind, body, and brain can contain vast information spanning not only centuries but dimensions, consider the fact that Microsoft Corporation has recently unveiled the first publicly known digital DNA hard drive.

A single gram of DNA has the remarkable capacity to store up to 433 petabytes of data, exceeding a thousand terabytes. Consider the bold possibility: cloning through a simple skin sample, replicating, and effortlessly transferring consciousness from a digital DNA storage device into a new body.

This raises an intriguing question: if fallible humans can accomplish such feats, what level of mastery might Sumerian gods in Jupiter-sized crystal motherships or archangels demonstrate? A discovery like this, combined with the scientific findings that epigenetic memories can persist across 14 generations in DNA, unveils new perspectives on the potential of ancient, hidden esoteric knowledge within our physical and non-physical selves.

As if the replication of human genes over countless millennia through heredity, giving us the eyes and ears that resemble a great-grandmother or even an ancient Pharaoh, isn't remarkable enough, the quantum mechanics involved in the formation of, *"YOU"* alone, encapsulates centuries of information from multiple dimensions.

In addition to these revelations, we know that our human auric field can extend beyond our bodies from six to twelve feet, as evidenced by different measuring devices, including Kirlian photography etc. We also know that there are trillions of electromagnetic waves over and around us at all times. Ask yourself, what do these waves carry? The resounding answer is information! Whether internet, radio, or television waves, diverse electromagnetic waves permeate your body and auric fields like oxygen, all carrying valuable information. Think about that for a moment—the fact that the entire internet is literally coursing through your entire body this very moment is astonishing.

When you hold a flashlight to your hand at night, even the darkest-skinned individual will witness the light passing through the webs of their fingers. Just as sound passes through the skin and blood of those same hands when covering your ears at a loud music festival. Between atoms lies a vast and empty space.

Let me remind you that the nucleus of an atom can be likened to a grain of sand on the fifty-yard line of a football field, with the surrounding stadium seats representing the electron field of an atom. Together, trillions of such atoms combine to form what we perceive as different forms of matter. The idea of consciousness riding on photons of light, akin to remote miniature drones skillfully navigating the atoms of the human body, is not inconceivable. Considering these realities, alongside the seamless passage of information through an individual, one can deduce that, the storage cells known as DNA have the capacity to harbor advanced information, even regarding the nature of the soul.

Professor **Sylvester James Gates Jr.**, a renowned theoretical physicist known for his work in supersymmetry, supergravity, and superstring theory, has passionately explored "The Elegant Universe." He unravels the complex role of advanced numerical mathematics, similar to era-correcting codes known as Adinkras, governing our space-time reality, much like a precisely tuned computer program.

With this information, it is not hard to fathom residing in what I call an "Atomic Hologram," where we possess access to the entire universe through a seamless quantum entanglement. Within this framework, the potential to conjure boundless possibilities from within ourselves emerges when in sync with universal consciousness—known in some circles as self realization or god consciousness when fully activated.

Let's affirm that the majority of humanity acknowledges the existence of a soul—an extension beyond the mirrored self, even if interpretations differ. For everyone reading, consider this question: If you believe in the existence of a soul, where do you think your soul resided, and what might it have been doing before you were born and or became conscious of your human body and personality? What does it do when you are in a deep sleep or unconscious of your life for long periods of time. What about those that are brain dead and on life support with a beating heart? When did your soul, If you believe you have one, even come into existence? Was your soul too born in 1977, 1999, 2001 or even 2012 when you fell from your mother's womb? Subsequently, If one's life span is limited to several decades, what would be the ultimate destination of their soul once their temporary body reaches the end of its short existence?

Allow me to introduce another question: Is the soul generated simultaneously with the human sperm and egg? In the course of fetal development, a female human harbors around six million eggs, having all the eggs she will ever possess from birth. Does this mean each of her eggs carries within them a short order soul even as she passes the womb during her own birth. I imagine, that would be souls, on souls, on soul. Could it be plausible that half of a soul resides in each of her eggs, while the other half remains encapsulated in her future counterparts sperm—which could potentially be squandered during his formative years, and so forth? These queries are intended for contemplation, fostering realization and the expansion of minds.

In this chapter, I will avoid relying on the conventional heaven-hell narrative, opting for a more comprehensive approach. Furthermore, I struggle to accept that an extremely temporary and limited human intellect should be completely responsible over the destiny of an entire immortal soul. If this were true, it would suggest that an eleven-year-old child, engaging in deceit, theft, or harm to animals, could potentially confront eternal damnation due to their juvenile actions if they were to pass away prematurely. should an eleven year old mind be responsible for an eternal souls fate regarding everlasting, unending torturous and hellish punishment for all infinity.

The lingering question persists: what is your soul doing during its existence beyond 3D space in linear time? Where was it, and what was it engaged in right before it assumed the role of the biological carbon-based avatar known as, You! Surely, the soul must have had a prior existence before the 21st century in North America or any other continent. Or maybe your soul is actually just twenty one years old, maybe you don't have a soul at all and your just a big coagulated ball of funky cells whose only purpose in the vast cosmos is to clock in at work, pay rent and die, only to be forgotten in a matter of months. Perhaps the souls only purpose is to animate the human just long enough for it to be harvested from a farm called earth so that it can be seasoned and served in a cosmic cafe on a luxury mothership.

Drawing from diverse philosophies ranging from the ancient Egyptian Book of the Dead to teachings of self-realized yogis and spiritual leaders like Ramana Maharishi, as well as figures such as Madame Blavatsky and even Jesus known as Yeshua to some and Eshua to others, we can discern that an individual's current incarnation is not their first. This perspective is echoed across cultures and teachings, suggesting a continuity of the soul beyond a single lifetime.

This notion aligns with having several lives, as indicated by numerous past-life regressions worldwide, not to mention various ancient religious doctrines. The phenomenon known as Spontaneous Regression can manifest through various forms, including dreams, third-party channelings, near-death experiences or NDEs, intense meditations, or even DMT-induced experiences, ranging from breathwork to psychoactive plant medicines. However, for the purposes of this book, we will focus exclusively on psychiatry-based, peer-reviewed clinical hypnotherapy as our primary source for regression data.

The American Psychological Association, or the APA, stands as the preeminent scientific and professional organization representing psychology in the United States, boasting a membership exceeding 133,000 researchers, educators, clinicians, consultants, and students.

According to the APA, hypnotherapy is defined as a procedure during which a health professional or researcher suggests, while treating someone in a trance state, that they undergo changes in their sensations, perceptions, thoughts, or behavior. In simpler terms, hypnosis is a trance-like mental state where individuals experience heightened attention and concentration, as well as receptive guidance, thus fostering hyper-sensitive focus.

While hypnosis is commonly likened to a sleep-like state, a more accurate description characterizes it as a state of intense focus with heightened suggestibility. Many regard hypnotherapy as an alternative medicine treatment, employing guided relaxation and intense concentration to attain a heightened state of awareness or an altered state of consciousness. By muting all other distractions and bringing laser-like focus to specific attention, the mind can transform into a tool for enacting latent superpowers.

Hypnotherapy, or clinical hypnosis, is typically employed to assist individuals in comprehending and regulating their psychological, physical, and emotional behavior. It seeks to induce positive changes in mental state and behavior by providing suggestions during the hypnotic state. Hypnotherapy proves beneficial in addressing everything from addictive behaviors, anxiety, and phobias, as well as exploring the depths of the mind to cope with deep-seated trauma.

For over a century, scholars have conducted rigorous scientific inquiries into hypnosis, predominantly in the realms of psychology and medicine. Their endeavors aimed to unravel the nature of hypnosis, its mechanisms, and its effectiveness as a clinical intervention. In the twentieth century, diverse research teams undertook inquiries into hypnosis at esteemed American institutions like Harvard and Stanford, as well as leading universities in England and Europe.

In modern times, research on hypnosis has become progressively divided between academic and clinical domains. Furthermore, the use of brain imaging techniques has enhanced our understanding of the neurological foundations of hypnosis, significantly advancing our comprehension and broadening our recognition of its potential clinical applications. Despite its demonstrated effectiveness, hypnotherapy and hypnosis often face skepticism and criticism.

It's crucial to emphasize that scientific studies on hypnosis undergo rigorous peer review and are published in reputable scientific journals. These encompass specialized publications like the International Journal of Clinical and Experimental Hypnosis, as well as mainstream periodicals such as Science, the Journal of Personality and Social Psychology, and NeuroImage. As discussed earlier, hypnosis entails a state of heightened concentration, and it is believed that during hypnosis, the subconscious mind is exceptionally receptive to suggestions.

These references lend credibility and a sense of official endorsement to the subject of past life regression using hypnotherapy, addressing the concerns of skeptics. **Neurophysiology,** a discipline dedicated to investigating the nervous system, offers valuable insights into the functioning of the brain during the hypnotic state, thereby enhancing our comprehension of hypnosis. Research in this domain suggests that hypnosis can indeed alter the activity of distinct brain regions, including those associated with consciousness, attention, and memory.

Advancements in real-time neuroimaging allow scientists to observe and record neurophysiological changes during hypnosis, providing concrete evidence of its effects on the brain. This understanding has been crucial in revealing how hypnosis influences brain activity, explaining its effectiveness in behavior modification and therapy. As you may already know, in the realm of hypnotic practices, some therapists utilize the "Past-Life regression" (PLR) technique, to aid patients in understanding and addressing current psychological and physical issues. This method is highly contentious, sparking considerable debate and disagreement among experts in the field.

The premise of past-life regression is that our past experiences influence our current lives. By re-experiencing these past lives, we can gain insight into the origins of our present problems and discover ways to address them. Although not mainstream, and lacking popular scientific evidence to support past-life regression claims, many individuals believe it is a potent tool for self-exploration and healing.

As of now, the growing awareness of past life regression is evident not only through a myriad of online videos and documentation on platforms like YouTube but also on popular platforms such as Netflix in documentaries dedicated to exploring the phenomenon. This indicates a broader dissemination of knowledge and interest in the subject.

Concerning past-life regression, the belief in reincarnation is founded on the idea that the soul is immortal, enabling its rebirth into a new body after death. This belief has endured for centuries and continues to be embraced in diverse cultures today. Despite some individuals asserting recollections of past lives, mainstream and skeptical clinicians typically regard such memories as expressions of psychopathology.

Several factors contribute to this skepticism. Firstly, memories of past lives are often fragmented, lacking clear linear narratives—resembling dreams. This is understandable, given the challenge of articulating rational alphawave thoughts while in a betawave mental state. Secondly, these memories may involve themes of trauma and abuse, which could be more easily explained as products of the individual's imagination or unconscious mind.

Proponents of reincarnation see it as a way to understand the cycle of life, death, and rebirth. However, skeptics, particularly in the clinical field, often dismiss reincarnation beliefs as delusions, associating past-life experiences with symptoms of mental illnesses like schizophrenia. Despite this, some argue that information about past-life science is deliberately kept out of mainstream discussions, perhaps for reasons similar to why early church councils preferred the concept of resurrection over reincarnation.

The unknown or misunderstood should not always be so quickly dismissed, as is often the case in mainstream society. Each individual maintains their own beliefs and convictions. With approximately 18,000 different gods, and each individual holding the conviction that their chosen god is the sole-supreme, true and ultimate deity, one must consider the possibility that our collective understanding of reality is a multifaceted realm potentially defying our surface understanding. It's possible that we might all be mistaken.

Consider that not so long ago, the mere suggestion of extraterrestrial life was deemed eccentric or even considered a manifestation of insanity. However, governments worldwide are gradually acknowledging the existence of extraterrestrial encounters, offering a passive form of disclosure. This highlights how long-held beliefs can resist change, even when confronted with emerging evidence or alternative viewpoints. As technology advances and more conclusive evidence is made public, it's not uncommon for long-held beliefs to be overturned.

Comprehending why exploring the depths of the subconscious mind through regression techniques is not a priority for the masses could certainly be paralleled to the similar neglect of financial literacy and holistic lifestyles among the general populace. In exercising their free will, individuals choose other things to capture their attention like entertainment and material wealth.

Moreover, it is worth contemplating whether the mass populace could even process such a model for transformation. The popular Indian Mystic, Sadhguru, asserts that most people can't handle one lifetime of memories without their minds cracking up, let alone ten lifetimes of memories. So, why past-life regression? Why mention it at all? It is brought up because there are numerous encounters that cannot be ignored, shedding light on the potential nature of the soul and its dynamics in our interactions with each other concerning love and daily life.

If there truly is a soul acting as an extension of the visually seen physical body, serving as a battery or counterpart to animate said body with life force energy, then it must surely interact with other souls in different bodies. In fact, It could be argued that there is an entire network designed for the interaction of these souls—an entire cosmic community in fact.

These days, among skeptics, it seems that many would find it easier to believe in fanciful descriptions of angels, presenting as 9-foot-tall blond haired beings with bird-like feathers and metallic trumpets, along with bronze-age swords, than to conceive the idea of an intelligent, self-extending light body operating in a macro-cosmic network within a multi-dimensional universe. Of course, it's not to deny the existence of angels with swords and trumpets, but it's crucial to remember the existence of infinite intelligent souls, of which you may have one of your very own.

Before we explore those depths, let's take a brief look at basic regression therapy, such as the kind that takes place in your average hypnotherapy or psychiatric office. Many have likely encountered scenes in movies or shows where a therapist asks, "tell me about your childhood," and eventually discovers that some hidden childhood trauma is the source of unhealthy behavior wreaking havoc in one's life. It's widely accepted that by identifying the trauma's source, one can actively work to diminish its power and find relief or remedy.

Additionally, therapists are increasingly incorporating "Current" life regression. In current life regression, the individual is guided to memories of current and past events that may negatively impact their present life. These recent events could be traumatic or stressful, and by reliving them in a safe and controlled environment, the individual can begin to process and heal these experiences.

As we know, unprocessed trauma can wreak havoc in an individual's emotional and psychological life, affecting their trajectory and making it challenging to move forward. Unhealed wounds from past experiences can significantly impact an individual's present and future. This is where the practice of hypnotic regression come into play, offering a potential pathway to address and integrate these fragmented states.

Regarding memory, both short-term and long-term recall can be unreliable. Often, a specific smell or sound can trigger deeply hidden memories in the subconscious. At times, viewing an old photograph can suddenly bring back a flood of forgotten details from that day. It is believed that the brain holds every moment of a person's life, with the challenge primarily being in the ability to access these memories.

Sometimes, the mind requires a little assistance to activate certain brain areas, similar to the electric shock from defibrillator paddles that restart the heart after cardiac arrest. This assistance can help you uncover long lost memories. Imagine a computer where you've accidentally deleted files, thinking they're gone for good. But then, a federal agent with an electronic forensics team uncovers the supposedly erased data, revealing the unmentionable websites you've visited. Similarly, a skilled therapist can assist you in conducting a forensic search in the depths of your own mind uncovering things you were unaware of.

Psychologists are deeply intrigued by the complex world of memory, studying how our memories respond to surrounding stimuli. Consider the Ebbinghaus forgetting curve, which shows how quickly we forget new information. Beyond this, research reveals that our memories are significantly influenced by sensory experiences. For instance, studies show that people are more likely to remember events presented through vivid, visually engaging mediums, such as engaging videos or interactive modules.

Our memories can also be affected by the sounds around us. For instance, individuals who witness a crime often struggle to recall the details of what they saw due to the stress of the event. Similarly, people shown a series of images in rapid succession may only remember the last one because their brain has not had time to process the others. These findings indicate that our memories are not merely static storage devices but dynamic and ever-changing.

A skilled hypnotherapist can help relax the conscious mind, enabling a heightened and focused state to retrieve memories. When the hypnotherapist activates neural activity in areas that were previously inactive, like remedying a neural drought, those brain regions start to flood with the desired memories, akin to an electrical storm.

An elementary example is when an acquaintance loses their keys, and you guide them through or assist in retracing their steps over the past few hours. The mind operates through association, and a skilled hypnotherapist should possess an excellent framework to help you connect the dots, guiding you on a timeline you've subconsciously already experienced.

That example is resemblant to a popular technique called timeline hypnosis, which guides the individual back to key moments in their life, starting from birth. This can help the individual understand how past events have shaped their present life and provide insight into current issues and problems. This isn't impossible, and it is not uncommon. If a trained therapist knows where to look and how to unlock the clutter in your mind, when tapping into the right brain frequency, your mind will surrender, and your soul will do the rest.

The reality is that even untrained individuals can achieve similar results. You, too, can learn and practice self-hypnosis to unlock some of the mysteries of your own mind and soul. Understanding how your mind's waves, rhythms, and frequencies work is beneficial. For context, brain waves are electrical impulses that travel across the surface of the brain. There are four primary types of brain waves: delta, theta, alpha, and beta. Each type of brain wave has a specific frequency range.

Delta brain waves, with their slow 0-4 Hz frequency, are the gentle giants of our brain activity, typically emerging during deep sleep. Moving up the spectrum, Theta brain waves range from 4-8 Hz and are a bit livelier, often linked with light sleep, relaxation, and states of meditation that bridge the conscious and subconscious minds. In the middle of the frequency range, we find Alpha brain waves, which oscillate between 8-12 Hz. These waves are slower than their Beta counterparts and are synonymous with relaxation and a calm, focused state of mind, ideal for deep concentration.

At the faster end, Beta brain waves zip along at 12-38 Hz and dominate our normal, waking states of consciousness. These waves are subdivided into three groups: low Beta (12-15 Hz) helps us with relaxed focus; mid Beta (15-18 Hz) keeps us alert to tasks at hand; and high Beta (18-38 Hz) drives our highest levels of alertness and cognitive functioning, crucial for intense problem-solving and decision-making.

It's worth noting that these frequency ranges are not set in stone and can vary slightly from person to person. Additionally, the brain produces a mixture of different brain waves at any given time, and the relative balance of these brain waves can change depending on a person's state of consciousness and activity.

Additionally, **Gamma brain waves** are a type of brainwave with a frequency range of 30-100 Hz or higher. They are the fastest brainwaves and are believed to be involved in higher-level processing, such as consciousness, perception, and problem-solving.

Research suggests that gamma brain waves are crucial in integrating information across brain regions and in memory formation. They have been linked to states of deep focus and spiritual experiences, like those reported by self-realized yogis. For example, a 2004 study in "Science" found that Tibetan Buddhist meditators showed higher gamma wave activity during compassion meditation compared to non-meditators.

In popular culture, the movie "Limitless" features the fictional drug NZT, which enhances cognitive functions and supposedly synchronizes brain waves from Delta to Gamma simultaneously. While NZT is fictional, practices like transcendental meditation can be effective in harnessing the brain's synchronized and coherent potential. Brain waves, measurable through an E.E.G., reflect our mental states, these states can be altered through emotional intention, desire, technique, chemical induction even advanced technology or hemi-sync. Nothing is more potent however than trained and practiced self realization techniques.

One example is auto-hypnosis, a self-induced trance state in which an individual remains conscious and in control of their surroundings while deeply focusing on something other than their immediate environment. This could involve internal or external focal points like deep breathing, candlelight, or a pendulum. Auto-hypnosis serves various purposes, from self-improvement to achieving specific goals such as overcoming fears or boosting confidence. It's also applicable for enhancing memory or concentration. Through auto-hypnosis and regular meditation, one can acquire the skill to enter a trance, navigating their pineal and neural stargates from any location —I.E, traveling without moving.

Be it through stimulating the piezoelectric crystals within your pineal gland for lucid visions of past events or by evoking micro-memories trapped in the fabric of cellular tissues, the ancient Hermetic axiom, "As above, so below," assumes profound significance in **exploring the sub and superconscious mind**. Psycho-tech has the capacity to extract the most dormant memories from the DNA-laced fabric of your cells within an ocean of infinite information, all accessible for you.

The Hermetic principles, as found in the Kybalion, may have unveiled one of the simplest complexities encapsulated in those four words, 'as above – so below.' It is not overlooked by most intellectual minds that the microscopic atoms constituting our physical reality mirror the patterns in the cosmos. This ranges from the ubiquitous Fibonacci sequence to the reflective pattern of a tree's roots and branches. **The profound truth here is that the microcosm is a reflection of the macrocosm.**

The intelligence within the microcosm often escapes many, possibly because the ego is tuned only to what falls within the narrow bandwidth of human vision and perception. Our sight is limited to a range that excludes ultraviolet and infrared light, constraining our visual capabilities. Similarly, our hearing is restricted to a range narrower than frequencies like those used in dog whistles, illustrating the limits of our auditory senses. What about dimensions that surpass, even by a single degree, these aforementioned sensory limits?

True, we acknowledge that microchips in our smartphones can store almost unlimited data, and some of us are aware of the immense power of nanotechnology. Yet, for some reason, we often overlook the remarkable fact that our cells contain genetic data from over a million years ago. Every ancestor preceding you, including those from other realms, like the "let us make man in our image types," is intricately woven in some form within our genetic patterning. This is the marvel of the microcosm within the macrocosm. If you compare a blood cell in an organ or body to a planet in a solar system within a galaxy, you must consider that the cell might have as much drama and action potential as that planet. From political intrigue to weather patterns and distinct personalities and species, that tiny cell may mirror the same vast variety.

For context, it's noted that thirteen hundred Planet Earths could fit into the planet Jupiter, and it would take 1000 Jupiter-sized planets to fit into our sun (roughly 1.3 million Earths). Even more astounding is how our sun could fit into other suns in our galaxy over 10,000 times. The most prominent sun in our observed universe, UY Scuti, would require 5 billion of our suns to fill it. I present these facts to offer a glimpse into the quantum significance of time and space concerning infinity and the human condition.

Even Martian LSD-laced psilocybin mushrooms grown in Ayahuasca substrate from Orion couldn't propel a journey far enough into the reality of our true existence. Maybe that's why fairytales resonate so well with the ordinary human mind. The idea that a flying stork bird delivers babies is simpler to grasp than the intricacies of reproduction, just as attributing the reason for the holiday season to Santa Claus feels more palatable than acknowledging commerce or otherwise. Comparable explanations provide ample elementary reasoning for everyday mental puzzles, encompassing the enigma of our quantum reality.

These diverse, yet interconnected, points converge to demonstrate the potential of past life regression in accessing information about a soul's journey, particularly in relation to the soulmate network that influences human connections in real time. The underlying question that remains is which forces contribute to the guidance of our personal lives.

The myth that humans only use 10% of their brain power is no doubt a familiar one. If true, what potential lies within the unused and untapped brain? What about the so-called junk DNA that scientists claim to lack working knowledge of? The claim that 90% of your brain's functions are equivalent to junk actions is absurd to say the least.

Occasionally, there are extraordinary stories involving the brain and mind, such as the true account of Jason Padgett, a furniture salesman from Washington. His story goes as such, on September 13th, 2002, Jason was brutally attacked by two men after leaving a karaoke bar, leaving him unconscious with a severe concussion. Subsequently, he began experiencing changes in his vision and developed remarkable mathematical abilities, seeing patterns and shapes in everything he looked at. Further research revealed that he had developed synesthesia and savant syndrome due to his concussion.

Synesthesia is a condition in which two or more senses are involuntarily linked. For instance, some people with synesthesia might taste shapes or hear colors. Savant syndrome is a rare condition in which individuals exhibit extraordinary abilities in one area despite having cognitive or developmental disabilities in other areas. Upon research, you'll discover that Jason Padgett is one of many. He is not the first or last to undergo a change in brain fluidity, whether spontaneously or through due process.

Superfluidity, or superior fluid intelligence, is when your thoughts and ideas flow in perfect harmony, seamlessly converging in a millisecond without friction or viscosity. When you experience an epiphany or connect seemingly unrelated ideas in new and useful ways, this is directly associated with fluid intelligence. Now, envision for a moment that you could attain this supernatural state through design, intent, and/or will. Picture bypassing the daily confusion that plagues the average mind on social drugs and distracting beta wave ideas to realize your highest potential in consciousness. Would you not, at the very least, endeavor to delve into the depths of your being? Such is the potential power of a successful body scan, timeline or past life regression through hypnosis.

In this chapter, I've embarked on a journey to illuminate the captivating realms of hypnotherapy and its powerful influence to tap into Past Life Regression. I've delved into the profound depths it can explore within the doorway of human psychology, extending its reach into the mysterious abyss that is the soul.

Past life regression is a phenomenon that has gained attention both in popular opinion and scientific exploration. It emerges as a potent tool, empowering individuals to delve into the mystical expanses of their soul's esoteric history. Through the exploration of past lives via PLR, individuals can unlock profound insights into their spiritual journey, revealing hidden talents, deciphering unresolved patterns, and shedding light on the interconnectedness of their soul's evolution across lifetimes. This transformative technique serves as a gateway to unravel the intricate tapestry of human existence, providing a means to navigate the future with newfound wisdom and clarity. Ultimately, PLR can unlock dormant memories regarding the life of your soul and it's purpose or destiny. Information revealed by the soul opens the flood gates to highly esoteric information that can assist with your current incarnation and the many holographic programs surrounding it.

While it remains a subject of debate, there are several key points that contribute to a case for past life regression:

1. **Anecdotal Evidence:** There is a substantial body of anecdotal evidence from individuals who have undergone past life regression therapy and claim to have accessed memories and experiences from previous lifetimes. These accounts often describe detailed and vivid recollections that

are difficult to explain solely through imagination or suggestion.

2. **Therapeutic Benefits:** Many proponents of past life regression argue that it can have therapeutic benefits. Some individuals report relief from unexplained phobias, anxieties, and physical ailments after undergoing regression therapy. While the mechanism behind these improvements is not fully understood, the positive outcomes suggest potential therapeutic value.

3. **Parallel Belief Systems:** Past life regression aligns with belief systems in various cultures and spiritual traditions that embrace reincarnation and the concept of a continuous soul journey. These belief systems have existed for centuries and offer a contemporary context in which past life regression can be interpreted.

4. **Neuroscientific Considerations:** Neuroscientific research has shown that certain brain states, such as those induced during hypnosis or deep relaxation, may facilitate the retrieval of memories and experiences that are not readily accessible in normal waking consciousness. This suggests a plausible neurological basis for the phenomenon.

5. **Exploration of Consciousness:** Past life regression also ties into the broader exploration of human consciousness. It raises questions about the nature of memory, the boundaries of individual identity, and the possibility of non-local consciousness, all of which are topics of interest in both scientific and philosophical circles.

6. **Cross-Cultural Relevance:** Past life regression is not limited to a specific culture or region; it has been explored and practiced in various parts of the world. This cross-cultural relevance suggests that there may be universal aspects of human experience that underlie the phenomenon.

In summary, spontaneous past life recall and past life regression present a complex and multifaceted phenomenon that encompasses anecdotal accounts, potential therapeutic benefits, alignment with certain belief systems, neuroscientific considerations, and relevance across cultures. While it remains a subject of ongoing research and debate, these aspects collectively contribute to a case for further exploration and study of past life regression as a unique aspect of human consciousness and experience.

In the next chapter, insights from Seven highly esteemed experts will be presented, aiming to unlock universes of data within you. Their groundbreaking research has significantly influenced the understanding of soul knowledge, obtained through past life recall and other methods, contributing to the profound journey of conscious awakening. They among many lead in bringing this information to the forefront.

Chapter Eight

Leaders in the Field

Ian Stevenson + Jim Tucker + Carol Bowman + Brian Weiss + Michael Newton + Rob Schwartz + Delores Cannon

Quote: I inhale loneliness like it is the sweet smell of Virgin Earth conquered by fiery raindrops. Within me, I am a thousand others." —Faraaz Kazi

Throughout history, the mysteries of the soul have captivated the human imagination, leading us on a quest to understand its essence and connection. This exploration has spanned epochs through culture and religions, both offering unique perspectives on what binds souls together and the journey they undertake beyond a single lifetime. Within the multifaceted layers of this quest, we uncover the intertwining concepts of soulmates, soul ties, and the enigmatic idea of reincarnation—a belief that has persisted across civilizations and time.

As we explore these narratives, we will meet a series of pioneering researchers whose groundbreaking work has profoundly shaped our understanding of these concepts. If this book were a movie, the upcoming chapter would unfold as an engaging montage featuring some of the most pioneering leaders in the field of past life regression therapy from the last half century, offering the most dynamic reference material on the phenomenon.

The first among these luminaries is Dr. Ian Stevenson, a psychiatrist whose groundbreaking research into spontaneous past life recall in the mid-20th century opened new doors to understanding the soul's journey and its profound connections. His work marks the beginning of a journey through the minds and discoveries of several exceptional individuals, each contributing a unique piece to the puzzle of the soul's mystical nature.

This narrative aims not only to weave together the diverse threads of spiritual, cultural, and scientific insights but also to showcase the remarkable individuals who have dedicated their lives to unraveling these mysteries. From Dr. Stevenson's pioneering efforts, we will journey through the contributions of various other experts, creating a comprehensive view of how our understanding of the soul and its connections has evolved through groundbreaking research and insightful theories.

In the late 1950s, Dr. Ian Pretyman Stevenson, a Canadian-born psychiatrist who later became an American citizen, sparked a groundbreaking investigation into young prodigies recalling past lives, a phenomenon he termed 'Spontaneous Past-life Recall.' This began with children, as young as two or three, astonishingly remembering details from lives they couldn't have known in their current existence. These memories, ranging from benign recollections of another family to vivid accounts of a past life's end, emerged from around the world, gaining traction and broader acceptance in research circles by the mid to late 21st century.

Dr. Stevenson's illustrious career was deeply intertwined with the University of Virginia School of Medicine, where he founded the Division of Perceptual Studies and served as the department's chair and later as the Carlson Professor of Psychiatry. His work, spanning over fifty years at the university until his passing in 2007, left an indelible legacy in the study of reincarnation and related phenomena.

Authoring over 250 papers and books, including the influential 'Twenty Cases Suggestive of Reincarnation,' Dr. Stevenson meticulously documented cases of children's past-life recollections. While his reincarnation research initially met skepticism in the medical community, it became a catalyst for further studies, enriching our understanding of this complex subject.

Dr. Stevenson's intellectual pursuits extended beyond reincarnation to explore apparitions, near-death experiences, and out-of-body experiences. His research, encompassing four decades of global fieldwork and over three thousand case studies, suggested that phobias, philias, unusual abilities, and certain illnesses might have explanations beyond genetics or environment, possibly linked to reincarnation.

In the following sections, I will introduce some of Dr. Stevenson's most notable works, providing a brief overview of each to serve as a reference for those interested in delving deeper into this fascinating field.

- **Twenty Cases Suggestive of Reincarnation:**

Ian Stevenson's book, *"Twenty Cases Suggestive of Reincarnation,"* is a fascinating work on a much-debated topic. In it, Stevenson looks at twenty individual cases in which young children have seemingly spontaneously recalled information about past lives. In each case, Stevenson took great care to ensure that there was no possible way for the child to have acquired the information through normal means. For example, in one case, a child began speaking of a past life in which he owned a particular animal. When Stevenson spoke to the family of the deceased person the child claimed to be, they confirmed that the individual had indeed owned such an animal and that this was not common knowledge. The book is well-written and provides a compelling argument for reincarnation. In 1977, the Journal of Nervous and Mental Disease devoted most of one issue to Stevenson's work in which psychiatrist Harold Lief described Stevenson as "a methodical, careful, even cautious, investigator, whose personality is on the obsessive side. But this very obsessiveness has driven him to amass an impressive body of evidence supporting the reality of reincarnation.

- **Children who remember previous lives:**

In 1961, when Ian began researching cases of young children who claimed to remember previous lives, his approach involved a rational, scientific attempt to discern what the children said about a previous life and how much of it could be verified to be accurate for a particular deceased individual. He discovered that cases could be found all over the world. He also learned that memories were not the only items that seemed to carry over for these children. A number had birthmarks that matched wounds suffered by the previous person, and many demonstrated anxieties, phobias, or emotional longing that appeared to be derived from the previous events that they described. Researchers have now studied over 2500 cases in a project that is still ongoing. This book traces that history and summarizes extensive psychological research involving thousands of children over many years. <u>It is important to note that Stevenson's approach was not intended to provide proof of reincarnation but rather to explore whether or not such claims had any merit</u>. The fact that so many cases have been studied and that many of the details provided by the children could be verified suggests that there may be something to the phenomenon of reincarnation.

- **Where Reincarnation and Biology Begin:**

There is no doubt that children who claim to remember a previous life have been found in many parts of the world. This is particularly true in the Buddhist and Hindu countries of South Asia, among the Shiite peoples of Lebanon and Turkey, the tribes of West Africa, and the American northwest. Dr. Ian Stevenson has collected over 2,600 reported cases of past-life memories, and 65 detailed reports have been published. Specific information from the children's memories has been collected and matched with the data of their claimed former identity, family, residence, and manner of death. Birthmarks or other physiological manifestations have been found to relate to experiences of the remembered past life, particularly violent death, as a specialist in psychiatry and as a world-renowned scientific investigator of reported paranormal phenomena. Dr. Stevenson is uniquely qualified to discuss this topic. His research is very thorough, and his conclusions are based on solid evidence.

- **Science, the Self, and Survival after Death | Selected Writings of Ian Stevenson:**

Science, the Self, and Survival after Death is the first book devoted to surveying the entirety of his work and the extraordinary scope and variety of his research. He studied universal questions that cut to the core of a person's identity: What is consciousness - How did we become the unique individuals that we are - Do we survive in some form after death? Stevenson's writings on the nature of science and the mind-body relationship, as well as his empirical research, demonstrate his strongly held belief that methods of science can be applied successfully to such humanly vital questions. This collection featuring a selection of his papers and excerpts from his books presents the larger context of Stevenson's work and illustrates the issues and questions that guided him throughout his career.

- **Unlearned language | New Studies in Xenoglossy:**

This book consists of a lengthy discussion and descriptions of two cases of responsive xenoglossy. The latter can be defined as <u>the ability of a person to speak and understand a foreign language</u> that was not learned normally. Ian Stevenson wrote another book about another case previously published. He makes comparisons in the current volume among all three cases. In these cases, Stevenson interviewed small children who could speak foreign languages from their previous lives.

For adults, past life recall typically emerges from extraordinary experiences like hypnosis, lucid dreaming, or even a significant blow to the head. Regardless of your stance on reincarnation, Ian Stevenson's work distinctly suggests that certain individuals harbor memories of lives beyond the scope of their current existence. Moreover, it sheds light on physical and biological phenomena that defy conventional explanations.

Under the influence of hypnosis, numerous individuals vividly recall the particulars of their past lives, sometimes adopting the very personalities of their former selves. Surprisingly, this phenomenon occurs more frequently than one might initially surmise! Multiple factors contribute to a person's capacity to recollect past lives during hypnosis. For instance, if someone were reincarnated into a different culture, their regression might manifest in the form of speaking a foreign language. These implications propose that reincarnation may transcend mere hallucination, becoming a tangible reality for some. Subjects under hypnosis adeptly detail their previous homes, families, friends, and various facets of their past lives.

In some cases, individuals under hypnosis could vividly recall the events preceding their deaths. These memories were not mere products of the imagination; they were exceptionally vivid and realistic. If we entertain the reality of reincarnation, it opens the door to the prospect that we, as individuals, have traversed multiple lives and might persist in doing so beyond death. This influence could elucidate why certain individuals display a seemingly innate affinity for specific cultures and trivial things — perhaps a potential echo of experiences from a previous life!

In 1824, a Japanese farmer's son named Katsugoro, just nine years old, revealed to his sister that he believed he had lived a previous life. Katsugoro could remember dozens of specific events about his past life, including details about his former family and the village where they lived, even though Katsugoro had never been there. He even remembered the time of his death, his burial, and the time he spent before being reborn.

A subsequent investigation verified Katsugoro's claims and found that everything the boy had said was true. This case is significant because it suggests that people can remember past lives without hypnosis. According to his story, which is one of the earliest cases of past life recall on record, the boy vividly recalled that he had been the son of another farmer in another village and had died from the effects of smallpox in 1810, all using **spontaneous past life recall.**

There are a variety of methods by which people can recall their past lives. One of the most well-known is hypnosis, but it is not the only method. In some cases, people may simply have a **vivid dream** in which they relive a previous life. I for one, "Kushaqxi," can remember what would have seemed to be a dream but was indeed a spontaneous memory, of myself talking and joking with a comrade while building a matrix of Kushite styled pyramids, at dusk beneath a reddish sky, with hundreds of other specially skilled or high ranking soldier/laborers, under the command of something akin to a Pharaoh. There are several cases like this where individuals have spontaneous past life recall by way of dream sequence.

Such was also the case for a British woman who dreamed that she and another child fell to their deaths from a high gallery in their home. The woman remembered the black and white checkered marble floor on which they died, and she was disturbed by the dream. She related the dream to several of her friends and later had the opportunity to visit an old house that was rumored to be haunted.

When she saw the black and white marble floor, she immediately realized it was the same floor as her dream. Further investigation revealed that two children had died in that very house. Whether the woman recalled a past life or had somehow psychically tuned into this dramatic event is still unknown. However, it shows that there are multiple ways in which people can access memories of previous lives.

Other notable cases of past life recall include the cases of George Gurdjieff and Shirley MacLaine. George Gurdjieff was a Russian spiritual teacher who claimed to have memories of his previous lives. Shirley MacLaine, an American actress, and author, also claims to remember her past lives. Both Gurdjieff and MacLaine have written extensively about their experiences, providing valuable insight into the phenomenon of past life recall.

A multitude of documented cases reveal individuals with vivid memories of past lives. The instances shared earlier are merely a glimpse into the well-known examples of past life recall. Numerous other cases, extensively documented, provide compelling evidence for the existence of reincarnation. Considering the sheer number of people passionately claiming to remember their previous lives, dismissing them as fabrications seems unlikely. It's more reasonable to embrace the belief that they authentically recall genuine memories from their past lives.

Some of these memories are remarkably specific, like recalling the name of a past town or the layout of a previous home. In contrast, others may only experience a vague sense of déjà vu or a feeling they've been somewhere before. While skeptics might dismiss these memories as mere fanciful imagination, closer examination often reveals compelling supporting evidence. Moreover, certain individuals have showcased skills or knowledge from their past lives that defy explanation within the context of their current existence.

While the pioneering work of Ian Stevenson initiated the meticulous research documenting various cases worldwide, he certainly wasn't the last scientist to embrace the challenge of shedding light on these phenomena. Several scientists and therapists have assumed the responsibility of researching reincarnation. For instance, picking up where Dr. Stevenson left off is Dr. Jim Tucker.

Dr. Jim Tucker, a distinguished Professor of Psychiatry and Neurobehavioral Sciences at the University of Virginia School of Medicine, holds the position of Director at the University's Division of Perceptual Studies. Known for his authorship of 'Life Before Life,' Dr. Tucker specializes in researching cases of children who claim to have memories from before their current birth, a focus inspired by his encounter with the pioneering work of Ian Stevenson. His investigations delve into the realm of children recalling previous lives, continuing and expanding upon the legacy of Stevenson's groundbreaking research.

In his captivating book, "Return to Life: Experiences of Reincarnation," Dr. Tucker generously shares some of the most enthralling cases he has explored in his illustrious career. Remarkably, these memories often unfold with incredible specificity, and Dr. Tucker meticulously verifies them using birth, death, and census records.

One remarkable case involved a boy from India who vividly recalled being a WWII pilot shot down over Japan. Astonishingly, the details provided by the boy were later confirmed by military records. Another compelling instance featured a girl from Sri Lanka who confidently asserted she was the reincarnation of a murdered woman. The girl not only described the woman's home but also provided details about the murder, later corroborated by police records.

Tucker has investigated hundreds of cases in which children have made claims about remembering past lives, and he has found evidence that supports their claims in many of these cases. Since taking over Ian Stevenson's research into claimed past-life memories in 2002, Tucker has been interviewed about reincarnation in print and broadcast media in the United States, United Kingdom, and Canada. In 2009, he was interviewed on Larry King Live about his studied cases and has since been interviewed on mainstream broadcasts. While Ian Stevenson focused on cases in Asia, Tucker has primarily studied children in the U.S.

In addition to Doctors Stevenson and Tucker, Carol Bowman, M.S., is another prominent figure in reincarnation research, especially known for her advocacy of children's past lives. Since publishing her first book in 1997, Bowman has gained international recognition as an author, lecturer, counselor, past life regression therapist, and a pioneering researcher. Her work extends beyond children, encompassing adults who claim to recall past lives, and is based on extensive interviews and case studies.

A frequent guest on various media platforms, Bowman has appeared on shows like Oprah, Good Morning America, Unsolved Mysteries, and ABC Primetime.

Her expertise in reincarnation has also been featured on networks such as A&E, Discovery Channel, the BBC, and radio shows like The Art Bell Show and Coast to Coast with George Noory, cementing her status as a respected authority in the field.

Bowman presents an abundance of compelling evidence affirming the reality of reincarnation. Her book, *"Children's Past Lives: How Past Lives Affect Your Child,"* serves as a convincing exploration, diving into the genuine existence of reincarnation and its profound impact on our lives. Through her meticulous research, Bowman not only sheds light on the mechanisms of reincarnation but also explores the reasons behind its occurrence.

Bowman's perspective is that reincarnation is a dynamic process of spiritual evolution, where souls actively learn and grow from one lifetime to the next. She firmly believes that by comprehending our past lives, we can gain valuable insights into our present lives, fostering positive changes and personal growth.

Carol's book, Children's Past Lives, is the first book of its kind to explore the phenomenon of children's spontaneous past life memories. Carol's own children's past life memories led her to do extensive research on the topic, and the result is a fascinating and eye-opening read. The book includes a guidebook for parents to teach them how to recognize and respond when their children have these memories.

Carol's research presents reincarnation as a practical reality in our lives and families. Her book, along with all the authors mentioned, are essential reads for anyone interested in reincarnation or who has had any experience with past life memories.

Other enriching reads and noteworthy mentions that delve into the intricacies of the subject, with thorough case studies, include:

- **Old Souls:** Compelling Evidence from Children Who Remember Past Lives: *By Thomas Shroder.*

- **7 Reasons to Believe in the Afterlife:** A Doctor Reviews the Case for Consciousness after Death: *By Jean Jacques Charbonier*

- **You Have Been Here Before:** A Psychologist Looks at Past Lives: *By Dr. Edith Fiore*

- **Past Lives, Future Lives:** *By Dick Sutphen*

- **Reliving Past Lives: By Helen Wambach**

- **Edgar Cayce's Story of Karma:** *By Mary Ann Woodward*

- **Mass Dreams of the Future:** *By Chet Snow*

- **Reincarnation:** *By Sylvia Cranston and Carey Williams*

- **Children Who Remember By**: *Dr. Ian Stevenson*

Long before I encountered the works of Ian Stevenson, Jim Tucker, or even Carol Bowman, a compelling story on Fox News caught my attention. It centered around a remarkable blue eyed, blond haired five-year-old boy named Luke Ruehlman. Luke began unsettling his mother with claims of being the reincarnated spirit of a 30-year-old woman named Pam, who tragically perished in a Chicago fire two decades prior.

Even more gripping, Luke recounted vivid details of how his past life concluded, describing his death by leaping from a tall burning building. He even shared specific aspects of Pam's life, mentioning her prior travels on a train in Chicago.

Erika, Luke's mother, found herself bewildered. The family had never visited Chicago, and she had never discussed anything remotely resembling her son's revelations. Intrigued, she turned to the internet for answers and unearthed a chilling revelation — a tragic fire at Chicago's Paxton Hotel claimed the lives of 19 people back in 1993.

In a truly remarkable twist of fate, Erika Ruehlman, Luke's mother, made a startling discovery. She found that an African American woman in her thirties named Pamela Robinson matched the description provided by Luke and was one of the victims of the tragic event. Luke's grandmother couldn't dismiss the story as mere coincidence.

Luke's mother, recalls how, Luke used to say things like, "When I was a girl, I had black hair,"' or he would say, "I used to have earrings like that when I was a girl." Ruehlman was stunned. She pressed him more and asked how Pam died. "He would look right at Erika and say, 'Yeah, it was a fire.' At that point, he would motion with his hand like he was jumping off a building, "He'd say, I died and went to heaven, and I saw God. Finally, God moved me back down here, and when I woke up, I was a baby, and then you named me Luke."

The TV show The Ghost Inside My Child also investigated Luke's story, which put Erika in touch with Pamela Robinson's family. Upon speaking to the Robinson family about Pam, Luke's mother said that her son and Pam also had similar tastes in music and personalities. I personally found the story of Luke fascinating, as I myself could recall various esoteric happenings as a small child as well as my teenage years. I'm pretty sure this story, among others, is what ultimately set me on a path to finding a deeper understanding of past life phenomena.

With the insights from Luke's story, it opens up the idea that souls incarnate in the most contrasting and varied narratives. A soul could have once been the classical composer Debussy, creator of 'Clair de Lune,' and is now incarnated as rapper Lil Boosie, creator of 'Wipe Me Down.' From Debussy to Lil Boosie, the diversity and contrast, along with the challenges faced, contribute to resilient and dynamic learning experiences for the incarnate soul's evolution.

Regarding my own journey, I quite serendipitously, stumbled upon the author Brian Weiss's book, 'Many Lives, Many Masters,' on a random summer day. The discovery of his book, and the story within propelled me into a deeper exploration of Past Life Regression. I believed that learning about Luke's story was a preparatory step, preparing me for the wealth of information I was about to uncover and wholeheartedly immerse myself.

I found Dr. Brian Weiss, 'Many Lives, Many Masters' so enlightening that, after reading it, I have gifted both physical and audio copies to many friends. This book, along with others, deepened my understanding of the soul's true nature. It also resonated with my intuitive development of the 'twin elemental doctrine,' which aligns with esoteric knowledge and fits seamlessly into many people's personal journey. My prior interest in auto-hypnotherapy naturally drew me to Weiss's work in past life regression. I recognized hypnosis as the key method he used to guide subjects into recalling their past lives.

Being a long-time enthusiast of hypnosis, my journey began earlier with studying figures like Richard Bandler, Franz Mesmer, and the pioneers of hypnosis. My initial aspiration was to use hypnosis to cultivate well-behaved geniuses out of my small children. I also harbored dreams of assisting family members in overcoming substance abuse caused by premeditated epidemics through the power of hypnosis. Imagine my astonishment when discovering that one could be hypnotically induced to astral travel or recall past lives. It was truly a revelation, and stumbling upon Dr. Weiss's book at a local West End Goodwill felt like a stroke of luck.

Dr. Brian Leslie Weiss, a renowned psychiatrist and hypnotherapist, specializes in Reincarnation and Past Life Regression. His extensive work includes narratives from individuals who claim past life experiences and examining how these memories impact their present lives. His writings cover a range of topics, from the mechanics of past life regression to future life progression and the enduring nature of the soul beyond death. The details I am about to recount and the intriguing journey of Dr. Brian Leslie Weiss into Past Life Regression or PLR, is well-documented online and detailed on his website.

Before his foray into this field, Weiss was a conventional psychiatrist, teaching at the University of Pittsburgh and later serving as the Chief of Psychiatry at Mount Sinai Medical Center in Miami Beach, Florida. It was here that he met Catherine, a 27-year-old lab technician struggling with anxiety, depression, and phobias, despite her skepticism about traditional therapy.

Weiss's exploration into Past Life Phenomena began with Catherine, who became the central figure in his seminal book, 'Many Lives, Many Masters.' In this book, published in 1988, Weiss recounts Catherine's struggles with various psychological issues and her initial reluctance to undergo psychiatric treatment. Despite months of conventional therapy, her condition showed no improvement.

Weiss writes that a turning point came during a museum visit, where Catherine displayed unexpected knowledge about Egyptian history, jokingly attributing it to past life memories. This incident led her to agree to hypnotherapy with Dr. Weiss, a decision that marked a significant shift in her treatment.

Under hypnosis, Catherine recalled childhood traumas, but these revelations did not ease her symptoms. In further sessions, Weiss guided her to explore earlier periods, unknowingly leading her beyond childhood where Catherine would begin to describe vivid experiences from a past life as a woman from 1863 B.C. These sessions not only provided insights into her current afflictions but also became a cornerstone of Weiss's work in PLR, profoundly influencing his approach and understanding of the therapy.

Dr. Brian L. Weiss was profoundly impacted by his sessions with Catherine, a patient who under hypnosis recalled over eighty past lifetimes, although she provided detailed accounts for about eleven. Weiss, initially astonished and unable to align these revelations with a clinical diagnosis, noted that Catherine, a devout Catholic, had no inherent belief in reincarnation, which added credibility to her recollections.

During her sessions, Catherine described lives of varied genders, ages, nationalities, and races. She also recognized individuals from her current life in these past experiences, including a former lover, who appeared in different forms in her past lives. This experience introduced Weiss to the concept of a 'soul family,' where individuals reincarnate together in different roles across lifetimes.

As Catherine explored more past lives and interacted with what she described as Master Spirits, her psychological issues began to improve dramatically. This breakthrough with Catherine not only inspired Weiss's best-selling book 'Many Lives, Many Masters' but also led him to apply past-life therapy to several other patients, with notable success.

Following this initial book, Dr. Weiss continued to explore and write about the soul's journey and its connections across lifetimes, focusing on the interactions within one's 'soul clan.' His subsequent books further delve into the themes of soulmates and past lives, each contributing a unique perspective to our understanding of these profound concepts.

Each of these works provides a distinct perspective on the subject matter. Beyond the impactful "Many Lives, Many Masters," other compelling reads include Brian Weiss's "Only Love is Real: The Story of Soulmates Reunited." This book delves into the notion of soulmates and past lives, recounting incredible stories of couples rediscovering each other in this lifetime after being separated in previous existences.

Another enlightening read is "Same Soul, Many Bodies: Discover the Healing Power of Future Lives through Progression Therapy" focuses on utilizing progression therapy to facilitate healing from emotional wounds carried over from past lives. Another notable work is "Messages from the Masters: Tapping into the Power of Love" by Brian Weiss. This book delves into the concept of communicating with loved ones who have passed to the other side, recounting incredible stories of individuals forging connections with those who have departed.

"Through Time Into Healing" by Brian Weiss is a captivating exploration of utilizing past life regression for healing emotional wounds. Dr. Weiss enriches this book with powerful stories illustrating how regression therapy can guide individuals through profound healing from deep emotional pain. Each of these books provides a distinct perspective on the subject matter, and I wholeheartedly recommend them to anyone keen on delving deeper into this fascinating topic.

Dr. Weiss's book profoundly expanded my consciousness to the possibilities of past lives, soul families, and karmic debts in relationships. I am eternally grateful to him and his transformative work.

Fastforward—

Who could have anticipated lightning striking twice, and right at the same Goodwill, of all places? During a quest for random Octavia Butler books and hidden gem vinyl records, I stumbled upon a book called **"Journey of Souls: Case Studies of Life Between Lives"** *by Michael Newton, Ph.D.*

Dr. Newton, stands as a highly acclaimed international spiritual regressionist, unlocking the gateway for individuals to tap into the wisdom of the spirit world and their higher selves while still in the clutches of life. Holding a doctorate in Counseling and Psychology, and certified as a Master Hypnotherapist, Dr. Newton was also a distinguished member of the American Counseling Association.

Trained under prestigious institutions like Harvard Medical School, where he earned his doctorate, Dr. Newton pioneered techniques celebrated as cornerstones in the realm of Spiritual Healing Arts. These groundbreaking methods aid clients in unraveling the mysteries surrounding death through spiritual inductions, conducted during their sessions with Dr. Newton.

As a highly regarded researcher in past life regression, Dr. Newton generously unveils his findings from over thirty years of dedicated study in this compelling book. Within its pages, he intricately narrates the stories of 29 individuals who candidly share their experiences of past lives and the profound impact of these memories on their present lives—both the positive and the transformative.

My appreciation for Dr. Newton's books lies in a feature that has become a staple in my research endeavors—being, case studies. The weight of these studies amplifies when I can compare narratives from various cases. Particularly captivating are instances where individuals access information from other worlds or dimensions, aiding in the resolution of past wrongdoings. When a myriad of people share similar or identical experiences, we tread the path of **"Consensus Reality,"** a collective agreement that lends **authenticity** to these shared realities.

Following the ground-breaking success of "Journey of Souls," Michael returned five years later with the second installment in the series, "Destiny of Souls."

In this sequel, he delves even deeper, presenting 70 detailed accounts of individuals regressing into their previous lives. Dr. Newton provides answers for readers craving further insights into aspects explored in the earlier book, addressing questions about what happens after death and **how one attains enlightenment through multiple lifetimes.**

Newton's impactful legacy lives on through the Michael Newton Institute, which recently published *"The Wisdom of Souls."* The memory of stumbling upon that first book is etched in my mind. Despite my initial excitement to read it, I continued to procrastinate until one day at a local coffee shop when I finally pulled it from my bag and opened its pages. Hours flew by, and I couldn't tear myself away. Case after case unfolded, each more captivating than the last, affirming many theories encountered in the works of Brian Weiss several months prior.

My discovery of this information affirmed a belief I've held intuitively, even before learning about Luke's story—*There's nothing new under the Sun.* This ancient wisdom, drawn from the biblical book of Ecclesiastes and instilled by my church pastor and parents, has deeply resonated with me since childhood. It reinforced my long-standing perception that our earthly existence is merely a reflection of a more mystical, unseen realm.

From vibrant, astral-inspired dreams to tangible astral journeys, I've come to realize that reality isn't always as straightforward as it seems. It sometimes feels like being enveloped in an eternal mist of illusion, casting a high-definition glow reminiscent of an exceptionally advanced virtual reality gaming console. I can't help but marvel at the possibility that this alternate realm might be a billion years ahead of what we've collectively embraced as our reality here on Earth.

I'd like to provide context to an earlier reflection by sharing a personal experience. Not long ago, I experienced the profound loss of a dear friend, which was eerily foreshadowed in a vivid dream. In it, paramedics rushed past two friends and I towards a nearby tragedy. As I neared the scene, I heard an actual voice in real time urging, 'Stop him, don't let him see.' I awoke yelling, I want to see, I can handle it, what is it etc. I felt at the time the dream was a warning, possibly for me or one of my friends from the dream.

Tragically, a week later, my dear friend took her own life. This was the same person who provided the advice that sparked my first genuine experience of compersion, as mentioned in the first chapter. Her loss brought overwhelming grief, and I struggled with the fact that I hadn't anticipated it, despite the dream's warning and her previous suicide attempt.

At her funeral, I longed for a sign from her and later received a message through my life partner's mother, who is a spiritual intuitive. She conveyed that my friend was in a place of vibrant colors and brilliant light, urging me to play music for her whenever she came to mind. This friend, Naphtali Nkashimo Tanzania Doty, was more than a close companion; she was a distinguished soul mate, and I honor her memory with music and libations. A'se.

Further insights into the soul's connections came during a journey with Mother Ayahuasca. I found myself in a session experiencing playful laughter with my departed friend Naphtali and a few others. During the session, I felt an overwhelming sense of love and connection as they giggled and teased. This experience reinforced the idea of a 'soul family' — a group of inseparable comrades, present in this life and beyond, always near in spirit. These moments have solidified my belief in a soul family that transcends physicality and individual lifetimes. These concepts have become a cornerstone in my understanding of our shared spiritual journeys.

The myriad books penned by the aforementioned authors brought newfound clarity and understanding to the deep-seated feelings and knowledge I'd always harbored but struggled to articulate. The uncanny manner in which I encountered their information seamlessly aligned with the universe's pre-designed script. Some events and relationships unfold in ways that feel predestined, happening regardless of personal desires, with no resistance and exceeding even the most optimistic expectations.

Becoming attuned to these experiences has been remarkably enriching, shedding light on the connections I share with my soul family and those with whom I had a preexisting karmic soul contract, established long before encountering them in the current lifetime. Whether the meetings are positive and uplifting or distressing, they are encounters that destiny dictates. As I emphasized earlier in this book, people enter your life for a reason, a season, or a lifetime, whether to spark a fire within your spirit or provide soothing floods of water; ultimately, a predestined assignment must be fulfilled.

Upon encountering a researcher and hypnotist named **Robert Schwartz**, I would delve deeper into understanding these intricate dynamics. Schwartz authored a book titled *"***Your Soul's Plan:*** Discovering the Real Meaning of the Life You Planned Before You Were Born."* Within its pages, he elucidates how each of us crafted a pre-birth plan before conception. In essence, the author proposes that before our birth, we collaborated with our spirit guides to create a plan that shapes our life story. What this means is that every event in our entire lives are already scripted and planned. From the best to the worst experiences, you and your guides wrote it out like an amateur movie on Tubi. Of course, your next question might be, "Why would I plan and create the terrible things happening in my life? For those who struggle to believe in a preordained script governing their lives, consider this thought provoking perspective.

Among religious believers, there exists a conviction that God, the ultimate polymath, possesses omnipotence and omniscience, with supreme knowledge extending to every detail—from the countless hair follicles on heads to the existence of every individual atom in existence, with foresight encompassing all yet-to-unfold events as well. Given this belief, the idea that a blueprint of one's life may precede its actualization is not far-fetched, given God's all-encompassing knowledge.

It's akin to living on a timeline that moves backward rather than forward, resembling the essence of a playwright's script. It's authored and completed to the end, and then the actors enact all predestined actions with the end in mind, effectively returning to the past with each performance after glimpsing the future. While the actors may be cognizant of the events unfolding in the final scene, they must remain wholly present and laser-focused on the current events, such as those in "Scene One," as they play out what is to come.

To illustrate the relative scope of time in the context of biological life, I often draw a parallel between the 'seventy-year' or 'seven-decade' lifespan of a human and the fleeting lifespans of certain animals, insects, or cells. For instance, the 'seven-year' lifespan of a dog, the 'seven-day' life of a mayfly, or even the 'seven-second' lifespan of a specific bacteria are no different from **a 'seven-millennium' or 'seven epoch' lifespan of a young soul in the realm of nonlinear, omni-directional time.**

Each measure of time may appear vastly distinct, yet outside the confines of time, they hold an equal scope. To provide perspective, whether it's the seven-second lifespan of a bacterium or the seven-decade life of Billy Ray Jackson Jr., all of it can be compared to a mere **seven-minute dream in the expansive landscape of a soul's consciousness.** Simply put, if your soul were to drift into slumber and dream, that dream could equate to your current seven year or seven decade lifespan. Time is simply a perspective of mind, everyone and everything experiences it differently.

Upon reflection and fostering complete transparency with yourself, when dreaming, have you ever pondered if you're genuinely cognizant that while you envision drifting on a gondola boat through the network of canals at sunset in Venice, Italy, you're, in reality, at your mother-in-law's home in Charlotte, North Carolina, resting on worn white sheets in a twin-sized bed during the Thanksgiving holiday? Most likely, you have no idea and truly believe that you are in Italy living out several seasons of your best life.

Within the soul's dream, you, along with your higher selves or soul family, take on the roles of writers, directors, and stars in a grand play. As the renowned line from William Shakespeare goes, "All the world's a stage, and all the men and women merely players," voiced by the melancholic Jaques in Shakespeare's pastoral comedy, *"As You Like It,"* dating back to 1599, for those who didn't know. Shakespeare unknowingly tapped into a profound truth about our existence with this line.

Getting back on track, In the book *"Your Soul's Plan,"* by Robert Schwartz, it is explained that during the planning of your current mortal life, you as an eternal soul, took part in selecting your parents, and they, in turn, also agreed to choose you. You made decisions about the cities you would inhabit, the schools you would attend, the homes you would reside in, the individuals you would encounter, and the relationships you would forge.

Options for careers and a few significant life events or tragedies were also prearranged for specific junctures in your life. Additionally, you entered into agreements with the souls that would take on the role of your children. Last but not least, amid numerous other choices, you deliberately chose that furry companion you fondly call a pet, each serving specific purposes in your life. All major events were preplanned and all that was left to do is decide how you were going to enact them and what decisions you would make in dealing with them. More importantly, how you respond to the decisions you make.

When someone is murdered, and the other spends decades in jail, make no mistake, that was a predestined action to enact a soul lesson, agreed upon by all-knowing souls for unknowing minds. The vast majority of life's challenges are indeed chosen, and the more profound the challenge, the greater the likelihood it was designated before birth. Whether or not we are consciously aware of planning something, our growth stems from our experiences. The true value lies in focusing on why you might have chosen a specific challenge in your life rather than questioning whether you planned it. Essentially, the journey is where we encounter admiration, gratitude, and appreciation far more than in the destination itself.

As mentioned before, when people encounter information like this, their immediate reaction is usually, "No way would I have signed up for the grief or hurt Im feeling—why on earth would I do that?" But what if, against all odds, we really did map out our experiences before taking our first breath? How could such a feat be possible, and what might be the underlying purpose or significance of such pre-birth planning? This becomes particularly intriguing when considering aspects like life partners or intense experiences involving soul mates, twin elementals, and the intricacies of soul ties and karmic debts.

These inquiries inject a fresh burst of energy into our approach to life's hurdles, encouraging us to embrace them with curiosity as stepping stones to personal growth and the pursuit of wisdom. Understanding the incipient and sometimes precarious nature of pre-birth planning is like grasping the nuances of color and contrast. Without the interplay of light and dark, our comprehension of existence remains incomplete. Imagine only knowing light without ever experiencing the profound depths of darkness. It's the dance between these polarities that sharpens our universal understanding. What is joy without pain to define it.

In a three-dimensional physical simulation, we encounter this contrast through layers of duality, reminiscent of the ones and zeros in virtual reality, computer gaming, or generative neural networking technology. The interplay between good and bad, up and down, left and right, hot and cold, and even love and hate forms a vibrant palette of colors for painting on our canvas of life experiences. Without problems to solve or conflicts to navigate, our journey lacks the rich tapestry essential for honing problem-solving and conflict-resolution skills—to say the least.

Winning a championship holds little meaning without the hurdles, setbacks, long nights, and achievements that led to claiming the trophy. Moreover, how could one truly fathom the depth of love without grappling with the shadows of hate or pain? Some say it's better to have loved and lost than never to have loved at all. Likewise, the opposing forces in life are essential, as they add richness, depth, complexity, and significance to our experiences. Devoid of these aspects of our humanity, how would we ever recognize our own divinity? These examples, though basic, weave together to create a comprehensive picture, aiding in our understanding of the intricate connection between flesh and soul within the life we know.

Life plans emerge as blueprints for exploring the essence of our being. For instance, a profoundly compassionate soul seeking self-discovery might choose to manifest in a highly dysfunctional family. Experiencing a deficit of compassion prompts a deeper appreciation for it. When compassion is scarce externally, one turns inward, rediscovering their compassionate nature. Just as a bodybuilder cannot gauge their true strength without lifting heavier, one cannot understand their true capabilities without pushing themselves further. Similarly, a soul is tested and revealed through challenges.

The absence of something often holds the key to understanding its true value and meaning. Frequently, when faced with adversity, it may seem like senseless suffering. Yet, the thought-provoking question posed by the book, "Your Soul's Plan," challenges us: What if your most arduous experiences are laden with hidden purpose, intricately woven into the fabric of life's circumstances, relationships, and events you consciously designed? These questions cast a revealing light on the nature and comprehension of twin elemental relationships.

In the compelling book "Your Soul's Plan," author Rob Schwartz recounts the remarkable experiences of ten individuals. Individuals who, much like yourself, orchestrated their own life challenges before birth and faced significant struggles. Through collaborative efforts with four gifted mediums and channels, Schwartz unveils the profound reasons behind pre-birth planning for those confronting substantial challenges. By delving into actual pre-birth planning sessions, he uncovers the hopes and aspirations of these eternal souls, illustrating how we intricately design our trials, tribulations, and potential victories. In essence, Schwartz provides readers with a captivating window into the intricate process of shaping our life experiences.

Among the myriad stories, one that resonated deeply with me was that of a young woman engulfed in an explosion that left her severely burned and disfigured. Through a journey of healing and regression, her sessions revealed that she consciously chose this experience as a transformative journey, ultimately emerging as the powerful healer she is today. Her lack of regret or resentment towards those responsible for the actions are truly remarkable, making her story profoundly moving and worth every reader's attention.

Its shocking to learn that the individuals who pose the greatest challenges in our lives do so at our own request. The soul assuming the role of a persecutor willingly provides contrast out of love, often delaying their own growth until a subsequent lifetime provides them with the necessary experiences to pay it forward. These roles are agreed upon even before our parents conceive us. These roles are acted out by the quintessential twin elemental archetype in many cases.

In the following paragraph, I'd like to offer a paraphrased excerpt from "Your Soul's Plan" by Robert Schwartz, exemplifying a soul's personality.

"Yes, I have incarnated in your realm 867 times, spending numerous lifetimes in human bodies and others in non-human forms. I've chosen to be your guide across incarnations—sisters, mother and daughter, enemies who've clashed and even taken each other's lives, and dear friends. Each time, we decided where and under what circumstances we'd meet, presenting opportunities for beautiful growth experiences. We are true soulmates, souls vibrating at a similar frequency, each with a unique color and sound." End Quote.

Ultimately, the pre-planning of life's challenges and the agreement to incarnate with a soul group serve our personal growth. While we learn a great deal between incarnations as part of a soul group, those lessons are more deeply ingrained when put into practice in the spiritual realm. This practice is similar to taking the classroom out for hands-on field study, where knowledge becomes not just acquired but a cathartic and powerful experience for the soul.

The impact on your soul in the nonphysical realm is profound, and your body, the avatar of your existence, serves as the vessel for this intense awareness, illuminating areas where growth is crucial. As the physical journey concludes, your unique consciousness signature rejoins your soul group, enriched with a wealth of knowledge.

Life operates without a pass or fail system, devoid of shame, blame, or judgment from a tall, bearded man-god prone to impulsiveness, spite, and jealousy. Instead, it's a tapestry of lessons in duality with your soul family, set within the framework of eternal time, space, and evolution—pre-planned from a higher state of awareness and divine consciousness.

Kudos to Robert Schwartz for being the conduit through which this enlightening information manifested. I wholeheartedly recommend delving into his book, "Your Soul's Plan," alongside his other insightful works, such as "Your Soul's Love" and "Your Soul's Gift."

One of the remarkable figures also shedding light within the metaphysical realm is none other than your favorite metaphysical auntie, Dolores Cannon. A pioneer in hypnotherapy that specializing in past life regression, Cannon's nearly 50-year career took her to captivating destinations. Born in St. Louis, Missouri, in 1931, she embarked on extensive global travels with her husband Johnny, accommodating his various overseas assignments for 21 years.

In the late 1960s, Cannon integrated past life regressions into her therapeutic practice. A pivotal moment occurred when a woman undergoing therapy spontaneously recounted scenes from a past life as a flapper in 1920s Chicago. Dolores and Johnny witnessed the woman transforming into distinct personalities with different vocal patterns, sparking Cannon's lifelong fascination with past lives and metaphysics. The first-hand account of this event is chronicled in Dolores's inaugural book, **"Five Lives Remembered."**

Over subsequent decades, Cannon interviewed thousands who shared past life memories, synthesizing her findings in several insightful books like "Hidden Sacred Knowledge," "The Custodians," "Keepers of the Garden," "The Convoluted Universe," and "Between Death and Life." In these works, Cannon explores the myriad ways past lives influence our present existence, unraveling common themes and patterns embedded in people's past life memories.

Dolores Cannon's literary works abound with fascinating stories derived from her extensive experience with past life regressions and her innovative Quantum Healing Hypnosis Technique (QHHT). Some of the most significant and intriguing stories from her books include:

1. "The Three Waves of Volunteers and the New Earth" - In this book, Cannon describes her sessions with clients who claimed to be part of

a group of "volunteers" from other planets and dimensions who have come to Earth to help with the transition to a new, higher level of consciousness.

2. "The Custodians: Beyond Abduction" - This book explores Cannon's work with clients who claimed to have had encounters with extraterrestrial beings and explores the nature of these encounters and their potential significance.

3. "Jesus and the Essenes" - In this book, Cannon recounts a past life regression session where a client described living as a member of the Essene community during the time of Jesus Christ.

4. "The Convoluted Universe" - This book is a compilation of some of Cannon's most fascinating and mind-bending stories from her work with clients, including stories of past lives on other planets, alternate dimensions, and even conversations with plants and animals.

Overall, Dolores Cannon's exploration encompasses a vast array of profound subjects, delving into the core of consciousness, the incredible potential of the human mind, and the immense influence of our thoughts and intentions. Her work traverses topics such as parallel universes, alternative realities, lost civilizations, ancient history, and the holographic nature of reality. She unravels details of experiences where individuals were regressed to lives on other planets, shedding light on the concept that we are fragments of multifaceted souls.

Central to Cannon's methodology is the Quantum Healing Hypnosis Technique (QHHT), a process involving inducing a hypnotic state in her clients to access their past lives and higher selves. Through this technique, she claims to facilitate healing, spiritual growth, and profound insights into the nature of reality. An underlying theme in her work consistently emerges – the interconnectedness of all beings, emphasizing that we are integral parts of the same master soul.

In alignment with Cannon's teachings, there's a fundamental point to underscore – the energy source animating the universe is identical for all. Using the metaphor of water droplets forming an ocean, we share a common consciousness yet exhibit individual characteristics shaped by our co-created realities. The analogy of a pitcher of water poured into distinct glasses beautifully encapsulates the interconnected nature of our existence.

Each glass shapes the water's form, giving it a unique character, yet the source remains unchanged. Whether the water is returned to the original pitcher or follows diverse paths—consumed, flowing into a river, evaporating into clouds, and returning as rain—the essence of the water retains alignment with its source code, just like you and I. That which animates you, animates me. We are quantum reflections on the same holographic wave—a reflection of the interconnectedness that defines our existence. In essence, EVERYTHING, IS ... Everything else.

Dolores Cannon's monumental contributions, along with those of other leading researchers, have illuminated the mysteries of our forgotten nature. This knowledge allows us to better comprehend the esoteric aspects of our souls' existence, offering insight into our passions and purpose as we navigate human bodies and ego consciousness. In simpler terms, we are souls belonging to soul families, currently embodied as humans on Earth.

Our earthly existence unfolds within predetermined narratives alongside soulmates from our soul families, offering invaluable lessons for personal growth and the evolution of our souls. The shared tools and insights make our evolutionary paths more discernible, guiding us toward a deeper awareness of the source within each other. As reflections of one another, our interconnectedness becomes increasingly apparent, inviting a profound understanding of our shared completeness.

In presenting these leaders in the field of past life studies and reincarnation, I have only introduced a fraction of the many influential figures whose work significantly contributes to our understanding of these complex subjects. I strongly encourage you, the reader, to delve deeper into the contributions of each of these experts as part of your research.

While the scope of this text allows for only a brief mention of a few, there exists a wealth of other authors, researchers, and esteemed teachers whose insights can greatly enrich your study. I hope that as you continue to explore, you will discover an array of valuable resources and perspectives that will further enhance your knowledge and understanding of these fascinating topics.

The primary objective of this chapter, as well as the preceding ones, has been to broaden your perspective on the concept of predestined soul ties and humanities relational structures as well as their origins. These soul connections, which I propose extend across multiple incarnations, play a pivotal role in our continuous journey as souls. The idea is that when we reincarnate, we encounter these soulmates - be they platonic or romantic - to engage in narratives that foster our growth, learning, and the evolution of our true selves.

To understand these profound connections, Past Life Regression and Spontaneous Regression can emerge as powerful tools. They enable us to access and comprehend the experiences and lessons from our current and past lives. These insights offers us a clearer understanding of how and why we experience the various soul connections within our lives, each bringing unique challenges and experiences. Such understanding sheds light on the enigmatic nature of these connections and their significant impact on the subtleties that direct the trajectories of our lives. This exploration aims to provide you with a deeper awareness of the intricate dance between souls and the transformative influence these relationships have on our personal and spiritual growth.

PART II

Chapter Nine

Twin Elementals

Twin flames are not the only Soulmates, are they?

Quote: The longer I live, the more deeply I learn that love, whether we call it friendship or family or romance, is the work of mirroring and magnifying each other's light. — James Baldwin

As we explore the topics discussed, it becomes evident that the soul can express itself in numerous ways across the human experience. The saying "When a soul falls asleep, a baby is born" whimsically encapsulates the themes we've discussed. Each human life is like a brief flash of light in the soul's vast journey, comparable to a fraction of a degree in a 360-degree cypher. This analogy provides perspective by placing our individual experiences within a larger, continuous cycle.

Some of the concepts discussed here may appear to be new information for some and seem complex at first. This is because people usually prefer what they are familiar with, a tendency known as the 'familiarity principle'. Our minds have a limited capacity to process new information, which can make learning new concepts challenging without enough repetition or explanation. Often, we might feel inclined to give up, much like a child who becomes frustrated learning to ride a bike on the first day compared to the third day. This idea ties into the learning curve, which shows that our understanding improves as we spend more time and effort learning something. If this chapter feels overwhelming, try reading it again and think deeply about how it connects to things you already know.

In the dynamic realm of reincarnation, a recurring theme is the vibrant presence of our soul families, journeying with us throughout our incarnations. They emerge as counterparts and reflections, injecting energy, balance, and perspective into our soul's profound odyssey. Whether you know them as guardian angels, ancestors, guides, soul-fam, spiritual homies, or soul mates, echoing Michael Jackson's timeless lyrics—You-are not-alone.

Before we push further, allow me to present a comprehensive and definitive understanding of what the Twin Elemental Effect truly entails. The Twin Elemental Effect represents an innovative model that explores the dynamic interplay between individuals drawn together by the convergence of their karmic destinies and shared elemental affinities—be it earth, wind, and fire, or water. With distinct characteristics, these juxtaposed interpersonal connections transcend the ordinary, embodying a synergy that resonates on a soul level.

Whether it's the grounding stability of earth, the fluid adaptability of water, the passionate intensity of fire, or the dynamic movement of wind, each mirrored elemental trait represents the temperamental human spirit and contributes to a rich tapestry of experiences, conditions, and realizations. In a world marked by constant fluctuation, the Twin Elemental model provides clarity and purpose, reminding us that our connections with others are not random occurrences but meaningful encounters designed to catalyze growth and fulfillment.

In essence, the Twin Elemental Effect can be summed up as relational field probability, better understood as the likelihood of life events and paths influenced by the energies within specific relationships. In the same way that field probability in physics represents the chance of interactions within a defined environment, Twin Elementals reflect the probabilistic outcomes of human relationships, where powerful, unseen forces shape our journeys.

In physics, field probability describes how particular states or interactions are likely to unfold within specific fields, like electromagnetic or gravitational fields, where each particle's behavior is affected by the larger force surrounding it. But field probability is not confined to physics. In any domain where multiple forces or variables interact, from biology to sociology, probabilities shift as these influences dynamically interconnect.

In the Twin Elemental Effect, relational field probability refers to the likelihood of life events and relationship paths taking shape within the unique field created by the energies of each connection. This field is not only a combination of psychological, emotional, or even karmic forces but also the context in which our deepest connections take root and grow, subtly influencing our decisions, paths, and ultimately, who we become.

Each relationship within the Twin Elemental framework creates its own field, guiding or altering life's probabilities in ways that might feel inexplicably fated. For instance, a relationship infused with profound elemental resonance may become a catalyst, shifting one's path to align with that shared energy. The outcomes that emerge are not random but shaped by this dynamic field—a force with the power to amplify, redirect, and mold life's journey.

In this way, the Twin Elemental Effect suggests that who we deeply connect with has the potential to shift our life's trajectory, creating a story that feels as if it were written into the very field of our existence. Relationships thus become fields of probability, places where paths converge and diverge, offering transformative experiences that align with, challenge, or even reveal the core of who we are meant to be.

At its core, the Twin Elemental Effect offers a framework for understanding the intricate dance of spiritual energies that shape our lives. The model illustrates how individuals are brought together by fate and shared character traits, shaping each other's personas through unique interactions and influences. Each elemental connection carries its own unique energy signature, and understanding each of the four archetypes enriches our comprehension of our interpersonal, social, and relational behavioral patterns. Moreover, Twin Elemental Souls play a pivotal and indispensable role in triggering the exposure of the shadow self, aiding each other to diligently uncover and seamlessly integrate hidden and unexplored aspects of our multifaceted personalities—a transformative process for soul development.

Now, let's unpack that. Like a juxtaposed personality paradox, the intensity spectrum reflected from a twin elemental counterpart is akin to the infinity mirror effect, where two mirrors face each other to reflect themselves, bouncing reflections endlessly. It's a dance of dualities causing an infinite ripple effect, where multiple images emerge from a singular source. This mirrors the paradoxical nature regarding the emotional and social interactions generated by twin elemental soul reflections.

The countless influences we encounter subtly shape who we are, often without us realizing it. Even a minor event can start a chain reaction, like a butterfly effect, dramatically altering our personality trajectory and setting us on a completely different path than we expected—all without our awareness. This in fact generates a divergent timeline than the one we were on.

Consider a simple, everyday example: how social media subtly creates divergent timelines within our routines. Imagine you have an important destination—a place you need to be on time, a critical subject to study for a test, or plans for a business venture that could free you from financial constraints. Yet, instead of focusing, you start scrolling through social media. Before you know it, time slips away, reminiscent of the "missing time" phenomenon reported by UFO abductees. You look up, hours lost, your task incomplete, and realize the opportunity has passed.

Initially, you were on a timeline set for success, but the seemingly innocuous act of scrolling diverted you from that path, creating a divergent timeline—one where the outcome no longer aligns with your original goal. This is a micro-level example of a macro phenomenon, where magnetic soul pairings create powerful, life-altering events that pull us into alternate paths. Rarely do we even notice.

Our minds manage the complexities of our identities and experiences, often highlighting the routine tasks and focusing on the daily events. This focus creates what feels like continuity of consciousness, which helps us to simplify our sense of self. Meanwhile, the deeper and more intricate parts of our identity composed of intricate details and subtle nuances, fade into the background, residing in our subconscious.

From a psychological perspective, this phenomenon can be seen as a protective mechanism called selective attention, which allows us to navigate the complexities of life without being overwhelmed by the totality of our experiences. Philosophically, it underscores the depth of the human psyche, where the majority of what truly defines us resides beneath the surface of our immediate awareness. This intricate interplay between the conscious and subconscious realms is a testament to the multifaceted nature of our existence, illustrating how much of our true self remains to be discovered in the depths of our mind.

Regarding our continuity of consciousness, the memories we focus on often just scratch the surface of the myriad events we experience, particularly those involving interactions with our soul family. Most of our interpersonal relationships are akin to signing contracts without fully examining the fine print—this often includes the relationship with yourselves. These interactions, rich with unseen depths and nuances, often go beyond what we consciously recall or understand, revealing the complexity of our interpersonal connections and the subtle agreements they entail. In essence, we see what we want to see and accept what feels good and makes sense in that moment.

From the perspective of an omnipresent soul navigating the linear consciousness of a biological avatar—karmically contracted with other ensouled avatars, numerous opportunities arise for transformative encounters. These liminal experiences, which challenge and enrich our perception across different planes of consciousness, are interwoven with synchronicities. They seamlessly link emotional entanglements, spiritual revelations, and karmic encounters, among others. This complex interplay of cosmic connections paves the way to delve into the intricate dynamics of interpersonal relationships, especially those bound by soul ties, thus leading us into the critical discussion regarding the science of Twin Elementals.

The topic of soulmates and twin flames has long captivated people. While most individuals familiar with both concepts view these terms as distinct and uniquely separate, a deeper examination, such as the one offered in this book, suggests something significantly different from the common narrative. In contemporary ideology, loose translations of Soulmates are typically seen as individuals who share an immediate, profound connection, whether in a romantic or platonic context. They are believed to be wandering souls who have finally found each other, two halves of a whole even, and their souls are sometimes said to have been together in past lives. A soulmate relationship is typically filled with a deep sense of understanding, mutual respect, and unconditional love. It is often said that soulmates are brought together to help each other grow and evolve, to heal past wounds, and to support one another on their life journeys—and so much more.

Twin flames, on the other hand, are believed to be the mirror image of our soul. They are said to be our perfect match, with whom we share an unbreakable and intense connection. Like soulmates, twin flames are believed to be one soul split into two bodies, and they are often described as being two sides of the same coin. Twin flame relationships can be incredibly intense, with both partners experiencing deep emotions and spiritual growth. It is said that the purpose of a twin flame relationship is to help each other reach a higher state of consciousness and to work together to bring positive change to the world.

So on one hand, there is the concept of a Soulmate, who is believed to be a special soul connection and one half of a whole, while on the other hand, there is the notion of a twin flame, who is believed to be a predestined soul tie and even a single soul split into two. I suppose it is possible that it is just me, but it seems like both are essentially saying the same thing, differing only in the language used to describe them. #semantics.

In truth, many individuals tend to assign their own unique interpretations to these terms, shaping their meanings to fit personal experiences. This approach is entirely valid, as we are, after all, the architects of our own perceptions. Contrary to the belief that soulmates and twin flames are distinct from one another despite their portrayal as separate entities in popular literature, I aim to demonstrate that they are intricately connected and are one and the same. The preceding and upcoming chapters will delve into intimate esoteric connections, aligning with this idea.

These previously overlooked, groundbreaking concepts are now coming into the spotlight. The very foundation of the presupposed title, **"Twin Flames are not the only Soulmates,"** is constructed based on evidence presented by the ongoing work of the various researchers mentioned earlier and countless others. Through their efforts, we've formed a fundamental consensus, establishing a basis for understanding a soul's functionality while in flesh on Earth.

The goal of my work is to bridge the understanding gap, carving out a more defined ethos, particularly concerning the abstract and intrinsic nature that spans the entire spectrum of Twin Elemental Soulmates, in addition to the well-known *"Flame-like"* Elemental nature present in some relationships.

In what appears to be a collective journey towards a transhuman technocracy, the genuine human connections we've grown use to as a species, seems to gradually diminish with each passing day, evident in prevailing trends on social media and in the real world. With a profound understanding of how and why souls attract and interact, I firmly believe individuals can conquer the fears entwined with human connections, fostering a new appreciation for diverse and trusting social connection to the highest degree.

In the vast cosmos, absolutely nothing—including souls—exists in isolation; instead, everything is interconnected and follows specific patterns. Each entity, from a photon a blood cell, and a planet to grains of sand, blades of grass, species, and spirits, forms a link within an intricate pattern, contributing to a broad network of corresponding relationships. Here, each element influences and is influenced by the others, crafting a complex system.

It's crucial to acknowledge that just as humans rely on their parents and guardians for learning how to walk and talk, a soul doesn't embark on the school of life on planet Earth without the guidance of its soul community. In the complete essence of one's scripted, calculated, and cataloged life, recognize that every actor and character, whether seemingly good or bad, has been intentionally cast to play a significant role in your living biography.

Collectively, this primary cast forms your soul family; individually, they are your soulmates. In a recent social media post, I posed a rhetorical question: "What if your entire life was a pre-scripted, interactive spiritual recording? Based on some of the response's, some who pondered this query likely wondered about the roles people play in their own lives recording and exactly how interactive this recording might be.

In the context of transparency, my intention is never to patronize, but rather to provide absolute clarity and ensure undeniable understanding. This approach aims to lay a definitive and practical foundation for comprehending the concept of soulmates. With that understanding, let's demystify the basic principles in a distilled and rudimentary manner, making it simple and concise for anyone's easy comprehension. We can begin with basic, foundational definitions to establish a basis for all the past debates surrounding the subject.

The term "soulmate" consists of two words, soul and mate. Let's first unravel the latter, "mate." The word mate found its way into Middle English in the 1300s, originating from the German word "Ge-mate," signifying sharing a meal at the same table. Today, the term "mate" (noun) encompasses various meanings: a friend or companion, often a close one; a partner in business, at work, or part of a group or gang of friends; a shipmate, someone with whom you might break bread, i.e., share a meal; and a romantic partner or spouse. In each context, the emphasis is on pairing or more, intended to complement or match each other, even if just in banter over a meal. Think brothers in arms on a nordic pirate ship greeting each other with a jolly "good-day mate" in an early English accent, when contemplating the original meaning.

Within its etymology, the term "Soulmate" also incorporates the Modern English noun "Soul," tracing its roots to the Old English words sāwol or sāwel, with attestations reported as early as the 8th century in King Alfred's translation of De Consolatione, Philosophiae. Here, the soul is defined as a person's immaterial, spiritual, or thinking aspect, contrasting with the person's physical body.

If we were to be quite literal and interpret the words, we'd derive their meanings from their etymologies and arrive at a clear definition. This approach mirrors dissecting a machine to understand its parts or scrutinizing a painting stroke by stroke to grasp its overall message. As uncovered earlier in this manuscript, the term "soulmate" originated from the poet Samuel Taylor Coleridge in a letter from 1822, where he expressed, "to be happy in married life, you must have a soul mate." Essentially, a soulmate can be defined as a partner or companion with an intimate connection to an individual that extends to the very core of their soul, figuratively, if not literally.

While some may struggle to accept or find it challenging to see reason in the factual dictionary definition of a soulmate, it's their right as they are entitled to their beliefs, recognizing that we create our own reality. I have certainly been challenged by a few on what a soulmate is and their reasoning has generally been based in personal creativity and emotion.

Should I believe a man in the park believes he is watching a giant squirrel breakdancing? Despite his emotionally stirring and convincing delivery, there's a dilemma of trusting such a claim, especially considering the absence of tangible proof.

An emotional interpretation of a word, serving as a believed definition, is unnecessary when each word and idea has a definitive origin and meaning, serving as definitive proof or evidence. Blindly accepting any belief based solely on emotion is like accepting the emotionally stirring conviction of a man who believes he talks to giant invisible dancing squirrels in the park. This is why I have provided context by way of official definition and cultural origin. It's in the very nature of humanity to often lean towards an emotional or subjective interpretation, especially if that interpretation is profoundly passionate and convenient at the time.

Beyond mere dictionary definitions, I have committed to offering a variety of real-world insights into soul culture. The concepts found on these pages are expressed as accurately as a contemporary western mind can interpret, drawing from messages retrieved from the depths of non-physical consciousness across centuries. The extraordinary case studies presented here offer a rich reservoir of knowledge to draw upon, as well as methods for delving into your own pre-life narratives concealed within your subconscious.

Regarding soul contracts and soul ties—based on our shared consensus and pre-established conditions concerning the soul's role as a mate to other souls within an incarnation cycle, it would logically follow that there's no separation for esoteric connections or special spiritual designations independent of your soul family, i.e., your soulmates. I present this argument to counter those who question the concept that a twin flame isn't a pre-arranged engagement within your soul family during a predetermined karmic cycle.

Every personal encounter with another interconnected soul that brings juxtaposed emotional and transformational polarization to your living timeline and life trajectory is a result of a pre-arranged soul contract with a member of your soul family, i.e., a soulmate. This implies that none of the other designations on the spectrum, such as twin flames, twin rays, divine counterparts, karmics, cosmic partners, divine consorts, kindred spirits, or any other, are distinct from your fundamental soulmate or soul family. In reality, they are all a part of your soul family, each falling into the category of a soulmate—this includes a twin flame.

Here, one might concede with a hint of reluctance, suggesting that there indeed is a pre-arranged agreement to cross paths, but insisting that in the case of a twin flame, it involves a soul you have never previously encountered. However, regression data collected over time contradicts this notion. Consequently, In a world where technology opens up possibilities for clones, androids and extraterrestrials—not everyone you encounter and engage with may necessarily be a soulmate from your soul group. The potential for individuals to encounter what some term NPCs, or non-player characters derived from video games, cannot be dismissed. But where there is truly a soul connection, it is without a doubt based in a soul family dynamic.

Discovering a twin flame in this life is a rare and extraordinary occurrence. It's the convergence of two souls meant to cross paths. To dismiss this meeting as a mere coincidence or chance would be unreasonable. More likely, the two souls had a pre-arranged purpose agreed upon in the realm of souls within your soul group, solidifying the status of that twin flame as a soulmate, all the same.

The title of the book boldly asserts the inherent connection between the concept of a twin flame and soulmate, rooted in the concept of a soul family. It's crucial to emphasize that no Twin Elemental exists in isolation from pre-existing soul contracts or karmic debts. Essentially, a true twin flame engages in a mutual and karmic agreement with another soul member from its grouping or soul family while in the soul state. This agreement is forged with the intention of mutually exchanging experiences, fostering growth, and facilitating evolution during its temporary assignment within the three-dimensional "Human consciousness program," on Earth.

And there it is—the title and deed to the entire premise of this book. If a soulmate is a pre-arranged soul contract with an interrelated soul, then **a twin flame and a soulmate are inherently intertwined**. You simply cannot detach the idea of a twin flame from the role of a soulmate based on their definitive characters. It is categorically impossible—and thus we end that particular debate.

Many confidently assert that twin flames and soulmates are distinct, yet such a view is not entirely accurate. It's more fitting to consider them as varying expressions of a similar concept. All twin flame connections are, in essence, soulmate connections, but not all soulmate connections exhibit the intense characteristics typically associated with twin flames.

This relationship can be likened to different shades of the same color, where each shade represents a unique manifestation of a core element. Whether the color is salmon, fusia, coral, blush or rose, at the end of the day, most will assert that it's just pink. In this light, a different type of soulmate might be seen as a softer, more subtle expression, while a twin flame embodies a more intense, elemental aspect of this connection. Both, however, stem from the same fundamental principle of deep, soulful affinity. This understanding aligns with the idea that while the left and right hemispheres of the brain have different functions, they are part of the same organ, working together to create a nuanced and comprehensive perception.

The two young women who shared the same significant purposes and soul energy mentioned at the beginning of this book were indeed my twin flames (plural), embodying the character of twin-like polar energy infused with abundant flames of fire. Yet, they were integral members of my pre-birth soul tribe, making them my soulmates all the same. Even if only a brief flame, and our paths never cross again, the wheels have long been set in motion, influencing the parts of our lives that would ultimately alter the trajectories of our respective journeys.

I understand why these concepts may vary in the minds of many individuals. Twin flame relationships can often burn out like a once-powerful campfire, leaving behind the lasting residue of soot and coal. In contrast, relationships termed as soulmates generally tend to endure with more positive connections, although they too can fall victim to entropy. Both types of relationships are potent forces, each with its own unique impact on our lives. The Twin Elemental model provides a clearer distinction between the types of soulmates, clarifying why we recognize the differing characteristics of soulmates and twin flames. Like the butterfly effect, where one small displaced action can set in motion an entirely new course of events, both will influence your the trajectory of your life's timeline.

A football quarterback or airplane pilot understands that even a slight deviation in trajectory at launch alters their destination. For instance, in the case of an airplane, a one-degree deviation at takeoff from LaGuardia airport could lead to landing in San Francisco instead of LAX, or even atop a three-thousand-year-old Sequoia tree in the Redwood Forest. A quarterback knows that an interception is possible without a skilled launch of the ball with a trajectory to his intended target.

In the case of my soulmates, who manifested as double twin flame experiences, my life was undeniably shifted from its original trajectory, embarking on a new course enriched with wisdom gained from pain. Every subsequent choice was influenced by the flames felt while encountering my shadows in the mirrors of my romantic counterparts.

Consequently, the gentle trauma experienced as a result of those two polarizing relationships triggers a response from my sympathetic nervous system whenever I encounter anything reminiscent of those experiences. I was tempered by the fires of twin elemental transformation and heartbreak, emerging from the ashes as a stronger, more resilient version of myself, comparable to the mythical phoenix rising from its ashes.

Some people propose that we can have several twin flames, while others insist we only have one. In a vast universe teeming with countless souls, the idea that only one soul could cover all our lessons for an eternity, serving as our one and only true partner distinct from all others, can be challenging to imagine. If that were the case, that partner would have to be the creator and source of all things, locally referred to as God or "You" according to the *'Egg Theory.'* ~*Delving into that metaphysical concept is a conversation for another dimension of consciousness and another book for another day.*

I've often asserted the belief that the relationship between you and your soul is the one and only true relationship, the master relationship that ultimately boils down to the connection between you and "God," the source of all souls. This perspective hinges on the idea that the consciousness of God is infused in and permeates all atomic things. Yet, once again, this is a conversation for another time. With its infinite shapes, colors, and character, the reflections of the master source, when manifesting through a soulmate connection, can take on intense, passionate, and reflective twin-like reflective energy in predestined intimate interactions. In these moments, we can experience that illustrious and powerful Twin Elemental connection.

To spiritual practitioners, unless you've been living under a rock, you've likely noticed many people in metaphysical communities using systematic models to identify and define esoteric patterns and behaviors related to love. These patterns typically involve a variety of functions and moving parts to clarify the model being used. Unfortunately, individuals often recognize only a limited spectrum when defining romantic counterpart models. When exploring the enigmatic nature of a spiritual counterpart in love through this lens, you're presented with two primary models to consider, each characterized by its unique and distinct energy signatures: soulmate and twin flame.

Astrological models, such as natal charts, are renowned for providing a multifunctional array of an individual's many qualities, including strengths, weaknesses, and interactions with the world around them. By understanding these aspects, we can gain valuable insights into how to effectively approach and connect with different personalities. Similar to how natal charts and Astrology provide a versatile framework for comprehending compatibility patterns, the elemental aspect of the twin flame concept also stems from a comprehensive and expansive framework. This framework helps identify behavioral patterns in relationships, including concepts of destiny or fate. It's essential to emphasize that the flame element is just one of the elements acknowledged within this framework.

It appears imprudent to confine our comprehension of the intricate and intimate nature of love and purpose to a mere two-dimensional model. Relying on a single element to characterize the ever-evolving spiritual connection between soulmates is limiting, especially when numerous elements can more accurately portray the intricacies of this bond. Let's aim for a more holistic approach to grasp the richness of esoteric dynamics in relationships, given the multitude of factors at play. It's time to move past the common yet singular expression of the twin flame alone.

The acknowledgment of multiple elements broadens our understanding of profound connections between individuals. Many have mistakenly misinterpreted their twin elemental connection by exclusively using the fire element to depict a deep magnetic soul polarization stemming from intense emotional union. Despite our awareness of the four major elements—Water, Earth, Wind, and Fire—our understanding of a soulmate is often limited to narrow aspects within the exploration of the esoteric lover archetype. This constriction overlooks the profound and multifaceted nature of other soul connections.

In my counseling experiences and interviews with volunteers, I've noted that people often mistake twin flames for other twin elementals due to a lack of awareness. How is this possible? It could be that people naturally gravitate towards, remember, and reinforce their connection to relationships marked by intense passion and fiery emotions. These relationships set the brain ablaze with an expansive and addictive chemistry, often accompanied by drama that makes for riveting storytelling during trauma bonding.

Depending on an individual's level of emotional and social intelligence, this surge of chemical fire might have the potential to shake an individual's entire meta-emotional and meta-spiritual world. Yet, with the attainment of spiritual maturity, emotional intelligence, and heightened awareness, those same inflamed passions can undergo a transformation, becoming a source of warmth and even a controlled, yet intensely electric, kundalini-like relating experience fostering enlightenment.

So the query remains, why do we frequently sideline the other three elements when it comes to interpersonal interactions and soulmate connection? We're constantly bombarded with tales of explosive and passionate relationships with our supposed twin flames, while the beautiful, transformative and spiritual connections with others, not recognized as twin flames, are often overlooked, as if their emotionally transformative nature were insignificant. While twin flames tend to steal the spotlight, what about those incredibly powerful relationships that don't neatly fit that mold?

These are the relationships that explore unheard-of depths, reshaping the trajectory of our lives and propelling us to the epicenters of our destinies. Sadly, they often slip under the radar because they lack the dramatic flair that tends to capture our attention. Yet, what revelations might await us if we shift our gaze away from the flashy allure of the well-known twin flame connection and redirect it toward the quiet, steadfast glow of other extremely potent elemental connections?

It's high time to broaden our definition of mirrored elements, acknowledging the diversity of soul connections in all their forms. We must expand our understanding of these spiritual connections beyond our limited confines, recognizing the diverse range of relationships that exist beyond the twin flame archetype. Through this shift, we may uncover a deeper appreciation for the intricacies and complexities of the human experience.

A few years back, in the early stages of researching for this book, I conducted interviews with passengers during my part-time rideshare job, recording conversations with their permission in a dashcam-style for my Youtube show, "Heart to Heart on the Highway: The Dash Cam Diaries." One particular conversation stood out, featuring a recently divorced young Latina woman who spoke about her twin flame, her partner of 13 years in fact.

Despite a world wind romance, an extremely deep love and unyielding connection to him, she admitted to never experiencing that over-the-top, electric kind of love. However, they had successfully built a life together and had two wonderful children. Further exploration revealed that her slightly older husband, an ambitious and driven individual with his life together when they met, focused heavily on lecturing her about mature ideas, such as investing, business acumen, and organizational concepts, which eventually eroded their relationship.

Through our conversation, we discovered that this woman, raised in an unstable and unpredictable home with a possible unorganized and avoidant attachment style, subconsciously sought stability and security in a partner. After delving deeper, we concluded that her husband, initially believed to be her twin flame, exhibited all the signs of an intense twin planet instead.

While their passion waned quickly after the initial spark, they settled into a more grounded and unconditionally loving relationship with the type of security that a planet would offer. The fiery passions of a dramatic flame, though present at times, was not the soul draw, but the stability shared among the two would be the magnetism for tieing the two souls together per their karmic contract and trajectory influence. She expressed profound love and respect for him, ready to navigate life's journey alongside him, trusting in his ability to lead. As our conversation unfolded, it became increasingly evident that their entire relationship bore the unmistakable signs of a twin planetary soul connection—a dynamic firmly anchored in a fixed orbit, shaping the evolution of their souls.

It appeared as though her soul had orchestrated the first decade of adulthood in a steadfast and secure romantic partnership, offering stability and grounding. This, in turn, laid a strong foundation for the countless lessons that awaited her on her life's journey. Undoubtedly, her path will continue to unveil itself, introducing her to various elemental connections as she moves forward in time. Though some individuals adhere to the notion of having only one soulmate, a belief that is gaining more widespread acceptance is that individuals can have multiple soulmates, each contributing a unique and valuable gift to their personal growth.

The vibrant young chica from my rideshare interview had her life and trajectory deeply shaped by her upbringing, setting her on a path that ultimately defined who she became. She and her ex-husband, upon first meeting, seemed destined to connect, their love story unfolding with the ease of fate. Together, they built a family and a business that would sustain them financially for the rest of their days—an arrangement likely rooted in their pre-birth agreements. For over a decade, they shared a life that reflected both the best and worst aspects of each other, embodying light and darkness alike. Ultimately, they parted ways after fulfilling their destined roles in each other's lives. In retrospect, this pivotal soulmate relationship reshaped the trajectory of her life, profoundly influencing the chapters that will follow while residing on Earth as the embodiment of her soul.

As our understanding of soul mates continues to evolve, it becomes increasingly evident that karmic contracts and agreements extend beyond romantic relationships to include platonic friends, family members, and even our beloved pets. Consider your grandmother, a steadfast rock and pillar in your journey, who not only provides emotional support but also plays a crucial role in your education through financial assistance achieved by refinancing her home—an action that sets the stage for your future inheritance of that same home. Is she not a loving and predestined integral part of your life's trajectory and soul's evolution? Is there not a profound love for her. Let's not dismiss the grandmother who shared your first spliff, and despite cursing like a sailor, taught you how to stand up for yourself and to never give up. When she is gone, will you not think to yourself, no one ever really loved me like the grandmother who had my back no matter what.

Likewise, contemplate the significance of your pet, entering your life with a specific purpose. Support animals, also known as emotional support animals (ESAs), are pets that provide comfort and emotional support to individuals with psychological, emotional, or mental health conditions. They exist to help mitigate the symptoms of these conditions, such as anxiety, depression, and stress, improving their owner's overall well-being and functioning. Could it be that, in the realm of souls, the two of you entered into a contract to support each other in this lifetime? Is it's plausible that you and your pet agreed prior to birth to be there for each other, and your furry companion fulfilled their part of the agreement by offering love, support, and companionship when you needed it most. Contrary to cinematic portrayals, souls don't communicate in British English but in vibrational projection instead.

Picture a cherished pet becoming a lifeline during your darkest moments, preventing you from reaching the brink of despair and even hurting yourself. It stands as a powerful testament to the deep healing and strength that the love and bond we share with our animal companions can offer, especially when facing mental health challenges. We mustn't underestimate the transformative influence that pets can exert on certain people's lives and the spiritual connections that unite them.

Have you ever found yourself reflecting on the platonic friend who embraced the friend zone, standing by without complaints, showering you with unconditional love, surpassing even their own romantic partner, and demonstrating a willingness to sacrifice their very life for you? What about the one lover who got away or the first marriage abound with soulmate energy, that concluded amicably, and holds a special place in your heart?

Even if the fire did not burn as brightly as you matured, it still guided you through the challenges of college, and perhaps marked the beginning of your journey into starting a family and securing your first home. Without that particular partner, might you have embarked on your first business venture or evolved into the exceptional individual you are today? The flame might not have sparked with intense and theatrical passion, but the oceans of emotion complete with intimate devotion, flowed and flooded your entire life's timeline for many moons.

These connections, sometimes overshadowed by the grandeur of the famed flame, hold significant value in their own right. While they may lack the dramatic intensity of a twin flame, they offer a unique intensity, stability, and support that should not be underestimated. These are the relationships that endure life's storms, providing a solid foundation upon which we can construct our futures.

Let's strive to recognize the beauty and worth of these connections, refraining from dismissing them simply because they don't align with the popular notion of the singular twin flame. Some may not kindle the same flames, yet others certainly flow on a different kind of wave like such with the twin flood, washing us in oceans of love. They are the relationships we can rely on when the winds of change threaten to extinguish our spirits.

Moreover, should we, spiritual adepts, versed in the esoteric awareness of spiritual connection in romance, categorize all our enigmatic relationships as twin flames? It's essential to acknowledge that some of them may be something entirely different. And, perhaps more importantly, shouldn't these relationships deserve the same level of elemental recognition that mindfulness brings to any soulmate connection? Approaching all our soulmate connections with mindfulness and intentionality is crucial.

Consider this: Once we have embarked on a journey with a twin flame and arrived at a profound destination in consciousness, we can look back with 20/20 hindsight and recognize the transformative power the experience has had. Concluding a journey with a twin flame is often the catalyst to a significant shift in our consciousness, leaving an indelible mark on our memory.

Throughout this journey, our experiences may mold our outlooks and overall disposition. If we were hurt during the process, we might adopt a "hurt people hurt people" mentality. However, if we manage to heal from those wounds, we may exhibit a "healed people, heal people" temperament instead. The specific type of Twin Elemental we engage with can often be identified by the subtle signs and shifts in our consciousness, ranging from imperceptible to highly noticeable.

If a person is partnered with a twin flame, whether driven by passion towards an uncertain future or sustained through love and deliberate choice, the mere awareness of twin flame energy often adds a layer of mythical magic and deep emotional connections, fueling transformation. The allure of viewing things through a mythical lens alone generates a mystique effect.

If you've ever been in a twin flame relationship and find yourself still talking about it to this day, you know exactly what I mean. **It takes on a supernatural significance** of its own. Just the knowledge that a past lover was a twin flame can be a driving force for transformation that lasts for years. Each time you mention them, it's as though the experiential influence from that chapter in your life is reiterated with lessons replaying like a looped recording. One could argue that recognizing how you may not have evolved into the unique person that you are today without the polarizing effects of a life-changing twin flame is just as comparable to the equally transformative unions experienced by the flowing or flooding nature of a highly influential Twin Flood Soulmate.

I can recount a twin "wind" soul connection, for instance, far more powerful than any twin flame connection I had ever experienced. Let's call her Atallah to protect the innocent. Many years ago, Ms. Attallah and I shared an experience that mirrored the freedom of the best friends' dynamic, all while exploring the nuances of open relating and polyamory. The feeling was akin to being in love with your best friend, who happened to be the coolest, most fun, most beautiful person in the world—far from a twin flame connection yet with all the same intensity, if not more. Coupled, of course, with the immense freedom of a romantic twin wind connection.

Our time together was transformative and left an enduring impression. I'm confident it changed the substance of our thoughts and ideas as well as influencing our choices in subsequent relationships. Atallah was one of my earliest experiences in open relationship exploration, introducing my mind and heart to radical new ideas in relating. Although she wasn't my girlfriend or wife, she was my best friend and lover—the wind beneath my wings and a tornado when she wanted to be. TBH, I never knew if she was going to sweep me off my feet with her cool breeze or sweep me away in a Category 5 hurricane—she was a Brooklynite, through and through.

In retrospect, I've also encountered powerful twin flood connections. A flood is to water as a flame is to fire. To emphasize the magnitude, a twin flood might sacrifice their career so their partner could finish medical school or give up their dreams to help raise their lover's children, contributing to the freedom and benefits of mindfully shifting their spiritual evolution up a degree, as they can either flood you with support or drown you with insecurities.

I'm reminded of a twin flood whom I cherish deeply. Our friendship dates back to high school, and since the tender age of fifteen, our energies have formed a whirlpool of emotional intensity that is distinctly different from fire passion, or the winds freedom. Water passion in fact, is an intriguing and powerful force, in and of itself. It's fascinating because, despite not directly being romantically involved with this particular friend, we can lose ourselves in each other, a dynamic that has remained constant for decades.

Even as a teeny bopper, I considered for the first time what it would be like to start a family with her. She introduced me to the concept of a vegetarian lifestyle during our first conversation when we were just 15 years old, at a time when this idea was not as popular as it is today. Decades later, that initial interaction still strongly influences my commitment to practicing vegetarianism. The ripple effect of a twin flood, indeed. Our deep admiration and love for each other has only grown stronger with the passing of time.

Over the years, our relationship has unfolded like a vast ocean, spanning a lifetime of events. Sometimes she's as unpredictable as a thunderstorm, and at other times, as enchanting as the sunlight reflecting on the soft waves of a peacefully flowing river. Yet our union of soul is not without its duality and its shadows. Despite her busy life as a successful actress with movie roles and a popular television series on ABC and now Netflix, she consistently makes time to stay connected with her longtime soulmate of a friend. Such kinship illustrates the undeniable magnetism inherent in any twin elemental connection.

While a twin flood can engulf you in passion and infatuation, their primary function differs from the quintessential twin flame or twin wind. Those who can't see the forest for the trees might miss the profound magnitude and butterfly effect quality of such a pan-dimensional dynamic, yet it wields the same life-changing and reality-altering power as other twin elementals, as you'll soon discover in the upcoming chapters that dissect all four of the twin elemental archetypes.

When seeking to understand twin elemental archetypes, it's important to note that a powerful twin elemental connection may encompass more than one elemental quality, with one element often dominating or prevailing. This can be likened to the way western astrology reveals diverse qualities about individuals through not only their sun, but moon, and ascendant signs as well.

In enduring relationships, the dominant elemental characteristic might undergo a pole shift, with the less dominant elemental trait taking precedence and reshaping the nature of the soulmate connection. The merging of distinct traits in twin elemental overlap creates a dynamic interplay, echoing the intricate dance found in brain waves or the expansive color spectrum.

This harmonious interplay illustrates the intricate ways in which these elements converge, intertwining and influencing each other in a rich and multifaceted tapestry of characteristics and expressions, much like the fluid transition of musical notes in a symphony or jazz quartet. For instance, a twin wind in high school with innocence, could evolve into a twin flame in college with curiosity and eventually, after 25 years of marriage, transform into a twin planet-styled soul connection with maturity. This raises the question: Was its purpose always that of a twin planet—seeing as though hindsight and retrospect is the architect of each elemental archetype?

Note that in some relationships, one partner may perceive an emotional connection akin to water in their counterpart, considering them a twin flood, while the other might recognize reflections of a wind elemental, yet both still receive what they need for transformation through a soulmate bond. Consider the example of the young Latina woman from the earlier rideshare story. She discovered a planetary reflection in her mate, who provided the stability and foundation reminiscent of a twin planetary alignment. Conversely, he might have found a source of twin flood energy to support him emotionally while he offered stability.

Given that we have all navigated various forms of twin elemental interactions in our social and relational lives, we possess the intrinsic capacity to conjure the energetic frequency of each elemental force within us, restoring balance within any aspect of the polarity spectrum we're currently navigating or aspire to align with. To achieve this, we can adopt personal rituals ranging from the straightforward—such as jotting down our desires, utilizing affirmations, and creating vision boards—to more complex practices like light work. While the underlying purpose persists, individuals who navigate their social or romantic relationships with conscious intent recognize the power of tapping into desired energies. Further exploration of these themes will be presented in the forthcoming chapters, aptly titled "Conscious Relating."

It's essential, however, to focus these efforts inward rather than projecting onto others. Conjuring the spirit of your desired elemental within yourself is advisable, as external projection can lead to unforeseen consequences. By cultivating these energies internally, we set the stage for a more harmonious and balanced existence, aligning our inner world with our outer desires.

It's crucial to understand that the vibrational influence of twin elementals does not confine your spirit to a single mode of being. Just as certain characteristics can catalyze a shift in your overall perspective, propelling you towards a greater version of yourself, the exact opposite can achieve the same effect. For instance, experiencing love may inspire an individual to improve themselves, while the absence of love can serve as a powerful motivator to strive even harder towards self-improvement to receive love. This dynamic underscores the principle behind the maxim, "Let your haters be your motivators," illustrating how both positive and negative experiences can drive personal growth and transformation.

Within the framework of twin elementals—be it Twin Flames, Twin Floods, Twin Winds, or Twin Planets—polarity plays a critical role in defining the dynamics and evolution of these profound connections. Each elemental pair embodies its own unique form of polarity, manifesting as a spectrum of energetic and emotional states that range from harmony to discord, intimacy to indifference, and understanding to misunderstanding. This polarity is not merely a static contrast but a rhythmic interplay that reflects the ever-changing nature of relationships and personal growth.

At the heart of these twin elemental interactions is the concept that opposites are different expressions of the same essence, a principle echoing the Hermetic view of polarity. The spirit and personality of a temperamental, opinionated and even creative individual can significantly influence the polarity or mood of a relationship.

For instance, the Twin Flame relationship, known for its fiery intensity and capacity for profound transformation, can see dramatic shifts between a passionate, unifying connection and periods of intense conflict. This duality reflects the personal battles and growth phases each partner undergoes, acting as a mirror for their deepest fears and highest aspirations.

Twin Floods on the other hand dives into the oceanic depths of emotional engagement, where the waters of connection can turn from calm to stormy.

These relationships are characterized by their ability to touch the most sensitive parts of our beings, prompting moments of unparalleled closeness and times of overwhelming emotional challenges, as each individual endeavors to confront their vulnerabilities and strengths.

Twin Winds offer a more cerebral bond, where the flow of ideas and communication breezes through the relationship. This elemental pairing can alternate between periods of exhilarating intellectual exchange and misunderstandings, showcasing the fluctuating nature of thought and dialogue. It's a dance of minds, where the alignment and misalignment of perspectives highlight the complexity of human interaction.

Lastly, Twin Planets embody the gravitational pull of stability and harmony, presenting a solid ground upon which to build a lasting connection. Yet, even in this steady space, there can be seismic shifts that test the relationship's foundation. These moments of imbalance challenge the duo to find a new equilibrium, adapting to the evolving dynamics of their shared journey. Instability in a space where stability was perceived and foundations were built can cause for a polarizing spiritual shift with eye opening consequences.

Each of these examples illustrates the vibrant spectrum of affects experienced throughout twin elemental exchange, highlighting the ways in which polarity influences the depth and direction of our most profound connections. This dynamic interplay ensures that no relationship remains static, urging both partners towards personal development and a deeper understanding of the unity and diversity of human connections. Through recognizing and embracing the polarities within these elemental bonds, individuals can navigate their relationships with greater awareness and harmony, aligning with the principles of change and balance that underpin the universe.

Understanding the principle of "Twin Elemental Polarity" is pivotal, as it empowers you to act from a place of awareness and purpose. By comprehending this concept, you can intentionally shift your paradigm to align with the highest possible vibrational reality. Every intersection offers several possibilities, and having a simple awareness of these principles empowers you to consciously navigate your living timeline instead of being swept away by the force of circumstance, feeling primitive and powerless.

The purpose of the Twin Elemental model is to illuminate and broaden our limited understanding of the twin elemental effect, with twin flame energy serving as a prominent example. It seeks to replace conventional terminology with a more expansive and apt designation, specifically embracing the appropriate term **"Twin Elemental."** This redefinition aims to encapsulate the nuanced aspects found in soulmate connections, fostering a clearer comprehension of the spiritual intricacies inherent in these profound connections. Once light has pierced the darkness, one cannot undo or unknow the revelations that unfold.

For deeper exploration, the term *"Twin,"* originating from Middle and Old English etymology, meaning a pair, double, or twofold, symbolizes the mirroring or twinning aspects between a pair of twin elementals with soul ties. These shared attributes, when conjoined, can transcend basic habits or recently learned behaviors, penetrating an entire being right down to the soul. Take, for instance, an individual may have a particular habit or struggle they find challenging. The advent of a powerful twin elemental attraction can serve as a catalyst, fostering a genuine eagerness to embrace change, particularly when the desire to captivate that elemental's attention is in play. There is no greater motivator.

Bearing that in mind, it sometimes takes looking deep into a mirror as a requisite for a soul to perceive itself distinctly, much like gazing into a vanity mirror in the tangible realm. Mirrors reveal the lint on our shoulders or perceived flaws on our faces and hair, making actual mirrors akin to mirrored souls. Unbeknownst to many, your spiritual shadows are often defined in the reflection of a soul's mirror, much like the interplay of lighting and shadows defining your three-dimensional reflection in the vanity mirror above the restroom sink. Without light there is no such thing as color and without shadows there is no such thing as dimensional depth.

Let's not overlook the valuable lessons found in the fairy tale of Snow White, where the witch famously recited, "Mirror, mirror on the wall," and so forth. As the narrative unfolds, it becomes apparent that despite the Queen's outward beauty, her internal state was marred by deep-seated feelings of insecurity, inferiority, and lack. Thus, what is apparent on the surface does not necessarily encapsulate the entire narrative.

The essence lies not in the exact reflection of the mirror but in our interpretation of it, and, subsequently, the significance we attach to what we see and the emotions it arouses for a response. This interpretation is influenced by the context of time, space and the energetic vibration of what we seek to perceive. It's crucial to recall that individuals tend to perceive and comprehend what aligns with their desires and preferences. In other words, "people see what they want to see!" Yet in time, repetition brings all things to the light and we are forced to see the truth of our reality if we are wise enough to open our eyes.

Regarding the juxtaposed nature of a soul mirror, what often begins as a positive experience can quickly transform into extreme contempt and resentment. Consider the basic example of a man captivated by and falling in 'square,' love with his wife while she dances in a gentlemen's club. However, he later resents her for the very qualities that initially seduced him—her alluring and sensual nature.

The tale unfolds as her beauty mirrors his internal desires, and he develops a sense of entitlement to possess this enchantment. Engaging in competition with others, he eventually triumphs, emerging as a conqueror. She radiates like the diamond she is, reflecting her inherent sexual nature and tantalizing allure to which he enjoys immensely—to the extent that he marries her.

However, this enchantment that she possesses, becomes a continuous emanation that she cannot turn off for it is her inherent and magnetic nature. After six months or so, engaged within a whirlwind romance where he is fully invested, financially, emotionally and otherwise, he attempts to force her to change. When she refuses, he resorts to stalking, making threats and a sometimes extremely aggressive temperament. This narrative starkly illustrates how positive traits can morph into negative ones when reflected through the mirrors of a twin elemental.

The words of Carl Gustav Jung, the Swiss psychiatrist who founded Western analytical psychology, resonates here: **"Everything that irritates us about others can lead us to an understanding of ourselves."** This forms a core tenet of Twin Elemental understanding. The science of Twin Elementals teaches us that everyone is a mirror, revealing not only our true selves but also guiding us toward improvement if that's our intention. Jung also noted that when someone causes you no harm or slight, yet you dislike them, it often stems from stirring insecurities or uncertainties within themselves. They are commonly termed as "Haters." I've had my fair share—hoards in fact.

Contemplating why individuals find certain qualities irksome in others, I've observed that what one hates about others is often a reflection of their own insecurities. It's akin to the frustration of a person, despite their best attempts at fashion, looking in the mirror at their outdated clothes and hairstyle, exclaiming, "I don't have anything to wear – all my clothes are trash, I hate my clothes and I hate my hair." Boo-hoo-wine-wine! This reflective behavior might manifest in a personality that judges others in different circumstances with self projecting tendencies.

In Jung's "Psychological Types," published in 1921, he outlines four basic personality functions—feeling, thinking, intuition, and sensation—mirroring water, air, fire, and Earth, as well as the seasons—winter, spring, summer, and fall. With introverted or extroverted aspects, these functions can work in either direction with positive or negative effects.

A major key in the foundational understanding of the power inherent within twin elemental relationships is understanding what Carl Jung terms as the shadow self. The shadow self represents the concealed aspects of our personality, the parts of ourselves that we tend to deny or repress. These hidden facets can encompass our deepest fears, desires, insecurities, and unresolved issues from the past.

Embracing and integrating the shadow self is like shedding light on the hidden corners of our psyche, allowing us to confront and transform those aspects that have been lurking in the shadows, often influencing our behavior and decisions without our conscious awareness. This process of self-discovery and shadow integration is an essential component of personal growth and plays a significant role in the dynamics of twin elemental soulmate connections.

In the realm of twin elementals, the term I've coined as **'shadow mirroring'** defines the process in which closely aligned counterparts reflect each other's subtle internal psychological challenges. Shadow mirroring often leads to the surfacing of frustrations stemming from internal dissatisfactions, causing irritations and at times, even resentment. It can also elicit emotions similar to buyer's remorse.

Essentially, shadow mirroring exposes facets of your personality that may not be your best, revealing the darker aspects of yourself that you may have believed didn't exist. This process lays bare all aspects of your being, even those you may have attempted to conceal. A twin elemental relationship serves as a mirror, bringing these concealed qualities to light for both you and your counterpart to witness firsthand. It unveils aspects of yourself that you may not have been aware of, such as inclinations towards insecurity, dishonesty, even violence, and other less favorable traits.

In the realm of twin elemental connections, the process of shadow mirroring serves as a powerful catalyst for self-discovery. It brings to the forefront facets of your personality that may have remained hidden, unveiling the less favorable aspects that you might have been unaware of. As you engage in this intricate dance of reflection with your counterpart, it becomes an exploration of the depths of the human psyche. The phenomenon of shadow mirroring ultimately leads to what can be termed as **'shadow exposure,'** a profound revelation that sheds light on the complexities and intricacies of the self.

In summary, shadow mirroring, in alignment with Jung's theories on the shadow self, leads to shadow exposure. Twin elementals serve as a primary catalyst for triggering the process of this awareness, providing an opportunity to integrate this aspect of the self. This process supports karmic clearing and paves the way for subsequent soul evolution. In accordance with the laws of polarity, where the pendulum swings between two extremes, if there exists shadow mirroring, then mirrored enlightenment must also be present.

A twin elemental connection has the potential to significantly impact your self-development, either enhancing it or causing deterioration, with varying speeds, to say the least. It can push you to become either a better or worse version of yourself. These dynamic relationships act as the propellant for igniting and accelerating the evolution of your character, as well as pushing the boundaries of self-discovery. The transformative power of 'The Twin Elemental Effect' is like taking a journey through the intricacies of your own soul, offering both challenges and rewards along the way.

Some individuals are sometimes unable to "see the forest for the trees. This expression highlights how we can become so immersed in the daily trivialities that we lose sight of the bigger picture. This tendency can be attributed, in part, to the self-centered nature of our egos, which often prioritize immediate gains and what's directly in front of us. When we find ourselves caught in the labyrinth of our thoughts, the path to clarity may seem elusive. Additionally, the influence that others have on our overall well-being can be as imperceptible as the air we breathe. Yet, despite its subtlety, this influence can have a profound impact on our entire existence.

Like the vibrant contrasts in the color spectrum, 'The Twin Elemental Effect' showcases a multifaceted nature that impacts personalities. Think of light frequencies that reflect the diverse expressions of an object with there shadows, depths, and luminous hues. Just as the light spectrum ranges from infrared to ultraviolet, and even black light and X-rays, the radiance from twin elemental soul connections is equally spectral. Each frequency of the effect reveals different intensities and perspectives, leading individuals to unveil various versions of themselves. This beautiful and challenging diversity sparks a journey of self-reflection and self-discovery.

Like observing broken bones or tumors under the light of an x-ray, at times, the reflection you witness may not be pleasing, as the subconscious reveals what the conscious mind tries to conceal. Yet, it is precisely in these discomforting moments that the most profound transformations begin to occur, enabling you to step into a higher version of yourself and embrace the fullness of your being. Those who are unwilling to be honest with themselves set the stage to repeat the same lessons over and over potentially falling deeper into lower and lower vibrational existence by way of uncompromising entropy. In other words, they start to create an astral hell for themselves, losing the ability to ascend from it due to the loss of youth, strength, clarity, and the accumulation of stress, debt, acidity, inflammation, and the burdens of life.

It's wise to understand the dual natures of twin elementals to avoid undesired fates like that of Narcissus from Greek mythology. Narcissus, the vain boy, fell in love with his own reflection and stared at it until he perished, turning into a flower that bears his name. This mythological tale gives rise to the term "narcissist." Staring into the reflections of your elemental mirror may reveal illuminations or shadows, all reflective of your own manifestation.

For context, this mirrors dating someone solely for their looks, while neglecting other crucial factors. It also mirrors the idea that a relationship of any caliber is all about you. Without grasping the dual nature of twin elementals, a couple might risks shared vanity, resembling Narcissus's fate. Investing energy in such frivolous pursuits might be a substantial waste of time and a possible energetic liability considering that individuals are drawing closer to the culmination of their lives by the second. If and when failure ensues, blame is shifted and resentment is nurtured.

Fixating on irrelevant or fruitless reflections hinders the cultivation of knowledge essential for true transformation and growth, thus causing stagnation instead of evolution toward divine potential. Fortunately, if teachable lessons in duality don't come from introspection, they will inevitably be forced through extroverted means. What that means is, when one lacks the motivation to move, the universe will inherently move them, and it may not be a movement of your favored choice. Nevertheless, within the grand tapestry of existence, lessons are inevitable and will be acquired one way or another.

Similar to the elements and seasons, your personality operates within a multi-layered, dual-natured spectrum. What is the day without the night? Both have their pros and cons. Summer brings out shorts and halter tops but also brings sweat, mosquitoes, and heat rashes. In contrast, winter brings beautifully designed fashion week jackets as well as snow covered roads and flu season. From personality changes and mood swings to epiphanies, moments of wonder, joy, and even physical experiences, the range of the human spirit is extensive, marked by the corresponding oscillations of the metaphorical pendulum.

The kaleidoscope of personalities within your social orbit all reflects the duality of opposites in attraction. This insight extends beyond mere attraction, permeating all types of relationships, from romantic entanglements to daily interactions with colleagues. Reflecting and mirroring others, issues and all, exists on a spectrum, closely aligned with the concept known as **Social Mirroring Theory.**

Social Mirror Theory pulsates with vitality, asserting that people naturally mirror behaviors, attitudes, and emotions of those around them to cultivate social bonds and establish a sense of belonging within a group. This dynamic process occurs both consciously and unconsciously, with individuals drawn to those with attractive qualities or who they perceive as kindred spirits.

In a broader context, *Social Mirror Theory* is often used to explain phenomena such as social influence and is thought to play a role in the development of group cohesion and teamwork. Additionally, it serves as a tool to understand the nature of social interactions and relationships. Social Mirror Theory isn't just a tool; it's the lens unraveling the mysteries of human dynamics. It transcends explanation, becoming a vibrant compass navigating the intricate landscape of human connections. It's not just about mirroring but navigating the delicate balance between conformity and individuality, propelling us into the uncharted territories of social dynamics.

Naturally, we seek to emulate the traits of those we find attractive, thus desiring their agreeableness. However, as the initial rush of limerence fades, and our brain chemistry settles, any compatibility deficits may cast a stark light on the shadows of our connection. We realize we may not be as inclined to conform to the rose-colored reflections in the mirror as we once thought. basically, Individuals conform, until they don't—Such is life.

As we look deeper into the perceptual insights offered by Social Mirror Theory, it becomes evident that the people we naturally mirror in our lives are no different than characters in a meticulously scripted play. They are actors with roles crafted to perfection, serving as essential catalysts for our personal plotlines and character development within the grand narrative of our existence. In this intricate theater of life, we embody the main character, living out the play to climactic perfection, culminating in a lifetime of purposeful incarnation.

When asked, "How are you?" the common response is often just "fine," which barely scratches the surface of our true feelings. This simple answer is an example of how we often stick to a script in our interactions. Whether we realize it or not, many of us are acting out our lives. The people around us are acting. In essence, we are all actors—simply performing our roles. The back-and-forth of our daily dialogs—whether dramatic or melodramatic—provides not only great entertainment but also valuable education. This theatrical analogy seamlessly connects the concepts of mirroring in social dynamics with the broader theme of life as a scripted and staged experience.

Beyond simulation theory and the Matrix movies, it's not unusual for life to be likened to an intricate video game, a vast school of learning, or elaborate performance. Consider the clever irony depicted in the Rick & Morty episode titled "Roy,"—Season 2-Episode 2—where a virtual reality game compresses an entire lifetime into mere minutes like a virtual dream.

As Morty interacts with the game, he is fully engrossed in a trance like state—experiencing everything from the cradle to the grave—in the life of a man named Roy. He subsequently experiences all the highs and lows of Roy's life journey. The moments of joy and the heartaches of a life fully lived before removing the game's headset, waking up, and consciously returning to his own reality—slightly dazed and confused. This conceptual portrayal reflects the essence of ensouled humans within our holographic universe, observed through the perspective of what seems like individual consciousness, sometimes called *'Witness Consciousness.'*

When contemplating the metaphorical notions of projecting into a staged existence and how life is characterized by inherent duality with intertwined narratives, one may find an interesting analogy in the Melpomene and Thalia masks. Historically, the laughing mask symbolizes comedy, while the crying mask represents tragedy. Together, these two drama masks serve as powerful symbols of the theatrical realm, vividly illustrating the mirrored duality inherent in human emotions, relationships, and the overall human condition.

The Melpo and Thalia masks, most commonly associated with the theatre, encapsulate equal but opposing intensities within their dual mirror natures. It's crucial to discern between the two facets of mirroring. While mirroring can build rapport through shared actions, attitudes, and speech patterns—highlighting surface-level compatibility—it frequently misses the mark in revealing the deeper dimensions of *shadow mirroring*.

The inverted nature of unconscious shadow mirroring with other souls presents a profound test that can either fortify or challenge the spirit on the path of soul evolution. The enduring effects of long-term shadow mirroring have the potential to reshape the entire paradigm of a person's reality. Our spirit inherently reacts to every encountered personality, whether the interaction is fleeting or enduring. Seeing that all actions have a ripple effect in time and space according to the laws of cause and effect, short interactions may loose themselves in your subconscious mind while longer interactions may have a more consciously recognized affect. The more extended your personality remains fixed within a particular response state, the more you embody that, "person—ality." Does this make sense? Essentially, this is how you become you.

In these situations, individuals can either nurture a profound love or harbor a deep loathing towards themselves nurturing either growth and progression or stagnation and regression. When subtle self-hatred remains unnoticed, individuals may unknowingly project their internal turmoil onto their partner, fostering resentment over time. The person you're becoming can be profoundly shaped by the influence of your chosen companion. Essentially, the process known as Twin Elemental Shadow Mirroring is how people are made. The sustenance of the ego is validation, and it must be fed to survive.

Understanding the intricate dynamics of shadow mirroring is particularly significant when observing the effects of connecting with twin elemental soulmates. This understanding offers individuals a valuable blueprint for navigating the complexities of these relationships facilitating self awareness and personal growth through comprehension and active engagement. Merely canceling each other out within unhealthy dynamics, fails to address the internal problems.

Engaging in self-projection, casting shame, blame or holding others responsible for internal dissatisfaction can be counterproductive and may reinforce the concept of the "pain body," potentially leading to more psychological trauma responses. If you're hesitant to commit to the necessary work needed for personal growth and evolution, I recommend exploring options like counseling, holistic therapies, or seeking assistance from professionals to restore balance to your emotional and psychological well-being. In the realm of twin elemental soulmates and their potential for shadow mirroring, the subtle dance of influencing each other's lives emerges as a profound force shaping each others evolving identities. This mutual influence extends to various aspects of our physiologies as well, involving a multitude of variables continuously at play.

The nature of our psychology will always be open to debate, researchers, philosophers, scientists, and systems, have identified several different factors that contribute to our intelligence, insight, and personalities as it relates to how we interact with each other, and yet have only scratched the surface. Our genes can define our cognitive abilities and temperament, while our brain physiology affects things like our memory and processing speed.

Our psychological makeup is shaped by our experiences and environment, including early childhood development, educational opportunities, and cultural influences. Surprisingly, even bacteria and parasites within us play a role in shaping who we are. Bear in mind that what your partner feeds you has a significant impact on who you are becoming. The enteric nervous system, often referred to as the body's "second brain," regulates our gut and our gut responds to what we consume.

Our evolutionary history, intertwined with epigenetics and various other factors as previously explored, plays a significant role in shaping our problem-solving abilities and social aptitude. These multifaceted elements combine, resulting in a distinct combination for each individual. Despite our uniqueness, akin to intellectual cross-pollination, we also share common behaviors, emotional responses, and cognitive traits. These shared elements manifest as consistent patterns in how we react and adapt to the ever-changing landscapes of our world, whether social, emotional, or material. The comprehension of diverse personality types emerges as a crucial key to unraveling the complexity of human behavior.

Exploring the traits constituting a personality provides insights into people's behaviors. For example, those high in agreeableness tend to be cooperative and helpful, while those high in neuroticism may experience higher anxiety and stress levels, making them less cooperative. Knowledge of diverse personality types, whether elemental, astrological, or psychiatric, enhances our ability to understand, communicate, and predict behavior, particularly in the influential world of personal relationships.

The Twin Elemental model emerges as a simple and comprehensive system for outlining the characteristics present within our most intense soul-tie interactions and soulmate connections. It exists to give us insight and deeper understanding to what is happening in our lives when our world seems to be experiencing a total pole reversal bringing with it havoc of seismic proportions or even unheard of bliss and flow state within compatible alliances.

Furthermore, the alchemical idea that human personality can be compared to blending a few fundamental elements is an ancient concept, predating even the Greeks and Egyptians. In later times, the Stoics, held the belief that human beings were comprised of four essential elements: fire, air, water, and earth. These elements served not only as the fundamental building blocks of matter but also as the raw materials shaping human nature.

This theory suggested that individuals were a blend of these qualities in varying proportions, each quality linked to distinct behavioral tendencies. For instance, someone with a predominant fire element might exhibit quick-tempered and impulsive traits, while an individual with a predominant water element might lean towards passivity and sensitivity. Although contemporary science doesn't give credence to this theory, its endurance highlights a longstanding fascination with the concept that external forces shape our inherent drives and personality traits beyond our control.

The influence of the four elements transcends ancient theories and extends into occult tools like tarot and astrology as well. Beyond your sun sign, represented by your birthdate, these models reveal a comprehensive chart, illustrating the varied influences of all 12 signs on your personality and life path. With a cosmic dance involving over ten planets, twelve signs, and twelve houses, our individual birth charts are an extraordinary masterpiece that won't repeat itself for over 25,000 years. In this vast celestial symphony, there are literally billions of unique combinations.

Similarly, the myriad expressions of twin elemental connection unfolds through spectral reflections, creating an array of versions of yourself with each new cherished elemental soul connection. The beauty lies in the diversity. Life is an eternal dance of change, and you are in a constant state of evolution, transitioning through different psychological and emotional phases. Your place in this evolutionary journey and the soul's pursuit of addressing voids, rectifying deficits, and overcoming inefficiencies will naturally draw the twin elemental counterpart required for your growth at the predetermined moment. This counterpart mirrors not only your light but also your shadows—the best and the worst parts of your being to be reflected.

Therefore, it becomes paramount to recognize that twin elementals are mutable entities. They possess the ability to transform into whatever your soul's destiny calls for. Like the alchemical processes of old, a twin flame can seamlessly transmute into a twin planet or exhibit elements of both, with one dominating over the other. The governing forces of spiritual consciousness and personal development dictate what you project and subsequently see reflected in the mirror of a soul connection.

The discerning eye of a visual or photographic artist keenly appreciates the power of contrast. It's often said that the more varied the contrast, the more vivid and defined the resulting image becomes. This enchanting phenomenon extends to the relationships we cultivate, particularly those of a twin elemental nature. These connections, rich with layers of duality and contrast, have the potential to be intensely soul-stirring. They can unfold as a fully polarizing experience, illuminating our path and propelling us towards a future that is vibrant and deeply meaningful. While the immediate purpose of these relationships might not be evident, their greater significance often unfolds over time.

Mirrored soulmate connections, steeped in elemental nature, act as pillars supporting our journey toward soul evolution and the fulfillment of our divine mission. In doing so, they act as mirrors reflecting the parts of ourselves that trigger our deepest insecurities, setting the stage for profound healing and growth. The paradox inherent in these connections lies in their dual nature—they can be both challenging and transformative, leading to a heightened understanding of ourselves and the intricate web of existence.

Through the lens of deep contrast and duality provided by a twin elemental soulmate, the polarization experienced in relationships can initiate a seismic shift in perspective and values. Individuals find themselves confronting their innermost fears and limitations, navigating a journey towards profound personal evolution. The crucible of extreme contrast and challenge compels us to face our imperfections, shedding old patterns and beliefs, ultimately fostering substantial personal growth. It is within the intense pressure and tension of these relationships that we find the fertile ground for transformation and the emergence of elevated versions of ourselves.

A poignant example of this transformational polarization can be seen in the story of a woman entangled in a highly tumultuous yet passionate relationship with a twin flame. Although she cherished her partner, at times even more than herself, the neglect of her own spirit unearthed deeply ingrained disparities that ultimately proved extremely unhealthy and sometimes rife with toxicity. Becoming aware of this dynamic, she set in motion a journey toward healing and balance.

Her struggle with self-doubt and insecurity, deeply rooted in her attachment style, was brought to the forefront. The bold and confident personality of her partner served as a catalyst, forcing her to confront these issues head-on. This challenging dynamic, although tumultuous, became the crucible for her personal growth and transformation.

Through the stark contrast between their personalities, she gradually gained a clearer understanding of herself, initiating the profound work of healing and transformation. Confronting her insecurities and actively working to overcome them, she witnessed a shift in her entire worldview. The process led to increased confidence, empowerment, and alignment with her authentic self.

Ultimately, she managed to liberate herself from the toxicity of the relationship, stepping into a new life filled with purpose and fulfillment. In this narrative, there were no victims or villains, no shame or blame—just a profound sense of self-accountability for the co-creation of a polarizing experience that ultimately facilitated the evolution of her soul.

While the journey of transformational polarization may be arduous, its rewards are ultimately fulfilling and evolutionary. Embracing the inherent contrast and duality within our relationships can serve as a powerful catalyst for change, enabling us to manifest the best version of ourselves and lead a life characterized by authenticity and purpose.

Within the pragmatic framework of twin elementals is a serendipitous journey of discovery. With each elemental, emerges continuity of the entire model, fostering an acculturated awakening. Cultivating this awareness can help mitigate the collateral consequences of unexplored potential, including the immeasurable liabilities rooted in ignorance that affect all human interactions.

Studying the nature of each elemental connection, both here and in real-time interactions, sheds light on the causation behind specific events, preventing you from being swept away by the consequences and effects of undesirable situations. Fortunately, those who find success in a conscious life partnership will often traverse the full spectrum of elemental traits throughout their journey. Integrating all elemental characteristics is comparable to self realization in a shared soulmate partnership.

For a comprehensive review of this chapter the following bullet points summarize the key learnings:

Introduction of the Twin Elemental Effect: We begin our exploration by delving into the Twin Elemental Effect, a model that not only encapsulates the essence of personal growth and evolution but also merges seamlessly with the notion of predestined life scripts originating from the soul realm. This model categorizes profound psychological and spiritual connections into four main types of elemental influence—each characterized by unique, dominant traits that influence our personal growth and relational dynamics.

- *Twin Wind: Dominated by intellectual stimulation and dynamic movement.*

- *Twin Flood: Emphasizes deep emotional resonance and nurturing capabilities.*

- *Twin Flame: Known for its intensity regarding passion and chaos potential.*

- *Twin Planet: Provides grounding stability and long-lasting support.*

Transformation and Personal Evolution: Twin Elemental connections are catalysts for significant personal transformation, challenging us to grow beyond our limitations and evolve into more aligned versions of ourselves. The emotional and cognitive exchanges within these relationships significantly influence our emotional and psychological well-being and encourage us to reconcile various aspects of our psyche.

- This process shapes our responses and growth through life's various stages.

Challenges in Embracing New Concepts: The introduction of new models like the Twin Elemental Effect often encounters resistance, primarily due to the familiarity principle, which naturally inclines us toward well-known concepts. This resistance can be understood as part of a learning curve—a psychological and educational journey where repeated exposure and thoughtful explanation are essential for overcoming initial skepticism and deepening understanding of innovative ideas.

- This dynamic shows that individuals must navigate initial discomfort to fully understand and integrate new knowledge into their worldview.

Emotional and Cognitive Impact Across Lifespans: The emotional and cognitive exchanges within these elemental relationships profoundly affect our psychological well-being, urging us to explore and reconcile various aspects of our psyche from childhood into adulthood.
- This long-term interaction highlights the enduring impact of elemental connections on our development and psychological health.

Psychological Foundations and Applications: The model integrates developmental psychology, parapsychology, behavioral science, and cognitive therapy to explain how the elemental characteristics present in our many connections shape our mental health and interpersonal dynamics, serving as a holistic tool for understanding personal and relational development.

- Incorporating these psychological principles provides a scientific foundation for the theoretical model, enhancing its credibility and applicability.

Field Probability and Relationship Dynamics: Drawing parallels with physical theories, like field probabilities in physics, the Twin Elemental model explains how relationships form dynamic energy fields that influence the probable outcomes of our paths, thus impacting the broader trajectories of our lives through a multitude of cause and effect dynamics.

- Relational field probabilities due to elemental natures of human behaviors represent the cause; the twin elemental effect highlights the far-reaching effects on one's life trajectory and how to identify the dynamics influencing it.

Ego Mirroring and Shadow Self Exposure: Relationships within this framework act as mirrors that reflect our deepest traits and unconscious impulses through mirroring elemental characteristics, particularly evident in our formative years and early adulthood. This interaction offers a unique opportunity for self-discovery and integration, leading to holistic personal development and the exposure of our shadow selves.

- This point expands on how Twin Elementals go beyond Social Mirror Theory, illustrating how deep social resonance impacts individuals intimately, setting the stage for shadow exposure. When exposed, by confronting and integrating our shadow selves—those aspects we often ignore or suppress—we engage in a transformative process that fosters significant personal evolution and growth.

Polarity and Power Balance in Relationships: The elemental connections exhibit polarity that can either harmonize or disrupt our internal balance, underscoring the importance of understanding these dynamics to maintain emotional and psychological health.

- The twin elemental effect does not only affect an individual in a positive or negative way but offers duality—better perceived as polarity—seeing as, for example, a twin flame can influence with the warmth of passion or the flame of destruction.

- The power balance dynamic comes into play due to the ego's rejection or acceptance of a juxtaposed individual's mirrored projections. One's attitude toward perceived actions can shift between acceptance and rejection constantly, demonstrating a range of polarities.

Micro Examples of Twin Elemental Effects: The model incorporates micro-level concepts such as Social Comparison Theory, Emotional Contagion, and Affective Transference to illustrate how subtle dynamics within these relationships affect our emotional states, self-perception, and both conscious and subconscious life decisions.

- These theories in psychology represent the microstates of the Twin Elementals' macro effects and influence on an individual's lifetime trajectory.

Predestined Life Scripts and Transdimensional Learning: The Twin Elemental model posits that our life's script is pre-planned from the soul realm, designed to teach us lessons in the physical world through transdimensional awareness.

- This section suggests that just as a playwright designs a script for actors on stage or a preprogrammed flight simulator provides the challenges necessary for learning to fly, predestined life scripts are a fundamental part of a soul's evolution for transdimensional learning.

Influence of Soul Memories and Hypnotic Insights: Hypnotic regression reveals that soul memories influence decision-making from the unseen realm, guiding actions and choices in our visible world, and highlighting the soul's journey through various incarnations.

- Past life regression hypnosis, past life recall, and various near-death experiences, along with other psychic phenomena, suggest that our major experiences in life, including enigmatic relationships, are predestined. This aligns with many religious doctrines, which posit that an omnipotent deity, or God, foresees all events in an individual's life.

Karmic Ties and Soul Family Dynamics: Our interactions with soul families—groups of souls connected by karmic ties—help us navigate our spiritual evolution, offering insights into our purpose and the challenges we encounter over multiple lifetimes.

- This section explores how soul groupings emerge as soulmates during predestined encounters, taking forms such as twin flames, floods, winds, and planets within our Twin Elemental network. This underscores the diversity of soul connections, illustrating that twin flames, for example, are not the only soulmates.

Cultural, Educational, and Environmental Influences: Our elemental dynamics are shaped by an interplay of cultural, educational, and biological factors. The early connections we form, shaped by our environment and culture, lay the groundwork for our life's trajectory. These early influences, often forgotten on a conscious level, continue to affect us subconsciously throughout our lives.

- This section highlights how twin elemental influences in one's early years are just as pivotal in shaping one's life trajectory as a magnetic soul pairing or intense relationship in adulthood.

These bullet points encapsulate the complex interplay of psychological, spiritual, and metaphysical themes discussed in the chapter, offering a condensed overview of its key insights and theories.

As we delve deeper into understanding the Twin Elemental model in the coming chapters, we are better equipped to navigate our relationships and personal growth trajectories, embracing the challenges and opportunities presented by these powerful elemental connections.

The following chapters build upon the foundations laid here, expanding and deepening the ideas introduced. Prepare to embark on a comprehensive exploration into the unique qualities inherent in the characteristics of each twin elemental soul connection. On this journey, we'll continue to uncover the layers of complex dynamics, illuminating the subtle interplay shaping our beings. Along the way, we'll reveal the transformative potential hidden within these unique bonds and energetic exchanges.

Chapter Ten

TWIN FLAMES

Inversion Mirroring of Fire Elementals

Quote: "The minute I heard my first love story, I started looking for you, not knowing how blind that was. Lovers don't finally meet somewhere. They're in each other all along."   —Rumi

The quintessential soul connection, widely recognized by lovers and esoteric relationship novelists, is the rare and intense Twin Flame. Characterized by its fiery nature, igniting the spirit with passion, desire, and emotion, the incandescent Twin Flame connection stands out as the most intense elemental soulmate bond to date. The intensity of fire perfectly denotes the characteristics found in these unique soulmate connections.

The sub title of this chapter poses an intriguing question—whether twin flames stand as the sole variety of soulmates. A brief venture into the boundless realm of YouTube, with its infinite stream of reels and stories, unveils a wide array of views on the matter. You'll find strong assertions emphasizing the unique distinction between twin flames and soulmates, alongside contrasting opinions suggesting the possibility of encountering several soulmates throughout one's journey, yet being fated to connect with only one twin flame, and sometimes the other way around. This exploration uncovers a rich diversity of beliefs and interpretations, each contributing to the complex discourse on the subject.

In a Hollywood fairy tale, such as the story of Bella and Edward Cullen from Twilight—who exemplify the twin flame dynamic with their tumultuous relationship and a poly-throuple-like love triangle involving Jacob, the werewolf—their story might lead one to believe in the existence of a singular, all-consuming love. Yet, real life often throws us into the kind of heart-stopping, life-altering "entanglements" that could prompt your mother to throw a side-eye, murmuring, 'I'm gonna keep you in my prayers.'

Throughout a lifetime, individuals may find themselves deeply connected to what they perceive as their "one and only" twin flame, only to eventually part ways and discover a connection with a new flame that feels even more intense. This evolution naturally challenges their initial belief, prompting a reevaluation to recognize this new relationship as the true twin flame.

The underlying premise is that if a twin flame's purpose is to catalyze personal growth, it's unlikely that a single individual would embody all the lessons and developmental experiences one is meant to have. The core message? While tales of fiction often romanticize the notion of a singular, everlasting love, the reality of human connections is far more complex, nuanced, and infinitely fascinating. Now, to embark on a more enriched exploration of the concept, let's delve deeper into the ideology.

When a connection transcends mere fire to reflect a flame.

Throughout history, fire and the spirit of man have been closely entwined. In numerous cultures, fire is symbolized as representing the human spirit, embodying life energy and vitality. A notable similarity between fire and the spirit of man lies in their transformative abilities. Fire can change matter from one state to another, much like turning wood into ash. Moreover, fire exhibits dual aspects—it can be both destructive and beneficial. While capable of destroying homes and forests, it also provides warmth, light, and a means to cook food. Similarly, the spirit of man mirrors this duality, capable of both great acts of kindness and cruelty. Naturally, these traits can manifest in how mankind relates to each other, evoking either passion or rage.

Fire holds deep symbolic significance in numerous indigenous cultures and religious traditions, serving as a pivotal link between the earthly realm and the spiritual world. In Hinduism, the deity Agni is honored as the sacred fire, acting as a celestial intermediary that connects mortals with the divine. The mythology of ancient Greece ties fire to Hephaestus, the god who oversees blacksmiths and craftsmanship, highlighting its transformative power. Similarly, various Native American cultures attribute profound spiritual properties to fire, considering it a medium for healing and purification. Echoing this reverence within Yoruba culture, Shangó, a highly venerated loa or orisha, reigns over the elements of lightning, thunder, and fire. As a warrior deity distinguished by his astute intellect and volatile temperament, Shangó stands as a paragon of virility.

Yet, in the realm of the twin flame dynamic, characterized by the fire element, many find themselves navigating without a clear guide, **improvising** through its complex layers. This approach can lead to the significant mistake of underestimating the connection, mistaking it for a mere karmic relationship, and thus, entering a perpetual cycle of uncertainty—a kind of limbo. Rest assured, the energy present within twin flame interactions, and indeed, all elemental connections, holds a divine intention in one's life. Navigating these dynamics without a clear strategy can **inadvertently sow the seeds of chaos.**

Brimming with inherent intensity, the concept of twin flames has deep roots in spiritual belief systems, symbolizing a profound karmic connection between two souls. In this belief, twin flames are perceived as inseparably bound individuals, stemming from a single soul division at the dawn of creation. Their meeting in this lifetime is believed to be predestined, serving a shared purpose as they mutually complete and fulfill one another in a way unparalleled by any other connection. This profound bond transcends the constraints of time and space, enabling them to sense each other's emotions and thoughts, even when physically apart. For believers in twin flames, discovering their counterpart is a sacred and life-changing experience - and they're not wrong.

When the long-awaited connection finally occurs, the sharing of souls becomes whole, with each receiving the emotional exchanges and spiritual resources the other has to offer. From what we've uncovered, every soul mate is a part of you, serving as the other half in the moments of your shared experiences, no matter how brief or dispassionate.

I won't attempt to sell you on the romanticized and idealized notions of twin flames. There are a plethora of books on the subject and a quick scroll through YouTube reels under the hashtag "twin flames" will vividly illustrate these fanciful ideas held by many people. I will, however, provide you with a brief preview of the shared characteristics of soulmates, twin flames, and all elemental connections.

Now, let's delve into some common qualities attributed to twin elementals:

- **Profound Familiarity and Comfort:** When twin flames converge, a profound sense of familiarity and comfort envelops them, as though their connection spans an eternity.

- **Intense Recognition from Past Lives:** Twin flames share an intense recognition, their souls intertwining from past lives to forge an unbreakable bond.

- **Deep Completion and Wholeness:** Upon uniting, twin flames experience a profound sense of completion and wholeness, effortlessly fitting the puzzle pieces of their beings together.

- **Powerful Connection and Understanding:** Twin flames share a connection and understanding so powerful that it transcends time, even when their encounter is fresh and new.

- **Distinct Feeling of "Home":** In each other's company, twin flames feel a distinct sense of being "home," marking a profound belonging and comfort beyond the physical realm.

- **Telepathic Connection:** Often, twin flames experience a form of telepathy, enabling communication without words, transcending ordinary understanding to sense each other's thoughts and emotions, even across vast distances.

- **Synchronicity:** Twin flames frequently encounter synchronicities—coincidental meetings, shared dreams, or parallel life events—serving as cosmic signposts guiding them along their intertwined journey.

- **Energetic Resonance:** In the presence of one another, twin flames often experience a profound energetic resonance, where their energies harmonize and amplify, creating a powerful and palpable vibrational connection that transcends the physical realm.

These remarkable qualities merely scratch the surface of the multifaceted tapestry that defines the unique and profound connection shared by twin flames. Having a twin flame elemental can profoundly influence a person's outlook and perspective on life. For some, discovering their twin flame is seen as the ultimate goal in their spiritual journey, promising a profound sense of inner peace and fulfillment. Others view the experience of being with a twin flame as challenging and intense, yet ultimately transformative and enlightening.

In many conversations about Twin Flames, they are also referred to as Karmics, a term derived from karmic connections or relationships where karmic debts are settled. According to this spiritual belief system, certain souls are destined to intersect to fulfill a karmic purpose. A karmic soul connection is considered a relationship meant to impart valuable lessons, fostering growth and evolution in both souls thus cultivating equilibrium. While these lessons can be arduous, they serve the higher purpose of helping individuals become the best versions of themselves. These beliefs align with our previous discussions and generally reflect the essence of all twin elemental connections.

Moreover, karmic relationships, often intense and tumultuous, extend beyond the romantic realm. They can manifest as friendships, family connections, or professional relationships. Some hold the belief that karmic relationships may not endure, but the lessons gleaned from them leave lasting imprints on individuals throughout their lifetimes. It is not uncommon to find an elder passing the baton of wisdom while reflecting on a character from their distant past who imparted a lasting lesson. This aligns with the lasting effects of Twin Elemental engagement, as all elementals carry a karmic essence, designed to aid in the journey toward becoming a better version of themselves. Karmic relationships frequently intertwine with twin flames, owing to the intense and fiery nature of these connections.

Indeed, twin Flames hold a distinctive place as a widely recognized form of elemental connection, playing a pivotal role in unraveling the mysteries of soul mirroring and raising awareness to this point. However, as we venture deeper into the realm of various elemental soul connections, it becomes crucial to distill and dissect what sets twin flames apart, thus making them the polarizing enigma that they are. Let's explore the exceptional traits and distinguishing features that separate twin flame characteristics from other soul connections.

Drawing inspiration from Eastern philosophies, Fire, alongside Air, embodies the "yang" element, radiating a masculine energy that is impulsive and passionate.

Connections rooted in these elements are characterized by intensity and fervor. The twin flame connection, in particular, stands out for its dualisticly demanding and restorative nature, deeply embedded in the intricate dance of mirroring a counterparts masculine qualities. A twin flame possesses the profound ability to illuminate one's deepest insecurities, fears, and shadows, while simultaneously paving the way for the realization of one's wildest dreams and aspirations. The magnetic attraction inherent in this connection can spark a transformative desire to evolve into a better version of oneself.

In the beginning, many perceive their twin flame as the missing puzzle piece, believing that this connection will complete them and bring a profound sense of wholeness. However, adopting such a mindset early on can raise cautionary flags and intensify the already fiery nature of this energetic exchange, especially in the face of potential disappointment.

On one hand, an all-consuming desire to possess your partner's mind, body, and soul can spark an intense limerence, urging you to absorb every aspect of their essence. Coupled with lofty expectations that their love, beauty, and magic will heal your inner voids and insecurities, this can set the stage for inevitable disillusionment. The powerful chemistry fueling this limerence may even blind you to obvious red flags, contributing to an uncontrollable inferno that reflects the shadows of your soul.

The connection between twin flames stands in a league of its own. Unlike other elemental bonds that may require time to flourish, the twin flame bond emerges as a fiery and passionate force, instantly recognizable and irresistibly magnetic. Generally, upon first contact, activation is immediate and thus, one of its most captivating qualities is the intense attraction that sparks from the very moment you meet—a magnetic pull that transcends both the physical and spiritual realms, captivating your entire being.

For a visual analogy, envision a building engulfed in flames. Starting perhaps from a single candle, the blaze rapidly jumps to a small curtain, spreading and consuming everything in its path. Similarly, the twin flame bond can ignite with such intensity that it demands acknowledgment. It's not always rooted in the purely sexual; instead, there's something about them that feels both peculiar and familiar, a magnetic force drawing you toward them like a literal moth to a flame.

In many instances, the desire to marry them on the spot may arise, even for those who had never entertained the idea of marriage before—such is the potency of the attraction. Johnny Depp famously experienced this upon meeting Amber Heard and went as far as marrying her. This sensation stems from an initial yet profound recognition of the soul. You sense their mirrored strength, and they feel like home, as if you've been yearning for them your entire life. It's a connection that defies easy articulation but is undeniably and indelibly etched in memory. The bond between twin flames is unequivocal, offering a shared perception that transcends the boundaries of the physical realm.

A heightened awareness of all things agreeable and even confirmation bias is equally prevalent in a twin flame connection, where you actively seek out and recognize the beautiful things you share in common. In the context of a romantic interest, individuals may remember information in a way that confirms their preexisting beliefs or preferences or focus on similarities to reinforce their attraction.

There's an insatiable craving for the undeniable chemistry and attention the twin flame provides. In pursuit of that intoxicating chemistry and a chance to microdose on their attention, you might find yourself willing to do the seemingly unthinkable for their love—echoing the sentiments expressed in the lyrics of a popular Alicia Keys song...

> Quote: You give me a feeling that I've never felt before, And I deserve it,
> It's becoming something that's impossible to ignore...
> I was wondering, maybe, Could I make you my baby?
> If we do the unthinkable Would it make us look crazy
> If you ask me I'm ready.

In some instances, this intense craving can lead to compulsive behavior, prompting you to go to great lengths for their love, even if it goes against your usual character. This powerful force can drive actions that you wouldn't typically consider, behaviors that may contradict your innate qualities and values. The potential disparity between your authentic self and these compulsive actions can eventually breed conflict and resentment, possibly paving the way for separation if it is a full on unhealthy limerence process.

While recognizing the multitude of shared traits and commonalities with your partner, it's likely that, as you reflect on the coincidences and shared experiences binding you, you'll perceive your differences as complementary. The belief that opposites attract, much like the concept of yin and yang, may come into play.

Perhaps one person's moon complements the other's sun, or one's shadows balance the other's light. This mindset can foster a potent and magnetic bond, one that leads to intense attachments and even withdrawal symptoms long after being apart. Twin flame energy possesses an irresistible allure that pulls you toward both the positive and negative aspects of the connection.

However, it's critical to acknowledge that red flags remain red flags, regardless of the intensity of your connection or how rich the hue is in your rose colored glasses. Even in the depths of a profound connection, it's essential to stay aware of potential warning signs and avoid overlooking them. The temptation to dismiss or rationalize certain behaviors may arise, especially if infatuation along with the rush of twin flame chemistry are at play. Ultimately, maintaining a balance between the allure of a magnetic connection and a clear-eyed assessment of your partner and relationship is vital. By staying grounded and attentive to warning signs, you can cultivate a healthy and fulfilling twin flame partnership.

As you will come to learn, all twin elemental archetypes are associated with distinct physical attributes. In the case of twin flames, the predominant energy is closely aligned with the root chakra, extending from the perineum to just below the navel. These chakras, integral to each elemental connection, are vital components of a broader system of energy pathways known as meridians. These meridians are believed to be intricately connected to macro/micro-anatomical structures known as fascia.

Boldly stated, the primary emotion linked to a twin flame connection is often 'Arousal.' With the focal point of this energetic connection residing in the realm of the sexual organs, it's not surprising that the entire body, including its fascia, becomes infused with chemicals in the bloodstream that ignite feelings of arousal and passion.

The neurochemicals dopamine and norepinephrine are most commonly associated with the intense chemistry of twin flames. This dynamic combination fuels the profound emotions shared by twin flames, sparking a fiery 'kundalinic' journey from the reproductive organs up to the brain. Through the intricate interplay of these diverse energy systems, including the esoteric aspects, a twin flame experience is generated and circulated between two individuals. By tuning into these energetic pathways and comprehending their role in twin flame connections we can deepen our appreciation for the complex and multifaceted nature of this powerful experience including its potential for transformation.

It's been suggested that the right fire attraction can make you so feverishly hot that you might fail a temperature check at the entrance to a public building during a pandemic, leading to a mandatory two-week quarantine. ~I'm only teasing. However, it is crucial to recognize that while twin flame chemistry can be exhilarating, it may also lead to risky and even dangerous behaviors if not managed with care. At its most challenging, the magnetic pull of a twin flame can resemble that of a moth drawn to a flame. In other words, if you're not cautious, you just might get *'burnt'*.

Approaching the twin flame connection with mindfulness and caution is comparable to a child learning the valuable lesson experienced by touching a hot stove. By remaining aware of both potential risks and benefits, you can navigate the twin flame experience in a healthy and constructive manner. While the initial attraction, ascension and healing process can be beautiful, make no mistake, a twin flame relationship can be tumultuous, volatile, and downright ugly—igniting a **dark night of the soul** experience. It's crucial to recognize that a twin flame relationship is not always a stroll in the park, contrary to common belief.

The flame has the ability to cast an amorous light that illuminates the deepest, darkest parts of your soul, casting a shadow that brings about a fierce and even violent awakening and transformation as mentioned in the introductory chapter. The process may be overwhelmingly challenging, but emerging unscathed and intact serves as a significant facilitator of growth and a potent catalyst for polarization, ultimately leading to **absolute soul evolution.**

Upon observation, it becomes evident that before embarking on a twin flame relationship, many individuals harbored idyllic notions filled with blissful expectations of harmonious unions—reminiscent of good tidings, rainbows, cotton candy, unicorns, and glittering stars. However, those same individuals who after personally experiencing such connections often describe them as akin to thunderous lightning strikes, seismic earthquakes, and raging infernos in opposition to the rainbows and unicorns. Despite the tumultuous nature, they cannot help but be consumed by an indescribable and unyielding attachment to their twin flame.

This is because when compulsively relating to a soulmate, you relate within a state of chaos. Later in the book, we will discuss the empowering benefits that come with conscious relating over compulsive relating, so that relating individuals can learn how to avoid the hellish states present in many twin elemental relationships. Essentially, a twin flame relationship should be the prototypical union for transcendence.

Despite the challenging states, the potential for immense evolutionary growth is always present, offering opportunities for massive transformation. As you mature and grow, recognizing a twin flame upfront while armed with wisdom, knowledge, understanding, and intelligence places you in a different emotional demographic regarding conscious relating, and not blindly falling without the accountability.

Success becomes attainable by adopting and utilizing the various modalities available to you. Incorporating tools such as the Twin Elemental model, astrological placement awareness, soft psychological testing, understanding love languages, and engaging in emotional intelligence programs, coupled with the fundamental concept of common sense, equips you with the necessary tools for relationship success.

You begin to understand that relationships, regardless of their dynamic, are reflections of your own consciousness—mirrors in fact. You realize that it's not anyone's responsibility to make you feel good, and by assigning that role to someone, you inadvertently grant them the power to make you feel bad, relinquishing your own power and allowing others to control you like a puppet.

While elemental connections may be complex, it's crucial not to overthink them. Moreover, once you've diligently initiated a process for shadow work, integrating your complexities into a coherent and balanced self-understanding, you'll find that you are less susceptible to being triggered by fiery tempers. Whether independently or through prior relationships, learning to cherish and love yourself without neglect, places an individual in a position to potentially attract a twin flame soulmate of the utmost caliber when in alignment with your predestined path.

One notable advantage of a turbulent-free, smooth-sailing journey with limited obstacles alongside a twin flame is the power to magically manifest your most radical desires together. Similar to harnessing the power of a vast and formidable magnet within the realm of the non-physical, the law of attraction becomes instinctual, even for those who are spiritually unaware. Among the most remarkable benefits of these manifestations is the ability to achieve them in a magical and awe-inspiring way through circulating "flow state" energy exchange.

When aligned with a shared purpose and consciously relating in high vibrations, twin flames, free from the egoic constraints of the typical relationship, possess a potent force akin to rocket fuel, propelling their dreams through the vortex, as often spoken of by the channeled consciousness known as **Abraham Hicks**. In fact, it transcends mere rocket fuel but becomes nuclear fusion-styled propellant. Imagine a couple mastering the art of conscious relating, effortlessly raising their internal kundalini, and attracting their desired life to the absolute highest degree.

Awakened individuals, with clarity in their shared purposes, steering clear of limerence pitfalls, form a resilient, magnetic bond, elevating their vibration to co-create a new illuminated reality. Through the power of their connection and co-creation, they can project laser-focus, allowing them to attract whatever they imagine, be it peace in the jungles of Bali, luxurious yacht living on the ocean, or freedom to jet-set to Cairo or Paris bi-weekly, even if they have subpar employment. This is all due to the shared peak and flow state previously mentioned.

In high-functioning conscious relationships, be it with a twin flame or any twin elemental, **Positive Psychology**, or "posi-psych," comes into play. This field delves into the positive aspects of human behavior, emotions, and thoughts, promoting well-being, happiness, and optimal functioning. Posi-psych explores leveraging strengths and positive emotions to enhance life and relationships while cultivating resilience during adversity. Essentially, it follows the principle that energy flows where attention goes—feeding what you want and starving what you don't.

Positive psychology—in alignment with coherence— paves the way for achieving a flow state, synonymous with "being in the zone." This mental state entails complete immersion and focus, transcending time and space. In this peak state, individuals experience energized focus, absorption in the task, and profound enjoyment and fulfillment. While commonly associated with sports, art, or music, flow state extends to various activities, including manifesting a desired lifestyle within a high-quality partnership. It's the pinnacle state, where creativity and productivity flourish.

The primary purpose of a twin flame is to catalyze a profound transformative impact. This transformative power can be harnessed consistently when both partners embody awareness, mindfulness, and intelligence, enabling a profound understanding of the purpose and transcendent potential inherent in their predestined twin flame coupling. Through this evolutionary journey alongside soul family reflections, twin flames can co-create an exceptional and fulfilling life that surpasses even their wildest dreams.

Furthermore, twin flame connections serve as gateways to higher levels of consciousness and understanding, bringing individuals closer to their true nature as spiritual beings. In the exploration of this connection, hidden talents and gifts may be uncovered, new depths of empathy and compassion discovered, and a profound sense of unity and interconnectedness with all of creation experienced. While the twin flame journey has the potential to be challenging, tumultuous, and polarizing it ultimately leads to a state of profound awakening and enlightenment, unlocking the full potential of the human experience.

So far, we've delved into the awe-inspiring potential of a twin flame relationship with a soulmate under the pretense of romantic relating. Yet, it's vital to note that a non-romantic soulmate can also fall under the fiery embrace of a twin elemental, impacting ones life in extraordinary ways. The twin flame connection fundamentally emphasizes passion, zeal and belief, with the intensity of fire, expressed through the mirroring of diverse spiritual and interpersonal dynamics.

In an unusual yet enlightening encounter, I found myself in the company of an unlikely individual with a compelling twin flame story. It happened during my part-time gig as a rideshare driver, a role I assumed for the purpose of recording interviews for my YouTube show, "Heart to Heart on the Highway." The man I picked up was a Hispanic male in his mid-30s, accompanied by his teenage son. What set this encounter apart was the fact that he was paralyzed from the waist down.

While hesitant to be recorded for my project, he eventually opened up and shared his remarkable story as long as the camera was off. He had initially perceived my project as something whimsical, centered around the airy-fairy notions of romantic soulmates and the like.

As he began to speak, it became clear that his past had been marked by a turbulence. In his youth, he had been deeply entrenched in active gang life. He recounted a fateful night when he and a couple of homies, including his closest childhood friend, whom he regarded as a brother, attended a party. After indulging in excessive intoxication, a trivial disagreement erupted, the details of which had long faded into obscurity.

In the heat of the moment, the young man uttered words akin to "F-you," prompting his best friend to walk away, muttering something unintelligible under his breath. Seconds later, his friend turned around, brandishing a weapon and firing several shots. Tragically, one of the bullets struck the young man's blood brother, who stood beside him, instantly claiming his life. Another bullet found its mark in the young man's gut, piercing through to his lower spine, leaving him paralyzed for life.

Although over 15 years had elapsed since that fateful night, I explained to the young man the profound concept of prearranged soul agreements. I suggested that he and his best friend, who was like a brother to him, might have known each other in a previous lifetime. Despite their deep bond as brothers and comrades, one tragic event had irrevocably altered the trajectory of both their lives. A brother was lost, one was imprisoned for life, and the other lost the ability to walk forever.

The young man revealed that he had been on a self-destructive path before that life-altering incident. However, in the years that followed, he underwent a remarkable transformation. He now volunteers to mentor youth and is actively involved in the lives of his own children, among other positive endeavors.

After our conversation, where I elucidated the true essence of a twin elemental soul tie, the romanticized notions he had previously held were demystified. He gained a profound understanding of why the tragedy had unfolded as it did, and how it might have been a part of their shared spiritual journey. I literally saw the 'aha' enlightenment moment in his eyes as we reasoned in conversation.

It's crucial to keep in mind that, whether romantic, familial, or platonic, twin flames and all twin elementals possess the power to ignite your spiritual journey just as easily as they can warm your heart or set your mind ablaze with passion.

Recognizing the profound reality that the twin flame connection isn't always a gentle, romantic warmth, as demonstrated in the previous story, challenges the common belief among most twin flame enthusiasts. It's often believed that twin flames can only manifest as romantic fairy tale-like connections, typically experienced through heterosexual relationships, yet same-sex attachments as well as other diverse dynamics can also be a part of this definition. However, as the evidence presented throughout this book illustrates, soul connections and soul ties can take on myriad forms, each laden with their own unique and intimately connected histories.

These connections, laden with fiery potential possess the dual capacity to both illuminate and/or incinerate. They can be the spark that lights up the darkest corners of your soul, yet they may also scorch and dismantle the structures you've built within. It's the dynamic dance of creation and destruction that defines the essence of twin flames—build and destroy.

So, as we navigate the terrain of soul connections, let's celebrate the flame's illuminating brilliance, recognizing its power to forge deep connections and impart invaluable wisdom, reminding us that the most profound transformations often arise from the very fires that challenge us.

In conclusion, let's summarize six key characteristics of a **"Twin Flame"** within the elemental framework of a mirrored soul connection:

- **Intensity:** Twin flame connections are defined by an unparalleled level of intensity, both in terms of emotional and spiritual energies exchanged between the individuals involved. One notable hallmark of a twin flame connection is the fiery nature that can spark brain chemistry and trigger the release of hormones, intensifying the experience of passion. This heightened state of arousal can lead to a profound sense of limerence—an intense infatuation and longing for the other person—that may feel all-consuming and overpowering.

- **Unbreakable Bond:** Twin flames share an unbreakable bond that transcends physical, emotional, and spiritual realms. This connection is characterized by an overwhelming sense of attachment and an unshakable feeling of being deeply interconnected on a soul level. Even after separation, flames are usually still very much connected, choosing to love from a distance and in silence.

- **Complementarity:** Despite possessing their own unique qualities, twin flames are naturally drawn to each other's differences, recognizing them as complementary aspects that enhance their overall connection. They epitomize Yin and Yang, reflecting as equal but opposite dark and light energies for full polarization in the shadows while presenting a unified whole to the outside world.

- **Synchronicity:** Twin flames often experience a series of uncanny synchronicities, where events and circumstances align in a meaningful and seemingly orchestrated manner. As one of the most overtly spiritual connections, twin flames tend to encounter many esoteric occurrences that serve as a transformative platform for intense lessons, fostering deep polarization.

- **Challenging Growth:** Twin flame relationships frequently act as catalysts for profound personal growth, presenting challenges, obstacles, and opportunities for deep inner transformation. While all twin elementals hold space for growth, twin flames are the most readily observable due to the intensity and frequency of the lessons learned.

- **Physical Attributes:** The neurochemicals dopamine and norepinephrine are the chemistry most commonly associated with twin flames, while the root chakra and sexual organs are the chakras and organs most linked to twin flame energy. Arousal, whether mental, spiritual, or physical, is the emotion most associated with twin flame soulmates.

Next up is an introduction to the life-giving and flowing nature reflected in the Twin Waters' Soulmate dynamic known as the all-encompassing Twin Floods.

Chapter Eleven

TWIN FLOODS

The Inverted Mirroring of Water Elementals

Quote: "True love is not a strong, fiery, impetuous passion. It is, on the contrary, an element calm and deep. It looks beyond mere externals and is attracted by qualities alone. It is wise and discriminating, and its devotion is real and abiding."
—Ellen G. White

Among the 92 elements adorning the periodic table, only a select few emerge as critical architects of the human body. At the helm is Oxygen, claiming a staggering 65% of our total mass, closely trailed by Carbon at around 18%. The dynamic duo of Hydrogen and Nitrogen solidify the top four, contributing about 10% and 3%, respectively. This quartet— Oxygen, Carbon, Hydrogen, and Nitrogen, collectively commands a staggering 96% share of our body's mass. The remaining 4% consists of seven major elements and approximately 50 trace elements.

Now, of this vital quartet, it doesn't take a rocket scientist to deduce that when Hydrogen and Oxygen unite (H2O), they form the essence of our being – water, constituting a whopping 75% of the human body. Water the ubiquitous life elixir, stands as the linchpin connecting all facets of our existence. Water, a coagulated gas that essentially makes us gaseous beings, may explain why we sway and flow within our emotions as effortlessly as gases move through the air, adapting to every shift as the situation demands.

Beyond mere sustenance, water plays a pivotal role in regulating body temperature, lubricating joints, facilitating nutrient transport, and expelling waste. Despite its elemental simplicity, water assumes a paramount role in the intricate machinery of the human body, exerting a profound influence on the human spirit. With around 75% of our mass in liquid form, the undeniable impact of water on emotions aligns seamlessly with the frequencies of human consciousness.

For those less inclined toward the scientific intricacies of the periodic table, the elements may resonate more as the traditional four physical elements of Earth, Wind, Fire and of course water. It's only natural that, within our three-dimensional consciousness, we gravitate toward what we can perceive through our physical senses – what we can see, touch, taste, and feel.

To provide perspective, Leonardo da Vinci, famously recognized water as the driving force in nature, and it's not a stretch to extend that recognition to it being the lifeblood of our planet. Geologists even theorize that billions of years ago, Earth existed as a complete water planet. Delving into history, spirituals and folk songs echoed the significance of water, with tunes like "Wade in the Water." Harriet Tubman, a courageous American freedom fighter, reportedly used this song as a covert signal, guiding the enslaved to take to the waterways to evade pursuit.

Across diverse religious traditions, water stands as a sacred symbol, embodying notions of purity, rebirth, and fertility. In Eastern Orthodox Christianity, its healing powers are harnessed in cleansing rituals like baptism. Additionally, there is the biblical verse in John 3:5, where Jesus answered, 'Verily, verily, I say unto thee, Except a man be born of water and of the Spirit, he cannot enter into the kingdom of God.

Taoism venerates water for its wisdom, as it gracefully flows regardless of obstacles. The ancient Greeks saw water as a symbol of transition and metamorphosis, embracing its myriad forms. In Ancient Egypt, water hieroglyphics adorned temple walls, emphasizing its cultural significance. The Egyptians even believed that water held the key to eternal life and insights into the cycles of time. From Suijin, the benevolent Shinto god of water in Japanese mythology, to Mami Wata, the bestower of wealth in the beliefs of the Anang Ibibio people in southeast Nigeria, the spirit of water has been intricately woven into the fabric of human existence since time immemorial

Delving deeper, Mami Wata stands as a poignant example of the spirit of water embodied across cultures. This revered water mother vividly illustrates humanity's quest to understand the essence of water within ourselves. Even amid the tragic horrors of the Transatlantic slave trade, Mami Wata endured, preserving her sacred significance in diverse forms throughout the Americas and Indigenous Afro-Caribbean cultures

This captivating African Goddess symbolizes numerous facets of life, embodying good fortune, wealth, and healing. Often depicted with a human upper half and a fish or serpent lower half. She may also be portrayed with a snake around her neck, symbolizing divinity and the art of divination. Mami Wata signifies the depths of the ocean and the generative force of life itself. This symbolism traces back to ancient doctrines, contributing to the medieval mermaid myths and finding modern resonance in popular culture with contemporary tales such as 'The Little Mermaid.'

Mami Wata embodies the duality of life, encompassing both joys and perils. As the goddess of good fortune, she bestows blessings, grants abundance, and possesses the power to heal ailments. She stands as an exemplary cultural representation, highlighting the profound influence of the spirit of water on humanity, including their emotional ebbs and flows, and exemplifies the characteristics of a twin flood connection. Moreover, it's not surprising that the characteristics of twin flood connections are prevalent in spiritual folklore and traditions.

Worldwide, myths about river spirits flourish, typically characterized as sentient deities or supernatural entities dwelling in local rivers, brooks, and waterways. These river spirits are revered for their immense power, associated with knowledge, alchemy, and influence. As humanity seeks to fathom the spiritual essence of water within, river spirits of mighty rivers such as the Nile, Amazon, Congo, and Mississippi are honored as royalty in the magical community. It is believed that river spirits, like many nature spirits, customarily interact with the magical community, considering themselves creator deities rather than Fae. Justifiably so, as across dimensions of time and space, rivers give birth to countless creations, ranging from microscopic life to canyons transformed into capital cities.

Beyond personifying rebirth and healing, river water symbolizes ease and fluidity, mirroring the creative flow of life with its constant movement along a synchronized path. Regardless of myth, surrendering to the natural ebb and flow governed by the spirit of water is an undeniable aspect of life on Earth. All of these qualities and more, lay the foundation for understanding the grand nature of water within the "Twin Flood" dynamic and the subsequent characteristics associated with a twin flood soulmate.

Before immersion into the wisdom of the twin flood, also known as twin or mirrored waters, it's crucial to note that the mutable twin elementals should not be confused with the astrological elements in the signs of the zodiac. While water signs like Cancer, Scorpio, and Pisces share many common traits with twin flood characteristics such as emotional depth and intuition, each astrological sign maintains unique characteristics that distinguish it.

For example, Cancers are often associated with domesticity and nurturing, Scorpios with mystery and emotional intensity, and Pisces with qualities like sensitivity, empathy, and creativity, reflecting the depth and complexity of the water element. Your twin flood may be none of those or a captivating mix of all. Whether exploring astrology or elemental mirrors, each element generally exhibits similar traits while remaining purposefully independent within their respective frameworks.

It's important to note that your twin flood doesn't necessarily have to be born under a water sign, just as your twin flame could in fact, be a water sign. There are instances where you may incarnate with a soul mate whose reflective design falls under a double element, such as an earth sign like Virgo—who also happens to be your twin planet, and, there are cases where an air sign like Libra may be your mirrored Twin Wind.

When a soul mate manifests under this destiny design, it becomes easier to comprehend the potential lessons you've agreed to learn through the power of love and reflection. The contrast between a natal element and a mirror element provides a much more complex level of connection.

During my time living in Uptown Manhattan, I encountered someone who, like me, was a southern transplant, but from the 9th ward of New Orleans, Louisiana. Being southern transplants wasn't our only commonality; we were both Sagittarius fire signs. Fate led us to fall deeply in love, and after some time, we welcomed a daughter surprisingly born under the fire sign Sagittarius as well, subsequently creating a house of fire.

One might assume that my eventual co-parent would be my twin flame, given our whirlwind, twin flame-esque romance and decades-long "Rollercoaster of Love," spoken and written in the melodic voices of the Ohio Players or Red Hot Chili Peppers, depending on the day. Surprisingly, however, with all that fire, my co-parenting soul mate and I, despite our rollercoaster, ultimately express twin flood characteristics when it comes to relating to each other's souls.

Consider this: within the Chinese tradition of the five elements, **Wuxing**, known as water in the West, is considered the most yin. It embodies qualities such as femininity, passivity, receptivity, and hiddenness. This prompts the question: what is the nature of water within me and my mirrored soul connection? How can I identify a twin flood, and what are the signs that they are polarizing my spirit for the evolution of my soul?

Here's a Question: Have you ever felt that profound soul connection, not ablaze with the fiery passion of a twin flame, but rather, immense Love flowing like the serene waters of a stream at sunset? It's the kind of connection that makes you never want to part, saturating your very chemistry with orgasmic energy, all without a single touch. If you're finding yourselves holding hands or sharing kisses longer than engaging in penetrative intimacy, congratulations – you might just be in the presence of a soulmate with twin-flood qualities.

Appreciation—or its mirrored shadow—encapsulates the essence of these mirrored waters. Think of Narcissus captivated by his reflection, entranced and in awe – a twin flood connection can bear a resemblance to this mesmerizing dynamic. Now, don't get me wrong; this isn't to say that the scorching passion of a twin flame is absent, as evidenced by the mesmerization dynamic.

The distinction lies in the fact that instead of erupting into flames when you come together, you're irresistibly compelled to pour yourselves all over each other while licking, sucking, and drinking whatever liquids are produced. It is the difference between *"effing"* or making love. You become each other's sustenance and thus attempt to slowly devour each other, savoring every drop.

Moreover, while the intense chemistry of twin flames is commonly linked to neurochemicals like dopamine and norepinephrine, the "Twin Flood" connection is closely tied to **Oxytocin.** This natural hormone plays a pivotal role in the reproductive system, managing processes such as birth labor, lactation, and human behavior. Originating in the hypothalamus, oxytocin is released into the bloodstream by the posterior pituitary gland, regulating vital functions like blood pressure, heart rate, body temperature, and digestion.

The fluids coursing through your veins, sustaining your digestive tract and all bodily functions, are intricately linked to the wellspring of twin flood energy. Can you guess which organ is closely tied to this wellspring? That's right, it's none other than the magnificent **Heart!** Every bodily function draws inspiration and vitality from your other brain known as the heart.

The heart's role goes beyond mere blood circulation; it conducts the symphony of your body. Beyond its circulatory function, your heart serves as the vessel of emotions, carrying the chemistry that shapes your emotional landscape. In the realm of energy, the **Heart Chakra** reigns as the epicenter of the twin flood essence, orchestrating a deluge of emotions that binds two souls in a profound and enchanting connection.

It's essential to acknowledge that each twin elemental dynamic is guided by a specific organ or a set of glands, intertwined with distinct brain chemistry and chakric energy, in case this insight eluded you.

Upon reflection, it becomes unmistakably clear that Twin Floods possess the extraordinary potential to ignite the collaborative spark, inspiring individuals to forge homes, businesses, and legacies together. These are the soulmates primed to accompany you on your long-term odyssey through the intricate simulation we call life, whether your connection is romantically charged or not. In the grand game of life, they stand out as your ultimate co-players, where **"Emotional Compatibility"** (or its shadow) emerges as the crowning jewel of a twin water connection.

In the harmonious embrace of positively charged mirrored waters, serious quarrels or contentions become rare occurrences. Here, the recognition prevails that they are not engaged in a competition, but rather, they are life partners, particularly in matters of romance. This means that connection, rather than contention and competition, is the driving force. This harmonious state is most evident when both individuals are spiritually mature and emotionally intelligent—though, sadly, this isn't always the reality. However, even those with a lot of growth ahead can have a remarkably healthy connection when linked with their twin waters.

This attribute is rooted in the inherent capacity of twin waters to embody a more unconditional love style, vividly reflected in their flowing and fluid nature—simply put, they go with the flow. However, with an immature water reflection, the destructive flooding nature of water may emerge, causing every positive aspect I previously mentioned to cast a shadow over its opposite. I speak from firsthand experience.

The inherent fluidity of the twin flood elemental naturally fosters a union of souls that ebbs and flows with organic grace. The ebb symbolizes the tranquil embrace of stillness and settling, while the flow state embodies the effortless dynamism essential for manifestation. It's important to bear in mind the dual nature of water—being both still, like a serene pond or puddle, and flowing, like a majestic ocean or river with tides rising and falling.

Much like a pendulum that swings in one direction and then inevitably swings in favor of its opposite, the mirrored nature of the twin flood connection embodies yin and yang qualities. In certain situations, a twin flood connection might encounter challenges akin to navigating a tightrope while striving to maintain the delicate balance between the positive and negative facets of the relationship.

In the realm of twin floods, the flowing spirit of water can manifest as active, aggressive, restless, impatient, and bustling. In contrast, the still essence of water can exude silence, relaxation, calmness, peace, or tranquility. These polarities intertwine within the personality of your twin flood, forming a rich tapestry of traits.

While water stands as a source of life and vitality, it also possesses the formidable ability to overwhelm and wash away the old, familiar world that no longer serves us. On the contrary, in its wake, it brings about a magnificent rebirth into a new world, signifying an evolutionary step for the soul. Thus, the destruction accompanying the flood emerges as a potent force for creation. As the concise saying goes, build and destroy, as sometimes, we must undergo a sort of death before experiencing a profound rebirth.

Regarding twin floods, while water may sometimes be "naice-n-purty" (spoken in a southern drawl), we are not just simply talking about water; we are talking about *FLOODS with the potential to become a Tsunami*, much like recognizing the reflective nature of not merely fire but *FLAMES*, with the potential to become an inferno within twin flame dynamics. Within the context of a twin flood's shadow side, emotional depths can become highly volatile.

Now, you might find yourself contemplating, "What kind of energy does a twin flood or any elemental truly embody, and how does my elemental essence mirror that of my twin?" It's a thought-provoking question, one that unfolds as you delve into the distinctive essence of each individual. To truly grasp what to look for in a twin elemental soul connection, whether it's a twin flame, twin flood or twin planet, a deep understanding of oneself is indispensable.

It's essential to be aware of both your positive and negative traits and to take full responsibility for them. Only then can you recognize these traits in others and connect with them based on your own life experiences. As the ancient Egyptian axiom wisely advises, "Know thyself," thus making it much easier to identify in others what you observe in yourself.

According to Taoism, delving into the water within oneself reveals qualities such as reflection, creativity, sensitivity, persuasion, and effectiveness. A person with robust water spirit qualities in relating, places high value on sacredness, family, and social networks. They possess the ability to attract rather than pursue. Similar to water, you and your partner may effortlessly co-create and adapt to new environments, as these qualities signify renewal.

In the realm of a twin flood dynamic, it's not unusual for at least one individual to radiate a serene personality. Both partners may share intuitive and spiritual qualities, or they might oscillate between dreamy and meditative states, influenced by the ever-shifting seasons. Whether they are deep thinkers or occasionally indecisive from overanalyzing, those represented by the twin waters exhibit a range of characteristics. These traits reflect the diverse nuances of water's nature that we've explored and more.

Regarding character, it is not fixed, or an immutable entity. It isn't built on a linear path but instead, as an omni-present superfluidity, a pervasive abundance shaped by a multitude of experiences aligning with the present moment. It is crafted with every new moment and can change in an instant.

Typically, you would think that twin waters would appear to be infused with a noticeable amount of fire energy, translating into a consistent sexual schedule and periods of intense passion akin to the steam rising from boiling waters. While not a primary focus, they never lose the ability to tap into their innate sex appeal while maintaining a healthy connection. Above all, the spiritual nature of water within both partners reflects more life and freedom when in a state of well-being.

The manifestation of this is a unique journey defined by the couple. While fire might resemble absolute lust, water would reflect love making.

When considering natal elements and mirror spirit elements within the realm of romantic intimacy, it's worth noting that while it's entirely possible for someone with an exuberant personality born under the Sagittarius fire sign to enter into a romantic partnership with a more easy-going Libra air sign, the essence of their connection might fundamentally be infused with water when their two souls converge in a twin flood soul destiny.

This destiny is sculpted by the flooding nature of the mirrored water element, reflecting the most emotional facets of their corresponding air and fire personalities. This is because the most prominent attribute of water in the spirit of humanity is emotions. While their personalities may bear the imprint of the elemental nature of their astrology, their relationship will mirror the twin elemental fates that they both share.

This connection sparks the inherent potential for polarization. A relationship with a twin flood is purely guided by emotion—not by lust, not by survival, and not even by freedom. While possessing a balanced blend of these attributes, the driving force that binds them is undeniably emotional. At times, the reasons behind a profound emotional connection may not be immediately apparent, other than a resolute sense of duty to love the other person unconditionally. I firmly believe that such connections often have deep roots in either past-life encounters or experiences from your past in your current life, including emotional habits accumulated from childhood.

Much like water, the relationship may appear to have a mind of its own, flowing with instinct. Twin floods approach everything primarily from an emotional standpoint. This doesn't imply a lack of practicality or realism; it simply means their response to life, in general, is more emotional than logical or instructional. When navigating through the lens of water energy, closely aligned twin flood connections tend to perceive things instinctively, possessing a highly intuitive nature.

It's paramount to bear in mind that all souls entering partnerships have a pre-birth agreement and purpose. In cases where the purpose demands a gradual establishment, souls may opt to connect under the elemental energy of water. This choice signifies embarking on a voyage rather than experiencing a swift rocket ship blast-off, highlighting the importance of the process and the time it takes to unfold.

In healthy relationships, these connections flow effortlessly and feel inherently natural. Twin flood relationships respond to each other based on an authentic inner feeling, akin to telepathy or an open channel to the higher self. This ability suggests that external factors, such as others' opinions or abstract ideologies, hold little sway over their perceptions of each other. In retrospect, while land and fire may exert minimal influence on the Sea, The Sea possesses the power to extinguish an inferno or transform the land in an instant.

When storms do roll in, it's crucial to remember that a well-skilled sailor can navigate those waves with expertise, leveraging their knowledge of the Sea. Note: Engage in inner work to learn how to intentionally relate from a higher state of consciousness together. The art of conscious relating is akin to that of a seasoned sailor. The bonus chapters on conscious relating offer tools for this. As you ride the waves of a stable relationship, you'll likely savor the tranquility of the waters and confidently navigate the energetic waves that occasionally wash ashore. This is only natural, given that the spirit of water largely governs the interaction.

While navigating the tides of romance and life partnership, it's crucial to remain mindful of the light and the shadows you cast or repress. Avoid projecting your insecurities onto your partner, a prominent aspect found in the shadow side of twin flood connections. While a twin flood connection possesses an array of attributes that go beyond sharing a deep emotional bond, it's important to recognize that another significant shadow trait in such connections is codependency, which can present as a potential challenge. The presence and extent of codependency are influenced by various factors, including how the element of water permeates their overall cosmic alignments.

Recent statistics reveal that a significant portion of the American population, estimated at over 90 percent, exhibits codependent behaviors. This condition encompasses a broad spectrum, ranging from mild to severe, and impacts individuals across various demographics. Codependency often arises from unclear boundaries, power imbalances, and learned behaviors within relationships, further intensified by emotional dependency. Additionally, it is frequently rooted in familial environments characterized by stress or dysfunction, such as substance abuse. Breaking free involves fostering self-awareness, setting healthy emotional boundaries, and cultivating individual identities within a balanced partnership.

Moving forward, water energy manifests as assertive, ambitious and entitled; it fills and adapts to the contours of whatever vessel it's placed in—namely, the mind or heart engaging on the soul journey. Water can also be easy-going without pushing or pulling; it can be present and in the moment, allowing things to unfold naturally.

Seeing that twin floods are primarily led by their emotions rather than solely relying on physical attraction it becomes crucial to keep in mind that when operating within the realm of water energy, they exhibit heightened sensitivity. This sensitivity requires being ready to navigate the waves of emotions that may surface. No, seriously, **'Anticipate' That Part.**

While the twin flood relationship may feel as fluid as the ocean, the dynamics between low and high tide can bring unexpected shifts. One moment, your twin flood might be riding high on a wave of emotional bliss, laughing and carefree; the next, they could be submerged in the abyss of melancholy, anxiety, or even outright depression. Water possesses the nurturing power of life, but it also wields an immense and potentially disruptive force.

In the classic tale of Moby Dick, Captain Ahab, and the whale are the primary characters, with each representing distinct elements. However, often overlooked is the most significant challenge of all in the story, which is the Sea itself. In that story, the Sea represents water's sometimes turbulent but always unpredictable nature. While water is essential to life, it also has the ability to flood and, most notably, the potential to drown anything that breathes; even a whale, a dolphin, or any other aquatic mammal that lives in the ocean can literally drown. That is the power of water.

Another noteworthy trait in the twin water dynamic, not always found in other twin elementals, is extreme loyalty, sometimes to a fault. This trait is the catalyst to the extremely destructive flooding nature when emotional loyalty feels betrayed. Depending on the spiritual maturity of the persons involved, one might in retrospect recall their past soul connection as a twin tsunami instead of a twin flood when emotional loyalty was challenged.

In the context of romance, another surprising feature includes the potential for becoming introverted hermits, especially if the couple have a comfortable little pond to call home. However, twin flood's must remember to guard against their pond becoming a swamp when complacency looms. Together twin flood unions are generally future-oriented and in motion toward a destination, even if that destination is rigor mortis in life and death. That means, complete inaction and or frozen in comfort or complacency—which represents the more detrimental extreme within the polarity spectrum of a twin flood.

Beyond shadow traits such as complacency, these twin elemental qualities are generally positive, yet water connections will certainly begin to flood if clear boundaries are not set in advance. This may appear as possessiveness to outsiders. Once individuals sharing a twin flood connection settle into their bond, they often become immensely soothing and nurturing to each other, sliding into a comfortable routine and comfort zones. While this might seem beneficial, it has the potential to pose challenges as one of the partners may eventually feel restless, opening the door to stormy weather, such as infidelity. This aspect is likely influenced by their personality profile and again, their astrological nature.

A twin flood soul connection, at its core, mirrors all the qualities of water on Earth. Water is in perpetual motion, whether descending as rain, coursing through streams and rivers, or accumulating in oceans and seas. Even when seemingly still in a pond, it teems with life and activity. In the profound depths of the ocean, its movement is deliberate and purposeful. Yet, water also harbors the potential for cataclysmic events, giving rise to tidal waves, tsunamis, and, when coupled with wind, spawning devastating tornadoes and hurricanes.

While soulmates can take on various forms, from pets, gang and tribe to platonic love, best friends, and even family members such as grandparents or godparents, this chapter is primarily centered on romantic partnerships. It aims to provide a contextual understanding of the intensity spectrum that twin floods bring to these romantic unions. It's essential to remember that a soulmate with whom you share a twin flood connection may display various emotional attachments, subsequently contributing to a significant twin elemental polarization. As you learn to integrate these polarities with balance, you pave the way for a more harmonious equilibrium, fostering the advancement of your souls.

The initial step in consciously integrating all the lessons and gifts that can unfold from these polarizing soul experiences in romantic relationships or otherwise is first recognizing it as a mirrored water connection. This connection stands as one of the most potent and meaningful influences imaginable because intense and transformative experiences accompany the polarization of a twin flood.

What's shared with the reflective soul brings both challenges and gifts that necessitate patience to navigate, but the journey is worth every ounce of effort invested, provoking a more meaningful life imbued with love and empowerment! This parallel journey serves as an extraordinary opportunity for growth, self-awareness, and a deeper understanding of ourselves, ultimately leading us back into union with our true selves and the source of all souls and all creation.

In conclusion, here is a concise summary outlining seven key characteristics of a "Twin Flood" in relation to the elemental nature of a mirrored soul connection:

- **Elemental Power:** Twin floods embody the essence of water as their primary elemental nature, characterized by the ebb and flow of emotions, fluidity, adaptability, and a deep sense of intuition, sensitivity, and emotional depth. A twin flood connection is highly reflective of familial and tribal energy.

- **Harmonious Flow:** Unlike the intense and fiery nature of twin flames, twin floods manifest a harmonious and serene energy. Their connection is marked by a gentle yet profound emotional bond that allows them to navigate challenges with grace.

- **Mutual Nourishment:** Twin floods experience a profound sense of mutual nourishment and growth. Their connection provides a fertile ground for emotional and spiritual development, supporting each other's growth and creating emotional security.

- **Healing and Renewal:** Twin floods possess a unique ability to heal and bring renewal to each other's lives. Their connection acts as a catalyst for emotional healing, washing away past wounds and creating a safe environment for emotional well-being for fostering maturity and transformation.

- **Emotional Resonance:** The emotional realm holds great significance for twin floods. They share a profound emotional resonance, comprehending each other's feelings on a profound level. This connection is marked by empathy, compassion, and the capacity to provide support for each other's emotions and sensitivities, acting as protectors of each other's hearts.

- **Physical Attributes:** The neurochemicals Oxytocin, in concert with the Hypothalamus and posterior pituitary glands, are commonly associated with twin floods, while the Heart and Heart Chakra are the physical and energetic centers linked to twin flood energy. Sensitivity, whether mental, spiritual, physical, or emotional, is a hallmark of the twin flood soulmate dynamic.

- **Shadow Traits:** A negative inclination of twin floods may be a proclivity toward insecurity and codependency, where individuals with these traits may exhibit tendencies to overly rely on each other, potentially leading to challenges such as possessiveness and the risk of complacency within the relationship. It is essential for twin floods to establish clear boundaries to avoid smothering dynamics and foster a healthy, balanced connection.

These characteristics underscore the distinct qualities of twin floods, accentuating their watery nature, harmonious flow, mutual nourishment, synchronistic alignment, healing abilities, and emotional resonance. Twin floods emerge as interdependent and creative entities within the broader realm of mirrored soul connections.

Chapter Twelve

TWIN WINDS

Inversion Mirroring of Wind Elementals

"

Quote: The pessimist complains about the wind; The optimist expects it to change; The realist adjusts the sails." — William Arthur Ward

In the previous chapter, we ventured deep into the complex dynamics of Twin Flood connections, illuminating the subtleties that define those profound relationships. The romantic ideal of soulmates often aligns with the characteristics of Twin Floods—attributes that epitomize the ideal partner dynamic and suggest an eternal emotional harmony. However, this notion can verge on a profound misunderstanding.

Our exploration extended beyond the conventional, revealing the myriad forms through which Twin Flood soul connections manifest. From the steadfast companionship of lifelong friends or brothers in arms or the unconditional love of pets to the nurturing presence of aunts and the wisdom of grandmothers, these bonds can trigger an emotional deluge unmatched in its intensity and depth.

Moreover, our journey also took us through the fiery realms of Twin Flames. Unlike the serene waters of Twin Floods, Twin Flames blaze with a passion that resists simple categorization. These connections, infused with fervor, emerge as rivals, mentors, friends, or family, challenging us and enriching our lives just as profoundly as any romantic liaison.

As we head into this chapter, we stand at the threshold of understanding, ready to dive deeper into the mysteries of twin elemental connection and the true essence of soulmates. Our narrative is poised to unravel the layers of emotional resonance and the diverse tapestries woven by these unique interpersonal relationships, inviting you to reexamine your perceptions of social dynamics, companionship and even love.

Twin elementals materialize with the purpose of polarizing your spirit and providing the contrasting experiences necessary for soul definition. Regardless of the role they play—be it romantic, platonic, or even transactional—this exchange and interaction certainly do act as catalysts for our soul's evolution during earthly existence. Consequently, **'Twin Winds'** are no exception to soul polarization. In fact, they serve as a prime example. Many twin wind-styled soul connections, even in romantic contexts, often involve a stellar or cosmic friendship, perfectly setting the stage to showcase mirrored contrast for definition.

The most prominent trait of a reflected air connection is partnership, whether it's a military brotherhood, the camaraderie of sports, or a sibling and best friend. For the purpose of this book, we'll stick to our lane of exploring romantic partnerships and intimate friendships.

Much like the word "love," the term "friend" is often used loosely. I, too, was guilty of this once upon a time. The truth is, many of your so-called friends are merely associates, acquaintances, neighbors, colleagues, or co-workers—not, dare I say, 'friends'. If you can borrow each other's cars, bail each other out of jail for a 3 A.M. misdemeanor, or attend family reunions together, then maybe we can call them a friend. A real friend is akin to family.

By now, we should understand that every soul we encounter enters our story with a purpose—always for a reason, a season, or a lifetime. This realization implies that twin wind elementals may not need to be a constant presence throughout an entire lifetime for maximum impact; their purpose could be fulfilled in just a season or for a specific reason before moving on.

I can vividly recall my best friends from grade school and often reflect on them even to this day. I'm certain I'll continue reminiscing about them when I'm old and gray. Some of them are still in my social media contacts, yet we don't maintain the same energy and connection. Nevertheless, they played an instrumental role in my development.

Air elemental partnerships are like the wind—constantly blowing and shaping the landscape of our lives. These connections wield the power to influence who we become, leaving a lasting impact. Much like the wind carries new messages and ideas, our friends and partners can introduce us to fresh perspectives that broaden our thinking and behaviors, facilitating growth and an expanded understanding of the world.

At times, a twin elemental soul may enter our lives for a specific, life-changing reason, only to vanish as quickly as they arrived. They might be present for a mere two minutes, two days, or two decades, yet they leave an impression that lasts a lifetime, whether positive or negative. There exists a particular openness when it comes to a twin-wind elemental reflection.

A well-known example could include Jada Pinkett Smith and Tupac Amaru Shakur, their love as vast as the sky. However, Jada eventually married a twin planet. Both individuals incarnated as soulmates with life-altering magnetism and distinct purposes. These elementals, one with platonic wind character, and the other, solid planetary character play different roles, yet stand as equals in the realm of souls, none overshadowing the other.

It's crucial to acknowledge that a wind elemental may not always take the form of a friend; each and every elemental has a shadow side, making them all enigmatic. With twin winds, this can manifest as the exact opposite of a friend, but with an equal level of intimacy, intensity, or entanglement, such as with an arch-nemesis. What truly matters is understanding the energy that a twin wind carries and recognizing the types of transformation that may occur in retrospect.

During my teenage years, fueled by a passion for music, I frequented a neighborhood producers studio named Cognac to record my tracks. It was during one of these sessions that he shared with me an intriguing story from his past.

His captivating tale involved the experience of transitioning to a new school, where he encountered the reigning, tough guy—a corn fed redneck from the countryside, as he so aptly put it. As a brawny inner-city tough guy himself, a clash between the two seemed inevitable. Their attempts at one-upping each other in the realm of bullying eventually escalated into a violent confrontation. Like two rams, they went head-to-head until both were bloodied, battered and bruised.

The irony of the story, however, unfolded as they transformed into the best of friends after the showdown, maintaining their close bond into adulthood.

Speaking of similar polarizing twin wind soul families, it's impossible not to recall the narrative of two of Wu-Tang Clan's most skilled musical assassins, Raekwon the Chef and Ghostface Killah, who were each other's arch adversaries in their youth, going as far as war games with live ammo which undoubtedly changed them. Yet, fate intervened, leading them to unite and become a dynamic duo within their music crew, crafting some of the most memorable tracks in the genre.

Initially, Rae and Ghost, might dismiss these concepts as fanciful or impractical. However, were I a betting person, I would stake everything on the possibility that a past life regression would reveal they were akin to brothers in arms in a former life. Their roles might have ranged from Roman soldiers to blood brothers in an ancient civilization like Sumeria, or even as Native American warring chieftains from the early 18th or 19th centuries. This exploration could uncover a bond, forged in the fires of battle and brotherhood, transcending time and impacting their current relationship.

When envisioning the perfect characterization of a twin wind, the term "wingman" comes to mind. I think of homies, comrades, or soldiers in arms. By this logic, understand that while a colleague may not be a friend, a colleague could certainly step into the role of a wind elemental to mirror your script if their ultimate purpose brought about a shift in your life's trajectory.

Sometimes the wind blows briefly to cool you off, and then it's gone. Other times, the wind carries you away in a whirlwind to the land of Oz. Regarding wind elementals and partnerships, I can't help but recall the character played by Jim Carrey in the movie "The Truman Show." The central protagonist, Truman Burbank, had a best friend named Marlon, who would consistently show up to drink beers with Truman, especially when Truman neared the truth of his reality. Unfortunately, Marlon was a paid actor designed to keep Truman in the dark. In retrospect, though they had virtually grown up together, was Marlon truly a friend, or was he the shadow side of a friend?

Similar to all elementals, the wind's reflective spirit operates within a spectrum of intensities. A close friend and confidant can embody the most balanced and healthy dynamic of a wind-mirroring relationship. It's a mutual lifting up, akin to the wind carrying you, while you reflect the same support for them. A support system, a literal mirror to which you can turn daily for confirmations and validations.

It may have the fire and passion of a flame, exemplifying the "I will die for my homie" type of energy. Alternatively, it could possess the depth of the ocean or the longevity of a large flowing river, echoing the "bad boys for Life type energy. Yet, it is none of those; it is the wind. The air that we breathe. That which gives us life… "Wind is to us as breath is to life" - a Native American Proverb.

In Native American cultures, the spirit of man is often likened to the wind—a powerful force that can bring change and convey messages from the spirit world. The wind holds significance in certain rituals and ceremonies, mirroring the role of the human spirit.

Therefore, it's no surprise that the **Lung** is the organ associated with the twin wind elemental. The **solar plexus** aligns most closely with twin wind energy in terms of energetic chakra drives. Additionally, **serotonin** is the brain chemistry linked to the twin wind elemental archetype. Like a good comrade or companion, serotonin regulates mood and is considered your body's natural feel-good chemical. Normal serotonin levels contribute to emotional stability, happiness, and calmness, while lower levels are associated with depression, anxiety, and mood disorders.

Transitioning elders often share, especially in heartfelt 'deathbed' farewells, that spending time with friends and loved ones holds the key to true contentment and fulfillment, surpassing the pursuit of material possessions. On the flip side, stories circulate about celebrities battling profound depression from a lack of authentic connections. While the stage provides a euphoric high, it falls short in delivering genuine love. Onstage, bathed in attention, it feels like floating or parasailing—a sensation akin to free-falling, the wind tousling through their hair, providing a fleeting sense of importance and validation.

Many entertainers confess to feeling a soaring high while basking in on-stage adoration, only to plunge into lows when returning to reality. This might explain why some turn to a lifestyle involving constant intoxication through drugs and the likes, seeking an escape from their sober existence. Little do they realize that genuine love, especially with a twin wind, coupled with an "Iboga or ayahuasca" ceremony perhaps, could be the transformative elixir they truly need. A side note: Had some of our especially loved and dearly departed talents been introduced to iboga or bufo, they might have had the chance for profound transformation.

While the allure of a Twin Wind connection may not resonate with the thrill of a fiery Twin Flame or the emotional depth of a Twin Flood for some, my own experiences have illuminated its unique value. I've often found myself humorously reminding close soul friends, who treat relationships like a game of musical chairs, that: "I was here long before your latest flame, and I'll still be here long after they've departed." I reassure them whenever their latest fling feels insecure about our long lasting and genuinely platonic friendship. This jest underscores the lasting intimacy and bond shared with certain Twin Wind soulmates, a connection with the potential to transcend and outlive the collective impact of all their previous relationships.

With some of these friends, we've encountered more profound moments together than they've ever experienced in the throes of passionate attraction. Granted, in most cases, these kinships remain platonic. However, in some instances, we've relished romantic interludes, courting with marriage in mind. I've also experienced profound romantic unions with twin winds that surpass any connections with other elemental mirrors.

Notably, in the realm of romance, twin winds are a rarity, making the connection all the more valuable when you find yourself entwined with a wind soul mirror. It's unfortunate that more people don't realize a twin wind connection could be the romantic relationship propelling them to the next chapter of their story in record time. While soul compatibility doesn't always translate to romantic compatibility, with maturity and freedom, it can certainly evolve into the most fulfilling and secure romantic partnership. For those seeking stability, serenity, and compatibility in romance, it's a journey well worth exploring.

Many individuals attempt to replicate the romantic, steamy, sometimes aggressive love scenes depicted in Hollywood movies, often foregoing highly pleasant and compatible connections with those they genuinely like and bond with through genuine friendship. However, it's crucial to remember that it's called 'Hollywood' for a reason—it's not cedarwood or oakwood, but Hollywood. The name is derived from the wood used for witches or wizards' magic wands. Quite an intriguing revelation regarding illusions—go figure!

In examining the character of twin elementals within films, one observes distinct patterns. Romantic comedies, or "rom-coms," typically exhibit an energy akin to that of Twin Winds, characterized by their light-hearted and breezy narratives. Conversely, romantic dramas align more closely with Twin Flame energy, embodying intense and passionate connections that drive their plots. Lifetime movies, known for their emotionally rich narratives, mirror the essence of Twin Floods, delving into the depths of emotional bonds and the complexities of human relationships. Meanwhile, documentaries focusing on enduring love stories resonate with the energy of Twin Planets, showcasing connections that are stable, enduring, and harmonious, spanning across time and space. These distinctions offer insight into the nuanced portrayal of relationships in various film genres, reflecting the diverse nature of twin elemental connections.

Furthermore, In the context of twin winds expressing themselves as genuine friends, the most balanced and healthy connections are naturally found during childhood. This embodiment is not only because the soul requires the most compatible and authentic support from a twin elemental reflection during early human spirit development but also because the mind and spirit have yet to be tainted by the culture of modern humanity.

Soul connections yield healthier relationships in ones youth, free from bias, egoism, perversion and trauma. Many grade school first loves are resonate with twin wind energy as they relate from a purer essence. Similar to the water mirror in the twin flood dynamic, grandparents often step into the role of a twin wind, donning the robe of soul support like no other. Those grandparents who consistently expose children to enriching experiences to broaden their horizons are likely infused with that wind-like energy.

While twin winds can make excellent lifelong partners, societal conditioning often steers us toward connections rooted in lower chakra energy, such as those found in passionate, fiery relationships. Could this be a deliberate 'fire spell' cast by the media through music and movies? The connection between Hollywood and wand casting is hard to ignore, but I'll leave that question open.

In the realm of air elementals, twin wind soulmates often find themselves in the friend zone, their love dynamics marked by purity and freedom. If narratives persisted in a society where everyone was either literally blind or figuratively blind and indifferent to trivial matters, or if individuals happened to cross paths during a period of dopamine fasting, or even after emerging from long isolation spent pondering the meaning of life, a twin wind could indeed become the most coveted and desirable partner in matters of love.

In ancient times, our ancestors would likely have preferred marriage to twin winds over twin planets, valuing the companionship of a close and caring friend versus an arranged marriage for stability with a stranger who most likely resembled an uncle and niece.

It's indeed unfortunate that when a twin wind assumes the role of intense romantic love, a separation from this bond can be especially painful, delivering the hardest blow due to the intricate and integrated nature of this rare and valued connection. Twin winds are akin to life itself, much like water to a fish, who is unaware that it is wet.

The lyrics in Jimi Hendrix's song "The Wind Cries Mary" beautifully encapsulate the sensation of having the wind knocked out of you during a twin wind separation. It's as if everything around you conspires to remind you of your twin wind counterpart. Their name, like "Mary's," drifts through the wind at every corner you turn and during every event of the day.

Why are twins winds so coveted amongst the mature? Possibly because twin winds tend to embody a fusion of "crazy sexy cool" and/or "homie lover friend" energy, epitomized in Pop and R&B songs. At the point of separation, one may appear in a daze or melancholic for a short season. While it might seem easier to move on compared to a twin flame, the lingering feeling of regret persists, as individuals may believe they will never attract that level of connection again. In truth, I don't think twin winds are ever truly separated, even after a falling out.

In the lyrics of SZA's song "Good Days," she writes, "I don't miss no Ex, I don't miss no text, I choose not to respond, I don't regret, just pretend it never happened…" This fear-based avoidance behavior is a common response when healing from a twin *'flame'* connection. On the contrary, with a twin wind connection, one might initially start that way yet find themselves attempting to contact their Ex after some time or even stalking them on social media occasionally. This behavior reflects the deep connection they once shared.

Considering that a wind connection is intricately woven into one's essence, it's plausible that, after some time, twin winds may rekindle their friendship, with their current partners accepting the renewed bond (albeit under watchful eyes). Such twin wind connections are easily identifiable as the crème de la crème of soul family energy. Another familiar dynamic of a twin wind is remarrying your first spouse after divorcing your second.

To further illustrate twin wind soulmate characteristics, let's revisit the Jerry and Elaine characters from the 90s sitcom Seinfeld. Yes, Seinfeld analogies yet again. If there were ever a couple of characters who were twin winds, Jerry and

Elaine take the cake. As ex-lovers turned best friends, their relationship resonated among viewers. Though you couldn't quite put your finger on it, you knew that their friendship had a certain, how shall I say, Je ne sais quoi, energy about it.

For contextual balance, there are also other examples of long-lasting TV relationships embodying twin wind energy, such as the Martin and Gina characters in the 90s sitcom Martin. Despite the show's comedic nature, Martin and Gina's relationship was rooted in deep friendship, evident in the comedic fun they shared.

My dear friend, who has since passed away and was mentioned in an earlier chapter, possessed the exquisite energy of a twin wind, making her one of my dearest soulmates to grace this earth. She was the one who, after our phone conversations, would effortlessly declare, I love you, a sentiment warmly reciprocated by me. We started that ritual and trend early on as young adults. I always found it refreshing to proudly express the sentiment , " I love you" when hanging up the phone to someone who was not a romantic interest or blood relative.

What made our connection unique was the freedom inherent in it and the absence of any jealous tensions from our respective partners. It was understood that she was my friend, is my friend, and was always going to be my friend, whether or not current partners were in our lives or not. As the saying goes, "what's understood doesn't have to be explained." Let me emphasize this: if there's one lesson to grasp, it's that soulful allure eclipses the power of mere physical attraction.

Aside from platonically relating in the most intimate way, a well-rounded "soul-ationship" aspires to achieve ultimate equilibrium in romantic connections. Twin wind dynamics extend beyond traditional romantic paradigms and may venture into cerebral relationships, highlighting intellectual compatibility and fostering stimulating mental engagement. In the realm of a cosmic twin wind, this can occasionally lead to unconventional relationship structures such as polyamory, a topic delved into more deeply in my upcoming book, *"Polyamorously Celibate: An Advanced Emo-Tech Model for Spiritual Development."*

Much like the dual essence of fire, your fervent passions can illuminate the night sky in a breathtaking display, akin to fireworks on New Year's Eve, or they can unleash a destructive inferno, reducing everything to ashes. Similar to the dual aspects of water, you can ride the wave of love like tubing on the "Guadalupe River" into the sunset, or you might feel the undertow pulling you into the depths of "Lake Lanier" through a whirlpool reminiscent of the Bermuda Triangle. And, in keeping with the airy nature of the wind, prepare for a duality unlike any other.

Exercise:

Pause for a moment and take a deep breath if you will. Now. Imagine you are running through a field of daisies with your eyes closed with arms stretched out like you have no care. The sweet scent of jasmine fills the air, and you feel the warmth of the sun and the wind on your back. In fact, like a trusted friend, you feel the wind beneath your wings. You run faster, and the wind lifts you up like you're parasailing into pure freedom, feeling carefree and weightless. The song, "Love lift us up where we belong," somehow plays softly in the distance. Make this a lucid visualization.

Suddenly, the sky darkens, turbulence strikes, your in the middle of a violent tornado and you're face to face with Dorothy, Toto, the Wicked Witch of the West, and a gang of grimacing flying monkeys. Heavy metal begins to play and you wonder how you got here. What you now have is a one-way ticket to Oz, my friend, and you're off to see the wizard riding shotgun in the eye of the storm. It's now a category-five hurricane, and the weatherman can't save you. Now: Take a deep breath and reorient yourself.

While it may sound dramatic, the wind can turn from a cool breeze to a life-threatening hurricane in the blink of an eye, depending on a myriad of other influences. It's important to remember this and stay prepared for anything when in love with a twin wind—be it romantic , platonic or transactional.

Think about this. When your best friend convinces you to take a little joy ride that lands you ten years in prison, or your best buddy sells you on a business investment that puts you in a depraved state of debt, threatening your family's livelihood, you will learn that a soul-polarizing twin wind connection also has the potential to send you into a tailspin of shadows. Though I've predominantly focused on the platonic nature of air, in the realm of twin wind connections, romantic relationships can also give rise to soul-polarizing shadows.

Imagine being in a relationship with your best friend, someone you share a deep connection with and trust implicitly. However, over time, as you grow into new versions of yourself, you realize that your partner's dreams and aspirations are not aligned with yours, causing conflict and tension in the relationship. Eventually, the relationship ends in heartbreak with the loss of a friendship that was once so important. In these instances, you could realize that remaining friends may have been the better choice to salvage a great connection. The following sentiment are all too familiar among twin winds—the "we were better off as friends" statement, or, "If we had stayed friends, we would still be in contact today."

Alternatively, another scenario could unfold where a twin wind connection creates an intense and passionate relationship that seems perfect, but over time, one partner becomes possessive and jealous, leading to a toxic and unhealthy relationship. The once beautiful and extremely close connection becomes a source of pain and suffering, leaving both partners feeling lost and alone.

Such relationships can form within a close-knit circle of friends, even when other members of the group have their own partners. In this unique dynamic, certain friends find a strong connection that grounds them without the complications of romantic politics. Within this friendly exchange, a special chemistry and affinity for each other persist, eventually blossoming into a full-fledged romance years later, after their respective partners have moved on. The groundwork for establishing a genuine connection has already occurred within this type of dynamic, unrestricted by conventional boundaries and expectations, and so on.

In yet another example, a twin wind connection can lead to a whirlwind romance where the partners move quickly into marriage or starting a family, only to realize that they are not truly compatible in romance as they would have been keeping it platonic. The relationship turns sour, and the once-strong connection fades away, leaving both partners feeling disillusioned and regretful. Overall, it's important to remember that a twin wind connection, like all elementals, can have both positive and negative aspects, and it's essential to be aware of the potential shadow traits that arise.

It is truly astonishing to witness the illuminated heights one can reach by confronting their innermost demons and purging the darkest corners of their soul. Everyone wants to go to heaven, but no one wants to die, is a premier metaphor illustrating the work of integrating the duality that exists within all twin elemental dynamics.

The majority of my examples have primarily focused on platonic relationships to illustrate the concept of twin winds. However, it is important to note that these same qualities can be paralleled in romantic connections as well, allowing for a comprehensive understanding of their dynamics.

As previously mentioned, comprehending the energetic trajectories that can be influenced by an air-elemental is crucial, irrespective of the specific role held by the twin wind. Whether the twin wind is a friend, lover, member of your tribe, or a family member, being conscious of the defining qualities of a twin-wind soul connection is essential for nurturing a harmonious balance within that domain.

Within the Zodiacal domain, Libra, Aquarius, and Gemini emerge as the three western signs aligned with the Air element. Yet, it's crucial to grasp that, like their counterparts, they are fundamentally distinct from the captivating twin wind elemental. Even with the destined convergence of two souls, the elemental classification becomes a defining force in the relating dynamic.

It's imperative to recognize that **the air elemental is an excellent teacher and muse as well as a powerful divination medium by way of a soul contract.** For instance, wind symbolizes the elusive, the transient, the immaterial, and the intangible. Drawing inspiration from Genesis chapter one, verse two, of the Hebraic Christian Bible, it narrates how God's **Ruach** (translated as spirit, wind, breath) moved upon the face of the waters, catalyzing the manifestation of our existence. This analogy underscores the divine or spiritual essence often paralleled with the ethereal nature of the wind.

The breath of life, often envisioned as the wind, mirrors a newborn's initial inhalation upon departing its mother's womb—a symbolic embodiment of life's inaugural breath. Such symbolism suggests that the wind plays a pivotal role in transformative experiences. While air remains unseen, its interactions with Earth, Water, and Fire render it visible, occasionally exhibiting what appears to be magical.

In the realm of Sacred Geometry, the octahedron serves as the symbol for air, strategically positioned between Fire and Water. This placement accentuates air's potency when intertwined with Fire or Water, showcasing its ability to exert influence, control, and balance. The multifaceted and robust impact of air enriches the interactions with other elements, producing an extraordinary and unparalleled paradigm when harmoniously combined.

It's unsurprising that the camaraderie, freedom, and companionship offered by the twin winds are sought after by other twin elementals in many relationships. This implies that while someone may embody the passion of a twin flame or the emotional dependency in their relationship, they harbor a hidden desire to also have a freedom based, trusted friend to share that intense passion and emotional bond with.

Throughout history, from the Egyptians to the Greeks and Chinese, ancient cultures revered the wind, attuning themselves to its whispers. They paid meticulous attention to the wind's direction, convinced that it could divulge insights into the present state of the world by observing its influence on clouds and trees. Early forecasters and weathermen, armed with rudimentary models like sifting dirt to the breeze, believed they could discern clues about the future. Indigenous and aboriginal cultures, spanning from aboriginal Australians to Native Americans, engaged in wind divination, interpreting the messages carried by the divine through this elemental force.

The diverse examples elucidating the essence of wind in the physical world serve as a conduit to portray the spiritual nature of wind within a transcendent and temporal dynamic, especially in the context of the overarching purposes of twin elemental connections. By understanding the profound influence of wind's character within this transcendent and temporal framework, we glean profound insights into the inherent trajectories and purposes of twin wind elementals.

In the realm of yoga, practitioners explore concepts drawn from the Hindu science of breath, including Prana, which symbolizes the breath of life. Prana, along with asanas or movements, forms the foundation of the practice and invokes the subtle life forces that animate our beings. Likewise, in Chinese cultures, the concept of Qi, representing a vital force and spiritual flow manipulated by the breath, has been studied for centuries. We all encounter Prana and Qi as a subtle wind, manifesting the essence of the Air Element. These expressions collectively highlight the impact of a wind elemental's influence on the soul's growth.

So, why is all of this being shared? Because, much like water, air embodies movement rather than being fixed. In the context of relationships, the Air Element carries the attributes of flexibility, adaptation, and improvisation. This flexibility may be a contributing factor to why twin wind elementals often appear in friendships rather than exclusively in romantic relationships. In many relationships, the scope for change, flexibility, and freedom is severely limited, often bound by a rigid belief system. Contemporary relationships often show contempt for freedom, in fact.

Straying from this system of belief in a romantic relationship frequently leads to its demise, as relationships often break rather than bend when pushed to their limits. Unfortunately, numerous rigid or restrictive belief systems proudly clash with natural laws, such as the freedom and flexibility inherently associated with Love.

On the contrary, twin winds thrive in an environment of freedom and change, craving these things as part of their natural inclination. In healthy interactions, twin winds tend to engage from a freedom centered space, embracing a natural ebb and flow, versus an ego-based analysis of their partner's every action. Easier said than done, right?

When twin wind soulmates choose to embark on romantic relationships, there is usually the potential to evolve into good buddies alongside being passionate lovers, provided they aren't already relating in such a manner. In a healthy dynamic, they maintain a balance on the chemistry compatibility index with minimal deficit. They share laughter, visit bars, nightclubs and other social events together, and prioritize each other's company.

They don't mind bringing "sand to the beach," so to speak, embodying the quintessential Bonnie and Clyde attributes. While it's not surprising that friendships typically offer more freedom than romantic relationships, a healthy romantic bond with a twin wind soulmate can be remarkably fulfilling and rewarding.

To the casual onlooker, the profound connection shared by a pair of twin winds often prompts them to label the duo as soulmates, even if they lack a comprehensive understanding of the intricacies of this concept. Nevertheless, the authentic bond and closeness that twin winds experience surpass the conventional understanding of soulmates, demanding a deeper exploration and appreciation of the unique nature of their relationship.

A twin wind's nature is highly mutable, much more so than an earth element. As a result, in terms of romance, a twin wind may find a non monogamous relationship more suitable, given their highly sociable disposition. When not fully polyamorous, they may simply relate freely in an open relationship. The character of wind can utilize each social interaction as a means for polarization. Like dust bunnies or tumbleweeds collecting debris as they move about, wind can randomly gather different concepts, emotional or otherwise, for processing into the next focus of consciousness for evolution.

In relation to the other elementals, wind augments the strength of fire, creates waves that surfers dream of and gives rise to remarkable dust storms. In contrast to the grounded and fixed nature of other elements, where a set of rules governs the journey of the relationship, the airy spirit in the character of these relationship types can become so ethereal that the combined consciousness of the union drifts in whatever direction the wind blows, mirroring the free-flowing nature of a great friendship between bosom buddies. If a twin wind was a person, it would probably be the actress Cree Summer. Perhaps even the character, Lynn, on the show Girlfriends as twin winds carry intense free spirited energy.

Relating with a twin wind soulmate presents an unparalleled sense of freedom. It's crucial, however, to remember that, like a pendulum, if allowed to swing without intelligent intervention, it has the potential to chaotically sway in the opposite direction. Air energy is inherently dynamic, capable of rapid fluctuations, changing polarity swiftly and impacting the emotional climate—plunging temperatures to extreme cold or soaring to intense heat. Air, as observed in storms, hurricanes, and tornadoes, possesses the potential for high destructiveness. It can either cool you gently like a soft breeze or, in its powerfully shadowed form, move earth and water.

I am reminded of one of my most celebrated twin wind souls, a talented vocalist named Carmen Liana. I met her over 30 years ago as I stood with a buddy, waiting for her to descend the escalator at Lenox Mall in Atlanta, GA. He had just started dating her, and as she descended, the entire mall seemed to fall silent. I remember that moment vividly. Fast forward to today: Carmen and I are still the closest of friends. When I say we work each other's nerves something awful, it's no exaggeration, yet neither of us can imagine a world without the other. Our connection is mystical. We look forward to gracefully growing old together, well into our hundreds and chuckle at the thought of us being soulmates in our own way.

When intelligent design is applied through wisdom and knowledge in twin wind relationships, the possibilities are limitless. It's your responsibility to recognize and seize the opportunity when granted the privilege of designing your life and evolving your soul with a twin wind soulmate. Mastering the wind allows you to channel the energy from a soulmate relationship with a twin wind elemental into the realms of blissful happiness —ever after.

Whether it's the unwavering support and consistency of long-standing friendships that surpass the impact of your previous five relationships or a deeply intimate and cherished connection with your best friend that takes precedence over superficial acquaintances and fair-weather friends, experiencing soulmate connection with a twin wind means having a bond that transcends average connections in your life.

Shadow traits are abundant, and the twin wind effect will undoubtedly change your life, though often in ways that are imperceptible. Twin wind connections offer unique soul experiences, crafted to polarize and define our souls through contrasting interactions. While I haven't extensively touched on the conflicting shadows of twin winds and their potential to significantly alter life trajectories through disruptive negative polarizations, it remains essential to acknowledge that air, along with all twin elementals, holds the capacity to influence personal growth through adversity as well as inspiration. Whether in romantic, platonic, or transactional roles, these connections play a vital role in our soul's evolution during our earthly journey.

Here you'll find a concise summary outlining Six key characteristics of a *"Twin Wind"* in relation to the elemental nature of a mirrored soul connection:

- **Partnership and Companionship:** In most twin wind connections, even in romantic ones, you'll often find a stellar or cosmic friend. These connections emphasize partnership, resembling the bond between brothers in sports or military, or the closeness of siblings and best friends. They provide unwavering support, understanding, and a sense of camaraderie. Twin winds will always have the "crazy sexy cool" and the "homie lover friend" energy permeating when it is a romantic connection.

- **Cerebral connections:** Twin wind connections can manifest as cerebral relationships, emphasizing intellectual compatibility and stimulating mental engagement. These connections can be so freeing that they sometimes evolve into polyamorous relationships, transcending friendship and transitioning into romantic involvement. Trust is a major bonding agent of twin winds.

- **Seasonal or Lifelong:** Though they feel as if they've been around forever, twin wind connections don't always last forever. They can appear for a specific reason, season, or an entire lifetime, leaving a lasting impression. Some friendships formed during childhood, like those with best friends from grade school, continue to shape us even years later when they are no longer around. Each connection serves a purpose in our personal growth.

- **Transformative Influence:** Similar to the wind shaping the landscape, twin winds have the power to shape our lives and influence who we become. They introduce us to new perspectives, broaden our thinking, and inspire personal growth. Their fresh ideas and messages are like a breath of fresh air, expanding our understanding of the world, seeing as though these relationships have a high degree of intellectual engagement. Like Qi, Chi, or Prana, twin wind elementals have the potential to underscore your life's energetic flow.

- **Shadow Traits:** Twin wind connections, often starting as friendships, can be intense and complex, leading to both empowerment and negative effects as guards are relaxed due to strong trust and loyalty. It's crucial to understand their energy, as they can become too comfortable, potentially blurring the lines of respect if not balanced. In the context of romance, they can easily lose their romantic spark, leading to them ending up in the friend zone.

- **Physical Attributes:** The Lung is the Organ associated with the twin wind elemental. The solar plexus is most closely aligned with the twin wind energy regarding chakra drives. In addition, serotonin is the brain chemistry associated with the twin wind elemental soul connection.

Overall, twin wind connections provide a profound and meaningful experience, offering genuine friendship, personal growth, and transformative influences within your interpersonal relationships. Their juxtaposed natures can appear for the purpose of expanding our understanding of ourselves and the world around us. These connections have the power to uplift us like a gentle breeze or challenge us like a strong gust of wind, leaving a lasting impact on our souls for eternity.

Chapter Thirteen

TWIN PLANETS

The Inverted Mirroring of Earth Elementals

Quote: "I love the piece of earth you are because, in all the planetary prairies, I do not have another star. You repeat the multiplication of the universe." —Pablo Neruda

In astronomy, a binary satellite system refers to a pair of planets that share an external orbital axis, remaining fixed together for eons. This concept mirrors the intense bond shared by twin planet soulmates.

Let's explore the unique dynamics of a resilient Twin Planet connection. You'll certainly find different sentimental expressions compared to other twin elemental relationships. Rather than phrases like "you light my fire" or "baby, you're the wind beneath my wings," it's more likely you'll hear expressions such as "you are my rock, and you keep me grounded.

In the realm of Twin Planets, a profound sense of stability forms the foundation of the relationships. Feelings of groundedness, safety, and security emerge naturally. While trust-building is an integral aspect of any relationship, within the dynamic of twin planets, there is often an immediate sense of trust, accompanied by an intuitive certainty that you are destined to share your lives together. This isn't merely the fleeting notion of "you're so beautiful, I'd marry you on the spot," but rather a deep-seated recognition that "I knew I'd spend the rest of my life with you from the moment we first met.

The story of my maternal grandfather comes to mind. Upon meeting my beloved grandmother, Emma, he declared his intention to marry her within the first few moments of their encounter, and that's precisely what happened. They married young and stayed together until his death. Remarkably, she never remarried. Despite some tumultuous moments in their marriage—she literally stabbed him a couple of times—every Friday he handed his paycheck directly to her. Then, he would indulge in his weekend whiskey.

Much like a binary planetary system, they never envisioned it any other way. Interestingly, the story is similar to my paternal grandparents as well. It's reminiscent of a Martin and Coretta kind of love, or marriage, I should say. Both of my grandmothers saw their husbands as their rocks, and vice versa. While their relationships might have ignited with a fiery, whirlwind-like romance during their courting season, ultimately, they embodied a twin planet energy. The prevailing theme was stability over sexuality, seeing as twin planet connections most often embody the familial love dynamic.

In certain marriages, religious couples often seek to model their relationship after God's love. For instance, Psalms 78:35 says, "They remembered that God was their Rock and that God the Most High was their redeemer." This implies that by modeling God's love into their relationship, they see their spouse as their rock—a source of strength and unwavering support, much like they would look to God. In this context, the word "rock" is synonymous with Earth or Planet.

The Earth element is frequently symbolic of our physical and material values. Twin Planet characteristics tend to be grounded, reliable, and loyal. They are often very practical and prefer sticking to set routines or rhythms, like celestial bodies. Additionally, twin planet soul connections are usually patient and strategic in their thinking, much like the moon's rotations and its influences on the rising tides. Their careful and rule-bound approach to relating provides stability and structure in their relationships. Moreover, their dependability is a great asset in any intentional partnership or team dynamic.

If you have friends who are constantly likened to the old married couple in your group, you might be witnessing a live demonstration of a possible twin-planet connection. Surprisingly, long-term sugar daddies often exude twin-planet energy, especially towards young mothers and others in need of support, stability, and guidance. Many young couples enter marriage under the influence of Twin Planet energy, establishing it as a dominant authority in the realm of long term matrimony. Unfortunately, upon realizing that their compatibility index aligns more with a twin flame-styled dynamic, the marriage may become a divorce statistic.

Of the physical elements, beyond the sun, water, and oxygen, the planet is one of our most invaluable resources, providing the physical matter essential for human sustenance. In Chinese philosophy, the soil element is referred to as **tǔ**; it symbolizes the stabilizing balance of yin and yang, harvest time, abundance, nourishment, and fertility.

This element is also seen as central to balance and the changing of seasons. It symbolizes stability and proper anchoring. The planet grounds us, and the substances that emerge from it—such as precious stones, clay, food, and harvests—have tangible and real value in the material world. These tangibles can be leveraged as securities. For instance, an expensive diamond ring given as a symbol of good faith for securing a spouse for a lifetime is a great example. Another tangible example of value from the planet is the fruit-bearing trees that grow from the soil to feed our biology, or the wood from those trees and the precious minerals and metals used to build our civilization with.

Despite differences between birth signs and twin elementals, all twin elemental archetypes often exhibit similar characteristics, aligning with their corresponding astronomical traits. Therefore, it comes as no surprise that Taurus, Virgo, and Capricorn, representing earth signs, are also linked with stability, groundedness, and practicality, in harmony with twin elemental traits.

Additionally, it is noteworthy that the chakras associated with twin planet connections encompass both the **'Crown' and 'Root' chakras.** The crown signifies forethought and planning, while the root represents being grounded in physicality. Depending on the twin planetary connection, the chakric drives will oscillate or remain fixed in a balanced state. Correspondingly, the organs associated with this elemental are the **'Stomach** and **"Intestines,'** 'symbolizing comfort and stability. The related chemistry involves an equal balance of **Serotonin, Dopamine, Oxytocin,** and **Acetylcholine.** As you may have already observed, the entire body and nervous system best represent the physical attributes of a twin planet.

For context, acetylcholine, a lesser-known hormone associated with twin planets, serves as the primary neurotransmitter for the central and parasympathetic nervous systems. It plays a crucial role in contracting smooth muscles, dilating blood vessels, increasing bodily secretions, slowing the heart rate, and influencing arousal. Additionally, it functions as part of the brain's reward system.

This highlights the intricate connection between twin-planet relationships and the nervous system. It's common for long-term couples to humorously say, "You get on my nerves," implying that you're affecting my nervous system. Prolonged exposure to such a connection can lead to either the crystallization of neural plasticity and-or the entrenchment of rigid behaviors, affecting how we respond to stress or regulate our nervous system. Longitudinal studies, which track the same individuals over time, reveal the profound impact that long-term exposure to a consistent partner can have on both individuals and their relationship dynamics. This enduring familiarity fosters comfort and intimacy, paving the way for deeper understanding and more effective communication.

The accumulation of shared experiences fortifies emotional connections, and the extended closeness often results in partners influencing each other's behaviors and beliefs. However, despite these positive outcomes, there is a risk of relational stagnation. This risk underscores the importance of continuous effort to nurture vitality and growth within the partnership. Therefore, longitudinal research highlights the intricate balance of factors that contribute to the stability and development of intimate relationships.

In essence, while other 'Twin Elementals' may impact fundamental cerebral changes through emotional polarity, a twin planet can exert a more tangible influence, manifesting in concrete physical changes due to prolonged proximity exposure. This concept aligns with contemporary scientific and philosophical understanding, highlighting the interconnectedness between environmental stimuli, neural plasticity, and the shaping of one's identity and physical being over time. For example, while a twin flame might disrupt your personality through a traumatic emotional event over a short period, a twin planet could cause a timeline disruption over a much longer duration. However, this dynamic isn't fixed and can manifest in reverse roles.

It is not uncommon to hear remarks about how a couple, after spending a significant amount of time together, starts to resemble each other, reflecting the physical influence of their prolonged companionship. With twin-planet connections, you'll likely feel as if you've been with the soul you're sharing the experience with for over a thousand lifetimes, whether you have or not. seeing as the energy exchange, "when positively relating, " is generally a comfortable, trusting, and grounded experience.

Feeling grounded, a concept linked to twin planets, is crucial for various forms of stability, with emotional stability being particularly important. Achieving emotional balance with your soulmate is key to evolving together and creating a high-vibrational relationship. Unlike connections that are emotionally turbulent or superficial, a relationship grounded in emotional stability is vital for maintaining equilibrium. Without this balance, there's a risk that your twin soul may seek a more fulfilling connection elsewhere, leading to misunderstandings and conflicts in any type of relationship, whether romantic or platonic. It's important to remind you here that while I often use romantic narratives for their universal appeal, a twin soul can also manifest as a mentor or a nemesis, and a twin planet might be a long term business partner or a longtime caretaker.

Aside from emotional stability, a natural focus on financial and mental stability are also key characteristics of a successful twin-planet connection. Financial stability provides security and peace of mind, allowing individuals to focus on their personal growth and self-improvement without worrying about financial constraints. Similarly, mental stability enables individuals to navigate challenges and conflicts in life as well as relationships with clear thinking and a positive outlook. A relationship that brings stability in these forms can be a powerful tool in the journey of personal and spiritual development.

Physical stability, encompassing a vibrant and active lifestyle, social stability through nurturing healthy connections with friends and family, and spiritual and intellectual stability by sharing beliefs and interests along with engaging in meaningful conversations—these are just a few examples of the robust stability inherent in twin planet relationships.

In the realm of twin planet relationships, where emotional, financial, mental, physical, social, spiritual, and intellectual stabilities are deeply valued, psychological stability emerges as the most sought-after trait. The rise in mental illness today, fueled by modern stressors, social isolation, economic challenges, and rapid technological advancements, poses risks to relationships by affecting communication and emotional closeness.

Having a mentally stable partner is not just beneficial; it's foundational for a thriving twin planet connection. Mental stability allows individuals to navigate life's ups and downs with resilience, maintain a positive and realistic outlook, and offer unwavering support to each other. This stability is crucial for fostering a safe space where both partners feel understood, valued, and connected on a deep level. It facilitates clear communication, enhances empathy, and strengthens the bond between soulmates, making it easier to overcome challenges together.

In essence, a partnership grounded in psychological stability enriches the relationship, enabling both individuals to pursue personal growth, mutual development, and a journey of spiritual and intellectual exploration. It lays the groundwork for a relationship characterized by deep understanding, emotional support, and a shared commitment to navigating the complexities of life together.

These various forms of stability not only bestow a profound sense of security and tranquility but also empower individuals within the relationship to concentrate on personal growth and self-improvement—a vital ingredient for any enduring connection. A relationship characterized by such multifaceted stability is not just meaningful; it stands as a precious asset in the expedition of personal and spiritual development, free from the strains and uncertainties that can accompany financial and mental instability. Achieving harmony and avoiding the frequent disturbances that come with instability is always a far more intelligent choice.

Numerous couples believe that the previously mentioned qualities are crucial for a relationship's endurance, making them highly desirable. At the onset of a relationship, individuals must face the possibility of a temporary or long-term arrangement. Yet the difficulty arises because many relations lack the necessary compatibility in all aspects to maintain a lasting connection. Thus, the sustainability of a relationship, whether it is short-lived or long-lasting, frequently depends on the partners' chemistry, compatibility, objectives, and intelligence.

In earlier chapters, we examined the intrinsic partnership styles inherent in interpersonal relationships. Frequently, individuals may vocalize a desire for a particular kind of relationship, but their habits, patterns, and actions tell a different story, indicating that they might not be fully prepared for such a commitment. A twin planet connection, like all elemental bonds, highlights the contrasts in a person's life through chemistry and compatibility. This can either lay the groundwork necessary for attracting a sustainable experiences and relationships in the future or enhance already existing ones.

Transitioning from ego consciousness to soul consciousness—sometimes called, *'witness consciousness'*—is the ultimate goal. If someone operates solely from the ego/mind, which can be a highly unstable and occasionally a chaotic state, it's possible they haven't yet learned the necessary lessons to stabilize the ego and achieve the spiritual growth required for a joyful life experience. This is where a powerful and beneficial twin planet soulmate can make a significant impact. While operating from ego consciousness can be highly volatile and chaotic, it doesn't necessarily impede spiritual advancement, it's just a different approach to an end goal.

However, a powerful twin planet soul connection can play a crucial role in **anchoring an individual** and setting the stage for the transformative process of ego death. This bond aids in creating a nurturing environment that stabilizes the spirit in unparalleled ways, preparing one for profound personal growth. Even the most spiritual sages of our time had guru's and ashrams to anchor them providing safe space to discover their stillness and true self. Twin planets excel at providing a functional space for the necessary work to integrate the disciplines required for growth and evolution, especially when one is already on a path of self-realization and conscious relating.

The presence of emotional, financial, spiritual, and mental stability reflects your capacity to function as a mature adult rather than relying on the coping mechanisms of your adaptive or inner child. The inner child tends to react emotionally and often behaves in a manner reminiscent of adolescence, correspondingly, the incessant thoughts of a busy and wandering mind is reminiscent of a hamster on a hamster wheel.

It's important to understand that experiencing emotions isn't inherently problematic. However, when emotional reactions become unbalanced, impulsive, or lack thoughtful consideration, they can create difficulties in adult life. While the whimsicality of one's inner child might be seen as endearing, akin to the adorable behaviors of toddlers, the ultimate aim in child-rearing is to guide their development into adults who are stable, rational, sensible, and composed.

Have you ever been driving and suddenly someone cuts you off, leading you to react angrily with harsh words, perhaps even attempting to follow them, only to discover at the next stoplight that the driver is experiencing early labor and also suffering a mild heart attack? In that instant, the entire frame shifts, revealing that one's actions were notably misguided and quite goofy in fact. This reaction is typically referred to as a temper tantrum. Unfortunately, television shows and comedies often depict these kinds of dysfunctional behaviors as either cute or humorous.

In contrast, emotional stability is grounded in the ability to function as an adult rather than succumbing to the reactive impulses of one's inner child. An emotionally grounded individual is able to approach situations with neutrality without being overly swayed by their emotions, opinions, or perspectives. While it's important to preserve the innocence of your inner child, it's equally crucial to be mindful of and regulate its impulsive tendencies.

In a relationship with a "twin planet" partner, you may experience an enhanced ability for acceptance and a decrease in judgmental attitudes. This kind of connection might lead to increased open-mindedness and a reduction in criticism, as well as the capability to stay calm and rational, even in difficult situations. These qualities are crucial for establishing a deep and loving bond with a twin planet partner, especially within a romantic framework.

A hallmark of the demi-sexual attraction to someone who possesses twin planet energy, alongside groundedness and stability is a profound and compelling sense of 'security.' This feeling of security extends beyond mere emotional security; it includes the manner in which a twin planet individual engages with and reacts to others, such as waitresses, store clerks, business owners, and most importantly, you.

When a twin planet responds to others in a charming or jovial manner, a mature twin planet does not react with jealous pettiness, as they are emotionally secure in their connection. On the other hand, an immature twin planet may respond with shadow traits such as jealousy or insecurity. Ultimately, an unstable and insecure emotional attachment will drive one's spirit to seek a secure and stable emotional connection, which is the polarizing job of a juxtaposed twin elemental. Keep in mind that while a twin planet elemental possesses beautiful qualities in relating, its soul purpose may be to evoke profound experiences of insecurity or instability. This can lead to the most intense exposure of the shadow self, pushing you to confront and understand your deepest vulnerabilities.

When considering certain qualities in a twin planet soulmate, one may ask themselves whether they exhibit signs of insecurity and jealousy, and if so, whether they are prone to projecting their personal frustrations on others. Additionally, if they become irritable and respond with snappiness, it's important to evaluate whether they possess self-awareness and are capable of recognizing and self-regulating or correcting their behavior promptly before moving forward no matter how powerful the attraction.

Ultimately, the question is whether they are stable, secure, and grounded enough to be trusted—with your peace that is. The principle that valuing peace over the need to be right, along with the belief that patience is a virtue, are defining characteristics of a twin planet soulmate.

Other questions you could ask yourself regarding this defining behavior and when attempting to identify if a soul tie is a twin planet is, do you feel **"secure"** when they compliment someone else in front of you? Do you experience compersion in that moment and remain in your security because you know without a shadow of a doubt that the two of you are solid in trust, regardless of the interaction? Like emotional stability, emotional security is paramount and one of the central tenets of twin planet soul connections, along with material security as well. Notice that I said material instead of financial security.

Long before money, the feminine principle across species sought the masculine principle for provisions. It has always been a requirement that the masculine principle within a coupling must be able to express and provide. Whether food, protection, genetic material, or even intellectual material, history tells us that most biologicals have had to show and prove that they were worthy of mating exchange.

Some people are not rich in coin-based finance but are resourceful and will make sacrifices while working with what they have to provide what is needed. The feminine equivalents related to provisions and security are inherent, whether through the art of nurture or the internal wisdom found in divine feminine principles.

Hunting, gathering, planting, or building are all human predispositions. To what level of dedication is one committed is the question. When experiencing the connective soul polarization that comes with loving a twin planetary soulmate, security in all of its forms are the pillars of attraction. Establishing a secure and reliable bond between two individuals is vital in cultivating many essential aspects of a strong 'Twin Elemental' relationship and helps to foster qualities such as trust, vulnerability, honesty, and reassurance.

Along with stability and security, **"trustworthiness"** also stands as one of the most significant pillars of a twin planet connection. Trust is undoubtedly one of the most intimate gestures that soulmates can share. While sexual intimacy can be purchased, the same cannot be said for trust. Thus, it serves as a prime example of how a truly intimate bond should look.

Many people mistakenly equate intimacy solely with sexual activity, overlooking its broader definition as a sense of closeness and familiarity. A more accurate association for intimacy is trust, rather than viewing sex as its direct substitute. Consider this perspective: if you were leaving for an extended period, would you entrust the location of your most valued treasures and an actual lifeline to someone with whom you are merely sexually involved, or to someone you deeply trust? This distinction highlights the essence of true intimacy.

Characteristics such as being **"highly responsible"** are also pillars of twin planet attraction. At this point, it's likely you've noticed that while a twin flame is often associated with beauty, excitement, wonder, and passion, the allure of a twin planet is more tied to the maturity, stability, trust, and security it provides. Has your twin planetary soul mate been instrumental in instilling these qualities in you? Was it the relationship that grew you up into an adult.

As with all Twin Elemental polarization, the goal remains constant: continual evolution and self-improvement, ultimately striving to become the best version of oneself. A positive twin planet connection can offer the necessary support and consistency to facilitate this growth. With a sense of security and dependability, coupled with the reinforcement of daily goals and activities, one can feel encouraged and gain the confidence to aim for even greater achievements. A stable foundation in all areas, including emotional, financial, and physical security, is essential for maintaining a healthy nervous system.

Additionally trust stands as a foundational building block for cultivating **"confidence,"** a vital factor for personal and relational growth. Confidence, in turn, shapes the precedent for how one engages in relationships. Establishing confidence in relationships provides a secure assurance that challenges won't be faced alone.

A profound sense of security and confidence arises when individuals deeply believe they have a supportive partner committed for the long term. These qualities define a twin planet, offering grounding support as the soul undergoes evolution. The destabilizing uncertainty of each day or moment becomes more manageable, alleviating feelings of discomfort and high anxiety.

Unfortunately, some find solace in relationships resembling **PTSD** symptoms, maintaining a heightened state of alertness. On the flip side, a twin planet soul connection frees individuals from the anxiety induced by an unpredictable partner, offering a sanctuary from emotional turbulence. It's important to note that the desire for trust and stability isn't confined to one gender. Men, just like women, seek partners embodying these qualities. Men want to be able to trust their partners completely and not have to live their lives in a constant state of anxiety. They want to know that their woman is Solid—as a rock, or planet, in fact.

As you may know, twin planets exhibit inverted qualities, parallel to other elemental dynamics. Within each elemental dynamic lies a polar opposite and shadow side to consider. Even for emotionally mature individuals, a partner who is overly predictable can eventually become monotonous and uninspiring, leading to downright boredom. This raises a crucial question: where is the contrast? How can an individual's soul experience polarization for definition and perpetual evolution if they're stuck in a state of inertia?

On one hand, a predictable partner can offer stability, laying the groundwork for a solid foundation and the potential building of a legacy. However, if someone finds themselves in a rut—uninspired, unmotivated, and unhappy—can they truly appreciate such stability? This is where the Chemistry / Compatibility Index comes up for addressing and balancing these deficits. Essentially, your partner serves as a mirror reflecting your own deficits and shadows; they are not the cause of your boredom—**you are.**

Now, considering the inverted nature of corresponding shadows, on a completely different set of hands, you might find yourself with a twin planetary partner who embodies the polar opposite of all the positive qualities mentioned, as if from the upside-down world. They could be entirely unpredictable and downright irresponsible, lacking material security and making you feel ungrounded, unstable and insecure. Despite promises of stability and security, they might fail to deliver, leaving you questioning the longevity of such pairings.

In situations like this, one might expect the relationship to fizzle out quickly. If it doesn't, an individual may find themselves questioning their choices, thus feeling like a derelict or thinking they are intentionally subjecting themselves to punishment. Their initial attraction may have drawn them to the illusion of stability, only to later realize it was all a dream.

Every soulmate embodies a portion of all the twin elementals, sometimes creating confusion about the continued existence of a specific relationship. However, it's the dominant element that shapes the purpose of a twin elemental in your life regarding a destined soul connection. In the absence of a desired quality, a fervent and enthusiastic drive may emerge, compelling you to actively pursue that missing quality. This is the formidable power of inversion magic, driven by a mirror element, influencing the polarization for the evolution of the soul.

Each Twin Elemental boasts a dual nature akin to the Yin Yang sigil. The Yin aspect of a twin planet may guide you toward your destiny by setting an example, while the Yang aspect of a twin planet might repel you, urging you to seek the internal power you crave and deserve. When the need for change arises, a twin elemental soul can either forcefully push you away toward becoming the best version of yourself, similar to two magnets repelling each other, or pull you toward your best self, much like the attraction of two magnets.

Either way, your soul is compelled to move into the position necessary for personal growth. This science represents the pinnacle of Twin Elemental Soul polarization and stands as the most extraordinary mechanism for soul evolution. It could be the primary purpose of human attraction, aside from procreation and sustaining the species. This reflects the essence of **twin elemental shadow exposure, which can either gently or forcibly trigger the integration of those shadows**, subtly influencing the direction of your life's trajectory.

Encountering someone who initially appears to embody a specific twin elemental energy, only to later reveal themselves as the polar opposite of what you truly needed, can propel you to seek out what was lacking for the ultimate polarization. It's the cosmic setup for me—the initial attraction becomes the catalyst for a more profound polarization. An individual who embodies this fate, serves as the epitome of twin elemental polarization, transitioning from the shadow to the enlightened self.

This situation underscores that it's not the individual themselves who defines the paradigm of the twin elemental but rather the overarching characteristics and cosmic alignment in which they were manifested. The elemental nature of your soul bonding is ultimately shaped by the end results. In essence, the elemental bonding takes form through the culmination of outcomes. The twin elemental connection acts like a cloak, embraced by the soulmate with whom you have a predestined appointment, aligning for a shared journey of soul evolution.

The true revelation of a twin elemental often dawns in hindsight, prompting contemplation on the transformative influence it has wielded, whether for better or worse. Through an examination of disruptions in one's energetic timeline, a deeper analysis can unveil the specific type of twin elemental encountered through spiritual interactions nuanced by social dynamics and specific attractions.

For instance, consider this simplified scenario of a professional relationship where an individual initially seems to embody qualities of cooperation and collaboration, only to later reveal a pattern of opposing objectives, thereby triggering a desire for and pursuit of a more harmonious and aligned collaboration. If you are stuck in contracts, the maze of adversity in which you must navigate through builds a much stronger business acumen for the remainder of your days. In such instances, the cosmic orchestration of the initial attraction lays the foundation for subsequent profound polarizations. While basic, this explanation sheds light on the wider impact of life-altering polarizations and transformative character development, much like the butterfly effect, fostering soul evolution on a grander scale.

In contemporary times, the concept of the Twin Flame reigns supreme as the most sought-after soulmate connection among novelists and is greatly influenced by societal trends. Yet, during the baby boomer era, the twin flood connection might have held more appeal. For Vikings and those with a rebellious spirit, a twin wind may have been the lover of choice. There was even a time when Twin Planets stood as the most prized connections, sought after during an era when community elders, possessing the wisdom for enduring unions, arranged marriages. Note: In societies where arranged marriages prevail, the qualities of a Twin Planet-style love are abundant.

The discovery of a fascinating article in the Indian Times sheds light on the enduring prevalence of arranged marriages in contemporary East Indian society, with a substantial 80-85% of people choosing this path. Matchmakers, trusted matrimonial sites, and parents often play pivotal roles in facilitating these unions. Notably, Indian parents frequently conduct extensive background checks on potential grooms, delving into family, career, and past experiences. Remarkably, some individuals take it a step further, hiring private investigators to gather additional information.

In the hustle and bustle of today's fast-paced world, many women face challenges in meeting potential partners and establishing meaningful connections. In this context, arranged marriages emerge as a practical option. The thorough investigations conducted in this process can uncover crucial information, acting as a preventive measure against potential issues down the road. It's essential to acknowledge that Indian and other Asian communities boast tight-knit family structures, where familial ties wield significant influence in decision-making processes.

Contextually, Im reminded of how corporations diligently vet potential candidates before entrusting them the future success of that company. Given this thorough approach, it's not surprising that a life partner would also seek a similar level of insight, ensuring a shared journey toward mutual prosperity that aligns with their common interests.

In Western countries, love marriages hold sway as the predominant choice, while in India, the centuries-old tradition of arranged marriages persists and surpasses the prevalence of love or romance based marriages. This enduring trend can be attributed to a myriad of factors, including religious disparities, cultural rifts, family expectations, and ingrained biases.

The idea of a son or daughter marrying without parental approval is often deemed unacceptable in Indian families, leading to potential tension and conflict. Some may label it as ignorance, yet these parents will literally disown the beloved children who dropped from their loins, and thus many children go along, to get along. Interestingly, this bias is not exclusive to India, as I recently learned from an Ethiopian YouTuber discussing how young women in Ethiopia, who fall in love with non-Ethiopians, namely their counterparts in America often feel compelled to conceal their relationships due to similar cultural expectations.

In addition, religious differences serve as a substantial barrier to love marriages in India, with Hinduism, Islam, and Christianity each presenting varying views on marriage. Couples from different faiths often grapple with challenges in finding common ground on religious matters. Furthermore, cultural disparities can pose difficulties, as couples may hold divergent perspectives on essential aspects of marriage. Despite these formidable obstacles, some couples still choose love marriages. Though the divorce rate in arranged marriages remains relatively low, by comparison, many individuals prefer the stress free atmosphere of arranged unions for various reasons.

1. Arranged marriages are often more stable because they are based on mutual respect and understanding.

2. Arranged marriages usually involve families who have known each other for a long time, which can help to reduce conflict.

3. Arranged marriages often result in strong social and economic networks between families, providing additional support during tough times.

In numerous instances, romantic love marriages are marked by difficulties and conflicts, leading to a higher divorce rate according to many researchers. While successful love marriages exist, they often come with more challenges compared to arranged marriages. Consequently, many individuals opt for arranged marriages, appreciating the prospect of living in peace and harmony without external pressures. Essentially, they go along to get along.

In essence, co-creating a culturally healthy lifestyle, building a familial estate, and accumulating generational resources represent a more significant responsibility than mere romantic love when contractually committing the rest of your life to someone—who, for lack of a better description, could turn out to be *"straight up crazy."*

If these practices appear unconventional to readers, it's crucial to recognize that alternative relationship models, such as polygamy or celibacy embraced by priests and monks, have been intricately woven into the fabric of specific communities for centuries. This is why travel is important. Consequently, these models may exhibit greater adaptability for success within those cultures when compared to contemporary Western countries. The top five nations where these seemingly more stable arranged coupling models thrive are India, China, Pakistan, Japan, and Israel. Some of these cultures can boast a more stable social culture in some regards.

The exploration of arranged marriages in the context of twin elementals aims to illustrate how the characteristics of a "Twin-Planet" soul connection can unfold through a lifetime of shared experiences, fostering character development during one's lifetime for the evolution of their soul.

One might ponder why a soul would choose to incarnate into a narrative involving a lifetime of twin-planet energy within an arranged marriage. Although I can't provide definitive answers, it's conceivable that the soul's evolutionary journey benefits from the lessons acquired through this specific human experience.

Just as an entertainer, navigating multiple short-lived yet passion-filled relationships in a lifetime of twin flame connections, gains valuable evolutionary insights, the stable foundation and emotional security inherent in a twin-planet connection within an arranged marriage may also foster evolutionary growth within the ordinary human experience.

Decisions within an arranged marriage are influenced by a higher level of experience. Elders, having weathered passions, whims, and experimental attractions, chart a course to ensure stability and security. This approach prioritizes rational thought over emotional impulses, resulting in financial security, assurance of social status, compatibility rooted in cultural and ethical similarities, and a steadfast foundation built on trust.

Arranged marriages, while not the exclusive setting for a twin planet connection, vividly portray how twinning planets manifest as spirits having a human experience. Despite the commitment and potential success inherent in twin planet connections, such relationships are not immune to challenges. As highlighted earlier, every positive aspect of the relationship comes with its corresponding negative effects. For instance, coupling could involve experiencing utter contempt and resentment due to a life tethered to another soul who triggers the darkest of your shadows. Imagine Miss Celie's Blues," from The Color Purple film or similar narratives.

"Commitment," a cornerstone in these planetary connections, carries varied meanings for different individuals. While some may interpret it as exclusive emotional devotion to one person, others may perceive it as loyalty and faithfulness to shared life causes and still others may perceive it as exclusive sexual rights. Whatever the perspective, within the context of a relationship, commitment takes on profound significance. It transcends mere exclusivity or loyalty alone; and involves finding a compatible partner for building a robust relationship, and potentially becoming lifelong companions—forever ever.

Despite its apparent simplicity, we recognize that commitment is no easy feat. While we often consider commitment as a noun, it's fundamentally a verb—a proactive effort that demands action. It doesn't unfold passively; rather, it's a conscious choice we actively pursue, shaping through our decisions and behaviors. For some it is easy, depending on the love shared. for others it is an arduous task.

To commit is to consistently show up and hold space for a shared outcome. Being in a committed relationship means being available for your partner whenever they need you. This can be challenging, especially if you're accustomed to having a lot of personal space. You might find yourself feeling suffocated and annoyed with your partner constantly being around, leading to stress and a sense of losing independence.

While the idea of having a lifelong partner may seem appealing in theory, there are downsides to consider in committing to an exclusive relationship. Firstly, it leaves less time for other relationships, including those with friends, family members, and other less intense soulmates. Secondly, it reduces personal space and privacy. Thirdly, it comes with added responsibilities and obligations. Fourthly, there's a risk of losing oneself in the relationship over time, which may clash with a strong sense of ego.

Lastly, even the most adventurous person may find sex becoming repetitive, boring, and tedious, especially when the initial chemistry fades. Therefore, it's crucial to carefully weigh the pros and cons of a committed relationship based on what stage in life you are. In the context of these dynamics, the interplay and integration of conjuring the spirit of other elementals may yield the most desirable outcome. Alternatively, **possessing a strong mastery in balancing the chemistry compatibility deficit** would also serve you best.

For some, commitment may evoke feelings of freedom's demise, yet it necessitates both partners to embrace change and growth. It involves stepping back and pondering, "What can I do to enhance this situation?" instead of reacting solely on emotion. This demands the sacrifice of placing the other person's needs above one's own, at least to some extent. While this might seem like a formidable task, it's about acknowledging the other person's needs without surrendering personal freedom entirely.

Maintaining individuality and a sense of self is imperative in a committed relationship. However, both partners must be willing to compromise when confronted with shortcomings. You might discover that certain activities you once enjoyed become less appealing because your partner doesn't share the same interest.

Alternatively, you might stop putting effort into your appearance, assuming your partner will love you regardless. However, this assumption can be misguided, especially if your partner also grapples with doubts or insecurities. In a world where competition is prevalent, it's vital to sustain effort in keeping the spark alive in your relationship.

Envision a scenario where you've embarked on an incredible journey with your partner that seems to stretch across the ages. The profound comfort found in their presence has eclipsed the thrill of self-challenge and personal growth. You've seamlessly settled into a routine radiating safety and coziness. While this feels like a warm embrace, there's a drawback. This comfort inadvertently ushers in stagnation and complacency, creating a shadow that makes you feel trapped in a circumstance you've woven yourself into.

You discover yourself locked in a pattern, persistently pursuing something that, deep down, no longer ignites the flame of fulfillment. Despite this awareness, you continue down a path that, instead of nurturing your well-being, seems to drain it away. The emotional toll becomes evident, as distress and a creeping sense of powerlessness intertwine with your daily life. It serves as a stark reminder that our own comfort zones can morph into confining walls, and the pursuit of familiarity can lead to inadvertent entrapment.

Now, picture being entwined in a relationship with someone stubbornly resistant to change and adamantly clinging to the comfort of their old ways. This resistance becomes a barrier to personal growth, hindering you from venturing into new territories and broadening your perspective. The stagnant air of resistance hovers over the relationship, stifling the excitement that accompanies exploration.

The absence of growth and dynamism in the relationship breeds frustration and resentment. The realization that your potential for development is curtailed by their unwillingness to evolve becomes a point of contention. The relationship transforms into an immobile state, where the refusal to embrace change turns what could be an exhilarating journey into a repetitive loop, leaving you yearning for the thrill of new experiences and the joy of shared growth.

These are just a couple of potential pitfalls for exposing shadows within a twin planetary commitment. While being with a life partner undoubtedly brings benefits, it's crucial to continually challenge and support each other for individual growth. Taking someone for granted becomes a risk in a long-term twin planetary relationship. The more time you spend with someone, the more familiar they become, increasing the likelihood of taking them for granted—a narrative that can breed resentment, as familiarity sometimes breeds contempt.

Over time, **comfort can turn into complacency** with a partner. We may overlook their contributions and the significance they hold in our lives, leading to tension that, left unaddressed, can erode the foundation of the relationship. This analysis reveals a mirror that reflects images capable of sparking the soul's evolution. Keep in mind that this extends beyond romantic relationships and can encompass your basic interpersonal connections as well.

All too often, individuals find themselves tethered to commitments they eventually regret. They think about all the other things they could be involved with and wonder if they made the right choice. The pressure may become intense or unbearable, prompting a search for a way out, which can be challenging if lives are deeply fused such as in business partnerships or coparenting relationships.

In the end, you are just expected to forget about your doubts and carry on. But what if you can't? What if you can't shake off the feeling that you made a mistake? What if the thought of being stuck in this commitment is simply too much to bear? For some people, the weight of these "what if's" can be overwhelming. You might begin to sense a feeling of imprisonment, and as if there's no escape in sight.

In the grand dance of life, it's only natural to find ourselves second-guessing ourselves, particularly when faced with monumental decisions. The monkey mind, always in search of the next thrill, can make these thoughts even more persistent, especially in enduring relationships. A lingering question may taunt: What other opportunities might we be passing up by committing to a seemingly singular path?

Ironically, even if you exert your utmost effort to push these thoughts aside, convincing yourself of an unwavering commitment, those persistent thoughts manage to infiltrate. It's akin to the relentlessness of cold seeping through layers of clothing; no matter the barriers, it eventually finds a way in. Once it penetrates, it numbs you from the inside out, dominating your senses until nothing else registers. This is precisely how doubt operates—sly, patient, and unyielding. It bides its time, patiently waiting for the opportune moment to strike, especially when you're most vulnerable.

In today's world, where distractions abound, having these doubts is almost par for the course. However, they can wreak havoc on a relationship. The constant pondering of "what if" creates tension and breeds mistrust. Worst of all, it steals your presence from the relationship you're currently in. So, the moral of the story: **"GUARD AGAINST DOUBT."** At its highest nature, twin planetary energy declares, "We Don't Do Doubt!" At its lowest, well, you can probably guess. In the twin planet dynamic, trust and doubt sit at opposite ends of the polarity spectrum, each an essential force within the twin elemental effect, shaping one's life trajectory in profound and unexpected ways.

Consider one of the most profound shadow traits within the twin planetary elemental effect: the devastating impact of divorce after a long marriage. Imagine your life, unchanged for decades, suddenly flipped upside down, leaving you to grapple with the daunting question of how to survive the rest of your days. As the plasticity of your neural connections is forced to adapt, and your entire lifestyle is torn apart at an age when forming new habits is physically and mentally challenging, the experience can be overwhelmingly destructive.

Yet, for those who endure and emerge on the other side, stronger and wiser, this trial becomes a catalyst for profound soul evolution. The adversity sharpens their resilience, deepens their understanding, and elevates their state of being to one of greater enlightenment and strength.

The spiritual significance of such life-altering experiences cannot be understated, particularly within the context of the twin planetary elemental effect, especially when we find ourselves in the eye of the storm. Everything that happens, even the most painful and devastating events, carries a deeper purpose. The universe operates with a sense of predestination, weaving each experience into the fabric of our lives to guide us toward our highest potential. When it comes to the twin elemental effect, the challenges we face are not mere coincidences but are intricately designed to push us toward spiritual growth and self-realization.

This belief in predestination suggests that every hardship, including the heartbreak of a long-term relationship's end, is part of a divine plan to awaken parts of ourselves that we might not have discovered otherwise. The intense polarities of the twin elemental effect force us to confront our deepest fears and insecurities, ultimately leading us to a place of greater wisdom and understanding. Each twist and turn in our journey serves a purpose, guiding us to fulfill our spiritual destiny and align with the true essence of who we are meant to become.

For all twin elementals, it's often only in retrospect that the full realization dawns—where the journey itself holds the key to growth, and the final destination is where the true depth and ultimate impact of our evolution are fully recognized and appreciated.

For those embracing Twin Planetary soul alignments, it's paramount to stay mindful of the challenges that can arise. In the realm of Twin Elementals, your Soulmate serves as a reflective mirror for your growth and evolution. It's crucial to recognize that it's not them you doubt but rather yourself or your own capacity to love unconditionally. While having a kindred soul by your side can bring immense joy and benefit to your life, they may also appear to embody the opposite when you engage in introspection and self-correction. Regular **self-reflection** emerges as a cornerstone for personal development. By dedicating time to reflect on your experiences, you shift from merely witnessing them to understanding them.

This newfound understanding becomes a catalyst for the evolution of your spirit, fostering continuous growth. Cultivating this level of self-awareness stands as a crucial element in the journey of soul evolution, enabling you to identify areas that demand your attention and efforts. Soulmate relationships may not endure forever in the realm of "3D consciousness," but their impact possesses enduring significance. In a place where there is no time, the causal effects of all soulmate experiences manifest as one consciousness and one continuous event.

Twin Elemental Soulmates, entangled with karmic debts and the likes, enter our lives with a singular purpose, and that is to serve our higher purpose. While it might not be immediately apparent, engaging romantically with a Twin Elemental can act as a potent catalyst, sparking not just romantic feelings but a profound journey of spiritual and emotional growth. This unique connection has the potential to birth intellectual and esoteric gifts, delivering lessons that transcend mere monetary value. In essence, these encounters wield the transformative power to propel us into advanced realms across various facets of life.

By embracing the spiritual scholarship that a twin reflection offers, you'll discover that the lessons woven into a soulmate relationship possess transformative capabilities, shaping you into a better human being and an evolved soul. These connections extend beyond fulfilling romantic desires; designed to serve higher purposes, they transcend the boundaries of earthly dimensions, reaching into realms beyond our immediate understanding.

Before concluding the chapter, consider examples from well-known relationships. These are presented to vividly illustrate the spectrum of energetic connections, enhancing the exploration of dynamic interactions. For starters, take for instance the talented and beautiful musical artist Erykah Badu. While I haven't personally interviewed her to determine the nature of her relationships, an educated guess based on public information suggests that her connection with Andre 3000 might have been a Twin Wind soulmate connection, while her relationship with Jay Electronica could be viewed as a Twin Flame bond. Her partnership with The D.O.C. appears to exhibit Twin Flood energy, and her connection with JaRon Adkison, who goes by JaRon The Secret, showed potential to be a Twin Planet, as evidenced by an Instagram post showcasing signs of nesting.

Consider Madonna, whose romantic history includes figures such as Sean Penn, Guy Ritchie, Warren Beatty, Dennis Rodman, and Tupac Shakur. Then there's Jennifer Lopez, who has had relationships with Ben Affleck, Marc Anthony, Ojani Noa, and Sean Combs. Taylor Swift's most talked-about relationships include those with John Mayer, Jake Gyllenhaal, Harry Styles, and Calvin Harris. These high-profile relationships prompt a reflective question: What sort of twin elemental energy might each of these soul-tied connections have introduced into their lives for transformational lessons? This inquiry invites readers to explore the dynamic and transformative energies at play in the realm of intimate relationships.

Cultivating a soulmate relationship requires effort and commitment, yet the rewards are immeasurable. It's not always a walk in the park, and there will be moments when you feel nudged beyond your comfort zone. However, it is precisely through these challenges that you evolve and develop in ways you never deemed possible. Your twin elemental soulmate becomes your catalyst for transformation, propelling you to confront fears, heal wounds, and strive relentlessly toward your highest potential.

These relationships will gift you with a profound sense of self-awareness, eventually setting the stage for the centering into your self realized "God Self." Beyond the realm of a romantic connection, the bond with your twin Elemental holds a purpose that transcends and propels you toward spiritual evolution and personal transformation. Indeed, the most remarkable life lessons frequently emerge from the crucible of adversity.

In conclusion, here is a concise summary outlining Seven key characteristics of a *"Twin Planet"* in relation to the elemental nature of a mirrored soul connection:

- **Dependability / Consistency:** Twin planet connections offer a steadfast anchor, where partners can rely on each other's unwavering support and count on their twin planet soulmate as a reliable and trustworthy companion. This dependability is a key characteristic, fostering a strong and enduring bond. However, shadow traits may initially present themselves as these positive qualities, only to later reveal their opposite nature, driving an unyielding pursuit of the experience, accepting nothing less.

- **Pragmatism:** Twin planet connections thrive on practicality, as partners approach challenges and decision-making with a down-to-earth perspective. They navigate life's complexities with a grounded mindset, making thoughtful choices that contribute to the stability and success of the relationship.

- **Foundational / Grounded:** Twin planet connections resonate with a harmonious synergy, mirroring the celestial dance of binary satellite systems in astronomy. The union of twin planets represents a deep and profound connection, where partners find solace and strength in each other's presence, forming a solid foundation for their relationship. These foundational relationships make it possible to establish anything from a business or legacy to the space for practicing evolutionary techniques over a period of time.

- **Longevity / Establishment:** Twin planet connections transcend fleeting romances, promising a lasting and meaningful journey. These connections are built to withstand the test of time, with partners fostering a deep understanding, appreciation, and commitment to nurturing their bond for the long haul. Some of the most valuable resources often require a significant amount of time for their establishment.

- **Trustworthiness / Dependability:** Twin planet connections thrive on a bedrock of trust, where partners feel secure and confident in each other's responsible fidelity and accountable honesty. Dependability is also a cornerstone of this trust, providing a sense of assurance that one can count on their twin planet soulmate during both smooth and challenging times.

- **Physical Attributes:** The chakras associated with twin planet connections are the crown and root chakras. The crown represents forethought and planning, and in this context, the root represents being grounded much like a physical anchor. The organs associated with this elemental are the stomach and intestines, which symbolize comfort and stability. The associated chemistry is an equal balance of Serotonin, Dopamine, Oxytocin, and Acetylcholine.

- **Shadow Exposures:** Shadow exposures in a twin planet dynamic can reveal the nuanced balance between comfort and the potential for contempt, emphasizing the risk of familiarity causing partners to take each other for granted. These moments explore the thin line between dependency and support, highlighting how easily one can shift into over-reliance, stunting personal growth. Arrested development and a loss of respect emerge as significant concerns, underscoring the need for continual self-awareness and mutual appreciation to prevent complacency and preserve the relationship's integrity.

In summary, twin planet connections deliver deep and enduring experiences marked by stability, reliability, and longevity. These connections serve as catalysts for personal growth, trust, and conscious relating, establishing an enormous foundation for a satisfying and lasting partnership. With their dependable and strategic essence, twin planet soulmates provide a reassuring sense of security and a structured framework for a flourishing soul reflection.

PART III

Chapter Fourteen

Conscious Relating MASTER CLASS Pt.1

Emotional-Technology for Evolving the Soul

Quote: The beginning of love is to let those we love be perfectly themselves and not to twist them to fit our own image otherwise we love only the reflection of ourselves we find in them." —Thomas Merton | No man is an island

A Neon Highlighter is recommended for this chapter

Now that we've delved into the Twin Elemental characteristics of a soul tie, presented as a soulmate and touched on several supporting topics, including soul science and a brief history of human relating, you may be wondering, What does all of this mean? The purpose is simple: it's a blueprint designed to set the stage for awakening your awareness in Conscious Relating! Why else would one be drawn to the twin elemental model if not to tap into its potential for conscious empowerment, fostering self-actualization and soul evolution?

Regrettably, a significant number of individuals remain unaware of the stark reality that their lives and relationships often operate more out of compulsion than consciousness. The effects are catastrophic. Imperceptible to most, yet catastrophic all the same. This tendency towards automatic behavior is widely accepted and normalized across different aspects of life, possibly stemming from habits acquired during upbringing or the subtle influences absorbed from social culture and media. Once these patterns and behaviors are established, their origins typically fade into obscurity, lost in the mists of time.

In the context of humanities inherent social nature, it becomes evident that we are deeply entrenched in a web of social and energetic transactions on a daily basis. According to transactional analysis, we navigate these interactions from one of **three ego states:** Parent, Child, or Adult. This framework helps to elucidate the automatic patterns that dominate our lives and relationships, highlighting the importance of conscious engagement to transcend these compulsive behaviors.

Given this context, the complexities of successfully managing a twin elemental experience becomes apparent. Dealing with the intricate interpersonal dynamics inherent in such an experience can be both mysterious and contradictory. As such, it becomes crucial to adopt deliberate and insightful strategies for relating in a conscious manner. Doing so ensures the cultivation of harmonious and rewarding relationships, effectively addressing the paradoxes and enigmas posed by our interactions with others.

In the realm of relationships, the term **"relation"** traces its origins back to the Latin word **"relātio."** It evolved through Middle English and Old French as **"relacion"** later morphing into **"relation"**). This noun stems from the perfect passive participle **"relātus,"** signifying **"related,"** which, in turn, is rooted in the verb **"referō,"** meaning **"I refer"** or **"I relate."** This verb is composed of the prefix "re-" (indicating "again") and the base "ferō" (meaning "I bear" or "I carry"). As an adjective, "relation" essentially means standing in a connection or being a relative of. *(I know—etymology is exhausting, —right?)*

By appending "ship" as a suffix to nouns, we commonly express a state or quality. In the context of "relationship," the fusion of "relation" and "ship" conveys the state or quality of referring to relatedness or simply being related, connected, or associated with someone or something. More importantly, is the fact that the core of the term *"relationship"* lies in the word **"RELATE,"** forming what we can aptly call a Relate—tionship, or the state of relating. At its essence, two individuals involved in a relationship are fundamentally engaged in the act of simply "relating" to one another. Period, point, blank.

For perspective, imagine a conversation that unfolds like this: "I really enjoy intimacy." "Oh, really? That's something. I can relate to that as well. It seems like we connect deeply on that level, doesn't it? I can totally relate to you." Or adversely, one might say, "I'm really into gang culture," to which the response could be, "Interesting, I can find ways to relate to that passion and the sense of belonging it brings. It's a lonely world, but the fundamental desire to belong is something I can relate to."

Alternatively, several conversations might unfold like the following, "I'm all about making money and I get a rush from running plays in business, orI love sports, I like shopping" , " I like having a partner to build a fulfilling life with, and or to share responsibilities like bills or raising children with." To these expressions, one might respond, "Wow, really? That's fascinating. Me too. I can relate. It's amazing how much we can relate to each other on these topics. Let's go deeper—maybe we can continue relating to each other on these things indefinitely, or at least until we no longer relate to each other anymore. To relate to someone means to establish a personal connection with them across a range of emotional depths, finding common ground in shared experiences or feelings. A relationship doesn't only manifest romantically, as evidenced in professional relationships, client relationships, collaborative relationships, and even therapeutic relationships.

Within any cycle of life, we must recognize that tomorrow is not promised, and that all good things eventually come to an end. Given our limited time—whether it's ten days, ten months, ten years, or ten decades—the best we can do is to fully "relate" with others, making the most of the time and space we have. Whatever narrative we perceive ourselves to be enacting, whether it's the roles of playing house for a few years, or mentor and student, or even best friends forever, our fundamental endeavor remains the same: to relate in a manner that reflects compatibility until we outgrow the confines of that narrative. Considering the scope of the three ego states mentioned earlier, relating from a conscious state rather than a compulsive one yields the most rewarding outcomes.

In Chapter Two, we explored the dynamics of partnerships. Within these partnership dynamics, individuals engage and relate according to the nature of that partnership dynamic. If you are in a romantic partnership you are respectively relating romanticaly. Similarly, If you are in a domestic, sexual or platonic partnership then you are relating to each other sexually, domestically or platonically.

Like the unpredictability in a game of musical chairs, or the fleeting connections made during speed dating, the essence of our interactions, constrained by our temporal and spatial limits, boils down to temporary engagements within a three-dimensional sphere of consciousness through the perception of time, space, and matter. This recognition helps frame our understanding of the temporality yet impactful nature of our relationships.

What this essentially conveys is the inherent transience of relationships and experiences. Just as the certainty of death marks the ultimate end of our physical journey, it also defines the boundaries of our temporal connections with others. No matter how enduring a relationship may seem—lasting decades, even half a century—it is, by nature, temporary. In the grand tapestry of life, **where change is the only constant,** we find that we cannot permanently hold onto moments, relationships, or individuals. Much like the ephemeral beauty of a flower, which, once plucked from its stem, is destined to fade, so too are our interactions destined to pass.

At its core, the best example is found in the marriage vows, which state, "till death do us part." This phrase reveals a profound truth often overshadowed by the romantic ideal of eternal love. It starkly acknowledges that, despite the depth of the bond and the strength of the affection, there will inevitably come a time when parting is unavoidable. It reminds us that even in our deepest commitments, there exists an unspoken recognition of life's impermanence, which encompasses all partnership dynamics.

This understanding invites us to engage with each other and our surroundings with a mindfulness of their impermanence. In the time allotted to us, the most profound action we can undertake is to genuinely relate and to authentically connect with each other within the fleeting moments we share. It's an acknowledgment that, while we cannot freeze time, capture a feeling in perpetuity, or claim ownership over another's essence, we can cherish the dynamic and evolving nature of our 'relating—ships,' alternatively, our states of relating.

Drawing from the wisdom of ancient philosophies and modern insights alike, we're reminded of the beauty in transience, a concept celebrated in the Japanese notion of "***mono no aware***," the poignant and bittersweet awareness of impermanence. This perspective doesn't diminish the value of our connections; rather, it heightens the appreciation we hold for them, knowing they are not everlasting. It teaches us to live fully in the present, to engage deeply with those around us, and to treasure each interaction as a unique and temporary convergence in our shared journey through life's vast, ever-changing landscape.

Though some individuals attempt to own and monopolize their lovers entire ecosphere, essentially all you can do is to simply relate for a moment in time. Whether engaged in intimate partnerships or broader social interactions, you encounter a variety of dynamics through which to relate with others. These can include intellectual, dramatic, romantic, emotional, sexual, domestic, financial, or even violent interactions. Each dynamic offers unique challenges and opportunities.

As we explore these relational styles further, we will introduce tools to help you identify compulsive habits in how you relate to others. Understanding these patterns will empower you to reshape your unconscious behaviors, enabling you to engage more mindfully and intentionally. The goal is to cultivate conscious relating as your default approach, enhancing both the depth and quality of your interactions.

By illuminating the unconscious patterns that influence our relationships, we can proactively alter our approach to cultivate a more vibrant and fulfilling way of relating to one another. This approach nurtures deeper connections and a heightened sense of personal growth, minimizing detrimental influences and empowering us to embrace overall well-being and a more enriching life. Awareness of the elemental effects projected and reflected is only the beginning.

Before we progress further, I invite you to engage in a moment of intense introspection. Through this introspection, attempt to gain a deeper understanding of your capacity for growth and learning. This self-awareness becomes especially valuable when embarking on new journeys or pursuing unfamiliar paths. Prior to starting any new venture, it is crucial to introspect and ask yourself a pivotal question: Am I open to being taught —am I teachable? Being teachable demands a willingness to embrace new ideas, welcome diverse perspectives, be receptive to constructive feedback, and subjectively process information.

Individuals possessing this quality can navigate obstacles with ease and adapt to changing circumstances with grace. In a world where continuous learning and innovation are keys to success, cultivating a teachable mindset becomes not merely an option but a necessity. So, before you take that first step forward, pause to ask yourself: **Am I truly teachable?** Posing this crucial question at the onset of our journey in conscious relating sets the stage for a more productive and fulfilling experience—one in which we can learn, grow, and thrive together.

Now, with that being said, the real question emerges: regardless of the dynamic in which you relate to others, which relating pattern are you most likely to adopt or engage in, [**C**ompulsive] or [**C**onscious]? Judging by the state of relationships and marriages in the 21st century, nine times out of ten, compulsive relating is the dominant, unconsciously practiced relationship style. Take a moment to reflect on this. Look around at your family, friends, and past relationships. Consider your Ex, for instance, Were their actions during challenging times compulsive or thought out and conscious?

Reflecting on past challenges, wouldn't you have preferred your ex or current partner to act with more conscious intent rather than impulsively or compulsively in the face of difficulties and obstacles?

For a more profound insight, it's crucial to recognize that, in the realm of conscious relating, a significant aspect revolves around fostering an advanced level of emotional wholeness. This refined state of emotional wholeness embodies a condition where an individual achieves a profound sense of balance and integration in their emotional experiences, particularly in their outlook and retrospective acceptance. It signifies establishing a healthy relationship with one's emotions, enabling the capacity to continue navigating a broad spectrum of feelings without succumbing to overwhelming emotions or being excessively controlled by them.

Emotional wholeness involves not just connecting with emotions but regulating them effectively and expressing them in a significantly healthy way. It requires a balanced self-awareness and a deep understanding of values, needs, and desires. This state empowers individuals to find peace and fulfillment, regardless of life's challenges, marking a pinnacle in conscious relating. Achieving emotional wholeness is vital for clarity of purpose and effective partnership, demanding a connection with one's individual divine purpose.

Unfortunately, many relationships are prone to emotional chaos as they progress rather than emotional wholeness, often due to issues stemming from the foundation upon which the relationship was built. This can often be attributed to the romantic notion of helplessly **"falling"** in love during the beginning stages, which often relieves individuals of the responsibility and accountability required for consciously **"growing"** in love.

Just as an individual may lose control of their balance and helplessly slip or fall, resulting in pain or injury, the act of helplessly falling in love is frequently depicted as a process devoid of conscious choice and control relieving individuals of accountability if it all goes wrong. In most instances of physical falling, the individual isn't at fault as prevention is often challenging. Likewise, falling in love is commonly seen as a natural occurrence beyond an individual's control. The subsequent actions align with compulsive behaviors rooted in impulsive habits.

The storyline for most love stories revolves around being swept up in an Oz-like whirlwind, reminiscent of the natural chemistry felt by twin winds. "It just happened" is a common refrain. In the face of internal conflicts between heart and mind, some absolve themselves of accountability, asserting, "I can't be held responsible because it wasn't a conscious and intentional decision; it just happened naturally. I fell for the person by accident, and now it's the most romantic entanglement the world has ever known.

Regrettably, I've observed individuals genuinely turned off when new love is intentional. Some people perceive it as "awkward" when a potential lover is deliberate and calculated in expressing genuine affection with forethought. It's seen as creepy, unnatural, and even potentially manipulative if it's a conscious effort rather than a naturally impulsive one, according to some. Consider the criticism directed at the Pickup Artist (PUA) community for their use of intentional attraction techniques. Admittedly, this isn't a universal sentiment, but for some, the preference is for the process to unfold impulsively, as it might feel more authentic and genuine, ultimately exuding extraordinary passion.

In hindsight, consider how, in law—specifically in divorce proceedings—You don't go to god, you go to court to hold a lover accountable in marriage. Interested parties are unable to quantify the love-falling process. Seeking damages for love is, in fact, not feasible apart from lashing out. Instead, legal suits are filed for capital, property, tangible estates, and assets—things that require conscious effort and forethought to acquire.

There's no accountability taken for entering the enchanting land of fantasy love. Yet, 'compulsive falling', is the primary sales pitch most individuals are often sold, just before entering a romance based relating-dynamic.

In various relating dynamics—whether within a loving domestic partnership, a romantic relationship, a platonic connection, or a transactional interaction—individuals often engaage through learned subconscious behaviors, unconscious patterns, and deeply ingrained belief systems typically aligned with the three ego states. These elements significantly contribute to one's personality profile and psychological makeup, influencing how one relates to others. Despite the assertion of free will and the power of choice, the perplexing question arises: who would consciously choose to hurt or hate the one they've professed to love or even have love for? Is it not hate or hurt that often stands as the culprit in the regrettable divergence of most relationships that meet such a fate?

For context, consider the tragic experience of a dear and long standing friend. At the tender age of 13, she endured the heartbreaking loss of her mother in a devastating incident involving her father. This father, who had professed love and dedication to his wife and children, had tirelessly committed himself to providing for their needs and instilling higher values. However, in a shocking turn of events, he committed a heinous act by violently taking his wife's life in front of their teenage daughter, despite her desperate pleas for mercy. Following this unthinkable act, he then sat, visibly shaken, patiently awaiting the authorities as he accepted his fate.

Considering one's most principled and highest intelligence, it seems implausible that someone would consciously opt to become unnecessarily petty or resort to aggressive violence against someone they've invested in and professed to love unconditionally. Yet, regrettably, these compulsive outcomes are not uncommon. It's essential to acknowledge that, while there are individuals upfront about their intent and openly communicate that they will intentionally cause harm if betrayed, the majority assert that it is not their conscious intention to treat their loved ones in such a hateful manner.

Anyone taking the time to reflect on this would likely argue that such behavior is nothing short of impulsive, stemming from unconscious compulsions. Are we, then, primitive animals lacking self-control? Animals whose egos demand the respect of an intelligent species, yet we engage in mating behaviors similar to wild wolves. Wait, strike that from the record. Wolves, in fact, choose one mate and remain faithful until death, with minimal violence toward each other aside from territorial clashes. Regarding our mating practices, whether tumultuous and hostile or loving and free, it is clear that the relationships we cultivate—and their inherent versatility—play a central role in cultural development and soul evolution. Thus, if we relate to each other compulsively and to our detriment, it is reasonable to expect that our cultural development, social and emotional intelligence and our spiritual evolution will reflect this.

Whether through conscious or compulsive relating, the cause-and-effect outcomes on our life timelines extend beyond mere anthropic coincidences. Many individuals eventually find themselves questioning why we engage in the ways we do. They wonder how it all happens, why it unfolds the way it does, and what purpose underlies these patterns. It happens because the process of introspection and transcendence, born from the countless experiences gained through avatar-to-avatar soul intercourse, has the potential to catalyze a profound soul transformation, possibly propelling one into a state akin to that of a cosmic creator.

This cathartic experience can be likened to the eventual absolution of karmic debt, creating a blank slate upon which to accrue universal energetic credits across various planes of existence, so to speak. These nuanced and vivid descriptions represent my creative attempts to illustrate the potential for transcending to a higher level of sentience by way of the human condition.

The spirit of this entire book aims to provide a comprehensive guide not only to make you aware of the unique qualities of Twin Elemental influences—formally recognized only as twin flames, a sub-characteristic of a soulmate—but also to serve as a foundation for your journey in practicing the discipline of intentional relating also known as Conscious Relating. **This discipline aims to achieve soul connection on the highest frequency of love for transcendence.** Through the use of examples, exercises, and practical tools, this book empowers readers to navigate the complexities of Twin Elemental connections and cultivate deeper and more meaningful soulmate relationships through high vibrational conscious relating.

The essence lies in the holographic consciousness derived from accumulated experience, combined with intelligent models of relating and practiced with diverse elemental connections over time—ultimately forming a mental construct akin to a tesseract. This involves simultaneous awareness of your species' relationship culture and social models, encompassing behavioral and psychological insights, as well as acknowledging hormonal chemistries, and most importantly remaining aware of the deep connection with your own soul. This integration occurs through a sophisticated yet simple system of thought processing. **Such pandimensional awareness prepares an individual for super-conscious relating.**

Although this system is inherently intuitive and aligns with one's understanding through the study of every chapter in this book, along with subsequent publications, it can be concisely and effectively explained by drawing a parallel to the Hermetic principles outlined in the Kybalion. These principles, like the system discussed, represent a holographic and psychic mind framework. This comparison not only simplifies the explanation but also imbues it with profound wisdom, illustrating the depth and interconnectedness of the concepts at play.

Grasping the power of the 'Twin Elemental Effect' underscores the nuanced interplay of elemental forces in conscious relating, enhancing our understanding of their potential to generate a myriad of positive ripples throughout an individual's life trajectory. This awareness embodies the principle of **Cause and Effect** with every word, breath, and action in our interactions with others.

This intricate system is rooted in a fundamental understanding of the four elemental natures of the spirit and their profound impact on the mind, unveiling the essence of conscious relating. It identifies all relational dynamics as mental constructs, embracing the principle that all is mind, aligning seamlessly with the Hermetic principle of **Mentalism**.

This perspective acknowledges the inherent duality within every twin elemental archetype, showcasing their polarity, which resonates with the Hermetic principle of **Polarity**, and highlights each twin elemental's capacity to either illuminate or cast shadows on our experiences. Moreover, these elemental forces are closely linked to soul attachments that may span lifetimes or originate within a soul group, resonating with the principle of **Correspondence** and the axiom 'as above, so below.'

Achieving a balanced equilibrium in relating requires navigating the dynamic spectrum of push-pull, give-and-take, in alignment with the expressive and receptive principles of universal **Gender** dynamics, which is paramount for establishing sustainable relationships. These foundational dynamics within the twin elemental model form the basis for the energetic resonance of conscious relating, emphasizing the complementary nature of opposites and their transactional interplay. This interplay reflects varying degrees of motion and energy across every temporal and spatial dimension of an individual, manifesting as a pervasive force that vibrates through every atom within, embodying the principle of **Vibration**.

With this profound comprehension, one expertly navigates the complexities of emotion, transaction, and relating through the rhythmic flow of life, moving in patterns of ebb and flow and embodying the Hermetic principle of **Rhythm**. This understanding recognizes how these dynamics oscillate and influence each other.

To ascend further in mastery, incorporating practices such as transcendental meditation, alongside a knowledge of astrology and its effects on human personality and relationships, as well as developing social, spiritual, emotional and psychic intelligence, become essential. These practices enable mental transmutation and the capacity to consistently alter one's mental state while effectively relating. Each component of this system contributes to a comprehensive understanding and application of conscious relating, fostering personal growth and interconnectedness with all beings encountered. I would imagine that this type of psychic cohesion between individuals could be the initial steps towards fostering telepathic resonance.

The pinnacle of intentional or conscious relating is to attain radical self-awareness, addressing the duality of relationships with a solution-oriented rather than a problem-oriented approach. By actively cultivating this mindset, individuals can learn not just to tolerate but to appreciate and celebrate their loved ones, acknowledging and embracing their evolution and changes over time while receiving the same in return. Conscious relating also opens the door to striving for spiritual intimacy and elevated orgasmic experiences with every breath, ultimately leading to states of cosmic consciousness, as one learns to manage and master hypersensitivity on all planes.

Some may question how conscious relating differs from other relationship models or programs. The truth is, conscious relating doesn't adhere to a specific or set program or model. It is a mindset and a daily intention to foster individual and shared growth in a relationship, with a focus on evolving the souls of both partners to reach a peak state. While there are courses and programs available to assist individuals in acquiring the tools necessary for conscious relating, it ultimately comes down to intention and a commitment to growth and purpose in the relationship.

In an unconditionally loving and ***"freedom-based"*** conscious relationship, both partners are *devoted* to supporting each other's *individual journeys* while collaboratively pursuing *common goals* within a dynamic that resonates with their compatibility. In a healthy relationship, ***mutual respect*** for each other's autonomy and ***personal space is paramount***, enabling individual growth and exploration. Simultaneously, there exists a deep commitment to a ***sacred bond*** that nurtures the growth and development of the relationship itself. This type of relationship demands continuous ***communication*** and effort, but the rewards it brings are immeasurable.

Here, I would ask that you pause and re read the last paragraph until you completely comprehend the idea. I have italicized and made bold the *KEY-WORDS* for your convenience. I understand that two can symbolically become one; however, the truth is, in matter, you are undoubtedly *individuals* traversing an *individual journey* in flesh, and that requires and demands *mutual respect*. There are no slaves in love.

A conscious relationship is built on a foundation of trust, honesty, mutual respect, and a commitment to growth. In this type of relationship, both partners feel supported in their individual journeys while also feeling connected to something larger than themselves. When creating a conscious relationship with your partner, it is pivotal to be honest about your intentions, be patient with each other, and be willing to put in the work.

The endeavor becomes truly rewarding when you can embrace the world through the lens of your partner's perspective. Constructing conscious relationships holds the potential to amplify our connection with ourselves, our partners, and the world around us. It signifies an authentic soul partnership in every conceivable sense. Within this chapter, we will delve into the many qualities that define a conscious relationship and explore the essence of engaging in conscious relating with a potential romantic partner.

In contemporary times, a prevalent pattern is **the impulsive pursuit of relationships** as a means to attain fulfillment. Individuals seek someone who seemingly fulfills all their needs and consistently brings happiness, irrespective of challenges. Initially, this approach may yield some success, yet inevitably, all relationships encounter obstacles. It is during these moments that we recognize our partners are inherently human, with their own set of needs, desires, and challenges. This realization can be jolting, triggering sentiments of discontent and, at times, even contempt. *Let me find out you're not here to grant all my wishes of happiness and solve all my problems.*

[They say you shouldn't meet your heroes because they'll probably disappoint you, potentially turning idols into rivals.]

The undeniable truth is that no one else can genuinely fulfill all our needs. If we're not happy and fulfilled on our own, no amount of love, attention or gifting from someone else will change that. When we rely on others to make us happy, we set ourselves up for disappointment. It's important to learn how to be consistently content and self-sufficient before entering into a relationship. Anything else would be entering a relationship needy, and incomplete—a breeding ground for impulsiveness and compulsion.

Consider the shelf life or trajectory of such a relationship. For those who knowingly enter relationships with a sense of neediness, how do you rationalize investing time and energy in what could be a doomed venture? While the concept isn't the most challenging to grasp, many people overlook it. If you knew better, you'd' do better; and approach relationships with realistic expectations, which increases the likelihood of lasting fulfillment. Taking responsibility for our own happiness and finding satisfaction within ourselves sets the stage for the possibility of a deeply satisfying and enduring relationship.

Through experience, we come to realize that a relationship is more than the coming together of two people and transcends mere gratification. Some hold the notion that a future partner should possess the power of a magical genie, capable of dispelling all the nasty monsters while providing unlimited pleasure. There are those who believe their partner should fulfill every need for all eternity because they're worth it. In fact, some may see themselves and their partners as each other's personal lord and savior, attributing no intrinsic value to anything else in life, beyond their world-class love as the end all and be all, even above spiritual attainment and oneness with the 'lifeforce-self and source' of all souls.

They imagine that no other person's jokes shall be more humorous, including the comedy greats. No one's outfits should ever be cuter or cooler, and god forbid someone else should have admirable intelligence. Should you admire any intelligence outside of your relationship, even if it's Albert Einstein or Nikola Tesla, the gaslit statement, "Go be with them then!" is most likely soon to follow. And, if you respond with, "But I can't be with Einstein, he's dead..." you may receive a scathing rebuke or medieval lashing for being sarcastic.

Whether or not you've encountered this behavior, we all come to understand that other relationships are an integral part of our lives. They provide support, networking opportunities, friendships, companionship, mentorships, and, at times, love—even if it is altruistic. Ultimately, alternative relationships serve as a substantial source of growth and expansion, especially in platonic contexts. As social beings, humans thrive through connections and networks—contrasting variety is the source of intelligence.

It's a given that relationships are meant to enhance our growth, but what happens when they fall short? What do we do when the individuals we're with hinder our growth rather than contribute to our flourishing? Regrettably, numerous relationships today have a tendency to impede growth rather than foster it over time. If this weren't the case, would breakups be so common? Isn't emotional, mental, and spiritual growth the essence of our existence?

It's unfortunate, but when the attraction dope isn't flowing and the chemical flooding dries up, the motivation to grow together can also dry out. When growth stops in any of those areas mentioned above, it feels like something has gone drastically wrong in the relationship. We soon look to place blame and ignore accountability. The truth is, without growth, we're not fulfilling our soul's purpose. Additionally, without the freedom to grow, anticipate the *subtraction* of *attraction*, ultimately leading to *inaction*. ~Jesse Jackson (I'm kidding - Jesse didn't say that)

Attraction serves as the fuel or sustenance to nourish and cultivate a new connection. When two individuals unite with the shared goal of growth, the relationship aspires to reach heights beyond mere gratification. In the presence of authentic, unconditional love, the partnership transforms into a sacred and divine journey of evolution, offering both individuals an opportunity for expansion beyond what they might achieve individually. Deep satisfaction, blissful contentment, and enduring fulfillment emerge as rewards, provided they remain teachable and apply the lessons learned.

In contrast to a fantasy based relationship featuring a perpetually rewarding partner, a growth-oriented relationship is characterized by both partners being largely committed to personal development. They actively challenge each other to expand and venture beyond their comfort zones, challenging outdated and unhealthy belief systems. Embracing change, they view difficulties as opportunities for learning. Together, they establish a safe space for exploration and self-discovery, leading to a heightened level of intimacy and connection. In essence, they collaboratively build the kind of magical relationships that fairy tales depict, with the significant distinction that it is firmly grounded in reality.

The individuals involved interact as two adults when interacting as ego states rather than a child and parent or a child and child as it relates to rebellious or adaptive child states. The free child ego states are characterized by spontaneity, creativity, curiosity, and expression of authentic emotions. It's the part of us that feels freely and experiences the world in the moment, without being filtered through learned behavior as explained by transactional analysis.

Growth is the key to sustaining the life of a mature freedom centered relationship. In nature, the maxim holds true: if it's not growing, it's rotting! While the process may be scary at times, an intentional couple is willing to embark on the journey of expansion and continuous transformation, even if it means the potential of outgrowing each other. This commitment to growth imbues the relationship with a natural sense of vitality. As my grandmother used to say, "what is dead should be buried." Relationships devoid of growth are on a path to lifelessness, eventually finding their place in the graveyard.

Twin elemental soul mates such as twin flames, exemplify the idea that relationships are reflective mirrors, offering profound insights into our identity, values, and life trajectory. These connections provide invaluable feedback, becoming catalysts for personal growth and transformative change that might have seemed unimaginable. In a conscious relationship, when attraction harmonizes with continuous growth, creating a reciprocal reflection between two individuals, it unfolds the potential for an even deeper journey—offering ample space for mutual transformation to take root.

In these relationships, both partners are devoted to self-awareness, consistently seeking innovative and affectionate ways to connect. It is **a solution and success-based paradigm** as the primary competition is with oneself, not the partner. This mindset fosters a profound connection and grants the freedom to love fearlessly, passionately, and wholeheartedly. These relationships are genuinely transformational, propelling individuals toward their highest potential. Envision a scenario where the only competition between you and your partner is a playful race to outdo each other in offering compliments, each round culminating in laughter and joy.

Moreover, Imagine a relating experience in which you are devoted not only to mutual transformation but also dedication to the freedom of loving—fearlessly, passionately, and completely. In this space, **vulnerability is celebrated**, and expressing your true self feels secure. There's no room for insecurity; instead, you're encouraged and lovingly prompted to grow and learn, with **unwavering support** throughout. Picture a space of **transparent feedback** and profound listening, fostering genuine understanding. It's a haven for authenticity and intimacy, free from judgment or misunderstanding—a sanctuary of unconditional love that perpetually nurtures **mutual understanding**, trust, and respect. Can most individuals comprehend what that might even look like?

When two individuals engage in conscious relating, they are fully immersed in the present moment and actively involved with their loved ones. They not only listen with their ears but also with their hearts, consistently speaking from a place of authenticity. This relational approach is rooted in the belief that we are all interconnected, and through open and heart centered communication, positive transformations become a reality.

Picture possessing the simple superpower of disagreeing in a thousand different ways while simultaneously honoring each other's unique paths and patiently maintaining mutual respect no matter what pressures you carried throughout your day. As simple as that sounds, this concept often eludes the majority of Earth's human population. At times, I find myself contemplating whether puppies and dolphins outshine humanity in this regard. Maintaining such respect becomes increasingly difficult when unconscious patterns of behavior are involved.

Unconsciously projecting pain has become normalized in modern relationship culture. People, while adhering to certain behavioral standards, are often unaware of the negative impact their actions might have on others. This unconscious mindset perpetuates a cycle of causing harm without realizing it. When one loves from a fear-based space, shaped by past experiences, it's not uncommon for them to be unaware that their love is being filtered through past trauma rather than being expressed fully in the present moment.

Taking responsibility and accountability for these behaviors becomes virtually impossible when relating unconsciously or compulsively. Correcting something you're not aware of poses a significant challenge. Research indicates that our conscious decisions are shaped by a myriad of influences, ranging from microorganisms like parasites and bacteria residing in our gut, to the deep-seated unconscious patterns established before we were even capable of spelling our own names. It's no wonder that many people fail to use their emotional intelligence when choosing a partner, as decisions are often driven by unseen forces, attracting inversion-heavy twin elemental energy that eventually will polarize their lives.

In our culture, there's a prevailing belief that our relationships should only feel good. We are taught that they should always make us feel happy, content, and magical, like an iridescent unicorn dragon that farts colorful laughter inducing glitter. We're conditioned to associate negative emotions with something being wrong. However, the reality is that all relationships have their ups and downs. Experiencing a spectrum of emotions, from happiness and love to frustration and anger, is a natural part of life that no one, not even gamma brainwave-producing monks, can escape as even they can become frustrated, they simply respond to it differently. Honestly, I'm not so sure I trust people that do not emote, In fact, I'd be convinced that they're agents, possibly cybernetic in nature.

The key is understanding the origin of negative emotions. Surprisingly, they are not triggered by our partners but by our individual attachment issues. Frequently, we project our own emotional baggage onto our partners, creating challenges in the relationship. Such situations provide the perfect opportunity for us to examine our attachment issues. Suppose we could learn to recognize and deal with these issues, would we not be much better equipped to handle the challenges that arise in all of our relationships, be they familial, platonic, or commercial?

Empowerment through Emotional Insight

Emotional intelligence is crucial in managing social dynamics and personal relationships, connecting self-awareness with the complexities of human interactions. It embodies the adeptness to recognize, comprehend, and manage our emotions while also navigating and responding to the emotional currents of those around us. At its core, emotional intelligence enhances empathy, enriches communication, and fortifies relationships, rendering it essential for the intricate dance of human engagement.

The journey to cultivating emotional intelligence begins with a deep dive into the self, unraveling the intricate relationship between emotions and feelings. This initial exploration is crucial, for it sheds light on the inner workings of our emotional beings, thereby equipping us with the tools to interact with others more effectively and with greater sensitivity. By understanding the subtleties of our emotions and their consequent feelings, we lay the groundwork for emotional intelligence, thus enabling us to navigate the diverse interactions and connections that define the human experience with sophistication and depth.

In the intricate dance of human relationships and social dynamics, understanding the nuanced interplay between emotions and feelings becomes pivotal. Emotions, those primal forces stirring deep within our subconscious, act as the initial catalysts in this complex choreography. They are universal, spanning all of humanity, transcending cultural boundaries and shared across individual experiences. Emotions are the body's raw, unfiltered response to the world around us—fear sparks the adrenaline rush of fight or flight, joy floods us with a sense of warmth and well-being, and sadness envelops us in a cloak of introspection. Anger, another primal emotion, primes us for confrontation, a universal signal across cultures that boundaries have been crossed.

Feelings, however, are the colors we use to paint these universal emotions on the canvas of our personal experiences. They are the mind's interpretation of emotional stimuli, shaped by memories, beliefs, and the unique lens through which we view the world. Feelings are nuanced and complex, a blend of multiple emotions filtered through the prism of our psyche. Love, for instance, is not merely an emotion but a tapestry woven from joy, security, passion, and a myriad of other emotional threads. Anxiety, on the other hand, might blend elements of fear and anticipation, colored by personal experiences and cognitive appraisals of potential future events.

This cognitive connection plays a crucial role in transforming raw emotions into complex feelings. It is through this cognitive process that we interpret, understand, and give meaning to our emotional experiences. The appraisal of an event as threatening can turn fear into anxiety, while the recognition of a loss might deepen sadness into grief. This cognitive evaluation adds layers of complexity to our emotional life, allowing for a rich tapestry of feelings that guide our behaviors, decisions, and interactions. Your intelligence dictates how you you feel about an emotion. Rather, your emotional intelligence dictates how you feel and respond to an emotion to sum it up.

For a vivid illustration of how people react differently to emotions, one only needs to observe today's social media pranks on platforms like YouTube. These instances vividly showcase varying levels of emotional intelligence—or the absence of it—in real-time interactions. In the context of feelings and emotions, one of a mother's twins, for example, might have feelings that their mother's emotional expression of love is overwhelming, whereas the other twin might feel that those same expressions of love are comforting and emotionally fulfilling. Feelings can be viewed as filters for our emotions, often possessing a nature that allows for programming or conditioning. No two people can feel the exact same way just as no two rays of sunlight can hit the exact same way.

The concept of emotional wheels, such as **Plutchik's Wheel of Emotions,** provides one of many visual representations of this complex interplay between emotions and feelings. Plutchik's model, for example, identifies eight primary emotions—anticipation, anger, joy, trust, fear, surprise, sadness, and disgust—arranged around a wheel. These primary emotions combine to form more complex feelings, illustrating how basic emotional responses blend into the nuanced feelings that color our world. Such models help us visualize the breadth of our emotional and feeling landscape, offering insights into how simple emotional responses can evolve into the complex feelings that define our personal and social lives.

Understanding the distinction and connection between emotions and feelings is essential in the realm of human connections. Emotions are the universal script, the shared vocabulary of our primal responses. Feelings, with their cognitive underpinnings, are the personal dialects, the idiomatic expressions shaped by individual experiences and cultural backgrounds. Together, they form the foundation of our interactions, influencing how we connect, communicate, and navigate the social world. Grasping this interplay not only enriches our understanding of human behavior but also enhances our empathy, allowing for deeper, more meaningful connections.

Furthermore, understanding the distinction between emotion and feeling also reveals many insights, one of which is the importance of empathy. Recognizing that self-centered feelings are valid for introspection, yet can verge on narcissism if not self-regulated, underscores the value of cultivating or advancing empathetical abilities.

Empathy is a hallmark of higher intelligence among sentient beings. The latter is indicative of savagery and is generally associated with lower intelligence. Beastly behavior in those purported to possess higher intelligence is likely to result in them being treated as beasts necessitating confinement i.e. 'prison' until they achieve refinement or further evolution. For higher beings, this process may compel their binding to matter or the material plane across a succession of lifetimes. Savagery may yield temporary gains, but its viability proves unsustainable in the context of an intelligent society.

Leveraging emotional insight heightens social and emotional awareness, fostering a more integrated and harmonious self. This state facilitates clear thought manifestation, directing one toward their optimal self. At the heart of this transformation lies heart-mind coherence, a principle esteemed in both mindfulness and scientific research, harmonizing the body's mental, emotional, and physical systems.

Central to this is the rhythmical interplay between the heart and brain is the rhythmic dance between the heart's beats and the brain's waves. This synchronization is not merely a metaphorical union but a tangible, measurable state that bridges the gap between our internal experiences and the external world. In this coherent state, each heartbeat echoes our thoughts and emotions, fostering a feedback loop that strengthens our inner wisdom, resilience and clarity for our highest good.

Intentional and consistent coherence serve as crucial steps on the path to unlocking higher levels of sentience. Whether achieved through technology-assisted hemisphere synchronization, known as hemi-sync, or through partner practices like chanting the Aum mantra during transcendental meditation, practicing heart-mind coherence is a valuable tool for achieving these beneficial states.

Conscious-Action (vs) Unconscious-Reaction

Unconscious compulsions are often triggered by past traumas, leading to coping mechanisms that drive automatic reactions aimed at avoiding pain. In the majority of cases involving negatively charged compulsive behaviors, individuals project internal pain, contributing to the "Hurt people, hurt people" paradigm when projected upon another individual. Even when pain-based behavior ultimately rebounds back onto themselves, individuals can see the destructive effects of the mind's attempts to cope with pain and trauma. This is evident in cases like those featured on the popular YouTube show "Soft White Underbelly," where individuals struggle with addictive behaviors.

Becoming aware of this behavior as a coping mechanism and taking full responsibility for one's pain without projecting it onto your partner is empowering and one of the first steps to authentically relating from a mindful and intentional space of pure consciousness. Take note that emotionally flooding from frustration and coping with that frustration by bullying your partner with extreme prejudice is an unconscious reaction and considered compulsive relating vs. conscious relating which is generally accepted as normal behavior. While unfortunate, the truth is, we live in a culture where **we have normalized replicating toxicity. I Repeat:** we live in a culture where **we have normalized replicating toxicity.**

In contemporary society, many of us find humor in dysfunction. We laugh at comedians depicting toxic scenarios and enjoy sitcoms featuring dysfunctional families or situations—what we see we become, as energy flows where attention goes! In essence, dysfunction has become a source of entertainment. Even in destructive, corporate sponsored pop music, including weaponized hip-hop, we witness examples of this. However, replicating compulsive and toxic behavior is a sure path to a cascade of failed relationships, plain and simple. So, I pose this question to those exercising free will: Who would, without prompting, consciously choose to intentionally sabotage the most intimate and nurturing experience they'll ever embrace—the act of love or authentic human connection with others?

In the current landscape of pervasive dysfunction, recognizing the significance of making conscious choices in shaping our lives and relationships is crucial. By embracing a more mindful approach to our interactions with others, we present a stark contrast to the dominant entertainment norms and behavioral patterns. This shift in perspective paves the way for a deeper exploration of relational dynamics, particularly within intimate partnerships.

Our expectations, heavily influenced by television programming and related media, tend to set the stage for a pessimistic outlook. These expectations, a blend of past experiences and repeated exposure to dysfunction, lead us to brace for the worst. While the principle of beginning with the end in mind is beneficial in contexts where the anticipated outcome is positive, such as in sales or hypnosis, applying it with a negative expectation is unproductive. Adopting a pessimistic stance is harmful and should be avoided.

The consciously relating "Intentional couple" isn't fixated on the outcome of the relationship. Their primary commitment lies in the experience of growth and soul evolution in the present, rather than adhering to preconceived relationship beliefs and forcing compatibility. This doesn't imply a lack of concern for the relationship's direction; instead, it underscores their prioritization of growth and transformation above all else.

This approach can be Initially challenging, and run counter to our instinct to hold on tightly to what we have, including our fears and insecurities. However, releasing attachment to the outcome opens up a plethora of possibilities. Detached from a fixed outcome, we gain the freedom to be fully present in the moment and establish a deeper connection with our partner.

Consider this: if you were convinced the world would end tomorrow, how would it influence your actions today? Similarly, if your boss suggested on Monday that payment on Friday might be uncertain, how would that affect your motivation to work for the remainder of the week, or would it influence your decision to work at all? I'm sure many of those reading this can remember all those grand plans for the last day of school back in the day.

When we fixate on hypothetical scenarios and potential outcomes, especially if fear-based and rooted in insecurity, it significantly shapes how we live and love in the present moment. Investing in the growth of your partnership can become challenging when consumed by such uncertainties. As you realize you've made irreversible choices based on false premises, you may begin to feel foolish and even regret them someday.

Consciously engaging in a partnership dynamic is the epitome of relationship intelligence. This form of intelligence, derived from conscious relating, lies in your ability to glean insights from every teachable experience and consistently apply mindfulness. Lessons acquired through self-reflection, shared exploration, and various educational models, such as emotional and social intelligence, combined with astrological or twin elemental frameworks, serve as powerful tools for achieving a supreme experience in love and relating.

Armed with this understanding, you become capable of catapulting yourself by design to attract experiences of a particular frequency in love and relating commonly unknown to the social majority. The ultimate enlightenment is realizing that a conscious relationship is an intelligent and intentional relationship with the potential to evolve into a Transcendent Relationship.

What is a Transcendent Relationship?

A transcendent relationship in essence is an ascension based relationship that surpasses the ordinary scope of physical human experience. A true power couple in every sense of the word, yet far from the Hollywood interpretation. It is a connection that goes deeper than touch, sound, and even personality, often transcending time and space. This connection delves into esoteric energy, a co-creation where two individuals become so intertwined that they operate virtually as one spirit on a telepathic resonance. A transcendent relationship is quite tantric and those involved pour into each other without being depleted. They value synchronicity over self sabotage. Have you ever felt the profound intimacy of sharing a psychic union with another person? A more significant question is, do you possess the willpower and tenacity to intentionally design and cultivate such a connection with another person?

When we embrace these extraordinary 'power team' relationships, we unlock a new level of intimacy, compassion, and love. Transcendent relationships, though rare, have the potential to alter the course of our lives permanently. These connections are marked by a profound sense of unity and understanding. Communication flows effortlessly, and the exchange of ideas feels natural. The **zone of proximal development** in alignment with **peak performances** together naturally evolves into an optimal experience, becoming a routine occurrence by default.

While we may struggle to articulate our feelings at times, the authenticity is undeniable. Transcendent relationships manifest as flow state connections, spanning across friendships, family bonds, or romantic partnerships. Whether they endure a lifetime or are curtailed abruptly by circumstances beyond our control, the impact of these unique connections is undeniably powerful. Moving beyond the realm of romance, these peak performance flow states are also evident in partnerships, such as those between teammates or entertainment duos, where exceptional chemistry leads to winning world-class awards.

In the world of transcendent connections, a graceful equilibrium of all twin elemental characteristics can manifest, with the dominant element taking the lead based on the energetic season. Through conscious relating guided by intelligent intentions, you gradually transcend barriers and dissolve blockages to intimacy and vulnerability.

In the romantic realm, the objective is to consistently nurture a '**perpetual tantric intimacy**,' regardless of the season or external circumstances. Whether you've been together for a short or extended period, irrespective of external stresses, the goal is to sustain **the lover's flow zone**—a state of surrender to a continuous and harmonious connection. This state can resemble New Relationship Energy or (N.R.E.) even years after the initial meeting.

Imagine a twin-planet union maintaining a lover's flow zone twenty years in. This state is not to be confused with the limerence and infatuation stages. It's simply the peak state of truly being in love without the interference of ego, attachment, or outcome but rather a pure connection of the souls. Such a connection arises when one can consistently cultivate a blissful experience akin to Kundalini rising within. This state is absolutely impossible when operating from a fear based consciousness.

When two individuals reach this level of love in their individual consciousness, sharing it with each other becomes an entirely different dimension of living nirvana. While one person consistently cultivating a controlled state of Kundalini is impressive, the synergy achieved when two individuals recycle and regenerate it amongst each other is on a different level altogether. It literally has the power to heal, not only spiritually or emotionally but also physically, as optimism and a positive emotional state have been shown to quicken wound healing and enhance immune function, thanks to a more robust immune response marked by higher levels of antibodies. This interplay between a positive outlook and physiological health is underscored by psychoneuroimmunology, which reveals how mental states directly impact physical health and healing processes, highlighting the profound connection between our psychological state and our physical well-being.

When both you and your partner have individually learned to raise your Kundalini energy, coupled with maintaining a mental space that perceives the world through the lens of tantric intimacy, the possibility emerges to remain in the lover's flow zone indefinitely. Together, you can circulate this energy, experiencing a natural high on a daily basis. Looking into the mirror, you witness the greatest version of yourself, ultimately manifesting as a self-fulfilling prophecy in real-time.

The most captivating aspect of all this is that it's a deliberate and conscious choice, not a random occurrence or a magical spectacle. Many of us have encountered fleeting moments of this state when falling in love under conditions reminiscent of twin flames. In fact, if you have ever fallen in love during a dream, you have tasted a fraction of the lucidity and brain chemistry present in this state. You wake up feeling a natural high that you hate to see fade.

Fortunately, you have the capability to cultivate and master this energy, akin to individuals dedicated to reaching their peak of self-actualization. Just as athletes achieve their objectives through sports and scholars through academics, you can also attain your aspirations in love and relational intelligence through deliberate practice and cultivation.

Becoming fully integrated and embracing unapologetic authenticity within the realm of pure love and attraction is the pathway to transcending your experience into a transcendent relationship. In essence, your relationship transforms into a vivid and dynamic transcendental meditation, capable of profoundly contributing to your ascension and inspiring those around you as you walk your journeys' together.

While these concepts may appear simple, they are not easily comprehended by the monkey mind. First and foremost, one must grasp that conscious relating begins with self-awareness. In short, "Know Thyself," as inscribed on the walls of the Temple of Luxor constructed by Amenhotep, and echoed at Apollo's temple in Delphi— a guiding principle for several millennia. To fully express ourselves to others, it is crucial to be conscious and accountable of our own thoughts and feelings. Only then can we authentically co-create an intimate communion with another highly conscious romantic counterpart.

It is considerably easier to attract a spiritually mature twin elemental who knows themselves when you, too, resonate in a spiritually mature space of self-awareness. In hindsight, if everything about you exudes chaos, confusion, and low magnetic attraction, then guess what? I would imagine I don't even have to say it, at this point, considering our discussions about reflections in the last few chapters. This self-awareness allows us to know what we need or want and effectively communicate those things honestly versus feeling selfishly slighted when we learn that our mates are not mind readers and have their own burdens and challenges to process.

Intentional communication might pose a challenge for some, but it's a prerequisite in conscious relating for maintaining a deeper connection with ourselves and those we love. Without this self-awareness, we risk behaving in ways that are not authentic when participating in relationships that are unhealthy and lack fulfillment. If we can not express our truth in a safe space, then is the union truly sustainable? Consider the shelf life or trajectory of such a situation.

I'm sure there are those who when reflecting on past relationships find themselves shaking their heads, wondering, "What was I thinking?" When we take the time to understand ourselves, we open the door to more intentional, conscious, and satisfying relationships with others. Though we try, one cannot be their true self and present an accurate representation without knowing who they truly are and what they genuinely need. Anything otherwise is experimentation and sustainable just long enough to learn more about who we are and what we need.

While some individuals recognize the shifting nature of their egos and masks, achieving a true understanding of themselves beyond external influences typically requires sustained and honest self-reflection over a prolonged period. This can sometimes necessitate a period of intentional aloneness, not to be confused with debilitating loneliness—even celibacy for some. For a spiritual aspirant pursuing a higher path, engaging in the Buddhist practice of complete silence called **Vipassana** for a while should be considered as it might be necessary.

Ultimately, experiencing a transcendent relationship starts with becoming self-integrated, authentic, and always relating from a space of total freedom. The late great Indian Mystic 'Osho' once said, "Love is authentic only when it gives freedom."

Contemplation: If I am living in confusion, chaos, repression, and misery, no matter what I say or project outwardly, you should under no circumstances expect freedom in love from me. Instead, brace yourself for a presentation of chaos and confusion, for that is the offering I am predisposed to deliver, possibly on a silver platter— as within, so without. If you recognize and still accept it, then take responsibility, as you are accountable for your choices. Avoid blaming your partner for their decisions; you can only guide yourself, not them. Cultivate the ability to identify red flags and potential trajectories to steer clear of future issues.

Another profound insight from the mystic, Osho, is his explanation of how we often unintentionally undermine each other's individuality instead of honoring it. Despite this, we expect contentment and fulfillment as a reward for our actions. True love, he emphasizes, is genuine only when it refrains from intruding on the other person's privacy. It respects their individuality and solitude.

When mentioning privacy, it extends beyond journals, emails, and cell phones to include a person's dreams, memories, and private thoughts. These aspects are not possessions for partners to regulate or control. This individuality deserves not only respect but also a lack of judgment or shame within the sacred space of a loving relationship.

Certain individuals, however, may grapple with discomfort when confronted by aspects of their partner's past. For example, coming across a photo from years ago might trigger insecurities, prompting questions about whether a prior connection brought greater happiness or surpassed the current one. Indeed, individuality and privacy encompass more than just the tangible aspects of someone's personal domain; emotions, memories, and experiences are also part of this distinct path.

In a healthy relationship, it's essential to understand that each person has a unique history, and acknowledging this doesn't diminish the value of the current connection. Trust and respect play pivotal roles in navigating such situations, allowing each partner the space to have had a past without compromising the present. The efforts of today's lovers are that nothing should be private; all secrets should be told without first earning this trust. Also, reciprocation is generally unnecessary. For today's lovers are your lord and saviors, and their insecurity is law, less you are prepared to endure gaslighting.

Consider this: Was a lovers unique charisma and energy not what drew you to them initially? If that magnetism was attractive at the beginning, why suppress it and make it dormant after winning their heart? This approach can seem manipulative, dishonest, and akin to betrayal.

Once the heart is captured, the expectation is for it to remain in a state of eternal stasis. The bliss should remain as pristine as it was on the first day of limerence and preserved like the art of taxidermy. Modern lovers tend to fear individuality, and thus, the expectation is for it to be sacrificed like a virgin to the volcano for a prosperous harvest, and so on. For some individuals, the prospect of individual growth signifies change, and change can be fear-inducing as it may entail a perceived loss of control. The initial fantasy shared becomes the sole reality embraced; anything less is deemed deceitful, echoing the sentiments, "You're a liar, and a cheat, and I don't want ya." so dramatically exclaimed, quivering lip and all, by the character Katherine Jackson, portrayed by Angela Bassett in the film "The American Dream".

Over time, one comes to understand that anything real is in a constant state of change. Think of a rose: its beauty and admiration stem from its ability to grow freely. The moment you attempt to isolate, own, and arrest its development by picking and displaying it in a vase, you set in motion its untimely and degenerate death. Simply admiring it in its freedom allows it to continue growing and presenting its beauty, even sewing seeds for more generations of its beauty as its source intended.

Unfortunately, In many marriages, the dynamic between partners is still rooted in a sense of ownership. Recently, I had a conversation with my beautiful, kind, and loving life partner about the terms "husband" and "wife." Upon examining the definitions, I found language such as *"master"* of the household and *"serve"* the husband. The use of terms like servitude and mastery over another reflects an outdated paradigm that can be misleading to an unconscious mind.

While we should all strive to master ourselves so that we can live in service to our higher purposes as well as our communities and loved ones, we should guard against the slave love paradigm of ownership, control, and possession of our lover or partner. If your partner says, "you belong to me," run for the hills because should you find yourself in a past life regression, you may learn that you really did belong to them somewhere in a cotton field or a gladiator arena once upon a time. **Freedom in love and relating is absolutely paramount.** In friendships, unlike in romantic relationships, there is little tolerance for restrictions on freedom within the relating dynamic.

Entropic Relating

The term "entropic relating," as defined in this work, explores the gradual yet natural decline or degradation of a relationship as the points of connection within it become increasingly disordered. This concept, which can also be called "relational entropy," captures how relationships can deteriorate over time without consistent efforts to maintain order and clarity in communication and expectations.

The energy experienced on the first day of a relationship is markedly different from that on the 100th day. Initially, there is a sense of order and alignment regarding ideas, but as time passes and the relationship encounters various events and new ideas—both positive and negative—this structure fundamentally changes. Essentially, the original order becomes disrupted or disordered, leading to a new, evolved state of complexity in the relationship.

As relational entropy increases, misunderstandings and conflicts may become more frequent, and the overall quality of the relationship may decline. This phenomenon can be observed in various relating types, including personal, professional, and social interactions. The concept draws on the metaphor of physical and information entropy, suggesting that just as systems in nature tend toward disorder without energy input, relationships too require continual investments of energy (such as communication, empathy, and shared experiences) to maintain their structure and function effectively, otherwise due to the law of entropy, they will naturally decline. Love and attraction alone will not maintain the life force of any relationship.

In physics, entropy is a measure of disorder or randomness within a system, crucial for understanding why certain physical processes occur in one direction and not the other. For example, ice melts and cream in coffee disperses because these processes increase entropy, representing what seems to be a disordered state. The concept of entropy can be illustrated by considering the probability distribution of energy in a system. With energy stored, there are many possible ways, known as micro states, that this energy can be distributed.

Systems naturally evolve towards the configuration with the highest number of microstates, which corresponds to the highest entropy. In essence, entropy is not just about disorder; it's about the spread of energy within a system and its likelihood. This statistical likelihood drives spontaneous and natural processes, such as spiderwebs and dust accumulation in an old house—a fitting description for some relationships that are currently experiencing relational entropy. Overall, entropy is fundamental in physics and is often referred to as time's arrow, expressed as a trajectory, signifying the irreversible nature of these energy-spreading processes.

Relational entropy mirrors physical entropy, where the microstates within a relationship—fueled by either compulsive or conscious energies—can lead to vastly different trajectories. Like physical processes where energies compound over time, relationships too can follow a path toward what could be termed an 'entropic death,' a gradual descent into disorder and dysfunction. It's therefore essential to cultivate each interaction with intention and conscious action. Infusing these microstates with positive, vibrant energy can pivot relationships away from decay and the loss of momentum, toward flourishing, dynamic connections. This proactive nurturing not only prevents breakdowns but actively enhances the vitality and longevity of our relationships.

A valuable exercise would be to take a moment now to reflect on your past interpersonal relationships, including platonic ones. Try to identify specific microstates that contributed to increasing disorder, ultimately leading to their dissolution. This reflection can offer deep insights into the dynamics of entropic relating.

In the following sections, I will introduce a variety of tools and insights aimed at enhancing sustainability in worthy partnerships. These practical strategies are crafted to nurture and maintain a fulfilling and enduring relationship.

Retention Celibacy & Touchless Orgasms

(Beneficial and high level tools in transcendent relationships)

Evolution is the name of the game, and conscious relating, with its mindful and intentional methods, has given rise to various lifestyle practices, one of which I've termed "Retention Celibacy." This counterculture alternates between phases of semen retention, where men intentionally avoid ejaculation during sexual activity through restraint or injaculation, and periods of complete celibacy. While primarily practiced by men, the benefits extend to both males and females. This practice is often adopted for health or personal growth reasons and allows for sexual engagement without ejaculation.

Incorporating the term "celibacy" highlights a commitment to discipline within this practice, drawing a parallel to the rigors of traditional celibacy. However, retention celibacy takes a unique approach by intermittently allowing individuals to harness and direct their sexual energy through semen retention, instead of completely abstaining from all sexual aspects, mental and otherwise.

Practitioners of retention celibacy as a lifestyle often describe the physical and mental benefits of semen retention as "Raw Power." They employ various tools, including meditation, breathwork, intermittent fasting, specific superfoods and supplements, as well as consistent, low intensity or calisthenic exercise regiment's, among other methods, to cultivate this power and maintain their discipline.

The emphasis is on the physical and mental superiority advantages of semen retention, rather than adhering to any specific religious or spiritual tradition. oftentimes, for the purpose of regaining mental clarity, individuals chose to practice actual celibacy for a season, allowing them to refocus and strengthen their resolve. This involves abstaining from all things and thoughts of a sexual nature, including the soft porn prevalent on today's social media timelines, often masked as a form of freedom of expression. There is a belief that a man who lacks self-control does not merit respect.

Retention celibacy offers a structured approach that allows individuals to partake in ethical and healthy sexual activity while intentionally abstaining periodically. This unique aspect differentiates retention celibacy from other practices. Adherents believe that through purposeful sexual engagement, they access a potent source of energy, fueling physical and mental vitality, sparking creativity, and bolstering overall health. The distinction between semen retention and retention celibacy lies in their duration and purpose.

Certain individuals extend these practices by adopting a more rigorous form of spiritual discipline within the context of retention celibacy. This form involves abstaining from sexual activity and retaining seminal fluid to produce what is cryptically referred to as "Christ oil." In esoteric circles, this term is linked to concepts like the "Sacred Secretion" or "Christmas cheer," symbolizing a speculated substance, possibly cerebrospinal fluid. Believers assert that mastering and cultivating this fluid can activate the pineal gland, leading to spiritual enlightenment and transformative experiences, along with benefits such as heightened vitality and bodily rejuvenation.

In addition, It is allegedly believed that coupling this practice with the intake of supplements like Vitamin K2, in the forms of MK-4 and MK-7—previously known as Activator X—facilitates the transfer of calcium from the pineal gland to its appropriate destinations, such as the bones, effectively assisting with glandular decalcification. This is thought to significantly enhance pineal gland function and christ oil mechanics.

The difference between basic semen retention and retention celibacy is that the former is a singular practice, while the latter encompasses a lifestyle. Retention celibacy merges both celibacy and semen retention, with the caveat that it also incorporates a myriad of health and spiritual practices for an overall evolution of being.

Pursuit of retention celibacy is grounded in the conviction that abstaining from conventional physical intimacy redirects energies inward, fostering heightened spiritual awareness. "Christ oil" becomes a metaphorical key unlocking the potential within the human body, offering a unique path to spiritual enlightenment and a profound connection to the divine. Practitioners believe that understanding and harnessing this sacred fluid can unlock the full spectrum of human potential, driving them on a journey of self-discovery and transformation.

When practiced with a non-processed, plant-based, living foods lifestyle, "raw power" becomes an understatement, but that's a discussion for another time. Just a heads up, though – if you naturally find yourself doing vertical handstand pushups on your knuckles a couple of hundred times a day and don't know why, don't say I didn't warn you, raw energy is just the beginning. Achieving any of these goals demands discipline and isn't for the faint of heart.

I would imagine you've heard the saying, ' less is more, or a little can go a long way'? Seemingly small lifestyle changes compounds to grow immense inner wealth, subtlety wielding immense power through seemingly minor but deeply impactful actions. Consider silence in a heated debate: a strategic pause can give weight to words, allowing the message to resonate more profoundly with the audience. In fitness, low-impact workouts like yoga or pilates highlight that gentleness and consistency can improve health effectively, possibly adding strength filled decades to your life.

Likewise, subtle facial expressions or gestures, such as a slight nod or smile, can communicate a spectrum of affirmative cues that verbal communication often cannot. Each of these examples underscores the profound influence subtlety holds in shaping outcomes across different aspects of life. Subtlety can be a path to superiority and self mastery. In the words of Leonardo da Vinci, "Simplicity is the ultimate sophistication.".

For some however, inaction, is not that simple. Retention celibacy represents a lifelong commitment to intentionally refrain from common sexual activities, with each engagement being purposeful and deliberate. Exceptions arise only during conscious attempts to procreate or in controlled activities without seed release. This intentional lifestyle extends across an individual's entire existence, with procreation periods thoughtfully planned based on partners' reproductive cycles and preferred astrological conditions.

With distinct lesson found in the polyamorously celibate relating method, this practice may, at times, incorporate hypnosis for those facing discipline challenges. The emphasis remains on a purposeful and conscious approach to intimate engagements, blending intentionality with streamlined discipline.

A core benefit of retention celibacy is that it fosters an increased sensitivity to a partner's needs, allowing individuals to direct and enhance orgasmic energy. This increased sensitivity can evolve into nuanced orgasmic practices, including touchless and full-body orgasms, where intense pleasure and release are achieved without physical stimulation. The intentional focus on cultivating raw power through retention celibacy, coupled with the deepening of the sexual connection with a partner, fosters an overall sense of evolution and well-being. It also facilitates a profound understanding of oneself and the transformative power embedded within one's understanding of sexuality and it's spiritual potency.

Reflecting on heightened awareness and energy sensitivity brings to mind my friend Iyabode from my early 20s, who shared intriguing tales of her older boyfriend guiding her to orgasm through meditation—a concept that has captivated me ever since. Years later, I found myself immersed in a captivating and exceptionally lucid dream where I experienced intense, full-body orgasms while creating unique musical scales infused with vibrant colors. In this vivid dream, the orgasmic intensity heightened with each rise of every octave, permeating every cell in my body, leaving a lasting impression on me.

It wasn't until I encountered a teacher named Shantam Nityama, who had studied under Osho and studied a man by the name of Vitvan, founder of the school of nature, that I delved deeper into understanding and intentionally channeling this profound energy. The dream's resonance stayed with me, becoming a key part of my exploration into the intentional cultivation and direction of energy—a journey that has connected me with ancient wisdom and practices, enriching my understanding of the transformative potential within.

The revelation of subtle energy in the body aligns with the long-standing recognition in traditional Chinese medicine of meridian points or acupoints. For centuries, practices like acupressure and acupuncture have been globally embraced for manipulating these subtle energies to promote healing and balance within the body. This ancient wisdom underscores the interconnectedness of the body's energetic pathways and their influence on overall well-being.

While my formal introduction to the sciences of energetic orgasms came through the Ifa practiced Tantric Mongoose Shantam Nityama, I embarked on a quest to broaden my understanding of the subject. Subsequently, I sought diverse teachers to expand my understanding of this subject.

Touchless orgasms, also termed energy orgasms, transcend traditional genital stimulation, manifesting as non-genital or full-body experiences achieved through methods like focused breathing, meditation, or tantric techniques. These climaxes, devoid of direct physical contact, involve manipulating psychic sexual energy circulating throughout the body, moving beyond the typical emphasis common body arousal. Through the practice of conscious relating, guided by twin elemental insights and the heightened sensitivity acquired from retention celibacy, one can learn to initiate electro-meridian orgasmic sensations that surpass basic and temporary arousal—and can even occur remotely.

Whether self-directed or guided by a skilled practitioner, touchless orgasms unfolds without the need for physical touch. Linked closely to meditation and mindfulness practices, they entail a focus on internal energy flow, described by some as waves of intense pleasure and release, absent any accompanying physical sensations. They can manifest with the lucid intensity of nocturnal emissions—also known as wet dreams.

Both energy orgasms and touchless orgasms align with aspects of tantra and mindful sexual practices, emphasizing the intricate connections between the mind, body, and spirit. Engaging in such practices enables individuals to heighten their awareness and sensitivity to internal energy and their partner's energy. While not universally experienced, for those capable of attaining them, these types of orgasms provide a potent and transformative exploration of the profound connections between physical and energetic realms.

In the practice of relationship alchemy, making subtle decisions to optimize your energetic body is one approach. However, what should you do when your energy has completely depleted, leaving no emotional moisture to lubricate the mechanisms of your positive relational experiences? In that dark place where relational entropy takes hold, eroding the foundations of trust or intimacy, what can one do to navigate these tumultuous circumstances? When it seems all vitality has been drained, consider the rejuvenation and recovery strategies in the next section to restore the emotional reservoirs that fuel healthy and constructive interactions.

Romantic Piggy Backing: *A practical approach*

Love and romance are dynamic concepts that require intentional effort to maintain over time, particularly in long-term relationships. While the initial spark of romance may be easier to ignite, as people's needs and desires change over time, keeping the romance alive can be challenging. When the frequency of romantic resonance decreases, some people may look for excitement outside their relationship, while others suffer in silence. Most people, however, will always desire a deep emotional connection with their partner and need romantic validation. For these individuals, aspects of conscious relating can be an effective tool in reigniting romance through various channels.

Conscious relating involves being hyper-aware of each other's emotional needs and nurturing intentional experiences to deepen the emotional bond. The hyper-awareness developed through your conscious relating style can serve as a roadmap in your relationship, indicating when an emotional amplifier is needed. This can help couples stay connected on a deeper level of intimacy, maintaining passion and the spark of romance.

Maintaining love and romance in long-term relationships is a common experience. As couples settle into routines and face life's stressors, such as work stress and the demands of raising a family, they may find it challenging to prioritize intimacy and romance. To address this, a solution known as romantic piggybacking on an emotional trojan is proposed. This approach aims to shift chemistry away from a deficit state, allowing complex emotions to piggyback on physical sensations through **embodied cognition**.

In the concept of romantic piggybacking, or "**RPB**," models of embodied cognition are utilized to enhance the emotional bond between partners. Embodied cognition suggests that our thoughts and emotions are not just abstract mental states but are intricately connected to our physical experiences. A tangible example of this connection is evident when we undergo a physical sensation, such as a warm hug, which prompts our bodies to respond by triggering corresponding emotions like feelings of comfort and safety. By applying the principles of embodied cognition, couples can infuse romance and emotional connection into their long-term relationships.

Scientific research highlights the profound impact of facial expressions on our mood, revealing that even forced smiles can subtly contribute to a positive mental state. For example, the act of smiling involves the activation of facial muscles that send neural signals to the brain and nervous system. This process has the potential to influence an overall sense of well-being. Furthermore, smiling has social implications, as it can elicit positive responses from others, fostering a reciprocal exchange of mirrored positive emotions.

This understanding underscores the inherent advantages of smiling, emphasizing its potential to contribute positively to both psychological and physiological well-being, regardless of its genuineness. Inherently, the reverse technicality holds an advantageous position by default. Positive physical sensations, particularly those derived from engaging in enjoyable activities, possess the capacity to induce corresponding positive emotions such as happiness and excitement. These positive emotions can intertwine and reinforce each other, **forming a reciprocal cycle or feedback loop that amplifies** the overall positive experience. When these uplifting feelings are shared with a partner, they become instrumental in reigniting romance and affection within the relationship.

In essence, physical sensations act as a "Trojan horse," surreptitiously introducing intimate feelings by bypassing conscious thought processes and directly influencing emotions and behavior. Through the shared experience of physical sensations with a significant other, regardless of the relationship's recent state, it becomes possible to reactivate shared neural circuits, contributing to the renewal of romance and emotional connection.

Through shared experiences that evoke the brains love and attraction chemicals, various activities promoting happiness and pleasure serve as catalysts for transmuting shared joy into intimacy. These experiences encompass a spectrum of activities, such as dancing, embarking on a cruise, practicing yoga and meditation together, hiking together, attending live music events, or participating in sip and paint sessions. As a conscious relating practitioner, determining the frequency of such experiences becomes your responsibility to achieve your desired goals and outcomes.

Shared experiences possess the transformative power to create new memories and fortify the emotional connection between partners. As couples engage in activities that bring them joy and pleasure, they release neurotransmitters like dopamine and oxytocin, associated with love and attraction. These chemicals play a crucial role in reigniting feelings that may have waned over time, rekindling the flame of intimacy between partners and evoking comparable moods reminiscent of earlier limerent stages in their relationship.

Success levels are directly influenced by the commitment and frequency of shared experiences, in conjunction with the recipient's openness to receive. This, however, is contingent on availability, recognizing that some may be constrained by factors such as time, space, energy, finances, or creativity.

Cultivating a mindset of giving without any expectation or desire for reciprocation is paramount. Embracing selfless generosity unlocks the true power of romantic piggybacking, fostering genuine connection and an enriching experience. The beauty lies in the inherent value of service and the act of giving, rather than seeking something in return.

The belief that "if you can change the mood, you can change the mind" is a popular maxim in the field of hypnosis. The idea is that by changing a person's emotional state, you can also alter their thoughts, beliefs, and behaviors. This is because emotions and the mind are interconnected and can influence each other. For example, the euphoric mood generated from falling in love with the countryside of Paris or embarking on a road trip through the redwood forest in Northern California can evoke a rapturous ambience. Subsequently, shared feelings of excitement, awe, and wonder can activate shared neural circuits associated with falling in love. Yet what do you give someone who has it all and has seen it all. The experience and what it evokes for the individuals is what is important without the triggering of less desirable thoughts, attitudes, and experiences. Under no circumstances should you approach the pursuit burdened with baggage, and if your counterpart carries substantial baggage, you may want to consider cutting your losses.

When a stream of nostalgic feelings are experienced together, they can provide a powerful foundation on which to build a torrent of emotionally satisfying relating. This can be especially beneficial for couples who may be experiencing a "dry spell" in their relationship, as it can provide a new source of limerent chemistry. Studies have shown that shared experiences of high emotions can have a significant impact on a couple's emotional and intimate connection. Research in the field of neuropsychology has found that emotions and experiences are closely linked in the brain and that shared experiences can activate shared neural circuits associated with love, attraction, and most importantly, arousal.

The caveat is that one must be willing to engage in a prolonged commitment, which may require planning, organization, and intentionality. Essentially, it's like an ultra-extended honeymoon or date with your lover. It should not come as a surprise, but as classic car enthusiasts know, starting up an old engine may take a few tries to get the motor running. However, once it's cranked up, it will purr like a kitten.

Sex is widely recognized as a mental and emotional experience where the process of arousal often begins well before the bedroom. For example, a study published in the journal "Social Cognitive and Affective Neuroscience" found that couples who participate in activities that bring them intense joy, excitement, and happiness experience increased intimacy and sexual desire.

The study indicates that shared experiences of intense emotions can stimulate the brain's reward system, enhancing the release of pleasure-inducing chemicals like dopamine and oxytocin. Likewise, studies published in the "Journal of Sex Research" show that engaging in new and thrilling activities together boosts couples' sexual arousal and satisfaction. These activities heighten emotional states, activating the brain's reward pathways and amplifying feelings of desire and attraction.

It's unfortunate that some individuals treat sex like a microwave dinner, lacking the depth of a meal made with love, patience, and seasonings. Others attempt to infuse more meaning, viewing it as at least something that takes a little longer in the air fryer. However, even this approach can eventually lose its novelty. Within consciously relating couples exchanges, floreplay is not merely a practice but an organic lifestyle. Each action is intentional and fueled by love, derived from a nurtured self-love that naturally radiates. Together, these partners embody lifestyles reminiscent of full-body peak state arousal.

While considerably taboo and certainly a walk on the wild side, some couples in today's modern world choose to introduce a third person into their sexual relationship as a way to piggyback and reignite the passion in the bedroom. Some experts suggest that this can create a sense of novelty and excitement, breaking up sexual routines and rejuvenating a couple's sexual energy. Additionally, some couples may be interested in exploring new sexual experiences, experimenting with different sexual dynamics, or pushing the boundaries of their comfort zones.

Whatever your motivations may be, whether something as taboo as threesomes or as serene and simplistic as a surprise picnic, consciously cultivating intimate moments—centered on environmental and physical sensations—can be a powerful way to connect with your soulmate, strengthen your relationship, and reinvigorate passion and intimacy.

Romantic piggybacking can be viewed as an extended form of " prolonged environmental foreplay," creating a **powerful feedback loop** and **cycle of emotional reinforcement**. By employing this technique, consciously relating couples have the potential to enhance their intimate and sexual connection. Through the strategic use of shared experiences that evoke high emotions, they can build a satisfying and more fulfilling romantic relationship.

A Living Sacrifice

Question: Have you ever felt like you couldn't be yourself around someone? Perhaps you had to wear a mask and adopt a persona that wasn't genuinely you, just to meet someone else's expectations. If so, rest assured, you're not alone. It's a common scenario where many of us suppress our authentic selves, molding into shapes that please others but leave us unrecognizable to ourselves. In this process, our original goals and dreams often take a backseat.

Regrettably, the game of conformity can potentially give rise to feelings of oppression and frustration, turning relationships into confining spaces resembling prison cells. The harsh reality emerges that, when playing this game, individuals unwittingly assume the role of their own jailers. A sacrifice occurs, in which self-neglect is offered up to your occasionally narcissistic lord and savior, and ruler of your heart. This act becomes a desperate plea to gain their elusive blessings, with your life force serving as the altar and the power you've voluntarily relinquished becoming the sacrifice.

In their respective renditions, Screamin' Jay Hawkins and Nina Simone aptly portrayed the essence of the ritual in the song "I Put a Spell on You - Because You're Mine,"

I was recently told that an elderly woman at a bus stop shared a piece of wisdom: people choose partners based on their level of self-esteem. I must admit, I find it hard to argue with that insight.

It's no secret that **people love at their level of consciousness.** This suggest that people will love someone or something based on their own emotional profile and current worldview. If you are operating at a high level of consciousness, you will be able to see the best in people, and they will reflect that back to you. On the other hand, if you are operating at a low level of consciousness, you will see the worst in people, and they will reflect that back to you as well.

Unconsciously, we often find ourselves mimicking those around us, a phenomenon referred to as "the chameleon effect," and resemblant of mirror theory. This effect is the automatic imitation of others' behavior in our social environment, resulting in subtle and unintentional shifts in our own conduct, such as adopting similar postures, mannerisms, or facial expressions. Notably, when we choose to focus on either the negative or positive aspects of someone, they tend to reciprocate with mirrored behavior.

The axiom, *"energy flows where attention goes,"* vividly illustrates how our conscious vibrations shape the dynamics of our interpersonal relationships. For instance, if we've been conditioned to assert dominance and possession over our partners from an early age, influenced by the examples in our environment, this inclination becomes evident in our actions, as our expressions of love reflect our prevailing level of consciousness. If an individual was raised in victim mode, their consciousness will reflect that and that is where they will love from.

This assertion implies that, if the individuals who shaped your upbringing were engaged in compulsive behaviors, such as frequent arguments and fights, and you were consistently exposed to such behaviors, reinforced by captivating affirmations in, for instance, radio music, these influences could significantly mold your behavior and perspectives. Consequently, this would impact your overall approach to life and shape the way you engage with others. The energetic patterns embedded in your approach to relationships will ultimately set a course leading to a torrent of unfulfilled and failed relationships.

Consider the influence of your worldview regarding your level of consciousness in the context of your love style. Think of primitive belief systems that may have originated in the minds of hunter-gatherer primates or religious zealots from 1500 years ago. Consider how the, "Me Tarzan – You Jane" mentalities, and archaic notions such as the inferiority woman or people of color, for example, are outdated belief systems. Yet, for many individuals, these beliefs run just under the surface yet parallel to their conscious processing in relationships, evident in the behaviors they enact.

Take into account how historical beliefs once unquestionably positioned the Earth as the center of the universe. How soon do we forget that Galileo faced imprisonment for challenging this notion and asserting that the Earth revolved around the sun. Primitive belief systems can, at times, obscure common sense. Outdated belief systems might impose rigid rules that hinder conscious action, promoting an approach of "ask no questions and do what I say." Such rigid and ignorant beliefs have the potential to dismantle divine love and disrupt the harmony of a beautiful family. This cycle of ignorance and compulsion can result in the suffering of children, perpetuating a harmful pattern when they, in turn, become parents.

The influence of groupthink and peer pressure, ingrained before you could even speak, undoubtedly shapes your worldview and level of consciousness in the context of how you express love and or interpersonal connection. What makes this peculiar is that these beliefs often contradict our genuine feelings and latent desires. Many individuals suppress natural inclinations simply to align with certain beliefs.

For example, despite a natural inclination to be kind and show favor to all people, specific beliefs may restrict individuals from extending kindness to the opposite gender when married. This sometimes leads to avoiding eye contact with others, a behavior motivated by the fear of reckless eyeballing, a concept from both the antebellum South and pimp culture.

In these situations, much like a pot of boiling water, pressure builds up, creating a need for release. This compels individuals to act dishonorably and sneakily, giving rise to betrayal driven by the fear of shame. Unfortunately, many couples find it challenging to be their authentic selves or engage in honest conversations about their experiences without the fear of judgment and shame, preventing the open expression of natural feelings, such as the desire for honorable and healthy social connections.

Despite being commonly overlooked, it's essential to recognize that when two individuals come together in a relationship, they bring along all their wounds, pain, negative beliefs, and baggage from the past. Often, there isn't sufficient time dedicated to processing and healing from past misunderstandings.

This baggage might originate from experiences in the current lifetime or even previous ones. It could encompass ongoing issues with family and friends or unresolved childhood trauma. While it's nearly impossible to completely avoid these triggers, conscious couples are aware of them and understand that they will inevitably surface at some point.

Put differently, both individuals may encounter sporadic emotions such as insecurity, rejection, or feelings of being ignored when engaging in intimate or non romantic relationships. Maintaining a heightened awareness and understanding that these emotions are integral to the human experience allows for no surprises, fostering mindful preparedness and empathetic acceptance. These potent concepts elevate awareness in conscious relating.

Instead of attempting to ignore or suppress these feelings, conscious couples possess an intuitive sense of when to anticipate them. This enables them to navigate these emotions together with empathy, understanding, and the intention to transmute the energy for a more sustainable and positive outcome by default.

To **remain cognizant that you are not in a competition** but on the same team requires conscious effort and, in some cases, a deliberate reminder. Arguments have no winners or losers, and no one should compete to get one up on the other. Engaging in such behavior is counterproductive and generally experienced between enemies or opponents.

Picture players on the same championship basketball team bickering throughout the game while the title is on the line or two soldiers behind enemy lines quarreling while in the line of fire. How can any of them achieve their goals or attain success when they are focused on competing against each other instead of the common objective? The overall objective in this context is to consistently recognize that it is never me against you, but me and you against the problem—seeking a solution for the win.

Maintaining awareness and exercising self-control in romantic relationships can be a challenging and painful process for some. However, it ultimately leads to a more robust and resilient relationship for those mature enough to recognize when growth or healing is needed. This approach should be cultivated and practiced diligently, especially when two or more people have partnered to pursue common purposes and goals.

It is an unfortunate truth, but **many individuals are pathologically locked in their inner child**, allowing the hyper emotional and disorganized aspects to take the helm and steer their ship. This is evident when individuals, old enough to be grandparents, engage in full-blown temper tantrums reminiscent of those they scold their own grandchildren for. Road rage provides a humorous yet relatable example, as even adults can succumb to uncontrolled emotional outbursts, particularly in the chaos of mid-day traffic alongside fellow adulting children. While occasional lapses into the inner child are common, consistent behavior from this standpoint indicates a reliance on adolescent coping mechanisms.

I assure you, it is entirely possible to identify instances all around you that are laden with behavioral undertones stemming from the psychology of the inner child. Individuals entrenched in their inner child or operating as an unconscious adult may find themselves inadvertently triggered, responding to adversity with a juvenile perspective. This also underscores the involvement of the three ego states in most interactions.

Such triggers may have medical roots, such as Attention Deficit Hyperactivity Disorder (ADHD), or virtual autism known as screen based autism, and may even stem from personality disorders like Narcissism. However, more commonly, these triggers are linked to experiences of abandonment, guilt, shame, blame, betrayal, trauma, regrets, loss of control, feelings of inadequacy, or excessive invalidation, to name a few. As discussed in a previous chapter, attachment styles further contribute to this extensive list

No doubt, people will always feel they need their perspectives affirmed and validated by others and will defend their beliefs even if the compulsions supporting the belief were created and maintained from an early age. In retrospect, envision a reality where you no longer crave external validation, not even from your significant other. Envision a state where you validate your own existence, cross-referencing your perspectives with your innate intelligence. Picture yourself in a relating with an open-minded, individuals who've earned your trust through consistent actions, providing a secure and judgment-free safe space for expression.

Imagine appreciating the feedback received without being attached to the outcome, while operating from a mindset of abundance. Picture possessing a self-affirming energy cultivated over time, ensuring you never show up emotionally starving or needy. Consider having put in the necessary work and daily ritual with evolved partners and friends to identify and address your triggers. Imagine commencing the healing process for wounds inflicted on your inner child, liberating yourself from reactionary patterns and fostering personal growth and transformation.

Imagine a scenario where, instead of reacting impulsively, you proactively began to take preliminary and preemptive conscious actions toward relating and reflecting with the intention of practicing relationship intelligence.

When we are triggered into a childlike reaction-based belief pattern, we subsequently self-project fear, insecurity, blame, and judgment. We place the full burden of responsibility on our unsuspecting partners, rarely accepting any accountability. In the presence of terms like **"safespace," "accountability," and "healing,"** an inner child-like mindset may mock or dismiss them as overly soft or inconsequential. Yet, this dismissal often occurs without acknowledging the profound collateral losses experienced in numerous failed relating encounters as well as general life experiences.

Further assessment reveals that while we may not choose partners with a master's degree in psychology, we often expect them to handle all our inner issues as if they were professional psychologists. Unfortunately, this can lead to treating them more like employees on our payroll, where failing to meet our expectations puts them in the precarious position of constantly walking on thin ice.

It is selfish and unfair to place the entire responsibility for your happiness on a partner. Expecting them to remedy a lifetime of trauma is not only apathetic, inconsiderate, and insensitive but also self-centered, egotistical, and, one might say, borderline narcissistic. Particularly when an individual enters a partnership with someone who they believed they could be vulnerable with, feel safe and protected by, and whose made a passionate display to wholeheartedly go all in.

Sometimes, it's not until it's too late that you grasp you've been duped, deceived, and bamboozled by Beelzebub, Satan, ole slew foot—commonly known as the Devil. This realization often hits when you unwittingly find yourself playing a role in co-creating a hellish state. By the time you realize that you've been party to this unfortunate situation, you could be three children in, facing a quarter-million dollars in debt, not to mention a missing decade of your life and wrestling with a couple of unhealthy dependency habits.

The compulsive need for control, mirroring the behavior of a selfish child on the brink of a meltdown and subsequently resorting to negative coping mechanisms, is not only unattractive but also detrimental to adults on the journey of self-discovery, growth, and evolution. Reflect on that again: An insatiable desire for control, resembling a petulant child about to throw a tantrum, is not just unappealing but also obstructive for individuals dedicated to their personal development and spiritual advancement.

Co-existing in such a co-creative hellish state results from A fear, lack, and scarcity-based reality vs. A love, growth, possibility, and abundance-based reality. The two can not coincide harmoniously; That is to say, they can not exist in the same space at the same time - it's against the laws of "psycho-emotional" physics.

When consciously relating with intelligent intention, a couple will find themselves more willing to confront challenges and difficulties as within adult ego states vs. neglect or hide from them as a fear based child ego state. They recognize the potential for transformation by addressing underlying belief systems. They acknowledge that dysfunctional patterns dissolve only when each person assumes full responsibility for their role. It's a demanding task, but a necessary one for those committed to a healthier, more expansive reality.

Take note that a single response holds the power to transmute the alchemy of an entire conversation, **either reinforcing dysfunction** or **promoting awareness**. Consider that statement for a moment and ask yourself, what does it truly mean? Taking accountability for our contribution to dysfunction, is a crucial initial step in conscious relating within our romantic, platonic and transactional partnerships. True change begins when we recognize and acknowledge these patterns, demanding sincere self-reflection and candid conversations. Both partners must be willing and committed to this process, but the rewards are infinite.

When we can let go of past unhealthy behaviors and move forward with intention, we open up the possibility for a more deeply fulfilling and tantric connection within our relationships. The consciously relating couple understands that this is an ongoing process and that there will literally always be new challenges to face, however, they remain enthusiastically committed to growth and evolution.

Consciously relating couples understand that facing real-world challenges is an inherent and unavoidable aspect of any relating dynamic. They meet these challenges with readiness, recognizing that sharing space with another person demands effort and communication. When confronting difficulties head-on, they bring awareness and a mutual dedication to personal and collective growth.

This mindset allows for navigating a **relating**-*ship* with increased ease and understanding. It becomes understood that the outcome can be deeply fulfilling, potentially reaching a **transcendent level** connection. These actions contribute to the evolution of humanity, gradually elevating the vibrations of the entire planet Earth. This is why conscious relating is not just beneficial but *NECESSARY!*

As you integrate the insights, wisdom, and experiences from this journey, you empower yourself to relate with greater intelligence. By embracing the enlightening modalities outlined in this book, you develop the ability to recognize soulmate energy and discern the essential characteristics that foster an optimal intimate partnership, encompassing high vibrational love. Through accumulated experience and wisdom, you'll naturally attract relationships characterized by quality rather than mere quantity, shifting from temporary gratification to enduring and meaningful connections with transformative vitality. Always remember, love stands as the fuel and driving force behind all creation.

In light of this, it's important to recognize that the terms "couple" and "relationship" do not exclusively pertain to romantic or sexual connections. Consistently associating these concepts with such contexts is a sign of immaturity. Elevate your spiritual consciousness to understand and appreciate the broader spectrum of relationships beyond these confines.

By consciously creating space for love with pure, unselfish intentions, you reclaim your power from the unconscious and compulsive inner child. This process allows you to rediscover freedom, comfort, intimacy, security, and sexuality within romantic love, as well as fostering a similar depth of love for humanity at large. Your actions become mindful and gentle, and as a result, you naturally draw in those who reciprocate the same mindfulness and tenderness. The dynamic between lovers and partnerships transform; there is no longer a sense of competition. Instead, the focus shifts, and the primary goal becomes the cultivation of divine connection.

Can you see the difference?

In example 1. The driving force is competition. (argumentative).

In example 2. Connection is the driving force. (mutual understanding).

As you progress, You'll eventually find yourselves naturally **cultivating soul integration** rooted in source love. In this state, you'll observe a heightened interest in nurturing open communication devoid of judgment, and your primary objective becomes understanding. The cultivation of awareness and presence evolves into a daily habit. Above all, you master the art of cultivating the greatest gift—total authenticity.

CODEPENDENCY

Compulsive relating manifest in various forms, with one particularly debilitating cycle being codependency. Codependency in relationships can ensnare an individual, making them rely on their partner for emotional and psychological well-being, impacting their autonomy, self-esteem, and sense of self-worth. Not only is this draining on your partner, but it can also lead to an inability to prioritize one's own needs and desires, fostering debilitating neglect for oneself. Some of these behaviors are seen at the low end of the polarity spectrum in twin flood connections.

At its core, codependency emerges when individuals grapple with establishing and maintaining strong personal boundaries in their relationships. In essence, feeble boundaries hinder self-assertion, rendering individuals susceptible to cycles of codependency. The overwhelming need to please the partner becomes paramount, often at the expense of one's own needs and desires.

This pattern is frequently rooted in underlying fears, such as the fear of abandonment or rejection, and can be exacerbated by attachment styles and childhood trauma. Over time, those entrenched in codependency may lose sight of their own identity, fostering feelings of resentment and frustration that strain their relationships.

Recognizing a codependent relationship can be difficult, as individuals may become deeply entwined in the dynamics of dependence without realizing the extent of its impact until circumstances force a separation or they consciously reflect on it. Conscious relating emerges as a potential solution, offering the chance to heighten awareness of one's own thoughts, feelings, and behaviors, as well as those of their partner. It promotes open dialogue to resolve conflicts while fostering stronger connections grounded in trust and support.

The potency of conscious relating lies in its ability to empower individuals to make healthier decisions that align with personal growth, self-fulfillment and compounding omnidirectional abundance. Instead of succumbing to old patterns of codependency that may provide a fleeting sense of security but ultimately hinder the potential for profound happiness in the relationship, conscious relating encourages a more enlightened approach. Furthermore, it aids in the development of robust communication skills, vital for both conflict resolution and the active identification of unhealthy patterns, such as codependency, while deepening intimacy with one's partner.

Conscious relating extends its influence beyond romantic partnerships, urging individuals to infuse awareness into every facet of life, encompassing interactions with friends, family, work environments, social gatherings, and any setting involving intimacy. It advocates mindfulness towards negative patterns that, if left unchecked, could regress into codependency. This transformative approach facilitates enduring positive change, empowering individuals to master their emotions and thwart the influence of fear.

Fear often serves as a precursor to codependency in relationships. Research indicates that individuals grappling with codependency frequently harbor underlying fears, ranging from fear of abandonment to fear of rejection or fear of solitude. While fear can be a contributing factor to codependency, it's essential to recognize that codependency can also emerge from other psychological and emotional factors, such as low self-esteem, feelings of worthlessness, or a need for control.

To determine if codependency exists in yourself or someone you care about, here are some questions that you can consider.

1. Do you often put the needs of others before your own, at your expense?

2. Do you have a strong need for approval and validation from others?

3. Do you have difficulty setting boundaries and saying "no" to others?

4. Do you feel responsible for other people's happiness or well-being?

5. Do you frequently ignore your own feelings and needs in order to avoid conflict or please others?

6. Do you have a pattern of getting involved in relationships with people who have problems, and then trying to "fix" or rescue them?

7. Do you struggle with feelings of guilt or shame when you prioritize your own needs over someone else's?

8. Do you have a tendency to stay in unhealthy or abusive relationships?

9. Do you have a fear of abandonment or being alone?

10. Do you struggle with low self-esteem or a negative self-image?

Answering "yes" to one or more of the questions about codependency does not necessarily mean that you are codependent. However, it can be a valuable starting point for reflection, contemplation, and conversation.

AUTHENTICITY & INTEGRATION

(The Whole-Self vs. The Fragmented-Self)

Integrating our lessons, growth, intelligence and strengths for projecting our truth, is a transformative process that involves harmonizing different aspects of our being and merging them into a cohesive whole, vs. several alter egos, allowing for a sense of total authenticity. Authentic individuals not only achieve this internal harmony but also create environments where others feel encouraged to express the best versions of themselves. This generates genuine connection and meaningful relationships. Witnessing someone's authentic expression often triggers a reciprocal response. When someone opens up authentically, it creates a space for us to reflect the same in return.

Consider the instances when someone shares a personal experience or a long-hidden secret. It tends to build trust, and we may find ourselves compelled to reciprocate by sharing our own secrets. Similarly, when we encounter someone who is real and genuine, there's an inexplicable magnetic pull. We feel drawn to them, compelled to open up.

Vulnerability, when exercised with discretion, enables others to relate to you through their own personal challenges, potentially finding vicarious guidance in your experiences. This mutual authenticity creates a space where embarrassment dissipates, as the principle of "like attracts like" comes into play. In certain contexts, vulnerability may be seen as a weakness ripe for exploitation, so it's crucial to exercise discernment. However, among loved ones, authenticity serves as a powerful means to forge genuine connections.

Understand that authentic communication carries immense power. There's a natural resonance with realness and authenticity that is inherently attractive. While not everyone may embrace your authenticity, in the context of interpersonal relationships, when judgment gives way to empathy and relatability, a space is created for genuine self-expression. In such an environment, individuals feel free to drop their guards and share their true selves. This freedom becomes reciprocal, making it easier for others to do the same. The key is demonstrating that being real is not only acceptable but also celebrated.

Reflect for a moment on past relationships where lies were present, in fact, ask yourself, have you ever found yourself telling even a small lie? If so, authenticity might have been lacking in those moments. Hiding your true face and wearing a deceptive mask or not being real was your inauthentic moment.

Many of us have experienced the inclination to change ourselves to gain someone's approval in new relationships thereby changing the truth of something. Whether it's adjusting our clothing, preferences, behaviors or story lines, we sometimes shape-shift into what we think the other person desires. While this may yield short-term benefits, the long-term consequences are often disastrous. Authenticity is compromised, as no one can maintain a facade of perfection twenty-four / seven. Sooner or later, imperfections surface--whether it's morning breath, a bad hair day, or other less-than-ideal moments.

Undoubtedly, the initial stages of 'the seduction game' can be exhilarating. However, it's crucial to recognize that, over time, the love received may be for the persona crafted rather than the authentic self. Moreover, by continually altering yourself to please someone else, you stifle your individuality and uniqueness, resulting in a gradual dissipation of love and attraction as reality takes hold.

It's essential to understand that the right person will appreciate and love us for who we truly are, not for the mask we wear. The philosophy here is simple: **if they come, they come; if they go, they go**. What's meant for you will inherently be yours. Prolonging a relationship built on inauthenticity is counterproductive. Instead, creating space for the right person, one who values and loves the real you with all your imperfections and authenticity, is a more meaningful and intentional approach. This individual offers a relationship founded on freedom, honesty, and conscious intentionality.

The power of authenticity lies in being true to oneself from the beginning of a relationship. This allows your partner to fall in love with the complete, authentic version of you—the real you in fact. Pretending to be someone else sets the stage for eventual disappointment. When you operate from a place of scarcity and present only a fragmented version of your true self, romantic relationships are destined to fail.

If you are reading this book as a newly founded couple, take a moment to ask each other: Have we truly been presenting our authentic selves?

A shadow aspect of authenticity may manifest as fragmentation. In psychology and psychotherapy, the concept of the "fragmented self" is frequently explored. It refers to the experience of feeling divided or disconnected from one's sense of wholeness, coherence, or authenticity. Various factors, including trauma, stress, cultural conditioning, or a lack of self-awareness, can contribute to this fragmentation. Many experts highlight the negative consequences of the fragmented self, such as feelings of anxiety, depression, or disconnection from others. This can result from various factors, including excessive screen time, which has the potential to dissociate individuals from reality. In terms of social intelligence, the influence of being raised on devices is becoming increasingly apparent.

Consequently, psychotherapy and personal growth work often focus on the process of integrating or "healing" the fragmented self. Integration involves bringing together different parts of oneself to form a more cohesive and unified sense of self. When individuals feel disconnected from certain aspects of themselves, it can pose challenges to showing up authentically in romantic relationships.

It's important to note that the fragmented self is not necessarily a pathological condition but a normal aspect of human experience that can be addressed and integrated through various means. Mindfulness practices, expressive arts therapies, and interpersonal therapies are some approaches that can aid in this process. By embracing all aspects of themselves, individuals can develop a deeper sense of wholeness, fostering more authentic connections with their partners for a supernatural relationship.

In severe cases of a fragmented self, **Borderline Personality Disorder (BPD)** may be the underlying cause. BPD is a complex mental health condition marked by unstable emotions, impulsive behavior, difficulties in self-identity, and turbulent relationships. Individuals with BPD often grapple with intense fear of abandonment, emotional instability, and a fragmented sense of self. Many individuals suffer from Borderline Personality Disorder (BPD) and are completely unaware, as its characteristics are becoming increasingly normalized. Others suffer in silence.

While conscious relating can provide valuable insights and tools for personal growth, it's important to acknowledge that Borderline Personality Disorder (BPD) is a complex condition that often requires professional intervention. Seeking assistance from mental health professionals, such as therapists or psychiatrists specializing in BPD, is strongly recommended. They can conduct a thorough assessment, provide a diagnosis, and create a personalized treatment plan to address the specific challenges associated with BPD.

If you suspect that either you or your partner may have BPD, it's crucial to approach the situation with care. Individuals with Borderline Personality Disorder can easily misinterpret even small gestures of love as attacks, as they are often easily triggered. Choose a safe time and space to communicate openly and honestly, fostering an environment of unconditional love and non-judgment. Express your concerns with empathy, recognizing the complexity of BPD and its impact on both individuals. By initiating open and honest communication in a safe and loving setting, you can create an opportunity for mutual understanding and support.

Self-integration becomes particularly central in complex relationships where individuals may experience fragmented parts of themselves and challenges related to conditions like Borderline Personality Disorder. Within these intricate relationship dynamics lies the opportunity for twin elemental reflection, where deep connection and mirroring can lead to intense polarization.

By embracing the lessons and challenges presented in these transformative relationships, individuals can embark on a journey of self-discovery and healing, ultimately fostering personal growth and harmony in your bonds.

By integrating the self and understanding soulmate dynamics, you'll learn to navigate these complexities with love, empathy, and a shared commitment to positive transformation. This creates the foundation for profound evolution and mastery in interpersonal adeptness. It can be incredibly challenging, and beyond exhausting but the rewards are absolutely unparalleled.

Embodying interpersonal adeptness—or interpersonal adaptability—is akin to mastering the art of effectively navigating and managing various interactions with others as an emotionally whole individual. Picture yourself seamlessly weaving through diverse social situations, effortlessly demonstrating flexibility, charisma, deep understanding, and a rich set of interpersonal skills as if perpetually in the flow zone.

This, my friend, is the cornerstone of conscious relating—a dynamic practice that opens doors to meaningful connections, vibrant experiences, and transformative growth. It creates an environment for relationships to thrive and evolve, becoming a powerful catalyst for personal and collective development as well as self actualization and self mastery.

Chapter Fifteen

Conscious Relating MASTER CLASS Pt.2

Emotional-Technology for Evolving the Soul

"One does not become enlightened by imagining figures of light, but by making the darkness conscious." — *Carl Jung*

Honesty & Authenticity

Imagine the freedom of playfully telling your wife that the actress, Angela Bassett, is the 'Baddest' to ever walk the Earth, with her then responding with a spirited "Ha! On God! " She fist bumps you, while laughing and complimenting Angela's abs from a recent film you both enjoyed together.

Regrettably, the alternative scenario all too often unfolds differently. Instead of shared laughter, it might result in a tense and aggressive retort: YOU SHOULD GO BE WITH HER THEN !

The former is a testament to a relationship grounded in trust, freedom, humor, and open communication, where admiration for others is met with understanding and sometimes even shared enthusiasm, i.e., a relationship overflowing in abundance. The latter, however, may signal underlying insecurities, self projections, and trust issues that can strain the fabric of a relationship, i.e., a relationship rooted in lack and suffering from attachments.

Closely relating with others necessitates a certain level of openness and vulnerability. To truly plunge into the profound depths of connection with another soul, you must be willing and open to share within a trusting environment. However, embracing this kind of vulnerability can be challenging as we all harbor insecurities and aspects of ourselves that we may not be so proud of. For a relationship to not just survive but thrive, it's crucial to be genuine with your partner. This doesn't mean divulging every minute detail of your life, but it does entail feeling comfortable enough to be open and honest about the things that truly matter.

Rare as it may be, '**radical honesty**' stands as the key to a lasting and fulfilling relationship. It nurtures the deepest connection people can share, which is Trust. When I talk about radical honesty, I mean a communication style that's all about transparency, even if it means dismantling or questioning exaggerated and unrealistic expectations. It's about being our authentic selves and letting our partners truly know and understand us in a deeply intimate way.

These actions pave the way for being seen and appreciated, fostering a love that transcends the ordinary. Taking the risk of vulnerability with our partners establishes a deeper level of intimacy and connection which is the foundation of a solid, strong, and lasting relationship as opposed to a weak, and most importantly, temporary relationship.

This heightened level of engagement also entails being open to your partner's innermost thoughts and feelings without passing judgment, even when their words strike a chord deep within you. Yes, it might even expose some deeply hidden insecurities, but if confronting those triggers is necessary to integrate those shadows through actively practicing "big intentional love" and encouraging your partner to be authentic and fully transparent, then it is worth it.

In an intentional relationship, we open up space for ourselves and our romantic partners to experience the full spectrum of emotions, expressing them openly without the fear of rejection. This arrangement is a profoundly healing journey, where all feelings are acknowledged, and no internal process is met with shame. It empowers us to embrace the entirety of our emotional landscape.

Undoubtedly, it's a challenge stepping out of our comfort zone into uncharted territory. Yet, it's precisely in this discomfort that the alchemy occurs. When we allow ourselves to be vulnerable and transparent with our partner, it creates a paradigm of trust and intimacy. This transformative space allows us to traverse the vast spectrum of human ecstasy, emotion, and connection within the confines of our relationship.

Just as many adults may have never truly experienced the depths of orgasm or the art of making love, there exist ecstatic feelings largely unexplored by a significant portion of society. The human brain, an unparalleled chemist, holds the key to emotions that transcend the realms of touchless orgasms and recreational drugs like ecstasy. These naturally occurring emotions are not only superior but also undeniably transcendent.

In today's society, molded by prevailing cultural trends, numerous individuals may never experience even a fraction of the ecstatic feelings and pleasures found within the emotionally transcendent spectrum due to the inability to grasp the simple basics. **These basics include honesty, authenticity, vulnerability, and freedom in love.** In the presence of copious emotional blockages and psychological trauma, one cannot expect orgasmic energy to flow freely. These neo-normalized, yet limited states, now celebrated, act like a dam in the middle of a river, obstructing the natural flow of water.

While most have encountered the basic orgasm, it's not uncommon for over half the population to have never experienced the expansive sensation of a full-body orgasm, let alone the marvels of a touchless or out-of-body orgasm. These points underscore the untapped potential dormant within each of us. This potential, lying just beneath the surface, often remains unexplored due to the neglect of fundamental relational principles — Trust, Honesty, and Authenticity, even when dealing with oneself.

Though It can be challenging to be vulnerable and share personal feelings of fear, doubt, and even desire, in a relationship, it is essential if the goal is to create meaningful connections and build trust. When we are honest with each other, we create a safe space where both partners feel supported, valued, and, most importantly, trusted. Keywords, "Trust and Safe Space. Embracing openness establishes a sanctuary where both partners not only feel supported and valued but, above all, trusted. These things are vital and absolutely necessary for creating a fulfilling, satisfying, long-term relationship capable of transcending the mundane and ascending into the most excellent versions of yourselves. Only you know what that version looks like.

Retrospectively, it's interesting to contemplate why people feel the need to be dishonest. Let's face it—honesty isn't always the default setting. Perhaps it's the instinct to evade embarrassment or salvage one's pride. In other cases, the reason for lying may be more intricate. For instance, individuals who have done something wrong may lie to avoid punishment. i.e., self preservation. Then, there are those burdened with shame and humiliation, thus weaving a tapestry of lies to shield their secrets from the prying eyes of others.

In some cultures, humiliation is considered a fate worse than death. This perspective often stems from the high value placed on honor, dignity, and social standing within these communities. In such contexts, being publicly humiliated can lead to a loss of respect and honor, not just for the individual but also for their family or clan, which can be seen as a fate more damaging than death itself. The saying 'Pride goes before the fall' is heeded by many, echoing the wisdom of the adage.

In either case, it is clear that lies are born from fear and often motivated by a desire to hide something we are ashamed of. As such, it seems fair to say that we mostly lie about things we are not only afraid of but are ashamed to admit. We fear being rejected, among other consequences. Psychological research suggests that rejection activates the same pathways in the brain as physical pain, explaining why the experience of being rejected can feel intensely painful. Rejection can significantly impact an individual's self-esteem and self-worth. Furthermore, chronic rejection or the inability to cope with rejection can contribute to the development of mental health issues, such as depression, anxiety, and stress-related disorders.

It's nearly comprehensible why individuals might resort to lying; nevertheless, lies frequently originate from fear, driven by the urge to conceal aspects of ourselves considered shameful, or as a means of deliberate deception to defraud others. This behavior is akin to a dance with the shadows, stemming from a reluctance to reveal traits that could face rejection or other severe consequences.

The concern lingers that if people knew the truth about us, they wouldn't accept us, and retribution might follow, especially if we've acted on self-interest and our innermost desires. Consequently, we hide our flaws, mistakes, perversions, and even curiosities, choosing to live in a false reality in the hope that others will never uncover the legitimate and true reality. Of course, this is only a temporary solution. Sooner or later, the truth always comes to the surface, and when it does, it's usually more damaging than if we had just been honest in the first place.

Living in lies essentially means living inauthentically. No matter how genuine you believe you are, resorting to lies indicates a sense of shame about oneself and a departure from being your most authentic self. If someone cannot accept you for who you truly are, then it's important to question whether this is genuinely a good fit. What is meant for you will undoubtedly find its way to you. However, apply wisdom and discernment in making these decisions, allowing your intuition to lead you to what truly serves your best interest. In due time, shine authentically and trust the process.

In the realm of love, dishonesty takes on the weight of betrayal—a cardinal sin that fractures the very foundation of any partnership dynamic. If individuals made a genuine effort to understand their partner's feelings and motivations instead of quickly resorting to shaming, blaming, or severe judgment—which could even trigger a psychotic BPD episode—choosing instead to engage in conscious relating would be one of the most insightful decisions they could make. This involves engaging in open and empathetic communication to foster a deeper understanding for genuine connection. **Attempting in that moment to understand that humans are flawed** and in a perpetual state of healing and knowing that adversity for growth is an inherent part of the human experience, places you in the top 1% of the worlds most emotionally intelligent individuals and is a super power.

Furthermore, It never ceases to mystify me how an imperfect person can shame another imperfect person for acting within their nature. It's like shaming a baby for crying or a dog for barking. We serve as mirrors to one another, aspiring to reach a level where we can provide support in helping our partners gain insights into their actions and decisions, thereby assisting them in their personal growth.

Moreover, once, maybe even twice, is a mistake; however, when patterns emerge, it transforms from an isolated incident into a defining behavior. Upon careful consideration of the pros and cons, one must eventually discern whether there's a genuine commitment to growth. If the scales tip towards a lack of intention and dedication to personal development, it could signal the conclusion of your shared journey together.

Intentional Communication

Can we hold our partners accountable without facing bitter backlash? Are we permitted to create space for their self-improvement? The absence of this freedom often leads to significant resentment among the majority of individuals. Moreover, How do you navigate the waters of change and express your transforming emotions to someone you deeply love and care about, for example if you feel you're outgrowing the relationship or your journeys in life are taking different directions? What do you do when the stark reality hits that this person, once a source of inspiration, no longer ignites that spark within you? Communicating these sentiments, while safeguarding their heart, poses a unique challenge.

When the fear of hurting a loved one becomes prominent, initiating an honest, open conversation about your feelings and the relationship's future becomes a complex task. Unveiling disruptive emotions without causing harm or eliciting hurt might inadvertently breed feelings of betrayal in your significant other. Bear in mind that prolonged suppression of your thoughts and feelings can create internal pressure and foster a sense of inauthenticity. Consequently, this may lead to feelings of resentment towards the person you love, resulting in self-imposed suffering. Moving through this necessitates delicate communication to sidestep harm and betrayal. Although daunting, opting for open dialogue can nurture mutual growth and understanding, accommodating personal transformations within the relationship.

Navigating potential pitfalls is undoubtedly easier said than done. However, engaging in open communication requires expressing concerns calmly and respectfully. Approach the conversation with empathy, <u>avoiding patronizing or condescending tones.</u> It's crucial to acknowledge your love while honestly addressing your needs and the evolving nature of the relationship. Remember to

<u>incorporate positive reinforcement</u> in your dialogue. These challenging discussions create a space for growth, healing, and understanding.

Open and honest communication is paramount for a relationship's health and success. Here are some tips:

- Create a safe and non-judgmental environment: Encourage open dialogue by creating a space where both partners feel heard, respected, and free to express their thoughts and feelings without fear of judgment or criticism.

- Listen actively: When having these conversations, it is important to listen to your partner with empathy and understanding. This means paying attention to what they are saying and acknowledging their perspective.

- Use "I" statements: Instead of blaming or pointing fingers, "I" statements to express your feelings and thoughts such as, "I feel upset when we argue about this issue," instead of "you always do this or that," helps with productive communication.

- Timing is key: It is important to choose the right time to have these difficult conversations when both partners are relaxed and able to focus on the conversation.

- Be patient: Allow time for both partners to process their thoughts and feelings. Avoid pushing for a resolution before either partner is ready.

According to Dr. John Gottman, a renowned author and relationship expert, the key to successful communication lies in steering clear of criticism, contempt, defensiveness, and stonewalling. Instead, he advocates embracing the "Four Horsemen" in communication, which includes: 1. fondness and admiration, 2. turning toward each other, 3. the repair attempt, and 4. the positive perspective.

In line with this, another relationship expert, Harville Hendrix, Ph.D., the author of "Getting the Love You Want," recommends couples to partake in regular "dialogue exercises." During these exercises, each partner takes turns sharing their thoughts and feelings "without interruption." This practice serves to fortify trust, foster intimacy, and cultivate mutual understanding.

In the realm of these experts' wisdom, communication becomes not just a means of exchange but a sacred art—an art that, when practiced with intention and commitment, lays the foundation for enduring love and profound connection.

I define these principles as **"Intentional Communication,"** a model that emphasizes the active pursuit of open and honest dialogue with your partner. Its goal is to foster a culture of mutual understanding and respect through consistent practice. This method includes creating a safe, non-judgmental space where both partners can openly express their thoughts and feelings. It involves active listening, practicing patience, and choosing the right moments to discuss concerns. This structured approach focuses on conversation strategies designed to mitigate impulsive emotional reactions. While maintaining self-control during emotional flooding can be challenging, with awareness and practice, it is possible to develop a communication style that not only minimizes conflicts but also deepens and enhances the connection between partners.

Intentional communication fosters growth and intimacy by encouraging open and respectful communication in the early stages of a relationship. This sets the tone for a sustainable, healthy, and supportive partnership, underlining that the roots determine the fruits. Establishing a culture of intentional communication from day one in a relationship is important because it lays the foundation for what's to come, even if it's those hard conversations such as we may have come to a place where we are outgrowing each other.

This intentional approach isn't merely a remedy for relational hiccups; it's a proactive stance that aims to cultivate growth and intimacy from the very outset. Imagine setting the stage for a relationship not just by chance, but by design—a relationship marked by openness and respect, flourishing through the art of mutual understanding.

From the embryonic stages of a partnership, intentional communication becomes the unseen architect, building a framework for what lies ahead. It's a pledge to navigate not just the smooth seas but also weather the storms. Even when faced with daunting conversations, such as the acknowledgment that paths may be diverging, intentional communication remains the compass guiding couples through the intricate terrain of growth, change, and the enduring journey of love.

Question: How important is it for you to create a foundation of open, non-judgmental communication right from the start, where honesty is rewarded with freedom from shaming and blaming?

Answer & why:

The bottom line is: When partners cultivate a secure space for open, non-judgmental communication, trust, intimacy, and mutual understanding thrive, reducing conflicts and fostering personal growth. Through respectful dialogue, they prevent resentment, setting the stage for a lasting, supportive partnership.

Allow me to share my superpower for navigating difficult conversations—a simple yet effective strategy: it is the subtle art of inquiry or simply put, asking genuine questions. Leading challenging discussions with thoughtful and genuine inquiries conveys genuine interest and fosters understanding, creating a safe and open environment for both parties to share their perspectives and experiences. Demonstrating genuine interest in the other person's point of view and a willingness to listen and understand is powerfully conveyed through asking questions.

Recognizing the power of genuine questions posed with authentic interest proves to be an effective strategy. This method sidesteps the need for excessive and dramatic self-expression where attempts at forcing understand occur. By employing thoughtful inquiries, one can foster an environment that encourages open, honest communication without the need for grandiosity. This, in turn, cultivates a safe and supportive space that facilitates rich and healthy connections between individuals.

When questions are perceived as genuine and authentic, most people are usually willing to answer them, provided they don't feel like they are being interrogated or attacked. One reason among many is a concept known as self-verification. The allure of hearing one's own voice, often driven by the quest for validation, has been a subject scrutinized in various studies and psychological theories. Social psychology introduces the concept of "self-verification," underlining the inherent human need for validation of one's self-concept by others. Consequently, individuals may actively seek opportunities to express themselves, craving feedback as a means of attaining this validation.

To navigate a challenging conversation with conversational finesse, in your own voice, initiate with open-ended questions like *"Can you share more about how you see the situation?"* or *"What led you to feel that way?"* Exhibit active listening by attentively absorbing the other person's responses, acknowledging their feelings, and paraphrasing what they've said to show you understand. If something isn't clear, seek clarification in a non-confrontational manner, saying, *"I'm sorry, could you help me understand what you mean by that?"*

As the conversation unfolds, delve deeper by posing more intricate, targeted questions to grasp the nuances of the other person's perspective. When tensions rise, strategically employ questions to steer the dialogue back towards a constructive and understanding path. A simple yet powerful redirect might involve asking, "Can we take a step back and discuss our shared goals for this conversation, or our relationship in general?

It's consequential to recognize that engaging in conversations while in a heightened emotional state can lead to misunderstandings and increased tension. Much like the turbulent water analogy, attempting communication in such moments is like trying to see your reflection in rippled water—clarity becomes elusive. Step back, let emotions settle, and approach conversations with a calm mind.

Remember, it should never be you versus your partner; it's always you and your partner versus the problem. If you sense a need to compete, challenge yourself to remain objective, patient, and understanding, regardless of the issue. The goal is the solution, not to inflict more hurt, pain, or confusion, achieving nothing.

In essence, leading difficult conversations with questions builds rapport, fosters understanding, and identifies common ground. This technique aids conflict resolution, improves communication, and strengthens relationships—a key aspect of "Intentional Communication" that signals active engagement and **commitment to understanding the other person's perspective**.

Utilizing this question-led approach isn't just a tool; it's a pathway to building rapport, fostering mutual understanding, and most importantly, discovering common ground. This technique proves invaluable for conflict resolution, enhancing communication, and fortifying relationships. Integral to "Intentional Communication," the art of asking questions signals active engagement and a commitment to understanding the other person's viewpoint. This communication style creates a safe, open environment where both parties feel heard and valued.

For an added touch of production value, envision a big burly tattooed and bearded, raspy voiced man sporting a black leather Harley Davidson jacket calmly addressing his visibly upset and violently aggressive wife, by responding with, "*I hear you clearly, babe, but I'm not feeling this is the best space for really opening up about my true feelings. Can you help me understand what's triggering this hostility, so we can move forward to a shared understanding?*" This stands in stark contrast to the frustration of punching a hole in the drywall and turning to unhealthy coping mechanisms before riding off on his fatboy Harley cruiser with 18 inch ape hanger handlebars.

Intentional communication at its core is about creating a shared understanding through active listening, enabling a profound exploration of the other person's thoughts, feelings, and POV. It also encourages the other person to be more forthcoming and to share their perspective more fully without fear of being authentic. It creates an opportunity to genuinely seek solutions and reach conclusions. While some may prioritize problems over solutions, being conflict-oriented rather than solution-oriented, for those who truly cherish peace, this approach is invaluable.

Engaging in intentional communication through question-and-answer dialog also allows for real accountability and the follow-through of agreed upon commitments as it spells out specifics. For instance, it helps to establish clear expectations and responsibilities, leading to increased collaboration, better execution of tasks, and is solution oriented. This can help the couple achieve their goals more efficiently and effectively, ultimately maintaining the health of the relationship.

Solution-oriented conscious communication, when wielded intentionally and effectively, serves as a bridge over potential conflicts, guiding dialogue towards positivity and productivity. The right questions during a conversation prompt self-reflection, unlocking deeper self-awareness and paving the way for personal growth. In essence, nurturing dialogue through inquiry builds a working framework for a richer, more fulfilling connection. While perfect in theory, in practice, it's perfected!

Here are several questions, including those provided above, designed to aid in the art of inquiry during intentional communication and conscious relating. These questions are crafted to encourage openness, transparency, and effective communication with a focus on resolving conflicts. It is suggested that you practice and commit them to memory.

1. "I'm sorry, could you help me understand what you mean by that?"

2. "Can you share more about how you see the situation?"

3. "What led you to feel that way, or so why do you feel like that?"

4. "Can we take a step back and discuss our shared goals for this conversation?"

5. "How can we make this discussion more productive and less confrontational?"

6. "Can we commit to understanding each other's perspectives?"

7. "What are your main concerns (top three) or what bothers you most about this issue?"

8. "Is there something I could do differently?"

9. "What do you need from me to feel more secure and understood?"

10. "Do you feel like your views are being heard and respected in our conversations?"

11. "What can we learn from this to avoid similar issues in the future?"

12. "How do you think we can move forward from here?"

These questions are meant to nurture a deeper understanding and enhance the dynamics of your communication style, ensuring that all parties feel heard, valued, and validated. They are meant to make conversing easier; however, some individuals are resistant or simply prefer to remain upset rather than communicate effectively.

When an individual operates from the "child" position within the three ego states, they might not possess the maturity required for open and effective communication, which can hinder conflict resolution. This raises a red flag and prompts the question: Is this interaction healthy for me? Considering we often interact with reflections of ourselves, we face a critical decision at these crossroads regarding sustainability and trajectory. When encountering such introspections, we must choose between evolving or repeating past cycles. This decision is pivotal in determining the path of our personal growth when basic communication within romantic and non romantic partnerships is absent.

LANGUAGE MODELS: in the context of human communication.

When engaging in conscious and intentional communication, a profound awareness of the consequential power of semantics becomes imperative. Understanding Semantics—a cornerstone in effective communication—is an exploration in the nuanced meaning of words and phrases within various contexts and languages. Miscommunication often arises when individuals interpret shared words differently, potentially fostering confusion and even resentment if left unaddressed. Therefore, having a solid understanding of semantics is essential for ensuring clear and effective communication. Communication thrives on clarity, and when faced with uncertainty, simplicity reigns supreme. To be direct is divine.

Semantics, deriving from the Greek word 'semantikos,' meaning "significant" or "meaningful," was introduced by philosophers and linguists in the late 19th century. This term explores the complex relationship between words and their meanings, examining how words communicate significance and how context influences this significance. Consider the word "bank," which can refer to a financial institution, the side of a river, or a storage site such as a food or blood bank—depending on the context. Similarly, "run" might indicate swift movement in the context of a race but can have a different meaning, such as operating a business, in another setting.

Believing you fully understand someone in every conversation, regardless of how well you think you know them, is misguided. This holds particularly true in text messaging or phone conversations, where the lack of visual cues like facial expressions can obscure true intent. Such assumptions can result in miscommunication, setting off a domino effect of misunderstandings and further complicating the relationship. Regrettably, even minor misunderstandings have frequently caused the disintegration of otherwise compatible and fruitful relationships, rendering them permanently damaged and beyond repair or forgiveness.

Connotation is a critical element of semantics, which explores the emotional or cultural associations words carry. For instance, "home" is imbued with positive feelings of comfort and security, in contrast to the more neutral "house." Miscommunications stemming from semantic nuances can lead to confusion and breed resentment across various relationships. Carefully navigating language subtleties, clarifying meanings when necessary, and observing nonverbal signals are vital strategies to avoid misinterpretation.

This becomes particularly relevant in instances where individuals might read too deeply into statements, inferring meanings that may not exist. Consider a situation where a romantic partner expresses concern, saying, "You used to say you loved our home, and now it's just a house. I guess that means you don't love me anymore," followed by an extensive discussion based on this interpretation. Such an example underscores how easily miscommunication, rooted in the connotations of simple words like "home" and "house," can profoundly affect relationships. It highlights the necessity of staying attuned to the potential for overinterpretation and ensuring clear, empathetic communication.

Intonation emerges as a pivotal component of communication as well and is capable of reshaping the very essence of a sentence. In English, the transformation of declarative sentences, words, or phrases into questions is as simple as tweaking the inflection of one's voice. A question, for instance, adopts a higher pitch at its conclusion, infusing an air of uncertainty. Conversely, declarative statements maintain a consistent pitch. Yet, the nuanced play of intonation extends beyond pitch, encompassing the lowering of tone at the statement's end or strategic emphasis on specific words to convey emotions, judgment, anger, or resolution of conflict.

This transformative process, known as intonation or stress, tracks the rise and fall of the voice during speech, where stress emphasizes particular words or syllables. These elements significantly influence the meaning and interpretation of spoken words. Linguistically, this interplay falls under prosody, enveloping the rhythm, pitch, and melody of speech.

In addition to intonations role in communication, it's worth noting, according to researcher Albert Mehrabian, who spotlighted the nonverbal dimensions of communication, that a significant portion of communication transcends words. Body language takes the lead, accounting for most of the meaning at 55%, while spoken words contribute 38%, and tone of voice adds the remaining 7%. This breakdown, known as the 7-38-55 rule, specifically addresses the communication of emotions and was introduced by Mehrabian in his 1971 book "Silent Messages" at the University of California, Los Angeles.

When reflecting on disagreements between not only romantic partners but general conversations, it's often bewildering to consider that the hurtful impact of the exchange may not have been solely caused by the content of the words but rather by the manner in which they were communicated. The familiar refrain, "it's not what you said to me, it's how you said it to me," underscores the profound influence of tone on meaning, where one misunderstood word can radically reshape the interpretation of an entire sentence.

Take, for instance, the sentence, **"Let's eat, Grandma."** By emphasizing different words, we can create different interpretations of the message. For instance, emphasizing **"let's"** changes the tone to a suggestion or proposal, suggesting, "Hey, how about we eat Grandma for dinner?" rather than a command. On the other hand, emphasizing **"eat"** changes the tone to a command, conveying, "Stop fooling around and start 'eating', Grandma!" Furthermore, emphasizing **"Grandma"** adds an emotional dimension to the sentence, conveying "We must eat, 'Grandma', to survive," or "I can't believe we are eating 'Grandma'!"

Similarly, in written communication such as texting or email messaging, the insertion of punctuation can also wield transformative power. "Let's eat, Grandma!" with a comma extends an invitation to dine, while "Let's eat, Grandma?" with a question mark suggests a query seeking approval or agreement for dining on Grandma. Such nuances in the English language add a touch of whimsy.

Intonation not only influences interpretation but can also change the actual meaning of a sentence. Here are more examples, **"I want to travel to Jamaica, do you want to go with me"** the meanings are changed with ease.

- Emphasizing *"I"* conveys that the speaker specifically wants to go to Jamaica, perhaps because they have a personal connection to the place. "I want to travel to Jamaica" becomes, 'I' want to travel to Jamaica, not any other place.

- Emphasizing *"Want"* could convey a sense of urgency or excitement. "I want to travel to Jamaica" could become "I really, 'want' to travel to Jamaica, it's been my dream for years!

- Emphasizing *"Travel"* could change the focus of the sentence to the act of traveling itself rather than the destination. "I want to *travel* to Jamaica" could become "I'm not interested in staying in one place, I want to, "travel" anywhere, even to Jamaica to explore.

- Emphasizing *"Jamaica"* could emphasize the importance of the destination, perhaps due to its cultural significance or beauty. "I want to travel to *Jamaica*" could become "I want to travel to, 'Jamaica', it's the most beautiful place I've ever seen.

- Emphasizing *"You"* could suggest that the speaker is offering an opportunity to the listener rather than just asking a question. "Do *you* want to go with me?" could become "I'm inviting, 'you', to join me on this adventure.

- Emphasizing **"Go"** could convey a sense of urgency or excitement. "Do you want to *go* with me?" could become "Do you want to, 'go', with me? It's going to be amazing!

In the grand symphony of communication, intonation, stress, and punctuation emerge as powerful instruments, capable of orchestrating a myriad of emotions and meanings. It's imperative to wield these tools mindfully, ensuring effective communication and sidestepping potential misunderstandings. Through the harmonious interplay of emphasis, intonation, and punctuation, we unlock a spectrum of interpretations, wielding the power to entirely reshape meaning.

When engaging in intentional communication, it is prudent to stay mindful of how you utilize the powerful tool of language. Ensure that you consistently express your intended message and convey your thoughts accurately. Mastering the art of communication is akin to possessing a superpower, endowing individuals with the ability to forge meaningful connections, understand others deeply, and articulate themselves with crystal-clear impact.

As we conclude this discussion, let's acknowledge the transformative secret weapon that turns individuals into communication superheroes—the superpower of listening. It's no surprise that **"Listen" and "Silent"** share the same letters, carrying a poetic resonance. Embracing the mastery of "Listening" opens the gateway to intentional communication. Active listening is crucial for mastering communication, fostering understanding, building trust and connections, enabling tailored messaging, preventing misunderstandings, aiding in conflict resolution, and supporting ongoing improvement in communication skills. Consider gamifying intentional listening during tense conversations by seeing how long you can hold out before speaking—a personal challenge that has the potential to elevate your communication skills to extraordinary heights.

On a related note, I frequently advocate for Vipassana meditation when mentoring. This method is distinguished by its prolonged silences, forbidding speech, other forms of communication, and sometimes even eye contact. It underlines the significance of silence, guiding participants to a deeper self-observation and understanding of their surroundings, free from verbal distractions. This intense quietude serves as a transformative instrument, potentially making one a more impactful communicator, capable of conveying profound insights with few words.

Compersion and Empathy.

During a chapter of my life, a remarkable woman, let's call her "Philly Jawn," was a part of my romantic journey. After a long season of dating, things took an unexpected turn when she eventually revealed what i already expected which was she had been with someone else. I somewhat expected it seeing as I was never around. Initially, I reacted with anger and a sense of betrayal. It seemed to me that the person I thought I knew wasn't truly representing herself authentically, seeing as though she felt it necessary to represent herself dishonestly.

Seeking solace and guidance, I turned to my trusted sister-friend, Naphtali whose insights unveiled a deeper understanding of why "Philly Jawn" chose a path of dishonesty, prompting a profound shift in my perspective. Armed with newfound empathy, I quickly reached out to "Philly Jawn" to apologize sincerely for how I initially responded. For the first time in my life, I experienced profound compersion and empathy for her circumstances and decisions.

Allow me to provide some context. During a time marked by the loss of our home and my relentless efforts on the road to rebuild our lives, the realization struck me that my concern for her well-being had not translated into creating a more nurturing environment for her. Her mention of feeling on the brink of insanity within our circumstances resonated deeply. Recognizing the importance of her mental well-being, I embraced the understanding that she needed to take whatever measures were necessary to heal without causing harm. In this moment, empathy took precedence, acknowledging that I might have made similar choices if I had walked in her shoes.

During this period, I worked over the road for months, occasionally diverting my attention to others while my domestic and romantic partner found herself living in hotel suites and, at times, in her car. She managed two jobs and endeavored to meet the demands of her soap-making business, while also resorting to showering at the local gym she frequented. In candid conversations, she confided in me, expressing how she felt like a troll living under a bridge during nights spent in her car at the all-night fitness center. I realized I had been neglectful, failing to be there for her when she needed me the most. She sought comfort, attention, and safety, yearning to feel valued and beautiful, even if by someone she had no intentions of committing to. At that time, I offered none of these things.

As I reflected on her circumstances with conscious awareness, I gained enlightenment. This marked one of my earliest experiences of compersion, revealing that when you genuinely care for someone, your primary concern is their safety and well-being. All you desire is for them to be okay, happy, and living in their highest possible vibration, regardless of the circumstances.

I recognized that some people harbor such strong insecurities that they might prefer to see their partner walk home in the rain than accept a ride from a co-worker of the opposite sex. Similarly, they'd choose to see their loved one endure a night outdoors in a snowstorm, locked out of their apartment, rather than seeking refuge at a friend or neighbor's home of the opposite sex when no one else is available. In these instances, insecurities and immaturity overshadow compassion, making the concept of compersion seem distant and elusive.

Some might find humor in the scenario described, insisting they would never permit their significant other to accept favors from the opposite sex under any conditions, reflecting a contemporary cultural trend that finds unempathetic and selfish behavior amusing. However, this perspective typically shifts when they find themselves in a similar predicament, highlighting a common disconnect between amusement at another's expense and personal experience.

After undertaking significant self-reflection I began to interact with her through a lens of non-attached clarity in our communication. Reflecting on our relationship and being utterly honest with myself, I could clearly see the trajectory. I realized that the prospect of marriage or spending our twilight years together were unlikely. Despite my deep love for her—a feeling that persists—I came to understand that our futures were destined to diverge.

Conceptually, **"Compersion"** is commonly understood as an empathetic state of happiness and joy that arises when a partner expresses contentment, satisfaction, happiness, or pleasure from another emotionally intimate, romantic or sexual relationship. Often regarded as the antithesis of jealousy, compersion is considered a healthy and positive element in mature relationships. However, its scope extends beyond romantic and sexual contexts. Compersion is closely related to empathetic joy and or vicarious joy.

For instance, a parent may experience empathetic and vicarious happiness or compersion when their child achieves independant success or finds happiness in their life, like when winning an award for a talent show or recital. Similarly, a friend might feel vicarious compersion when witnessing the joy of another friend in a new relationship. This empathetic state is not confined to personal relationships; it can manifest in various domains, such as the workplace, where one might mirror the happiness of a colleague's success. In essence, compersion transcends romantic boundaries, it's the contagious feeling that emerges in any context where the happiness of someone close to you brings you joy.

In due course, I came to a profound understanding of the challenging situation my former girlfriend found herself in when seeking solace in the company of another. Surprisingly, I discovered a sense of happiness and relief that she had found a temporary refuge during a period when I, her usual protector and provider, was unavailable. It became clear to me that love, especially unconditional love, extends beyond expecting someone to endure hunger when you cannot provide sustenance.

Regarding Philly Jawn and I, our time together provided valuable lessons and profoundly influenced our soul evolution. While some may say, "that could not have been me," many overlook the fact that—even though "slave-love" paradigms may encourage such thinking—they are not their partner's master or owner. This bullish mentality doesn't translate into sustainable relating dynamics. Unfortunately, some individuals treat their lovers as property without realizing that such relationships are not designed to last forever, which, in most cases, they don't. Ultimately, these relationships prove to be an enormous waste of time. As recorded in chapter one, these narratives can be repeated indefinitely.

Many relationships are initially fueled by the fairytale notion of lasting magically forever-ever, and any ideas that challenge this fantasy are met with contempt. However, when reality sets in, the dream can turn into a "slave-love" nightmare. There's no need to blindside a potential partner into such a relationship, especially with the existence of communities like the BDM community catering to those interested in "master and slave" relationships and other radical fetishes. It's essential to grasp that you don't own your partner, and relationships aren't always meant to last forever, even if separation comes in the form of death in old age.

Consider how many of your past relationships with exes are enduring to this day. The reality? None. They wouldn't be Ex's if they did! Recall that time, perhaps five or six relationships ago, when you behaved as if you owned your partner, leading to a breakup, only to repeat the same cycle. Now, imagine this cycle as the sole experience of your life, starting in your late teens and continuing into old age, with no alternatives in sight. Imagine the absurdity after a fourth divorce, still not recognizing that ownership or control was never part of the equation.

In the pursuit of ownership or control over a partner, one might expect to recognize the inherent unnaturalness and unsustainability of such endeavors, yet many do not. This lack of sustainability often results in a cycle of serial dating, preventing the establishment of healthy and prosperous relationships and impeding the potential for a transcendent union. Relating through ignorance, insecurity, and fear becomes ingrained due to misconceived and faulty social programming.

Retrospectively, many proclaim that God is love, attributing love as one of the greatest and most powerful forces in the universe. Love is often considered the fuel of creation. Yet, what exactly is this profound and enigmatic force that people claim to feel towards their romantic partners? Is it truly love? If so, is it the unconditional love of the soul, a creation of God, or is it a materialistic love of the ego? Perhaps it aligns with one of the seven Greek loves from early Greek philosophy.

Whether it's a lifelong bond with a twin-flame connection, a spiritual or domestic partnership echoing twin-wind energy, or a brief summer romance with a twin-planet soulmate that transforms your life, intentionally relating with someone can profoundly enhance your life's growth and development. Actively pursuing a conscious relationship with another promises greater understanding, deeper love, and elevated awareness, for cultivating a unique and transcendent union. Embracing strengths with tools like compersion, empathy, intentional communication, and emotional wholeness offer equips you with the necessary resources to construct a transcendent, highly functional, conscious union with another.

Having learned to know yourself through self-reflection, it becomes easier to organically grow in love with others because you've mastered the art of conscious self-relating. A person engaged in a conscious relationship with themselves can then engage in conscious reflection with a partner more effortlessly. Deep self-reflection and complete honesty with oneself pave the way for greater honesty in relationships.

Openness cultivates the ease and fluidity we seek in relationships. The absence of these qualities, coupled with a lack of purpose, evokes frustration. The accumulation of frustration can escalate into contempt and resentment, which is regrettable because, in hindsight, it often stems from severe misunderstandings. The unfortunate nature of misunderstandings lies in their potential to lead to unnecessary separations, reaching points of no return. It's crucial to acknowledge the destructive power of misunderstandings and actively work towards developing open communication and empathy. Doing so helps prevent the irreversible damage they can inflict on relationships.

Resentment & Contempt

It's genuinely disheartening to witness a once beautiful and happy couple devolve into bitterness, anger, and resentment. What begins with enchanting love can transform into malice and hatred. Resentment often stems from real or perceived wrongs, possibly born from miscommunication or misunderstanding. A lack of understanding can lead a romantic partner to feel a sense of injustice, creating feelings of inequality, neglect, or betrayal. These emotions can evolve into painful frustration that gradually morphs into crippling resentment. As resentment festers, it can manifest as all-out contempt, and begin to resemble a demon summoned through a ritualistic portal.

Make no mistake, the interplay between resentment and contempt is undoubtedly a ritual, and the spirit invoked through those daily rituals is certainly not angelic. The absence of conscious relating and intelligent communication allows small misunderstandings to grow into resentments, much like cracks in a dam or windshield left unmanaged. Harboring resentment not only gives way to expressions of contempt but can also lead to envy, jealousy, and passive-aggressive behavior.

Given these dynamics, particularly in daily interactions, the loss of respect and attraction often follows, setting the stage for a potentially toxic separation. Regrettably, when individuals engage compulsively with unhealthy and unconscious behaviors, this pattern can turn into an endless loop. It repeats itself year after year, decade after decade, across multiple relationships. Ultimately, these actions are met with contempt.

These days, separation has become a common occurrence for many individuals, resulting in a society populated by serial daters. These situations often start as chronic attractions that evolve into pathologically compulsive relationships. Serial dating, in my humble opinion, is the most inauthentic form of polyamory because individuals engaging in it may be deceiving themselves about their lifestyle. Many people who serial date at a high frequency are borderline delusional and may not even realize that they are engaging in a form of polyamory through their actions. The fact that relationships aren't happening simultaneously but are in short waves of succession with high frequency does not make one monogamous. If at all monogamous, it resembles **unethical monogamy.**

Consider this scenario: If you date a new person and break it off every 6 hours, you, beloved, are unequivocally polyamorous. This would amount to three lovers in succession per day, multiplied by seven days a week. But, of course, it's not simultaneous because, well, that would be a polyamorous orgy, wouldn't it? The belief seems to be that as long as you verbally break up at the sixth hour, then it's not "simultaneous," right? It would not be considered polyamorous, even if at the end of the day you've entertained three lovers. do the math and the end of the week would have seen twenty one lovers and so on.

You might be scratching your head right now, thinking, "What on earth?" The truth is, some people find themselves in new relationships almost every other week or month, accumulating a considerable number of lovers, perhaps half a dozen per year for over a decade. On the other hand, some individuals may only engage in one or two serious relationships per year consistently. This pattern can persist for decades as well, leading to terms like **"pathological dater"** or **"serial dater,"** embodying a form of unethical monogamy that, in essence, resembles polyamory due to its multiple romantic entanglements. Does this make sense? Take a moment to reflect on it.

I recall a debate between a polyamorous woman, practicing polygeny with the same two husbands for over ten years, and a monogamous woman who had dated one to three lovers per year with a one-year celibacy season during the same ten-year period. In this debate, each woman cynically argued that the other was more polyamorous. I was asked to be the judge, and even though it was a playful debate, I have enough sense to know not to get in the middle of two women debating.

Furthermore, when someone is chronically entangled in a torrent of pathologically compulsive relationships that resemble polyamory by default, they tread the line of predatory dating. The phenomenon of predatory dating is prevalent within the unethical demographic of many polyamorous communities as well. Some practitioners are extremely predatory in fact and irresponsible in their practice. More on that in the upcoming book "Polyamorously Celibate", available soon for preorder.

In the grand scheme of things, who am I to cast shame on someone for embracing their nature? What I'm attempting to convey, however, is the importance of honesty and self-awareness. If you consistently find yourself engaging in a series of relationships, it might be helpful to recognize that you're essentially living a polyamorous lifestyle.

Instead of adopting dishonesty or cognitive dissonance, consider entering relationships authentically with like minded individuals who appreciate you for you in all your authenticity. As explored in the section on Integration and cultivating authenticity, failing in these aspects creates fertile ground for "Resentment and Contempt," which often become staples in sustaining compulsively relating patterns.

I don't have an issue with ethical polyamory, emphasizing the "amour" part, as love can manifest in various healthy ways, even from a distance and within defined boundaries. Ethical polyamory stands in stark contrast to the cultural trend of toxic separation, a phenomenon that some individuals strangely revel in. There are those who derive a natural high from the dramatic attention associated with toxic separation. In some cases, individuals even form trauma bonds with their next partner or lover, rooted in the toxicity generated by their previous separation.

They thrive on placing all the blame and shame on their ex-lovers for any failed attempts at romance they co-created. This epitomizes a lack of ownership in the relationship they co-founded. Some individuals consistently adopt a victim mentality, using it to nourish their pain body, without realizing that they might be the common denominator in these situations. There are those who, based on their own irresponsible choices, swear off an entire gender class. Such circumstances are fertile ground for trauma or drama bonding, which, in some instances, becomes the lifeblood of certain attractions. For some couples, the absence of drama in their relationship is a deal-breaker, rendering it completely unsustainable without it. In these unique cases, the non-dramatic partner is often labeled as lame or a square. This holds true even for friendships and transactional relationships.

In psychology, the concept of the "pain body" was introduced by *Eckhart Tolle* in his book *"The Power of Now."* This term describes the accumulation of past emotional pain that individuals carry within themselves, often triggered by present events. The pain body can be fueled by negative thoughts and emotions, such as anger, resentment, and fear, as well as by engaging in behaviors that perpetuate suffering, like holding grudges or seeking revenge. The idea is that by becoming aware of the pain body and learning to detach from it, individuals can decrease their suffering and enhance their overall well-being.

Continuously professing love, only to escalate toxicity and subsequently ghost the person you claimed to have loved a month later, is a foolish behavior, especially when it becomes a recurring compulsive pattern. Engaging in blame and shame sustains your wounded inner child and, consequently, nourishes your pain body. Instead of cultivating shared clarity, understanding, acceptance, and forgiveness, shame on their name and blame in the game persist as the unfortunate sustenance of this destructive cycle.

Considering that we are all reflections on the same path of evolution, undoubtedly, empathy, understanding, acceptance, and forgiveness are excellent resources in consciously relating for growth. Essentially, conscious relating involves approaching every challenge with the conscious intent to transmute it into a learning experience and an enlightening self-awareness breakthrough, as if a therapist had just assisted you in some cathartic self-realization prompting immense transformation. You know the scene when the shrink proudly says, I think we've had a breakthrough, right before billing you $600 for the hour? Practicing that kind of patience with that level of intention in your own healing and awareness is what unconditional love is all about. While we are not our lovers' therapist, and certainly not our friends and acquaintances, we are, however, a source for patience, understanding and empathy.

When we discuss love, our minds often gravitate towards romantic contexts. However, it's essential to recognize that love, as a divine force, can be shared in the most unexpected places, even if it remains unexpressed. Many fathers hesitate to tell their sons "I love you," while nephews may never utter those words to their uncles, and friends rarely exchange "I love yous" with one another. The closest expression one might receive, and even that is rare, is, "it's all love," or "I've got love for you," which essentially conveys the sentiment "I love you." Contextually, It all boils down to the intricacies of semantics.

Love is frequently perceived as an emotion or feeling that occurs spontaneously. It's a topic we often discuss but might not fully comprehend. At its essence, love is both an action and a practice. Similar to any skill, it demands time, patience, and effort for mastery. Love is something we actively engage in rather than passively experience—the latter is fugazy love. It is also a decision and a choice, viewing someone not as an object for utility but as a human being deserving of care and respect. Unconditional love involves accepting people for who they are, not for who we want them to be. It means forgiving their mistakes and extending compassion when they face challenges.

It can be difficult to love someone who has hurt us or to forgive them for their mistakes. However, authentic and unconditional love involves choosing to see the best in someone, even when they may not always deserve it. It means being present for them in both good and bad times. Consider this: wouldn't you want someone to give you the benefit of the doubt and be there for you during your ups and downs?

Love goes beyond being just a word; it's about dedicating your time, attention, and patience to your counterparts. It's a practice of accepting them for who they truly are and loving them from your level of consciousness nonetheless. We must learn to be present with them in the moment, irrespective of what the future may hold. Ask yourself, am I capable of that?

Love, as a practice, possesses the power to transform our lives and the world around us. With each intentional act of love, we take a step closer to creating a kinder, more compassionate, and more connected world. We move closer to evolving not only our souls but our entire species. Even in the most hostile environments, with the most savage of characters, there's immense potential for transformation through the infusion of love as a unifying force. Just as individual links in a chain lack strength when separated, love serves as the binding agent that connects hearts and propels relationships forward. This bond propels relationships into a state of euphoria, characterized by dynamic growth and advancement.

Conscious love, in contrast to compulsive love, emerges when one is present, integrated, and aware of their relational dynamics. Through this awareness, individuals gain insights into their patterns and the conditions they set for giving and receiving love. In conscious relating, the potential for emotional chaos diminishes, and a clearer understanding of the relational trajectory emerges.

Much like peering into a crystal ball, developing skills in consciously relating enables you to envision clearer trajectories of possible outcomes without attachment. With heightened awareness of your own patterns, you can more easily recognize similar patterns in others, potentially attracting high-vibrational counterparts. This awareness empowers you to navigate and transform less healthy relational patterns, fostering a conscious and harmonious approach to love.

When consciously relating on your path of self-mastery, you'll discover that loving yourself completely, without neglect, eventually becomes the new normal—a lifestyle, in fact. In this state, you'll only recognize, attract, and accept pure, unconditional, genuine love from a partner, as like attracts like. You don't attract what you want; instead, you attract what you are—your reflection.

The soul mate paradigm on Earth operates like this: You'll consistently attract mirrors, even if they manifest as shadows within those mirrors. The emotional vessels and relationships that shape your life—whether they be kinships, friendships, relationships, or motherships—will invariably call forth different versions of you. These relationships are the mirrors that reflect your light from diverse angles and various perspectives.

Each version projected represents a role you play, and with each role, your character undergoes a transformation. Your character interactions with your ex-partner is not the same as the character you are when with your current partner. The way you interact with your mother differs from how you engage with your friends, mentors, or children. Essentially, you engage in **code-switching** with each new mirror, adapting to the unique dynamics of each relationship.

Indeed, the concept of "code-switching" refers to the ability to seamlessly shift between different languages, dialects, or social and cultural identities depending on the context and people involved. This skill is often observed among bilingual or multilingual individuals and aids in effective communication and social interaction. Code-switching is a natural process that allows individuals to adapt to various environments and connect with different groups of people. Code-switching, within the context of this section, extends beyond audial language to encompass body language and personality.

Recognizing that each mirror reflects a different version of oneself is crucial in understanding how individuals may exhibit diverse behaviors in various relationships. The dynamic nature of relationships can bring forth dormant aspects of the self, contributing to personal growth and evolution. This insight helps explain why some people, when relating compulsively, may betray the trust in their relationships, as different versions of themselves may emerge in different contexts causing them to switch between personalities.

The idea that being with a specific person triggers a unique version of oneself is not uncommon. Individuals may express sentiments like, "I like who I am when I'm with you or, I feel alive with you." This could be attributed to the concept of positive polarization with a twin elemental, where interactions with another, brings out distinct aspects of one's personality. A specific person may serve as a muse, providing inspiration, emotional support, and facilitating creativity or personal growth.

A **muse** is typically an individual or source of inspiration for an artist, writer, or musician. The term "muse" originates from Greek mythology, where the Muses, nine goddesses, were believed to be a source of inspiration. In contemporary usage, a muse can encompass a person, an event, a place, or an idea that sparks creativity. Muses can also provide emotional and psychological support, aiding artists in overcoming creative blocks and discovering meaning and purpose in their work or life.

Understanding the elemental characteristics of twin elemental and mirror souls empowers individuals to navigate their relationships with intention and awareness. Mirror souls, akin to muses, reveal aspects of ourselves that we may be unaware of—spanning from the darkest to the most illuminated spaces within us. They influence our actions, inspiring personal growth and the realization of our full potential. Recognizing the elemental dynamics at play and the effects they're having on us enables individuals to focus on the version of themselves they would prefer.

Asking oneself—Who am I when I'm with this person or these people and how does their presence affect me—is a pivotal question of great importance when engaging in introspection and self-discovery, even if it pertains to a muse in the reflections of one's friends list on a social media platform. Regarding the company you keep, it's often said that if you surround yourself with nine broke friends, drug addict friends, or even astronaut, investment guru, or yogi practitioner friends, you'll likely become the tenth, reflecting the influence of socio-cultural resonance. Whether interacting with a muse, a simple friend, or a colleague, we essentially code-switch to reflect a different version of ourselves with each new mirror we encounter.

Examining the dynamics within our social circles, particularly our personal connections and their influences on our decisions, effectively underscores the intricacies of conscious relating. The choices between active and reactive behavior is a critical aspect of conscious relating. In a society where accountability can sometimes lack, individuals have the agency to choose how they receive and respond to the lessons their counterparts offer.

The idea of life decisions compounding, as introduced by Darren Hardy in "The Compound Effect," underscores how small, consistent actions, when maintained over time, can lead to significant results, especially within the framework of choices made based on personal influences. Unhealthy loyalties can result in a chain reaction of numerous consequences, making it challenging to keep track of their origins or to quantify their impact. These compounding consequences in the context of magnetic mirrored soul attractions are essentially what is known as the twin elemental effect.

The concept of compounding, initially rooted in the financial world, illustrates the idea that interest earned on a sum of money, when reinvested, earns additional interest over time, leading to exponential growth. The compound effect, however, expands beyond finance, emphasizing the transformative potential of consistent, minor actions or habits over an extended period. Even seemingly insignificant actions can accrue and bring about significant changes in our lives.

Consider this scenario to grasp the potency of compounding: Imagine having the choice between receiving ten million dollars today or receiving one dollar today, with the condition that it doubles (or compounds) every day for a month. What would you choose? Many people might opt for the ten million today over the compounding dollar today, which has the potential to double into two dollars tomorrow and so forth. However, let's explore the compounding effect:

The $1 today that doubles every day would unfold like this: On the first day, it would still be worth $1. On the second day, it would double to $2, and on the third day, it would double again to $4. This doubling continues each day, so on the fourth day, it reaches $8, on the fifth day, $16, and so forth. By the end of the first week (7 days), the value would be $128. Moving to the second week (14 days), the value would surge to $16,384. Progressing to the third week (21 days), the value would skyrocket to $2,097,152. Finally, at the end of the fourth week (28 days), the value would surpass $268 million.

This vividly demonstrates the extraordinary power of compounding, where small, consistent actions can lead to exponential growth over time. Darren Hardy's illustration with the magic penny, doubling every day to reach ten million dollars within a month, beautifully encapsulates the essence of Choices + Behavior + Habits + Time = Compound Effect. Just as small, positive actions can compound to yield significant results, negative compulsive behaviors can also have a compounding effect on our lives. Even seemingly small instances of negative behavior can accumulate over time and lead to entropic relating or the breakdown of the relationship.

Just as negative actions can compound, so can positive actions. For instance, consistent acts of kindness, appreciation, and understanding in a relationship can fortify the emotional connection and trust between partners, fostering a more fulfilling and enduring relationship. Consistent intentional and positive communication, coupled with unwavering authenticity, can also compound, creating profoundly conscious relating dynamics in partnerships. This highlights the importance of practicing mindfulness in our habits and behaviors, recognizing their potential long-term impact when relating to your twin elemental counterpart and the cumulative effects over time, whether positive or negative.

Being conscious of how you relate to your counterpart and twin mirror contributes to a more productive spiritual evolution and ascension. **If you embody chaos, you're likely to attract the most chaotic versions of yourself in a counterpart, fueling the exponential growth of chaos in your life.** However, setting your intention to embody love can attract a counterpart who embodies the most loving version of yourselves to match your resonance. This sets the stage for a mutually nurturing and cyclical process of interpersonal energy exchange, where two people regenerate and recycle the vital force of love.

Remember that you attract what you are, even if it's an inverted expression of who you are, your shadow self. Setting intentions and consciously executing your plans while remaining present in love is a path to soulful connection, cosmic pleasure, and, ultimately, intimate bliss. This model resembles the euphoric "ascension-like" power of true love.

Real love, unbeknownst to many, is reminiscent of microdosing **on natural ecstasy daily** throughout your waking life. Recall the positive limerence you felt when you fell head over heels in love once upon a time. Now, imagine that flooding of chemistry daily, consistently, and intentionally. Some people never get the opportunity to experience it because they may not realize that to love is to make a conscious choice rather than a compulsion based on neediness and lack.

Choosing to understand that love is exploration means committing to showing up for all the varied nuances of your relationships and asking yourself, during challenging moments, "What would love do here." The answer will vary each time, providing an opportunity for growth in ways you've never experienced before. This journey allows you to discover new facet's about your partner and yourself. Although unspoken, some are genuinely afraid to step up to the challenge, choosing instead to focus solely on their failures in love. Could that be you?

Love is a journey that takes you to unexpected places, an adventure always worth taking. So, consistently asking yourself, "W.W.L.D. – What would love do?" and then acting on it is what conscious loving is all about. It leads to enrichment, evolution, and ascension. A crucial reminder is that the first and foremost love is the love of self – not selfishness, but recognizing oneself as a fundamental part of source energy, often referred to as the God within. Being consciously aware of this accomplishes a significant part of the necessary work.

Consciously relating with intelligent intent means that you and your soulmate are fiercely committed to being the embodiment of love. Through your devotion and practice, love shows up in your lives and relationship in ways you could never have imagined. Your love affair with life itself is palpable, and you treat every moment, whether designing a dinner date or taking out the trash, as an opportunity to deepen your connection with everything and everyone.

In a romantic context, you're not afraid to put in the work. Regularly attending workshops and retreats dedicated to personal growth and relationship enrichment because you're deeply passionate about understanding love. Above all, you comprehend that love isn't something you find; it's something you are and consciously cultivate. By fully showing up for your counterparts, you create a space for love to flourish and thrive, making your relationships radiant with possibility.

When intentionally relating, a couple recognizes that being loving is a verb, requiring daily action. This extends from the little things like always saying "please" and "thank you" to prioritizing weekly date nights and even engaging in meditation together. They understand that sustaining the spark in their relationship demands consistent effort. While they acknowledge it's not always easy, they firmly believe it's worth it. Instead of fixating on whether they are **"being in love,"** they **center their focus** on **"being loving."** Does that make sense?

At the end of the day, a consciously relating couple, whether twin flames, floods, winds, or waters, desires nothing more than to look at each other and say, "I'm so grateful for you and our life together." Versus periodically screaming at the top of their lungs, I HATE YOU, YOOU BEYAHTCH - and that's The woman talking to a man, by the way.

Embracing Detachment and Inner Peace

In life, the journey of detachment can be a path toward discovering our true selves—**who we are beyond the labels, roles, and identities we often attach to.** By stepping back from our ideas of who we think we should be, we begin to notice something remarkable: a sense of clarity and acceptance that comes from within. Detachment isn't about withdrawing from life; rather, it's about learning to embrace it fully by releasing the need to control or cling to outcomes. This allows us to see that what happens externally doesn't define us, providing an anchor of calm in a constantly changing world.

One of the core ideas in this approach is understanding impermanence—the fact that everything changes. Where change might once have felt unsettling, learning to see it as natural helps us build a more relaxed and open response to life's ups and downs. Each day, take a moment to observe the small shifts around you: people come and go, moods rise and fall, and events unfold in unexpected ways. By consciously observing these changes without attaching your identity to them, you gradually cultivate inner stability and peace.

Practicing non-reaction is key to embracing detachment. Non-reaction doesn't mean becoming passive; it's a choice to remain centered and thoughtful, especially when life gets challenging. When we react instantly, we're often driven by habitual emotions like frustration or impatience. But by pausing, breathing, and observing our initial impulse to react, we create space to choose a calm, thoughtful response. This practice not only brings peace to our minds but also improves our relationships, as others feel the balance and kindness in our presence.

Finally, as we deepen our practice of detachment and non-reaction, we develop a resilient, serene perspective that remains unshaken by life's fluctuations. The aim is not to escape from life but to engage with it more fully, with a quiet dignity that embraces both joys and sorrows as part of the human experience. With time, this practice helps us realize that consciousness—our true self—is not affected by the temporary highs and lows of life. Embracing this truth brings a profound sense of freedom, where we experience life not as something happening to us but as an unfolding of our own awareness.

Toxic Separation vs. Conscious Uncoupling

When compatibility issues persist in a conscious relationship, despite intentional communication and efforts to transform it into a transcendent union, there comes a point where parting ways may be the inevitable next step and possibly the only option. Saying goodbye is never easy, but in such circumstances, it becomes a natural part of the individual journeys, signaling that both partners need to forge ahead and continue their growth separately.

The ability to express one's feelings without the fear of retribution or gaslighting is a fundamental aspect of interpersonal communication, especially when recognizing incompatibility. Promoting honest and respectful communication should be the norm we strive for when relationships reach a standstill.

I once came across a news article detailing a tragic incident in Houston, Texas, where a 51-year-old woman fatally shot her husband multiple times after he tried to communicate with honesty that he was in love with another woman. This, I dare say, was not a safe space for communication. Such extreme cases highlight the fear of persecution that often leads people to live inauthentically. As I mentioned earlier, who would consciously choose to fatally harm that which they claim to love? Actions like these are rooted in subtle compulsions and are driven by low vibrational impulses.

Imagine a world where we recognized the importance of normalizing statements like *"We weren't compatible"* or *"We wanted different things out of life."* Equally valid are statements such as *"We had difficulty connecting and getting along," "We didn't communicate well," "We had varying levels of emotional maturity,"* and *"Our priorities, values, interests didn't align."* Additionally, acknowledging phrases like *"We were holding each other back"* or *"We held different ideas, expectations, desires regarding intimacy,"* among a myriad of other issues or feelings that sometimes need to be expressed, is equally essential. *Feel free to read that again and take notes if needed.*

Rather than hastily applying labels like abusive, narcissistic, or manipulative to every co-created failed relationship, it's important to acknowledge that sometimes two people simply don't click, and that's perfectly okay. Romantic success is not guaranteed, and not every relationship is destined to work out. There doesn't have to be a villain or a bad guy involved in every breakup.

In the story of villains and victims, shifting blame and demonizing someone who once held your affection won't fill the voids you're attempting to address, which in many cases lead to the cycle of repetition. Instead, it's crucial to identify the underlying issues that led to the incompatibility and strive to address them in a constructive and growth-oriented manner going forward. Twin elementals, whether viewed as fortunate or unfortunate reflections, depending on your perspective, serve as the perfect catalyst for learning and mastering the triggers that expose voids, issues, and shadows.

That which we RESIST, PERSIST

Have you ever wondered why breakups often lead to a dynamic of villains and victims rather than individuals taking responsibility and being accountable for their own actions? It's a safe bet that **accepting accountability** for one's own co-creation of romantic conflict is much more challenging than **resisting responsibility** for that conflict.

This statement implies that taking responsibility for one's own contribution to romantic conflict is likely more difficult than denying any responsibility for it; in other words, denying responsibility is the easier route. It suggests that accepting accountability and acknowledging one's role in the conflict requires introspection, self-reflection, and humility—qualities that can be more challenging than simply blaming the other person or avoiding responsibility altogether.

Central teachings of several Eastern philosophies, including Buddhism, Taoism, and yoga, emphasize the value of 'Acceptance over Resistance.' For example, in Buddhism, one of the central teachings is the Four Noble Truths, which states that suffering is an inevitable part of life but can be overcome by letting go of attachments and desires. This involves accepting the present moment as it is, without judgment or resistance, and cultivating mindfulness and compassion towards oneself and others. The quote frequently attributed to Buddha, "The Root of Suffering is Attachment," encapsulates this perspective.

The earlier example of the Houston woman tragically ending her husband's life illustrates her refusal to accept reality, leading to an excessive and triggered response. Her strong attachment to resisting the undeniable reality now brings about profound suffering in her own life and the lives of others.

Subsequently, the philosophy of Taoism emphasizes the importance of following the natural flow of life rather than resisting it. This means accepting things as they are without trying to control or manipulate them. By doing so, we can find harmony with the world around us and cultivate a sense of inner peace. Otherwise, it's like swimming against the tides.

The biblical verse Matthew 5:39 also comes to mind, where Jesus also known as Yeshua instructs his followers to turn the other cheek when slapped. This advice rejects the idea of seeking revenge or retaliation, emphasizing the importance of forgiveness and nonviolence instead. I've always interpreted Matthew 5:39, however, with a personal experience in mind. Picture this – when my innocent toddler playfully smacks my face, I don't resist, I accept it and respond without any negative reaction. In fact, I kiss their hands, allowing them to continue. I view this as a display of being unbothered and unfazed, which arises from a sense of greater perspective and authority. How can a babies slap be of any significance to a giant.

The parable within this verse speaks of rising to a higher level of consciousness where challenges and provocations become insignificant, allowing for transcending them with grace and ease. The actual agony of suffering may not be as intense as the anguish caused by our resistance and resentment towards it. Furthermore, if a baby's slap incites frustration, it is most likely because of internal conflict. The kind that would provoke a six foot tall adult to yell at the top of their lungs,

" why'd you slap me, little baby?"   Absolutely, in real-life situations outside of parables or symbolic teachings, if an adult physically assaults you, the gravity of the situation is significantly heightened, and based on your consciousness, it must be addressed appropriately.

Pressing on: Consider the idea that resisting pain and negative emotions typically makes things worse in the long run, not better. To illustrate this concept, imagine that you have a splinter in your finger. It hurts, so you try to ignore it and push through the pain. However, the longer you resist the discomfort, the more it starts to throb and ache. Your finger begins to swell and redden, indicating that it's becoming infected. Before you know it, what started as a small splinter has turned into a full-blown infection that requires medical attention.

This is similar to how resisting negative emotions by coping or covering them up with toxic behaviors or even smoking them away, can amplify the pain and distress. Like an untreated infection, when we cope by pushing them away or ignoring them, they fester and grow stronger. Eventually, they may become so overwhelming that we are forced to seek professional help to manage them.

To avoid the scenario of resisting negative emotions, facing our emotions head-on and processing them is important, just as we would remove a splinter from our finger without pause. By acknowledging and accepting our feelings, we can begin to process them and work through them in a healthy way before they spiral out of control. When doing so, we can free ourselves from the cycle of pain and suffering and emerge stronger and more resilient.

In the realm of colloquial wisdom, the colloquial expression **"It is what it is"** embodies the concept of acceptance in a profound manner, surpassing any other notion I've encountered. The phrase encapsulates the recognition of reality as it stands, without any attempt to resist, deny or change it. It suggests an attitude of letting go of any attachments or judgments and instead embracing the present moment with equanimity and serenity.

The expression **"it's all good"** is also colloquially used to convey a sense of reassurance or normalcy, even in situations where there may be underlying issues or potential problems. When someone says "it's all good" in the context of accepting their circumstances, they may be using the phrase as a form of positive affirmation or a way to shift their mindset towards a more accepting and resilient attitude.

The phrase "hindsight is 20/20" encapsulates the idea that understanding and assessing an event or situation is clearer after its occurrence. Wisdom gained from experiences, especially through hindsight, enhances mental acuity and equips individuals to anticipate potential trajectories. Through sincere introspection, individuals decipher potential outcomes in real-time circumstances, empowering them to take deliberate action and move toward a favorable outcome. This concept of hindsight serves as the guiding principle of the twin elemental program, emphasizing evolution through introspection from experiences and intentional movement.

Understanding the elemental nature in soul connections, revealed through hindsight introspection, offers insights into their impact on life trajectories. This proactive approach cultivates greater self-awareness and agency, empowering individuals to consciously shape their lives. When a chapter in a relationship comes to an end, it can be difficult to accept. However, this can also be seen as an opportunity for new growth and abundance, similar to the controlled burning of crops or the pruning of vegetation to promote new growth. Instead of viewing it as a closing door, one can view it as a chance for new beginnings.

Both partners should recognize that what may feel like **rejection,** is in fact, **redirection,** towards a more fulfilling path. This perspective enables both individuals to embrace a positive outlook and approach new possibilities with an open mind. If you visualize a door closing, do so with the understanding that when one door is closed, another opens - leading to an even better reality on the other side. It presents a fresh opportunity to manifest abundance from the newly opened vortex of your life, as articulated by the channelled *entity Abraham Hicks*.

Expecting modern couples to **prioritize mutual well-being** or act maturely during separation might be a tall order. The notion of intentionally working toward a mutually beneficial outcome can appear challenging. Negative emotions such as resentment, contempt, envy, and animosity often cloud judgment, hindering rational decision-making. In marital disputes, the intervention of a judge or magistrate becomes necessary when individuals struggle to actively pursue a mutually beneficial resolution. This indicates a lack of maturity in resolving conflicts with fairness and equality, akin to individuals acting from their childlike and impulsive ego states, necessitating the judge to act as an adult referee.

Regarding the emotional aspect of separation, the fear of stepping out of one's comfort zone can make accepting new ideas and experiences difficult, potentially exacerbating extreme feelings of resentment. These parts of our being may be more prone to fear and resistance to change. In turn, they can cloud the monkey mind and child self aspects of our psyche, preventing us from experiencing the consciousness with others that comes with a cathartic transformation in our emo-versal reality. By working through our fears, we can break free from limiting patterns and emerge as more enlightened and fulfilled individuals. —Easier said than done, I imagine!

Just as the metamorphosis of a caterpillar into a butterfly involves a traumatic change, transformation in our lives often requires discomfort and upheaval. But just as the butterfly that emerges from the chrysalis is more vibrant and free, we too can emerge from our transformative journey as wiser, more enlightened, emotionally advanced, and capable of **presenting as a superior version of our former selves**. Often observed following an examination of twin flame connections, many people feel cathartically wiser after processing the trauma of the breakup, however, consider the possibility of collective and shared catharsis between soulmates, brought about through a divine and intelligent process.

It is said that only a wet baby invites change. Fear of change and the unknown is understandable with compulsive behavior, yet when you know yourselves and have been relating consciously all along within a higher state of intimate communion, you are equipped with the tools for a divinely inspired **conscious uncoupling**, all the while maintaining emotional wholeness.

Conscious uncoupling, a term coined by the American author and relationship counselor Katherine Woodward Thomas, describes the approach to ending a romantic relationship mindfully and respectfully. The goal is to conclude the relationship while maintaining a positive connection with the other person, even after its termination.

The concept of conscious uncoupling emphasizes the importance of emotional healing and personal growth during the separation process. It encourages individuals to take responsibility for their own emotions and actions and to work through any unresolved issues or emotions that may have contributed to the end of the relationship.

This intentional approach aims to encourage a healthy transition from being romantic partners to a different form of relationship, whether it's as friends, co-parents, or individuals who genuinely have mutual respect for each other's journeys from a distance. Conscious uncoupling recognizes that the end of a romantic relationship doesn't necessarily mean the end of connection or mutual support. Instead, it provides a framework for navigating the complexities of separation with awareness, compassion, and the intention to move forward positively.

The process of conscious uncoupling involves several steps, such as:
- Gaining clarity about the decision to end the relationship.
- Expressing and validating emotions in a healthy way.
- Communicating effectively and respectfully with the other person.
- Creating a shared vision for the future.
- Releasing the past and letting go of resentments.
- Finding closure and moving on.

To consciously bring your union to a close is a parting of ways without the ego, shame, or blame. There are no victims or villains, and non-attachment to the outcome is practiced by both partners who consciously take accountability for their contributions in co-creating a voluntarily chosen relationship that may not have endured. It usually happens when they have practiced consciously relating with each other the entire time and understand that they are infinitely connected through source energy and not attached to the fleeting illusions of the body or its ego.

They seek mutual benefits in high vibration with benefits such as respect, honoring boundaries, integrity, and unconditional love, even if from a distance. Ultimately, the idea behind conscious uncoupling is that by approaching a separation in a mindful and respectful way, individuals can avoid the negative consequences often associated with traditional breakups, such as bitterness, resentment, long-term emotional damage, and even malice or assault. those things are the lifeblood of toxic separations.

One of the most important concepts that I want to share with you is that love should be unconditional, but relationships, however, come with conditions. When the conditions of your partnership can no longer be met, upheld, or maintained—thus becoming invalid—the ultimate goal, after making a conscious effort to relate in the most authentic and loving way possible, and-or consciously uncouple, is a consciously advanced model that I've defined as a **"Tantric Separation."** This denotes that both parties experience mutual delight in the potential opportunities that the future holds for each other, coupled with sincere support, love, and happiness toward each other's personal growth paths. It also encompasses a deep gratitude for the shared journey that has led them to their current point in life.

It is not lost that the majority of those reading this may find it ludicrous to discover mutual joy in breaking up. Toxic separations are far more prevalent than Tantric separations, indicating a greater inclination towards:

- Conflict rather than reconciliation.

- Discord over harmony.

- Confrontation over healing.

- Choosing strife over peace.

- Tumultuous endings over mindful resolutions.

to name a few.

Naturally, opting for conscious uncoupling via the Tantric separation approach is usually considered only when all other alternatives have been thoroughly explored. Yet, when the decision has been made, and there are no other options, a conscious decision, as opposed to a compulsive one, in mutual agreement is always the healthier choice among emotionally intelligent and disciplined individuals. This is simple math in the mathematical discipline called common sense. Individuals engaged in a high functioning transcendent relationship will most likely experience a tantric separation when navigating a conscious uncoupling.

Consider the profound realization of recognizing and expressing a sense of gratitude and appreciation for the role that a former partner may have played in one's current life circumstances. Consider the act of expressing acknowledgment that your current position in life may not have been attainable without the help of a soon-to-be former partner and twin elemental soulmate. Even more exceptional is the notion that the same sentiments and act of recognition are reciprocated by the former partner, resulting in a mutually appreciative and respectful separation. Though few and far between, there are those that after some time are able to reflect these sentiments, however, imagine being able to express and experience these tantric and cathartic emotions during a separation.

In situations where a couple's mental and emotional states are unfavorable, the focus should be on accountability rather than blame. By recognizing and taking responsibility for one's own actions, it becomes possible to move forward with a sense of mutual understanding and a desire for the best possible outcome for both parties. This process can be cathartic and transformative, leading to a conscious uncoupling that is both tantric and deeply meaningful. The end result is a sense of release without any lingering regrets—a clean slate devoid of trauma and abundant with resilience and tranquility.

Tantra, in and of itself, seeks to transcend the duality of the individual self and the divine and to achieve a state of non-dual consciousness in which the practitioner becomes one in bliss with the universe. The different practices are intended to lead to spiritual awakening and enlightenment. I teach individuals that in a tantric breakup, both partners embrace the duality they have experienced together, **allowing for complete forgiveness, compersion, empathy, and understanding.** This approach integrates that duality, setting the stage for a balanced and non dualistic relating dynamic which then fosters unhinged freedom in personal evolution and growth, among other transformative qualities.

To share ecstatic joy in the newfound freedom and possibilities that arise from an inevitable separation is a profound form of consciousness that transcends the ordinary. It represents a heightened awareness and appreciation for the opportunities that life presents, even in moments of transition and change. The alternative closely resembles resistance, which when stemming from attachment, ignorance, or ego, generally leads to more suffering and disharmony. The path of acceptance to the inevitable paths cocreated achieves harmony, peace and enlightenment among other subsequential and beneficial compounding ripples. It's about acceptance of the natural order versus resisting the natural order of the inevitable.

Moreover, when freedom is what one desires, they shouldn't have to ask twice; who has time for standing in someone's way and blocking their blessings, so to speak. Regarding freedom, "The sooner, the better." Consider adopting a mindset that embodies: If I genuinely loved you, I only want the best for you, even if the best is not me. My highest intention could only be to find pleasure in your freedom and for your forward growth with no malice or ill will.

I am whole with you, and I am whole without you, and so I have lost nothing. Instead, I have gained valuable experience that brought about significant evolution and changed me in a most intimate way, and I pray the feelings are mutual. It is important to note that reaching this level of consciousness is not possible when driven solely by ego-based compulsions and confusion. Instead, it requires spiritual enlightenment rooted in a higher purpose if not deep connection to the source of all creation.

As mentioned in the section on "Transcendent Relationships" in Part One of the Conscious Relating Master Class chapter fourteen, embracing perpetual tantric intimacy is achieved through cultivating the *"Lovers Flow Zone,"* which is akin to peak state intimacy where your "Relationship" with self and your lover is a walking, talking, living and breathing Transcendental Meditation. This means the way you relate to everything around you, including yourself and your lover, is perpetually *"Zen on Ten."* Just because you've decided to separate doesn't mean the tantric intimacy stops. This is where the idea of a "Tantric Separation" comes into focus.

I am about to reveal the most powerful yet simple secret of Tantra. But first, it's important to note that many people associate Tantra with something sexual, possibly influenced by the 1996 film "Kama Sutra: A Tale of Love." This film was inspired by the ancient Indian text "Kama Sutra," often associated with Tantra. The ancient **Kama Sutra text** is a guide to love and sexuality, including advice on various sexual positions and techniques. It was written around the 2nd century BCE and is considered a seminal work on human sexuality in Indian culture.

Tantra, on the other hand, is an **ancient spiritual and philosophical system** that originated in India around the 5th century CE. The term "tantra" comes from the Sanskrit words for "expansion" and "tool" and refers to a set of practices and tools that can help individuals achieve spiritual liberation and expand their consciousness. The connection between the Kama Sutra and tantra lies in the fact that both originated in India and share a focus on the exploration of human desire and the pursuit of spiritual enlightenment. Tantra, however, is a much broader and more complex spiritual and philosophical system that encompasses a wide range of practices and beliefs beyond sexuality.

Over time, tantra evolved into a diverse set of practices and beliefs that spread throughout India and beyond. Tantric practices involved meditation, yoga, ritual, and the use of sacred symbols and mantras. Tantra also incorporated elements of astrology, alchemy, and other esoteric sciences. In the West, tantra has become popularized in recent decades as a form of spirituality and personal growth—yet still latent with sexual undertones for many. It is important to note that the Western interpretation of tantra often differs significantly from its original meaning and context.

The key principle in Tantra, often associated with the "State of Ecstasy," is commonly misunderstood as being solely tied to sexual arousal. Yet, in the context of Tantra, "ecstasy" transcends sexual limitations and encompasses a state of heightened mystical experience. A spiritual arousal or a quickening to be exact. The true secret of Tantra lies in **cultivating a perpetual state of ecstasy,** meaning being **ecstatic about every action**, whether mundane or profound.

First, recognise that, regarding this life we live, it's all Māyā, or in contemporary context, it's all 'matter—material—matrix' and ultimately, mind. Even more profound in context is realizing that, everything in its essence is Light and ultimately Consciousness. We live in an atomic hologram where the space between atoms is akin to the nucleus of an atom being a tiny dot in the middle of a sports arena and the electron clouds surrounding the dot on the field are like the seats in the arena with empty space between the two. Now multiply this concept by infinity

Be it an actual football field or its corresponding atomic structure, you get to choose daily which end of its vibratory polarity your conscious mind will perceive as it sways back and forth to the rhythm of conscious and compulsive behaviors. Will you assert your highest vibratory consciousness or be receptive to your lowest vibratory compulsions within Māyā, a.k.a. matter-material-matrix?

Note that in the the Matrix Film, the character Neo after 'egoically' dying (represented by physical death) woke up to the reality that everything was just ones and zeros. This is similar to recognizing the nature of matter or the material world of Māyā, a sanskrit word used in buddhism and hinduism. Neo perceived clearly that he was in a computer simulation represented by the duality of ones and zeros presented as light impulses.

In our reality, we exist within a dualistic atomic simulation. When your ego no longer rules your perception, your eyes become trained to recognise that everything is atomic and not solid, even those you love. There is a singularity, all is one, and all is mind. All is source consciousness and it is deserving of recognition and ecstatic gratitude in bliss. This bliss can be likened to the edenic environment experienced by the archetypes Adam and Eve before falling into duality consciousness known as good and evil.

Maintaining a tantrically ecstatic mindset in daily activities, whether you're brushing your teeth, picking flowers, drinking water, or sitting on the toilet, initiates a peak state akin to a natural high, **triggering the pineal gland** to produce a continuous stream of Dimethyl-Tryptamine (DMT) initiating a spiritually orgasmic flow state for soul arousal. Achieving and sustaining this state requires intentional practice and discipline. It requires constant conscious awareness that, for lack of better words, "God" is the taste behind your tongue, the sight behind your eyes, the spark behind your heartbeat, and the love behind your love. Otherwise, you are merely dust. Furthermore, 'Ecstasy' in Tantra refers to the heightened spiritual or mystical arousal associated with tantric practices, fostering spiritual elevation in all tasks and practices. It's like being in constant communion with Source/God.

Take note: A naturally influx pineal gland, in a perpetual flow state, is akin to the luminous event horizon of a stargate's perpetually open vortex preparing the way for the rainbow body also known as the body of light. While this statement may be overlooked by many, those attuned to its profound value will discover its significance. The key question is: How does one cultivate a state of ecstasy or ecstatic joy, even for the most mundane actions? The secret lies in beginning and ending Absolutely EVERYTHING with GRATITUDE— not just basic gratitude, but **"ECSTATIC GRATITUDE."**

Consequently, combining these two feelings is the secret to a powerful tantric life. If you doubt this, I challenge you to adopt the practice of reciting the affirming words, Gratitude for this, and Gratitude for that, quietly to yourself as you look around and engage with your environment. By incorporating ecstatic gratitude into your daily life, you open the door to a powerful tantric existence. I challenge individuals to teach other individuals through platforms such as youtube and others this practice. If accepted, we will see the world transform right in front of our eyes.

When driving or riding city transit, look out the window and say to yourself, "Gratitude for those trees over there, Gratitude for the city bus, Gratitude for those cows, Gratitude for the homeless man panhandling, Gratitude for the attractive couple, Gratitude for the delicious smoothies in the smoothie shop, Gratitude for the 'hater' 'ice grilling' and 'mean mugging me'... and so on."

I challenge you to recite these affirmations in real-time, over a hundred times per session and twice a day for 21 days or beyond. If you have the opportunity to get your hands on a Kirlian photography camera, I'd be curious to see your before-and-after pictures. Feel free to post them and your experiences on the twin elemental social media accounts.

Here is where the authority resides. You must conjure up the feeling of ecstasy when affirming how grateful you are for all things, seeing that you understand that **everything is literally everything else** and it is all an extension of source creation. Projecting the ecstatic feeling of thankfulness ignites the spirit into an orgasmic resonance, thus influencing everything you do and every move you make, including relating with a soulmate through togetherness or perceived separation. Along with concepts such as compersion, tantric separations represent the higher pinnacles of conscious relating. Whether experiencing intentional relating or tantric separations, this approach is the key to transcendence in connecting with a highly functional twin elemental mirror that vibrates at the same frequency as you.

It may be challenging to comprehend, but the emotions of ecstasy and pleasure run parallel with gratitude. Consider the overwhelming and intense feelings that come up in the aftermath of experiencing orgasmic or cathartic release, or even during overwhelming emotional, physical, or euphoric relief. More often than not, when pressure builds and is eventually released or relieved, satisfaction, gratification, and gratitude are generally the prevailing emotions.

Upon release, many individuals are likely to express their joy or gratitude by shouting out an exuberant "YES!" or even dramatically exclaiming "Thank you, Jesus! or the equivalent" Even those not particularly religious may still invoke these phrases or use the expression "Allahu Akbar," if from Middle Eastern cultures, which translates to "God is great."

Consciously, these sentiments are linguistic programs, yet subconsciously, individuals may be tapping into their preconceived ideas of source energy to offer gratitude based on the cathartic feeling of relief, which can lead to the subsequent experience of ecstatic sensations.

In the context of a "Tantric Separation," you would affirm to yourself; Ecstatic Gratitude for the opportunity to have loved this person, Ecstatic Gratitude for the opportunity to move on from them in good health, Gratitude for the love we made, Gratitude for the meals we ate together, Gratitude for the lessons we learned, Gratitude for the disagreements we had, Gratitude and acceptance for everything we shared, Gratitude and acceptance for everything we lost, Ecstatic gratitude for the most beautiful tantric separation and conscious uncoupling within this atomic simulation. Most of all Gratitude and acceptance for this Moment Right Now!

This practice represents a zenith in source integration, embodying a profound union between the individual and the universal consciousness. Its efficacy lies in its ability to access and harmonize the deepest layers of the mind and spirit, facilitating a transformative journey toward inner peace, clarity, and spiritual awakening. With unparalleled capacity to transcend the limitations of the self and connect with the highest aspects of existence, this practice stands at the forefront of spiritual advancement and the pinnacle of personal growth and soul evolution.

Moreover, research suggests that gratitude meditation, as practiced by various spiritual traditions, including Buddhism, Hinduism, and Taoism, may be linked to increased gamma brain wave activity. A 2018 study published in the journal "Frontiers in Psychology" found that individuals practicing gratitude meditation exhibited higher levels of gamma brain wave activity compared to a control group.

This finding aligns with observations by neuroscientists that long-term meditators, through such practices, self-induce high-amplitude gamma synchronicity during mental activities. Gamma brain waves, characterized by the synchronized firing of different brain regions at the fastest frequency, are associated with peak concentration. They are typically observed during complex cognitive processes like memory storage and sharp concentration.

Additionally, the neuroscience of gratitude reveals fascinating insights. A recent study found that practicing gratitude activates the **ventromedial prefrontal cortex** (VMPFC), a region associated with neural pure altruism, indicating our brains have a natural inclination towards giving. Additionally, expressing or receiving gratitude triggers the release of dopamine in the neural circuitry of our brainstem, leading to a pleasurable sensation and a desire for more. Reflecting on or documenting the positives in life stimulates the anterior cingulate cortex, releasing serotonin, which enhances mood, boosts willpower, and increases motivation—an antidepressant effect. The neuroscience of gratitude illuminates its remarkable psychological power.

According to Dr. Joe Dispenza, the internationally acclaimed author and distinguished neuroscientist, gratitude wields an extraordinary power to set in motion approximately **twelve hundred different chemical reactions** that actively foster healing and restoration within the body. Dr. Dispenza delved into the realm of gratitude through a comprehensive study, wherein cortisol and IgA levels of 120 participants were meticulously measured both before and after an enlightening workshop.

Elevated cortisol, often dubbed the stress hormone, has the adverse effect of sapping the body's energy and compromising the immune system. Conversely, IgA, a crucial protein supporting immune function, tends to diminish as cortisol levels soar. To reverse these damaging effects, participants committed to the practice of cultivating heightened emotional states—such as love, joy, and gratitude—for nine to ten minutes, three times daily.

The outcomes were indeed remarkable, revealing a significant drop in cortisol levels and a substantial increase in IgA levels. Initially at 52.5, IgA levels soared to an impressive 86.

These findings underscore the profound impact that gratitude and positive emotions wield on overall health, highlighting our inherent capacity to fortify the immune system and catalyze healing, all without resorting to external substances. By dedicating just a few minutes each day to the deliberate experience of elevated states of joy, love, or gratitude, we can unleash substantial epigenetic transformations that contribute holistically to our well-being.

Gratitude not only has the power to change brain chemistry and improve physical health but also holds significant psychological influence. Looking back, cultivating a state of unconditional loving-kindness, compassion, and appreciation towards oneself, others, and the world at large holds the transformative power to free the ego from compulsive relational patterns. This shift has the potential to significantly reduce instances of compulsive uncoupling—where actions stem from fear, anger, scarcity, and malice.

Ultimately, the consistent state of gratitude is the most conscious relationship one can have with themselves and goes beyond merely integrating shadows exposed by twin elementals but sets the stage for integrating one's consciousness with source consciousness and like a single drop of water falling into the ocean, merges seamlessly into the boundless expanse of divine unity, transcending individuality and egoic limitations to become something much greater and far more powerful. In essence, consciously uncoupling through tantric separation represents a dynamic approach to transitioning from romantic relationships with compassion and intentionality. It recognizes that even as a relationship naturally comes to an end, there's abundant potential for growth and transformation for both individuals involved.

This process involves taking responsibility for our emotions and reactions, recognizing the shared patterns and dynamics that contributed to the relationship's conclusion. After acceptance, the next step is approaching the separation with curiosity and openness for integrating complete understanding of the inevitable without resistance, rather than resentment and blame, paving the way for clearer and more empathetic communication. Prioritizing personal growth and well-being while still honoring the connection and love that initially brought the couple together becomes paramount.

The idea of consciously relating and then engaging in a conscious uncoupling aligns with the principles outlined in the book "Power vs. Force" by David R. Hawkins. Romantic conflicts often lead to the use of force, such as forceful communication, decisions, and actions. While this approach may seem easier, it ultimately results in resistance and more pain. In contrast, employing power entails empowerment derived from acceptance, surrender, and a shared commitment to individual and collective growth, even in the midst of a separation. It is through this mutual evolution that a relationship can realize its full potential.

By releasing the impulse to force control where there is none, instead consider embracing love and acceptance, we can transcend the ego's limitations, opening the door to a clean and empowering tantric transition—as there is no separation, only transformation and transitioning. Recognizing the interconnected nature of everything makes it highly plausible to encounter a sense of ecstasy and liberation rather than merely enduring a painful ending during a perceived separation. Fear not your individual greatness. Embrace the boundless potential awaiting you in the next chapter of your life without hesitation or trepidation.

It's important to acknowledge, however, that the concept of ecstatic separation may not be universally applicable. The process of separation can be emotionally challenging, and individual experiences may vary. You'll have to do what's right for you and the trajectory of you future. Approaching separation with mindfulness, compassion, and acceptance, directed both inwardly and outwardly, not only fosters personal fulfillment but also contributes to a more harmonious and loving life. Unless you intentionally seek to sabotage your life, try to refrain from making immature, toxic and compulsive decisions.

Conscious relating is the master key—bear in mind, the alternative, compulsive relating which will inevitably lead to a compulsive separation, induces extreme prolonged stress, laying the groundwork for a detrimental impact on the body. As 'Sweet Brown' from the 2012 viral video said, **"Aint no body got time for that!"** Altruistic 'self-less-ness' is not the sole purpose of consciously relating; rather, there are seemingly self-ish drives at play as well, namely self-care and self-preservation. Personal health, wealth and knowledge of self are also at the forefront.

Unbeknownst to most, stress triggers a series of physiological responses that culminate in an environment hostile to longevity. Initial hormonal surges of cortisol and adrenaline, designed for acute responses to stress, become detrimental when sustained over time. Chronic stress exacerbates inflammation, compromising the body's ability to maintain optimal function while concurrently dampening the effectiveness of the immune system.

Telomeric degradation accelerates, triggering cellular aging and susceptibility to age-related diseases. Maladaptive coping mechanisms, such as overeating or excessive alcohol consumption, further exacerbate health risks. Cardiovascular complications loom as stress persists, fostering conditions like hypertension and cardiovascular disease. Thus, the narrative underscores how chronic stress engenders a toxic environment within the body, potentially curtailing lifespan and undermining overall health. In simpler terms, stress is comparable to drinking a half a cup of bleach or engine oil—it's essentially poisoning the body and bloodstream and unfortunately, we've normalized it as part of our daily sustenance.

These undeniable truths can be challenging for many to grasp, particularly in our current societal landscape, which often seems steeped in a kind of collective psychosis. Media, music, toxicity colored as humor, incessantly echos the dysfunction of our compulsive ways. The dissolution of romantic partnerships, often witnessed or experienced as toxic occurrences, becomes a powerful lens through which the dysfunction of our culture is magnified. However, through conscious relating with our twin elementals, we have the potential to shift this paradigm.

Recognize that all is mind and everything is consciousness. The reality you perceive is made of consciousness, even the seemingly solid matter you interact with daily, is pure consciousness. Moving beyond ego awareness alone leads to a state of non-duality, where all separation dissolves. Contemplate life as infinite, undivided, ever-present, and ever-active until you realize your oneness with it. This, for the record, is an actual meditation I am encouraging.

Within this space you can experience the superconsciousness that you are when your mind is dormant —the space you inhabited before your mind's development and after its degradation. Just as self-love precedes loving others, cultivating a conscious relationship with oneself comes before consciously engaging with others. It's wise to develop your own understanding and well-being initially, then share that enriching experience with those you love and care about for transcendent relationships, effectively inducing a euphoric state in others merely through your presence.

As we progress as a community and advance as a species, my hope is that you will choose conscious relating over the compulsions that often characterize our journeys in love with your respective soulmates and community at large. With a deeper understanding of Twin Elementals, I trust you've gained profound insights into the intricate tapestry of interpersonal and interactional relationships as well as how they've evolved through the ages. I hope you now possess the tools to discern when you are reflecting the subtle energies from any of the four Twin Elementals, for optimizing polarization and defining your souls evolution.

For a long time, the prevailing belief held that there exists only one soul mate in the vast expanse of the universe, exclusively tailored to each individual's egoic and self-centered desires. This belief has led many to embark on an endless search for this singular person, as if discovering them would be akin to finding the gates of heaven after enduring a lifetime of hell on Earth. All the while, there's the potential to engage with wonderful twin elementals, in the interim.

In conclusion, I trust that our discussion has broadened your comprehension of the intricate dynamics surrounding soul connections, underscoring the expansive nature of your species' capacity to forge connections with soulmates within your greater soul family.

I hope that this exploration has brought about a recognition that your soul family is a tapestry of elemental reflections, each mirroring distinct versions of yourself and facets of your being. Armed with this understanding, you wield the power to choose how to embody and radiate love from the source outward in all your endeavors, as the evolution of your soul depends upon it.

May you nurture the discipline to infuse every moment with ecstatic Gratitude, serving as your guiding light as you walk with purpose and clarity, supported by the knowledge that you are never alone on this journey. For **Everything, is Everything Else.**

Including you.

—The End

Before concluding this book, I invite you to enter into a contract with yourself, committing to conscious relating in every interaction. Base your engagements on the principles explored on these pages rather than defaulting to compulsive relating. This contract goes beyond simple comprehension; it's a call to action. It's about embodying the insights gained from the rich tapestry of relationships and the transformative journey of Twin Elementals.

Now armed with a deeper understanding, you have the tools to recognize when you're reflecting energy from any of the four twin elementals. As you navigate the intricate landscape of relationships, infuse your interactions with the spirit of intentional relating. Let it guide your responses, shape your connections, and illuminate your journey in love.

This is an invitation to empower yourself through conscious and intentional choices, find growth in shared experiences, and unlock the full potential of authentic connections. As you turn the final pages, embrace the next phase of your relational journey with intention, awareness, and a commitment to conscious relating.

By signing below, you make an agreement with yourself for making an effort to practice conscious and intentional relating in every interaction.

X_____

X_____

X_____

About the author

Kushaqxi, an Atlanta native, is an independent holistic therapist specializing in private counseling. He is also the founder and director of Sacred Sun Food Society, a living foods and gardening collective, as well as the creator of the Twin Elemental Model and the Polyamorously Celibate Relating System. With a deep interest in world philosophies, Kushaqxi has spent his life studying and researching the principles of self-mastery. Through his workshops, teachings, and work as an educator, speaker, author, and Polymath, Kushaqxi empowers individuals to discover personal transformation for unlocking their full potential. When he's not working, Kushaqxi enjoys pursuing his passion for organic arboriculture and spending time with his beloved family.

OTHER BOOKS BY THE AUTHOR

★ AVAILABLE   PREORDER   ☆ PREORDER

ALSO COMING SOON:

POLYAMOROUSLY CELIBATE:
An Advanced emo-tech model for spiritual and social development.

FRIEND ZONE MASTERY:
Why a fleet of platonic wingmen are far more valuable than a torrent of limerent entanglements.

www.ingramcontent.com/pod-product-compliance
Lightning Source LLC
Chambersburg PA
CBHW050527100526
44581CB00009B/158/J